LABOUR'S DILEMMA:
THE GENDER POLITICS OF AUTO WORKERS
IN CANADA, 1937–1979

The growth of the United Auto Workers in Canada dramatically improved the lives of thousands of workers. Not only did it achieve impressive bargaining gains, but the UAW was regarded as one of the most democratic and socially progressive of the major industrial unions in North America. However, workers in the automotive sector, who constituted the largest segment of the UAW membership, witnessed blatant gender inequalities. From 1937 to 1979, UAW leaders did little to challenge these inequalities. Both the union and the workplace remained highly masculine settings in which male workers and bosses played out the gender politics of the times.

Pamela Sugiman draws on archival materials and in-depth interviews with workers and union representatives to explore the ways in which the small groups of women in southern Ontario auto plants fought for dignity, respect, and rights within this restrictive context. During the Second World War, women auto workers formed close bonds with one another – bonds that rested largely around their identification as a sex. By the late 1960s, they were drawing on a growing union consciousness, the modern women's movement, and their gender identity, to launch an organized collective struggle for sexual equality.

In describing the women's experiences, Sugiman employs the concept of a 'gendered strategy.' A gendered strategy incorporates both reasoned decisions and emotional responses, calculated interests and compromises. Within a context of gender and class divisions and inequalities, workers developed strategies of coping, resistance, and control. *Labour's Dilemma* reveals how people may be simultaneously agents and victims, compliant and resistant.

PAMELA SUGIMAN is Assistant Professor of Sociology, McMaster University.

PAMELA SUGIMAN

Labour's Dilemma: The Gender Politics of Auto Workers in Canada, 1937–1979

UNIVERSITY OF TORONTO PRESS
Toronto Buffalo London

© University of Toronto Press Incorporated 1994
Toronto Buffalo London
Printed in Canada

ISBN 0-8020-2895-0 (cloth)
ISBN 0-8020-7403-0 (paper)

♾

Printed on acid-free paper

Canadian Cataloguing in Publication Data

Sugiman, Pamela H. (Pamela Haruchiyo), 1958–
Labour's Dilemma : the gender politics of auto
workers in Canada, 1937–1979

Includes bibliographical references and index.
ISBN 0-8020-2895-0 (bound) ISBN 0-8020-7403-0 (pbk.)

1. Women automobile industry workers – Ontario.
2. International Union, United Automobile,
Aerospace, and Agricultural Implement Workers of
America.   3. Sex discrimination in employment –
Ontario.   4. Trade-unions – Automobile industry
workers – Canada.   5. Women in trade-unions – Ontario.
I. Title.

HD6073.A82C37 1994   331.4'7811629222'0971   C94-931771-3

University of Toronto Press acknowledges the financial assistance to its
publishing program of the Canada Council and the Ontario Arts Council.

This book has been published with the help of a grant from the Social Science
Federation of Canada, using funds provided by the Social Sciences and
Humanities Research Council of Canada.

To Ritsuko Sugiman
and in memory of Ross Tatsuro Sugiman,
who taught me to value working-class experience

Contents

viii Contents

Acknowledgments

Like the women whose words fill the pages of this book, I have experienced both small and dramatic changes since I started this project as a PhD dissertation over seven years ago. These seven years have presented new challenges and opportunities, disappointments and hope, hurdles and triumphs. With the transitions in my own life, my thinking about sociology and social history has also taken on new dimensions. I began this project in an effort to answer the seemingly straightforward question, why has the auto manufacturing industry remained sex-segregated for a period spanning more than seventy years? I complete this manuscript with the understanding that people's lives are more complicated than an intellectual analysis of the logic of capitalism and patriarchy suggest. I recognize the importance, therefore, of talking to workers themselves in an effort to understand their past. Moreover, as I listen to growing numbers of workers of colour, I acknowledge the need to seriously address the ways in which the politics of race, as well as gender and class, has shaped industry and labour's agenda.

I worked through most of these ideas in dialogue with a small group of people. For many years, Lorna Marsden skillfully guided my intellectual development. Over the course of these years, she asked key questions at the right times. Most important, she always allowed me to provide the answers. I have tried to learn from her broad intellect, wisdom, pragmatism, and political savvy. Bonnie Fox brought her penetrating analytical powers to this project. She gave me cautious guidance, delivered in friendship, with honesty and understanding. Ruth Pierson was able to draw out significant themes in my work. And by example, she taught me the importance of careful and creative historical scholarship. In addition, I am grateful to Ruth Milkman, Dan Benedict, Ian Radforth, and two anonymous reviewers, for carefully assessing my work and for providing incisive comments. I also placed great value on the critical reading of my manuscript by members of the feminist study group in Toronto, Sedef Arat-Koc, Meg Luxton, Julia O'Connor, and Ester Reiter. Their highly constructive thoughts helped to fuel my confidence.

The research process was facilitated by the support of various people and agencies. I express special thanks to the Canadian Auto Workers Union National Office and CAW Locals 199 and 222. In particular, Leroy Bell, Kathy Bennett, Pat Clancy, John Clout, Pat Creighton, Sam Gindin, the late Betty Kerr, John Kovacs, Bev McCloskey, Betty Murray, Jim Nimigon, May Partridge, Maurie Shorten, Tom Saunders, John Sinclair, and Robert White gave generously of their time, expertise, and other resources. Gayle Hosack deserves special credit for sharing her technical skills, often with little warning and during odd hours. I also appreciate the help of the many archivists, librarians, and clerical staff of the Archives of Labor and Urban Affairs at Wayne State University, Peter DeLottinville of the Public Archives of Canada, and Reginald Barlow of the Windsor Public Library. As well, Karl Beveridge and Carol Conde kindly shared their interviews with members of Local 222. David Sobel helped me to locate valuable photographs of auto workers. Janet and Eric Beauchesne provided meals, accommodation, and a sense of family during research stints in Ottawa. In addition, I am grateful for financial assistance from the Social Sciences and Humanities Research Council of Canada and the Henry J. Kaiser Family Foundation at Wayne State University.

A number of people have also indirectly contributed to this book. Throughout my years at the University of Toronto, Bernd Baldus, Robert Brym, Harry Nishio, Richard Roman, and Janet Salaff offered me intellectual guidance and encouragement. Ann Duffy introduced me to feminist analysis. Her lectures were pivotal in helping me foster a critical sociological perspective. The solid friendship of Heather Lank Fortier, Lydia Danylciw, Vappu Tyyska, and especially Momoye Sugiman has been an important resource. These individuals provided a safe retreat, perspective, and replenishment, when needed. My special appreciation goes to Robert Storey, who offered intellectual counsel and emotional sustenance as I juggled the completion of this book with the rigours of teaching, new research projects, and the daily demands of life. His warmth, wit, and irreverence have brought bursts of colour to long, grey days in the academy.

My mother, Ritsuko Sugiman, my father, the late Ross Sugiman, and the late Betty Sugiman each taught me about inner strength and struggle.

They encouraged me to strive towards goals, and they kept me in touch with my origins – with working-class life, spirit and sensibilities. Hassan Yussuff gave an incredible amount of himself to this project. It is his and mine, equally. His passion for politics inspired this book, and his enduring patience and love saw it to fruition. Finally, I thank all the workers I interviewed – for being so true.

LABOUR'S DILEMMA:
THE GENDER POLITICS OF AUTO WORKERS
IN CANADA, 1937–1979

Introduction

Contradictions, Dilemmas, and the Politics of Gender

I tried to see contradictions not as problems to be ironed out ... but as the *goal* of the research. Such elaborations of paradox and confusion are painstaking and often painful. But it is precisely out of the process of bringing such contradictions to consciousness and facing up to illogicality or inconsistency, that a person takes a grip on his or her own fate. Politically it is of vital importance that we understand how we change.

Cynthia Cockburn, *Brothers*, 1983

How do people make changes in a context of social inequality? How do wage-earning women, in particular, secure dignity, respect, and rights in a patriarchal capitalist society? In order to answer these questions we need to understand how people interpret their world, what personal and societal developments prompt them to challenge familiar and longstanding arrangements, and what forces shape the nature and outcome of their struggles. As Cynthia Cockburn suggests, people are constrained by their location in society – as a woman or a man, a worker or an employer, a person of colour or a member of the dominant racial group. However, people also make changes and shape their lives. Structure moulds and limits, but it does not prevent agency. Sometimes we simply try to get through the day without directly confronting the complexity of our lives. Sometimes we hesitate and procrastinate. But often we resist, assert ourselves in small ways, and alter the structures in which we live.

The mechanism that 'prompts a break, a redirection, in either a person's practices or ideas,' says Cockburn, 'is the mechanism of contradiction' (1986: 10). People's lives are full of contradictions and individuals are usually painfully aware of them. Contradictions make us uncomfortable and present us with dilemmas. However, as these tensions rise within us, we seek resolutions. While individuals often seek to resolve these tensions by independently changing their own lives, they also do so collectively in social protest movements. Social movements for societal change heighten the sense of contradiction, involve the mobilization of resources, bring individuals together, and present them with alternatives.

Throughout the twentieth century, the labour movement has unquestionably offered workers an alternative vision, a discourse with which to critique existing arrangements, and the resources with which to improve their lives and make better sense of their world. For women, however, unionism has presented its own set of contradictions and dilemmas. Wage-earning women have long had an ambivalent relationship to the labour movement.[1] Indeed, the history of women and organized labour is largely one of contradictions. It is a history of workers' struggles to sort through the resulting dilemmas.

CONTRADICTIONS IN THE UAW CANADIAN REGION

One of the most significant developments in the growth of the labour movement in Canada was the establishment of the United Auto Workers Union (UAW) in the late 1930s.[2] In many respects, the UAW dramatically changed the lives of thousands of workers. Not only did it achieve impressive gains through collective bargaining in the area of wages, benefits, and job security, but in the past the UAW was widely regarded as one of the most socially active and progressive of the large industrial unions in North America.

Notably, the union firmly supported the movement for women's rights in employment and in the wider society. UAW members and leaders were active in the formation of feminist groups and the passage of equal rights legislation, and they participated in various community-based activities for the improvement of women's lives (Gabin, 1990, 1984; Meyerowitz, 1985; Milkman, 1987).[3]

The union also had a reputation for being a highly democratic organization (Stiebner, 1962; Yates, 1993). This reputation largely rested on the establishment of the UAW Public Review Board, a self-contained, internal body that governed the union's ethics, and the UAW District Council, a forum in which rank-and-file members could raise their specific concerns and openly challenge the decisions of their leaders.

Yet while the union achieved an outstanding record on social activism, the pursuit of justice, and the democratic process, the largest segment of its membership witnessed blatant and persistent gender and racial divisions and inequalities – as workers in the automotive sector.[4] Since its establishment in the early 1900s, automobile manufacturing has been overwhelmingly dominated by white men, of Anglo-Saxon and Eastern European origins, while white women and black, Chinese, and Armenian men have constituted a small minority of the workforce. Very few women of colour have ever worked in the industry. Furthermore, white women and men of colour were confined to certain plants and, within these plants, employers allocated them to a narrow range of jobs in a limited number of departments.[5]

From 1937 to 1979 UAW leaders made few attempts to alter these patterns. Thus, apart from anomalies during the Second World War, female representation in the industry has remained low. Most striking is that gender segregation and inequality have long withstood dramatic changes in both the workforce and society. Indeed, sex segregation in the auto plants did not begin to break down until 1970.

This central paradox uncovers a series of inconsistencies in the history of the union and the industry. For instance, both women and men workers strongly fought to establish the seniority principle as a symbol of fairness and uniformity, a means by which to avoid the favouritism and arbitrary dismissals of early times. This principle ensured that employers strictly adhere to a 'last hired, first fired' policy. Yet while the seniority rule was motivated by concerns about democracy and impartiality, union leaders agreed to institute sex-based seniority rights. In effect, this provision gave women the right to transfer only into jobs that were labelled 'female.' Women's seniority was thus severely circumscribed. In practice, unionists used the seniority rule to legitimate and entrench one form of discrimination, even though they had initially sought this principle as a means to combat discriminatory favouritism.

In addition, both the union and the auto plants were highly sexist environments that in various ways reinforced the unequal position of women. Nevertheless, it is within these settings that women began to defy conventional gender prescriptions. Through their experiences as dues-paying unionists and wage-earners, women became radicalized and attempted to alter the very structures in which they were oppressed. The women's activism is especially striking insofar as they were a seemingly powerless group. They represented a tiny segment of the huge automotive workforce, had a marginal standing in the union, were subordinated as a sex, and were unskilled manual workers who possessed little formal education and few employment options.

A further twist is that while sex-based seniority placed women in an inferior position in the industry, they drew on the general principle of seniority to uphold even their restricted rights to employment. With its premise of neutrality, the seniority rule appealed to women's sense of justice, even when this conception was shaped within a patriarchal framework that stressed their subordination to a male breadwinner.

WORKER CONSCIOUSNESS AND ACTION: GENDERED STRATEGIES

These contradictions reveal a need to heighten our understanding of workers and the politics of labour. With a sensitivity to gender, we need to specifically re-examine the complex development and multidimensional nature of worker consciousness, resistance, struggle, and movements for social change.

Early feminist research has demonstrated the importance of looking at both the system of *patriarchy* and *capitalism* in theorizing labour history.[6] In these writings, we see that worker solidarity not only develops around the experience of class, but it also emerges from people's common experiences as a sex. In addition, feminist theory has highlighted the ways in which the capitalist sphere of production intersects with the realm of social reproduction, and together they shape the political views and strategies of waged labour.

Working within this conceptual framework, for many years socialist feminists engaged in a somewhat perplexing, esoteric debate about the specific relationship between patriarchy and capitalism (see Sargent, 1981, for some articles in the debate). The primacy of one system over the other, their (relative) autonomy, and the functional importance of each, were central concerns in the early writings. This debate was largely a reaction to the tendency of Marxist theorists to reduce women's subordination as a sex to the exploitation of the working class as a whole.

Recently, some feminist writers have offered a more textured analysis, focusing on the lived experience of *gender* and *class*, concepts that are analytically distinct from, yet central to, the functioning of each 'system.' This research represents an attempt to understand how 'exploitation and oppression' are 'simultaneously interwoven' (West cited in Collinson and Knights, 1986) and 'interpenetrating' (Thompson cited in Collinson and Knights, 1986: 143), and it explores the ways in which gender and class mediate one another in shaping workers' perceptions and struggles.

From her research on secretaries in Australia, Rosemary Pringle concludes that 'classes are always already gendered while men and women experience their gender in class terms ... Class has different meanings for men and women and cannot be separated from these gender meanings.

A "proletarian" woman never occupies an identical class space to that of a "proletarian" man even though they may have been subject to many of the same processes' (1988: 199–200). Similarly, Joy Parr claims that 'any systematic approach that assumes that "everything falls into one category or another, but cannot belong to more than one category at the same time" belies the wholeness of consciousness and experience. Life as we live it is not subdivided sequentially. We exist simultaneously, rather than sequentially, in the social relations of class and gender' (1990: 8). Insofar as individuals experience them simultaneously, attempts to order these concepts are both futile and inconsequential. In order to fully understand worker consciousness and action we must recognize the ways in which gender and class are inseparable in lived experience. Only by treating them as purely abstract concepts can we view them as distinct.

Adamson, Briskin, and McPhail state that we need to move beyond both class reductionism and gender reductionism. Rather than 'prioritize' or 'rank' the relations of power inherent in class, race, gender, and sexual orientation in an abstract way, we should focus on 'the ways they intertwine, reinforce, and contradict each other. The relative strength and import of these relations to groups, individuals, and political practice is determined within the context of particular historical conjunctures' (1988: 109).

In highlighting the importance of the historical context in which people live, and the ongoing process by which they experience the world, sociologists can present a more nuanced account of worker solidarity, resistance, and struggle. Much of the research in this area, however, has been highly interpretive and speculative, giving insufficient weight to historical specificity. The literature thereby fails to adequately explain the complexity of people's thoughts and actions.

Discussions of worker consciousness have tended to reflect one of two basic approaches: the study of fixed (quantifiable) attitudes or the analysis of structural imperatives. Rick Fantasia (1988) notes that American sociologists have typically adopted the former approach. American sociology's study of worker consciousness, says Fantasia, is based on surveys designed to measure worker attitudes on indices, such as class identification, work satisfaction and dissatisfaction, class animosities, and political preferences. Researchers then correlate these attitudinal measures with independent variables, such as skill level, racial and ethnic identification, age, sex, and the like. On the basis of these findings, they draw conclusions about the degree of 'class consciousness' in a given population of workers.[7]

Structural theorists, in comparison, have tended to focus on the workings of the economy, the industry, and less often on the firm. These writers focus on the political and economic 'logic' of a system, and the 'motives' of the various actors within it. Assuming that employees and bosses think and act predictably and consistently, according to their distinct and opposing positions in the (narrowly defined) class structure, these theorists make reasoned claims about the nature and degree of consciousness and workers' propensity to resist. On the basis of their own intellectual expectations, then, they think for the workers.[8]

Both of these approaches are limited in that they fail to examine the historical process and thus they do not see that 'the world may be a paradoxical and contradictory place to those negotiating it' (Fantasia, 1988: 5). They overlook the unintended and often unpredictable outcomes that people encounter in daily living, the material and personal resources on which they must draw in order to seek and achieve social change, and the subjective motivations behind some of their assertions and actions. When we consider the objective 'realities' of their lives, along with their perceptions of the social structure, and the process by which they encounter the world around them, we can better understand why workers sometimes act and speak in ways that may seem irrational – in ways that appear to contribute to the perpetuation of their own subordination.

In adopting a social-historical perspective, we can see that people do not always act according to a predetermined logic, nor are their views static.[9] Workers' responses to industry, the emergence and development of consciousness, and the outcomes of their struggles all rest on the *dynamic interplay* of various components of their lives. Workers' subjective experience of gender and class, conceptions of masculine and feminine, and perceptions of themselves as members of families, all influence the ways in which they see and act. Furthermore, their location in the division of labour, the material resources at their disposal, and hegemonic and alternative ideologies shape their 'reality.'

The concept of a *gendered strategy*[10] helps us to understand the configuration of these forces at particular historical junctures.[11] Within a context of gender and class divisions and inequalities, workers develop gendered strategies of coping and resistance. A gendered strategy is not a purely rational plan of action. Rather, it incorporates both reasoned decisions and emotional responses, calculated interests and compromises. It reveals how people may be simultaneously victims and agents; compliant and resistant.

The relationship among these various components is not random. Gendered strategies are shaped by the structure of power relations in society.

This does not, however, preclude choice on the part of workers. The particular form that a gendered strategy assumes rests on the extent to which structure impinges on 'choice' at different points in history. Workers modify their strategies as their ideas and perceptions change, and as the world around them is transformed. By looking at changing gendered strategies over time, we can better understand the complex relationship between subjectivity and consciousness, reason and intent, ideology, structure, and struggles for social change. Under what conditions do people challenge the structure? What happens to those who push through the boundaries? What shapes the outcomes of their struggles? And how do these results shape people's consciousness?

In an effort to better understand these relationships, this book traces the working lives of the small groups of women who were employed in the male-dominated auto manufacturing industry in southern Ontario. Focusing on the years 1937 to 1979, I explore the ways in which different cohorts of women experienced auto work and their union, from decade to decade, in the face of numerous developments. Throughout these years, we can observe transformations in the women's perception of themselves as individuals, consciousness as workers, and strategies of coping and resistance.

At a more general level, this book is about the politics of gender in industry and in the labour movement. The claim that workers' politics are gendered, however, does not rest on the demonstration of female/male differences. For this reason, I do not offer a point-by-point comparison of the experiences and responses of women and men workers. While such comparisons are often useful and informative, I maintain that one does not have to directly study men in order to understand women. In doing so, we run the risk of defining woman as the 'other.' Women become whatever men are not.

Women's struggles were *gendered* insofar as they were shaped by the gender politics of the day. Female auto employees lived and worked in a highly restrictive context. Like most workers, their history is largely one of struggle – an ongoing struggle for dignity, respect, and rights. However, women employed distinct strategies for achieving these goals – strategies that were based on their unique experiences as women wage-earners in a patriarchal capitalist setting.

When we consider women's experiences, the discussion of equality and social change becomes more complicated. When we take gender into account, we can see the many dimensions of social inequality and the complications in remedying it. For women, securing dignity, respect, and rights in a patriarchal capitalist milieu poses dilemmas. This book is about women's dilemmas, visions, and the realities of their lives. It also illustrates a larger process – how issues are shaped according to men's lives, men's visions, and men's needs. When we listen to women's voices, we can recognize this. When women workers make demands in the industry and in their union they uncover the masculine biases. When women try to rewrite the agenda, some men resist. There is conflict and struggle. We can see the gender politics of the union. This is labour's dilemma.

1

A Gendered Setting: The Southern Ontario Auto Industry and the UAW Canadian Region

The relationship between the 'Big Three' auto manufacturers (General Motors, Ford, and Chrysler) and the United Auto Workers Union has been the subject of extensive scholarly and journalistic research (for example, Abella, 1974; Gabin, 1990, 1984; Jeffreys, 1986; Lichtenstein, 1989; Meier and Rudwick, 1979; Meyerowitz, 1985; Milkman, 1987; Serrin, 1973; Wells, 1986; Widick, 1976). As one of the largest and most powerful unions in North America, the UAW has been at the forefront of the labour movement.[1] Indeed, the emergence of the UAW was central to the growth of industrial unionism in Canada.

Unionization was largely a response on the part of Canadian workers to general social, political, and economic maladies. Financial hardship and insecurity, along with extremely poor industrial conditions, had long characterized workers' lives. More specifically, uncertainty, favouritism, and arbitrary supervision had plagued the auto industry from the early 1900s and into the years of the Second World War. Reflecting the precarious nature of auto work during the 1920s and 1930s, workers could seldom count on fixed hours of employment. Rather, their work schedules varied unpredictably, according to the fluctuating demands of the production process. Whenever the company ran out of materials, GM management would send employees home, even if they had been on the job for just a couple of hours. Workers were expected to return to the plant later in the day. Upon returning, however, they often discovered that supplies were still unavailable. Hence, they were forced to leave and come back yet again. Given that the company paid them only for the hours they actually spent on the job, auto employees were without a steady income.[2]

Throughout this period, auto employment was also subject to seasonal fluctuations, with the production season usually lasting from September or October to May, at which time the firms retooled for the manufacture of new car models. With the changeover, managements would shut down plants and consequently lay off workers in large numbers. While laid off, some people built houses or survived by performing temporary jobs in lower-paying industries. Others relied on public relief.[3] In spite of the length of their employment in the firm, workers had no guarantee that they would be recalled when production recommenced.

Middle-aged and older men had an especially uncertain status in the industry. After the firms retooled each summer, company doctors customarily gave employees compulsory medical examinations. And on the basis of these evaluations, management decided who was and was not 'fit' for assembly work. Typically, GM officials determined that men aged forty to fifty were unfit for work and therefore unsuitable for re-entry into the plants the following season.

Before unionization, favouritism was also rampant in the auto plants. 'If the boss didn't like you, he'd fire you on the spot. [He would simply say] "Go on home!"' explained auto worker Celia Wigg. Another employee recalled, '[T]here was no union in there and they could do just what they liked with you.' Given management's arbitrary power to hire and fire, employees felt obligated to perform special tasks for their supervisor. These favours were necessary if people wanted to secure some overtime hours and/or simply keep their jobs. Workers referred to this practice as 'looking after' the boss.[4] According to George Thomson, a GM worker in the 1920s, employees came to work with baskets of vegetables for the foreman. They also brought in bottles of liquor, cut the boss's lawn, and performed various household chores. 'They did anything for the foreman,' said Thomson, 'go and shovel their sidewalk, put on their storm windows and all the rest of it ... because there was always this lay-off and this is what we dreaded.'[5]

For women, favouritism had a sexual undercurrent. According to Janet Kent, an employee of the original McLaughlin Carriage Company (later GM) in 1923, the boss was 'women-crazy.' 'He had his favourites and they're the ones that used to get in the overtime or the extra work,' she remarked. Other observers reported that in St Catharines, certain bosses visited the homes of male Armenian workers and coerced their wives to perform 'sexual favours' in order to secure their husband's employment. A sizeable number of Armenian immigrants resided in low-cost housing that GM had constructed opposite the plant and rented to the workers.

Auto manufacturers could resort to these tactics because the oversupply of labour made job-seekers easily replaceable and therefore extremely vulnerable. During the pre-war years, the unemployed stood in long lines at the factory gates or at the government employment office on a daily or weekly basis, hoping to be hired. Some people sought employment daily for many months on end. Celia Wigg recalled that women as well as men just 'waited and waited' outside General Motors. 'Soon noon would come ... and they'd [the company] say they're closing. You'd have to come back in the afternoon ... And if you're called, you're lucky ... but if you weren't you just [kept] coming and coming.'

Although auto work is considered today to be relatively well paid, the instability of employment in the 1920s and 1930s meant that few workers were financially secure. Moreover, the Southern Ontario auto plants did not offer notably high rates of pay before unionization. In 1923, Janet Kent earned 17 cents per hour. And in 1927, Celia Wigg started to work in the same firm at 16 cents an hour. 'You had to go and ask for a raise,' recalled Wigg. 'Sometimes the boss would give it to you and other times, well you know, they didn't have to give you a raise if they didn't want to ... You were afraid to go for fear that he'd show you the door. So there'd be maybe two or three of us and we'd go together.' Rarely did workers win a wage increase, however. In 1934, Effie Baldwin worked as an inspector in GM at 27 cents per hour, while the day workers in her department received 25 cents. The following year, another woman also started with the company at 25 cents per hour.[6]

Adding to these insecurities, hours of work in the industry were excessively long. In some plants, employees worked seventy to eighty hours per week. They also worked overtime throughout the week, including Saturday and Sunday.[7] McKinnon employees typically worked a nine-hour day from Monday to Thursday, and an eight-hour shift on Friday, in a forty-four-hour week.[8] Women in GM's Oshawa plant worked from 7:00 a.m. to 6:00 p.m. They rested for one hour and returned to the plant at 7:00 p.m. and worked until 9:00 p.m. According to former GM employee, George Burt, 'We worked Saturday for nine hours. We used to say that we had half a day off on Saturday from five o'clock in the afternoon. We worked so fast we did not have time to go to the bathroom or get a drink at the fountain.'[9] After the economic crash in 1929, moreover, auto manufacturers intensified the daily pace of production, and shortened the production season. Said Burt, 'The speedup was so bad that many times I saw my fellow workers in the Body Shop throw down their tools and break into tears. We were reminded by supervision that if we fell behind, there were a hundred men outside the plant ready to take our jobs.'[10]

Health and safety conditions in the plants were furthermore appalling. According to Doug Clark, a GM worker in the 1930s, 'The only time the plant was shut down was when my Father died, when he was killed, they shut the plant right up. They refused to work ... at that time they used to build the cars $1/2$ of wood and he was foreman of the Mill room and he was talking to one of his men on one of the machines and this damn big blade broke away from one of the machines and cut his head off. Flew off the machine right through the air. No protection or nothin' on the machine, you know, and my uncle wouldn't do a damn thing about it because he was afraid of losing his job. He was working there at the time, see ... They shut the plant down for just one day, they refused to work anymore that day.'[11]

This was not an isolated incident. Former auto worker Harry Benson drew on a similarly painful memory. 'My brother was over there in the stamping plant, this was in 1930, and I was driving the truck ... this thing came down and it was just like a big hook ... No safety catch on it or anything see ... I said, that'll be killin' somebody yet and it killed my brother ... It was going down over him, this big thing. He went up with a load and laded [sic] it and he was coming back down, but it was swinging and it unhooked and came down and hit him and drove his head down in between his shoulders, and he left a wife and 5 kids. They gave compensation, you know what they done, his wife and 2,000 life insurance, she did, and they (co.) gave her a lousy 56 a month to live and keep 5 kids. Now that was compensation.'[12] In the absence of a formal grievance procedure, management often arbitrarily fired workers who openly criticized the company. Employers claimed that they were willing to discuss unfair and unsafe working conditions, but in practice workers who raised complaints were either let go or forgotten at the start of a new production season.[13]

Having long endured this situation, in the 1930s small groups of workers fought tenaciously to win union representation in the industry. This was a determined struggle that grew over the course of many years, in the face of concerted opposition from employers. Recognizing the likelihood of an organized challenge by the workforce, the companies employed spies to identify and contain actual or potential union agitators. Labour activists and sympathizers were thus forced to meet underground in one another's basements and devise various tactics to elude the investigators. Effective methods of concealment were extremely important because during this time the consequences of union involvement were serious. Even though their suspicions were frequently unfounded, management fired, and promoted less often, workers whom they suspected of union activity.[14]

However, inspired by the success of the central labour body, the Congress of Industrial Organizations (CIO), in unionizing workers across the border, as well as by the ability of American auto employees to secure concessions from GM through sit-down strikes, GM workers in Oshawa heightened their efforts to collectively achieve some measure of job security and improve the terms of their employment. As the Canadian economy became increasingly bouyant in 1937 and 1938, workers grew even more confident of their ability to secure these ends.

In 1936 American auto workers broke away from the American Federation of Labour (AFL) and formed the United Automobile Workers Union under the leadership of Homer Martin. At the union's second annual convention, their Canadian counterparts created the Canadian Region of the UAW (originally Region 12 and later Region 7). On 2 March 1937 workers in Oshawa formed UAW Local 222, and GM employees elected a seven-person committee to bargain with management for basic rights, such as union recognition, a grievance procedure, seniority rights, and a recognized work week. After many unsuccessful meetings with the company, however, the auto workers walked off their jobs. The now famous Oshawa strike of 1937 lasted fifteen days and resulted in a contract that marked the beginning of a new trend in labour relations in Canada.[15]

In December 1936 the UAW-CIO also granted a charter to eighteen men in St Catharines to form UAW Local 199.[16] Workers elected Jack Crozier as president of the local and George Campbell as their bargaining representative in the McKinnon plant. However, because union leaders devoted most of their resources in Canada to organizing efforts in Oshawa, Local 199 launched a relatively low-profile union campaign. Negotiations between the McKinnon shop committee and management began on 26 April 1937, the day the Oshawa workers returned to work. The following day, Ontario Department of Labour conciliator Louis Fine announced a settlement between the company and the union.[17]

The St Catharines agreement was based on the Oshawa settlement. Both contracts specified the reduction of working hours to forty-four per week, the payment of one-and-a-half-times a worker's regular pay if she or he exceeded these hours, and wage increases of 5 cents per hour to all employees under the age of twenty-one, all female workers, and all day workers on an hourly basis. In addition, the company agreed to pay workers every other Friday, rather than once a month as in the past. Both settlements, furthermore, provided employees with non-interchangeable sex-specific seniority rights, a grievance procedure, and a 'no-discrimination' clause that specified trade union activity as the sole basis of potential discrimination.[18]

After these initial gains, however, the UAW still faced a formidable challenge. Their central task was to maintain union support among the membership. This was difficult because in the face of steadfast opposition from employers, UAW leaders could not produce the immediate and dramatic improvements that some workers desired. In 1938 the grievance procedure was not functioning smoothly, management frequently violated the seniority clause, and health and welfare measures for employees were inadequate. Consequently, union membership dropped at an alarming rate that year.

This decline prompted UAW leaders to establish a 'reorganization committee.' Made up of a few dedicated unionists, the committee spent countless hours in a door-to-door campaign to foster support for the union. Union leaders also attempted to mobilize workers through (masculine) social and recreational pursuits. For example, in 1938, the UAW in Oshawa organized a rod and gun club that was exclusive to (male) union members. The club generated considerable interest among working men, and it fostered their active participation in shooting and fishing contests. Similarly, they arranged bowling tournaments and the union's league eventually became the largest in Canada. Over time, they added hockey, hardball, and softball to their roster of activities.[19]

These strategies were effective. Indeed, some people argue that the rod and gun club and bowling teams not only helped to rebuild the membership, but played a central role in saving the union from dissolution. In 1939 UAW Locals 199 and 222 tripled their memberships. As labour gained strength and leverage in the midst of wartime labour shortages, the numbers continued to rise. By the end of 1942 UAW membership in Canada had increased by 50 per cent, marking the largest gain of any region of the International Union. In addition, Ford workers in Windsor (who were originally members of UAW Local 195) formed UAW Local 200, with a separate charter. In November 1941 they won recognition of the UAW as their exclusive bargaining agent. The following year Chrysler Canada workers (who also had initially been members of Local 195) joined the union as well (Yates, 1988: 100). By the end of the Second World War, the UAW had become the largest industrial union in Canada, with membership averaging 51,000 (Yates, 1988: 134).

The growth of the UAW is significant, for it resulted in substantial improvements in the lives of thousands of workers. Its emergence also highlights some of the fundamental principles of industrial unionism, which may be viewed as both political strategy and ideology. Gaining strength in 1935 when a group of unionists in the United States established the Congress of Industrial Organizations, its development represented a significant departure from the American Federation of Labour craft-based unions that had dominated the early labour movement. At this time, many workers were critical of the elitism and conservatism of the AFL and its Canadian counterpart, the Trades and Labour Congress (TLC). AFL and TLC leaders expressed a distinct 'business' orientation to labour-management relations and were reluctant to organize masses of unskilled workers by industry (Abella, 1974; Laxer, 1976). Industrial unionism, conversely, was premised on the notion that all workers in an industry must be organized, regardless of their skills or incomes. This approach was based on a belief in impartiality and uniformity among workers.

One of the forces behind the growth of industrial unionism in Canada was a demand on the part of workers for greater job security. Job security, however, can be achieved through various means (Storey, 1981). For auto workers, job security was intimately tied to seniority rights.[20] Auto workers were keenly aware that the oldest workers in both age and tenure of employment were the most likely to lose their jobs. Thus, seniority became a key facet of what Gersuny and Kaufman (1985) term their 'moral economy.' Indeed, most UAW members regarded the seniority principle as their most important gain. In 1939 a UAW organizer stated: 'More than anything else we built the union to end favoritism. Before we had a union the foreman decided who would work – who would be laid off – who would be called back – and it didn't depend on seniority.'[21] Workers' struggle for seniority rights was an attempt to assert some measure of control over their employment. It represented an alternative 'political economy and morality to that of laissez-faire' (Thompson cited in Gersuny and Kaufman, 1985: 403). Premised on the notion of bureaucratic impartiality, it was specifically an assault on the unrestrained freedom of management to treat workers in a highly arbitrary and discriminatory manner, with little regard for the years the employees had spent in the plant.

Some writers have argued that the UAW, consistently with these principles of fairness and neutrality, also emphasized the liberal democratic process and placed a high value on rank-and-file participation in internal union affairs. According to Charlotte Yates (1988), the Canadian Region of the UAW reflected a 'culture of democracy.' Communist and left-wing allies, says Yates (81), 'injected into the union a militant discourse and culture of workplace activism and solidarity.' Unionists thus 'articulated a strategy of militant, mobilization politics' that 'fed the membership's commitment to democratic control of the union.'

Yates (1988: 82) argues that these democratic tendencies were rooted in the union's internal structure – a structure that revolved around the UAW District Council. Formed in 1939, District Council 26 (Canadian Region) was a policy-making body and provided a forum for debate between and among council delegates and the UAW leadership. Local delegates were elected to the council on a proportional basis and they met six times annually. At these meetings the regional director presented reports on the union's current concerns and International Executive Board decisions, and delegates had the opportunity to assess the positions taken by their leaders.

From its earliest days the UAW also took a strong position on social issues and participated in both community affairs and national politics. Nancy Gabin (1984: 1) refers to the union as 'one of the most liberal and egalitarian labor organizations' in the United States. Similarly, Ruth Meyerowitz (1985: 3) calls the UAW 'one of the most progressive unions' in that country. As noted above, UAW leaders were particularly active in the women's rights movement. During the Second World War the UAW set a precedent in establishing a women's department to address the particular concerns of female workers. In 1976 the department's original director, Mildred Jeffrey, became chair of the U.S. National Women's Political Caucus; two UAW leaders also helped found the National Organization for Women; and the UAW was the first international union to support the U.S. Equal Rights Amendment (Meyerowitz, 1984: 25; Gabin, 1990).

GENDERED DIVISIONS IN AUTO WORK

The history of auto workers and their union, however, contains a fundamental contradiction. Notwithstanding these concerns about social justice and democracy, the majority of UAW members worked in automobile manufacturing – an industry that was characterized by blatant gender and racial segregation as well as sexually discriminatory policies. As noted, both before and after unionization, white, primarily Anglo-Saxon and Eastern European women and men of colour each occupied distinct and non-interchangeable positions in the auto plants. Both groups were segregated from white men, though they did not compete with one another for jobs.

Few people of colour worked in GM's Oshawa plant, while a significant number of black men could be found in McKinnon Industries and Ford's Windsor plant. In both locations, these men were concentrated in the foundries. During the Second World War Ford also employed some Chinese men and Chinese-Canadian men. McKinnon Industries employed Armenian immigrants. These men tended to perform the dirtiest, hardest, heaviest, most hazardous, and least desirable types of work in the plants. Observers reported that some auto makers believed that blacks were most suited to foundry jobs because of an innate ability to withstand high temperatures.[22] The fallaciousness of this logic, however, is evident in that the auto makers specifically recruited blacks from Nova Scotia and Toronto. Undoubtedly this recruitment was prompted by the repeated refusal of white men to perform foundry work.

Women have always been a small minority in the industry. In 1918, for example, they comprised less than 6 per cent of GM's total hourly workforce.[23] During the Second World War, however, female representation increased notably, as sizeable pockets of women could be found in various auto-parts plants across the province. For instance, in 1942, Eaton-Wilcox-Rich, a parts supplier for the production of military vehicles, employed approximately 300 workers, many of whom were women. The company trained women as inspectors and machine operators.[24] By 1943 some Ford dealerships had turned showrooms and unused parts of their shop into production units, and they too employed women.[25] Similarly, the government-financed, GM-managed Border Cities Industries in Windsor boasted 'a small army of skilled young women' who had been trained at a local vocational school to produce automatic machine guns.[26]

The Big Three auto makers employed women on a smaller scale. Furthermore, female employment in these plants reflected the interfirm and interplant differences that were typical of the pre-war period. Unlike at its American parent, there were no women in production work at Ford Canada. Indeed, in 1942 all of the firm's 200 female employees worked in clerical and secretarial jobs.[27] Similarly, Chrysler Canada largely relegated women to its auto parts and trim plants. By 1944 UAW Local 127 in Chatham, Ontario, reported approximately 125 women in Chrysler and Ontario Steel Products.[28] After the war, however, there was a sizeable female workforce in the trim plant in Ajax, Ontario.

General Motors employed by far the largest female workforce of the Big Three. During the Second World War, the company trained at least

750 women at the Windsor Vocational School to work in its newly constructed machine-gun plant.[29] Similarly, most of the 1,000 employees in
the new GM Regina Industries were women who were trained on preci-
sion machinery.[30] Although they continued to represent only a small
portion of the total GM workforce, the number of women employees
increased dramatically between 1942 and 1943. In 1942 the Oshawa plant
employed only 200 women, but by March 1943 this figure had risen to
400 out of a total workforce of 4,000.[31]

Rapid expansion of production as well as growing labour shortages
drew even more women into McKinnon Industries. Although many male
workers left the plant for war duties, the 'McKinnon family' grew from
1,800 to nearly 4,600 in just a few months. As the plant settled to steady
production, the workforce dropped to approximately 4,000. Much of this
new workforce was female. Where previously women had made up about
8 per cent of the total personnel, their proportion increased to 25 per
cent.[32] According to UAW estimates, the female workforce in McKinnon
rose from 600 in 1942 to 1,200 out of a total workforce of 4,500 in 1943.[33]

McKinnon Industries, in fact, recruited women to St Catharines from
Northern Ontario and the Canadian West. The company also attracted
many farmers and farm workers from the surrounding areas. In Oshawa
GM management tended to hire locally, though some Oshawa residents
complained that the company hired workers from surrounding towns,
while they overlooked labour in the immediate vicinity.

Many firms employed female personnel officers specifically to recruit
women workers. In McKinnon Industries, for example, a 'women's co-
ordinator' interviewed all female job applicants.[34] As well, employers
were required to list available positions with the nearest government
employment office.[35] In Oshawa a government employee named Mrs
Baxter screened most of the women who sought industrial employment.
Mrs Baxter's formal position gave her much influence. Celia Wigg recalled
that 'Baxter used to be *the* lady.' One did not get into the Motors without
getting by Mrs Baxter. 'The ladies [who] were gettin' work ... used to
bring her chicken and they brought her eggs and stuff like that ... And
Mrs Baxter liked it.'

One might expect that rule-bound firms, such as GM and Chrysler,
would have relied on complex and stringent hiring procedures, but their
recruitment decisions were, in fact, simple and non-bureaucratic. Few
women war workers were formally interviewed or asked many questions
about their technical skills or work-related experiences. At most, they
underwent routine medical examinations. 'They just hired you. Just like

that,' recalled Bea Parkin. 'It was really easy because it went into war production and they needed so many more people for, say, the army trucks and all that.' 'Everybody was gettin' work,' another employee recalled.

Like most wartime employers, the auto manufacturers publicly highlighted women's involvement in the war effort. For instance, McKinnon officials regularly placed portraits of new women employees in company publications such as *McKinnon Doings* and *McKinnon People*. In 1943 Elaine Madigan was featured on the cover of one such magazine as their thousandth 'girl.' 'Elaine,' wrote company publicists, 'finds her work on Dynamotor Armatures very interesting and entirely different from anything she has ever done.' The magazine also featured a woman named Frances Reilly. Before the war, Reilly spent nine years on McKinnon's armature line and four years on the spark plug line, and thus had the longest service record of any woman employee in the plant. In addition, management applauded Diane Cross for her ten years of service to the firm. 'Can you imagine what good a motor would be with the distributor missing from the ignition system?' asked the author. 'It wouldn't be much good would it? For the past ten years Diane Cross has been helping to produce those vital distributors not only for passenger cars but for thousands of military vehicles.'[36] In the summer of 1943 McKinnon Industries also promoted women's war work in local department store windows. In public view, the women performed the jobs that they undertook daily in the plant. The theme of the display was 'the major role being played by Canadian women on the industrial front.' Company officials reported that over 10,000 visitors viewed the exhibit.[37]

The industry's new sex composition was an outstanding theme in wartime propaganda. Both employers and governments focused on the sexiness and drama of women's involvement in this male-dominated setting. An issue of *McKinnon Doings*, for instance, read, 'It used to be that homemaking was the avocation of most women. Today the trend is away from the home and into any job that will further the cause of right ... In Vancouver the women have invaded the shipyards. The Burrard Drydock now employs women as welders ... This is working out quite satisfactorily and the Director of Personnel has indicated his willingness to take on as many women as he can get ... Bringing the picture closer to home our Gear Division now employs girls on lines. This is a new venture for McKinnon girls.'[38]

Wartime propaganda, however, was misleading. Women's employment in the auto plants was not nearly as radical or as provocative and uncomplicated as these articles and personal profiles suggest. Rather, it was restricted by employers' persistent beliefs in the existence and legitimacy of a family with a male breadwinner and their prejudices about women's distinct capabilities.[39] In this sense wartime propaganda confirmed rather than challenged women's circumscribed position in industry.[40] Focusing on general industrial trends, auto employers largely ignored the dynamics within work organizations. An analysis of internal labour markets and workers' shop-floor experiences reveals the resilience of gendered divisions and inequalities, but employers preferred to stress sexy large-scale changes. They neglected the less appealing and less seductive aspects of women's wartime employment.

In haste to meet production demands, auto makers used ascriptive traits such as gender, race, and age to match workers and jobs.[41] Workers reported hearing, at times, that GM was specifically recruiting women. At other times, the firm was accepting applications from married women. Yet in other periods they sought black men.[42] In other words, job calls were not issued exclusively on the basis of skill or technical capacity. Rather, employers tended to make assumptions about the skills, experiences, and preferences of workers according to the social category in which they fit. Relying strongly on prevailing gender and racial stereotypes and prescriptions, employers largely determined the suitability of job applicants, without consulting the applicants themselves. One woman stated, 'They put me on a sewing machine when I first went over there [GM] and I had never run a sewing machine in my life. And they put me on a great big sewing machine. And a two-needle machine to start with. And I wasn't very good at it. So they asked me one day if I would rather work off the sewing machine on a bench job. And I said I sure would. I went on a bench job making up things ready for the girls on the machines.' A retired auto worker bluntly explained that in General Motors 'girls were girls' and 'men were men.'[43]

In the Oshawa plant, both before and during the war, most women worked in the sewing department in the west plant.[44] It was huge. 'A monster of a room,' declared one employee. On one side of the room, women worked on a line of benches and on the other side they worked at sewing machines. In the middle, they inspected work at long tables. Further down, women and men worked on huge bolts of material in the adjoining cutting room.

Men, a minority in this department, used large electric machines to cut patterns out of the material. Typically, two men would work on a table cutting material, while two women sorted, tied, and marked it. Occasionally male mechanics also entered the sewing department to repair the machines. As well, stock men periodically brought carts of supplies and unloaded them for the women. A limited number of men also worked in this department as inspectors.

The sex-typing of jobs ensured that adult men would not perform the work of female sewing machine operators, however. While some of the men who repaired the machines were excellent sewers, they did not perform the job. 'I couldn't have pictured my father or brother sitting down and sewing at a sewing machine,' stated GM worker Helen Beaugrand. 'You never seen a man sit down in the sewing room,' said another woman. 'Never.'[45]

The wire and harness department, commonly referred to as the 'north plant,' was the other big women's department in GM's Oshawa complex. Wire and harness employees assembled wiring and electrical parts for vehicles. Like the sewing room women, they were employed in 'the Motors' long before the war. Apart from this similarity, however, the two groups were quite distinct. The north plant women performed intricate, tedious operations on fine wires. In the 1940s they did all the work by hand. One woman explained, 'We would have to get these wires and ... we'd be given clips and a pliers and we'd have to put a clip around and take the pliers and tighten it and hold it, take it to a sodering pot and hope to goodness they stayed together till we got them in the sodering pot ... After that, we had to tape all that ... My fingers were just blistered from these pliers and the heavy wires that I had to join together.'

Men cut the wires, while various female operators added terminals to the products. A woman might have to join as many as thirteen wires. These operations were both highly detailed and fast-paced. 'You had to keep your wits about you to make sure that you got all those wires and that you got the right length and you had the right terminal and the right socket and everything on it,' recounted one worker.

During the Second World War, women also worked in GM's aircraft division, located in the west plant above the sewing room. This was largely a makeshift facility that was designed exclusively for the production of war materials. As many plants in Canada remained on partial domestic production during the early years of the war, management placed new female employees in this section, while experienced workers remained in the cutting and sewing and wire and harness departments. This meant that the aircraft division was largely composed of women who were hired for the duration of the war only. In addition, some sewing room workers voluntarily transferred into this department because it was the only place in GM that was open to married women. When there was insufficient work in the sewing department, the surplus of workers also temporarily moved to the aircraft division.

In McKinnon Industries women worked in a wider range of departments. Nevertheless, they too were confined to fewer jobs than men. In 1946 women worked in only thirteen out of a total of 158 occupational classifications in the firm.[46]

Margaret Heritz, an assembler of blocks for the engine-cores, explained the nature of the work she performed in the foundry. 'You're all standing in a row and you're doing your part and passing it on to the next person to do their part ... I think there might have been about 10 stages of that from the start. One person might get the bottom slab and then you had all of this stuff to – supplied by people in the background ... Some of those lines were at least about 25 feet.' Although it was female-dominated, some boys and disabled men also worked with her. Heritz estimated that in her area there were four women to every one man. Reflecting a perception that able-bodied women and disabled men were rough equivalents in the workplace, management often placed the latter group on the women's jobs and paid them a woman's rate. Some male suppliers also worked on this line, but they did not undertake the same operations as these two groups. The equation of women and physically incapacitated males strongly informs our understanding of the constitution of the female gender, whereby a woman was inferior to an able-bodied man and comparable in value to a disabled man.

The company employed female matrons in addition to production workers. The law required that there be a matron in any plant that employed women. In GM the matron maintained the women's washroom, and at break times, she prepared tea on a small electric stove. In the early years matrons worked on a part-time basis. Moreover they were not covered by the collective agreement, even though they were members of the union.[47] Their status was thus unique. 'I guess you could say they were with the company, they were independent from us,' remarked one worker.[48]

Both workers and employers attempted to explain sex segregation by drawing on dichotomous thinking about women's and men's work-related capacities. One worker, for example, noted that men performed the heavy jobs, while women performed the light and detailed jobs. Another employee explained that women, unlike many men, worked on the assembly of small objects. Likewise, McKinnon management boasted that products in the female-dominated Delco division were 'exacting to produce.' An article in a company publication, for instance, read, 'Parts are so delicate all machining operations partake of jeweller's methods and procedures. Much smaller than merely minute – parts are microscopic. This is especially true of the bearings turned on the jeweller's lathe ... When these are completed they are not inspected – they are "microscopically observed!" Inserting 36 coils of wire which, with insulation is much finer than human hair, is a trick that requires deftness to the nth degree ... The parts in this entire operation are so delicate that all work is performed in specially cleansed air under controlled conditions.'[49]

Employers furthermore reinforced sex segregation by promoting the idea that women were temporary workers, merely supportive of absentee men. Patriotism was indeed an outstanding theme in employers' and governments' depiction of women workers in this period.[50] Featuring photographs of eleven female employees, an article in *McKinnon Doings* read, 'During the war years while men went forth to fight, 4 million Canadian women toiled on the home front to produce material and maintain morale. The unity of Canadian women is exemplified here at McKinnon's with representatives from every province. Such unity as this has helped achieve the unconditional surrender of Germany and brought us to the half-way mark in the collapse of our enemies.'[51] In mobilizing female workers during the war, both the National Selective Service and the federal Department of Labour viewed women as a large reserve of labour, placing emphasis on women's patriotic obligation to work, not their right to employment (Pierson, 1986: 22–3). The auto makers similarly called on women workers to perform voluntary services and donate blood. 'Every woman in the Allied nations has a part to play,' read one article. 'There are still a large number of the younger women, who although working on munitions and in other defense industries, have not been able to avail themselves of the privileges of any of our present organizations. With this thought before them, a group of our local women have started a movement that will embody those who have not enrolled elsewhere This movement ... is rapidly taking shape under the guidance of the Canadian Women's Voluntary Service.'[52]

Historian Ruth Pierson explains that 'someone had to collect the salvage and the contributions to Victory Loans and to pass out information on how to practise domestic economies necessary for the war effort' (1986: 35). Not surprisingly, at the local level, women performed most of this work. Regardless of employment status, women provided voluntary labour that supported a huge network of wartime services and activities. In 1941 the Department of National War Services established a Women's

Voluntary Service Division to coordinate these efforts, and one month prior to this a group of Toronto women formed the Canadian Women's Voluntary Services (Ontario Division) (Pierson, 1986: 35–6).

These activities were undoubtedly crucial to the war effort, and many Canadian women enthusiastically initiated such work. Nevertheless, women's wartime experiences were still highly circumscribed. In confining women to specific jobs in the plants, in regarding them as temporary labour, and in presenting their employment as a purely patriotic mission, employers never fully relinquished the image of women as secondary wage earners, undeserving of full rights in the workplace.

SUMMARY

This is the general framework in which women and men, workers and employers, waged their struggles. In the first few decades of the twentieth century, powerful U.S.-based auto makers were establishing themselves in Southern Ontario and workers eagerly sought jobs in this promising industry. Yet auto employment was characterized by extremely brutal working conditions, and in the face of this brutality some determined and defiant workers formed the UAW. The UAW embodied the principles of industrial unionism – a movement that stressed uniformity and impartiality, pursued justice, and encouraged social and political activism. These principles stood in stark contrast to the exclusiveness, hierarchy, and strict economism of the crafts unions. In spite of these tenets, however, the auto industry was characterized by clear gender divisions and inequalities. Long before the industry was unionized, auto manufacturers allocated labour on the basis of sex and race. Although the Second World War produced a dramatic change in the economy and thus drew many women into this sector, employers upheld their initial policies regarding 'female labour.'

Management's treatment of women workers during these early years set the parameters for subsequent interactions. Although employers did not determine workers' ideas and actions, they set limits on their perceptions and shaped the nature and extent of social change.

2

The Gender Politics of Men in the UAW (1937–1945)

The influx of women into the auto plants during the Second World War created the potential for fundamental shifts in the composition, structure, and direction of both the union and the industry. However, rather than fully embrace women war workers, UAW leaders regarded them with reservation and ambivalence.[1] Guided by an assumption that women were financial dependents and that men were, and should be, breadwinners, male unionists adopted a family wage strategy that was premised on the notion that, as breadwinners, men deserved and required higher wages and better jobs than other workers.

Yet despite the centrality of these beliefs, it was not always possible for working men to freely act on them. As production demands in industry rose, and male labourers left factories to join the armed forces, auto manufacturers hired increasing numbers of women, some of whom worked on 'men's jobs.' This shift in both the sexual composition and the division of wage labour compelled male union leaders to directly address women as a significant group within the industrial workforce. Thus, during the war years the UAW stepped up the recruitment of women as members and directly challenged unequal pay for equal work among the sexes. Both of these moves were politically and economically motivated. They were reasoned insofar as they had distinct implications for working men's position in the labour market.

As individuals, however, many working men opposed these new policies. While some male unionists could recognize the expediency of such measures, many continued to act on the idea that working men deserved to occupy a privileged position in the industry, and that they should maintain an exclusively male union and workplace. Conventional gender ideologies, along with employers' sexually divisive practices, often obfuscated the deleterious consequences of gender discrimination for the working class as a whole. Employers' use of female labour as cheap and expendable, for example, obscured the common industrial experiences of the sexes. Moreover, it encouraged working men to view women employees as a threat, rather than as partners in a unified struggle.

It is because of the strength of such perceptions that many unionists tolerated employers' unfair treatment of women workers and ignored the gender component of social inequality. These ideas contributed to the entrenchment of workplace inequalities, fractured worker resistance, and resulted in the marginalization of women in the UAW and the construction of unionism as a masculine pursuit – all of which set limits on social change and fuelled controversy around gender politics in the years to come.

ORGANIZING WOMEN AUTO WORKERS

Recognizing that women's entry into auto employment was inevitable in the midst of wartime labour shortages and increased production needs, UAW leaders attempted to organize female war workers. This measure was necessary because during the war years, prior to the establishment of the union dues check-off policy, new employees would not automatically become members of the union. Reflecting growing concerns about the recruitment of female workers, in April 1940, before approximately 400 St Catharines and Merritton Ontario auto-parts workers, UAW President R.J. Thomas asked, 'Where are the 250 woman [sic] whom I understand are employed at the plant here?' Thomas encouraged UAW leaders to think about women's weak participation in the union and act on it immediately.[2] Two months later Local 199 officials reiterated this concern. In fact, unionist George Campbell identified 'the problem of organizing the girls in the plant' as 'one of the most important organizational questions confronting the local.' Although over 1,000 'girls and women' were employed in McKinnon Industries, he stated that the union was weak among them.[3]

Claiming that women members could best teach their sisters the benefits of unionism and show them that they too could play 'a leading role in the UAW-CIO,' union leaders left the organizing task to women workers themselves (Gabin, 1984: 27). In response, delegates to the seventh UAW-CIO Convention in 1942 resolved to instruct the UAW International to hire women UAW members as organizers, when needed.[4]

The union, however, employed female organizers on a temporary basis, and unlike union drives directed at black men, the efforts directed at women employees could not be placed within a specific and well-devised program that addressed the unique concerns of this segment of the membership (Gabin, 1984: 27). Indeed, in the Southern Ontario auto plants, women-centred organizing campaigns were fairly haphazard, with rank-and-file workers rather than full-time UAW staff initiating the process. In Oshawa, for example, GM employee Ethel Thomson was responsible for organizing her female co-workers. After successfully agitating for makeshift improvements in their department, she and a co-worker held meetings in the plant when management went home for lunch. The company eventually learned about her agitation and issued her 'walking papers,' but Thomson nevertheless got the UAW campaign rolling among women workers.[5] Mary Turner was another dedicated rank-and-file organizer. Turner was newly employed in GM's aircraft division when the president of Local 222 asked her to help recruit union members. Her goal was to unionize all the women in her section and she successfully signed up thirty-eight out of forty.[6]

Many male unionists, however, were less enthusiastic about organizing women. One reason for their hesitancy was that female workers were often tardy in paying their union dues, at a time when there was no automatic deduction from the employee's pay cheque. Some UAW officials recognized that the source of this problem was women's inability to pay and not opposition or indifference to the union. In August 1943, for example, representatives of Local 252 in Toronto reported that even though women were backward in their dues payments, they strongly supported the UAW. Local 426 officials likewise claimed that dues collection was handicapped in locations where 'girls' earned only 25 cents and 30 cents per hour.[7] Acknowledging this handicap, Local 199 leaders offered reduced union dues to women who worked in McKinnon Industries. The McKinnon bargaining committee granted women a one-dollar initiation fee and 50-cent-per-month union dues until the end of the organizing drive. After this time, they planned to raise the initiation fee to two dollars and increase their dues to one dollar.[8] In April 1945 the local even requested permission to exonerate women members from paying the international assessment, though the UAW International Executive Board denied this request.[9]

Other union men, however, believed that women were inherently conservative, and they therefore approached female workers with caution and distrust (Gabin, 1984: 28). For example, in 1942 Local 240 officials in Windsor claimed that women's entry into the plants was the cause of their membership problems. In their view females were especially difficult to organize.[10] The following year R.J. Thomas disclosed similar beliefs. Thomas repeatedly warned unionists of the urgent need to get the 'girls' interested in the UAW, and he rooted this sense of urgency in the notion that women are a dangerously reactionary group. With a hint of hostility, he referred to women workers as 'pretty little things in slacks' who 'may destroy the trade union movement' if they are not activated. He declared,

There is a tremendous job of education to be done – a job that must be done now, if our unions are not to be destroyed by these women who are new to the membership lists of organized labor. Many of them think of us – if they think at all – as radicals and trouble makers. Others have that dangerous 'little knowledge,' which is even more difficult to combat than ignorance. They are the reactionaries who are easy prey to insidious anti-labor propaganda. They may form the backbone of conspiracies against unions. Unless all organized labor acts to influence and educate these women workers, the work of years, the slow and painful building up of the trade union movement, may be destroyed. Uneducated in unionism, they represent a potential danger to the labor movement; educated they can be a constructive and powerful part of it and contribute much to its further advancement. But we must get there first – before management has won them over. We need them in industry, need them badly, but we cannot afford to run the risk of allowing others to destroy our unions.[11]

WOMEN'S UNION LOYALTIES

While Thomas was expressing the sentiments of many working men, the words and actions of the women themselves suggest that these beliefs had almost no foundation. Indeed, women played an important role in building the UAW. Only when we view union loyalties and worker consciousness narrowly, from an institutional lens, are we likely to draw such conclusions. When we measure political commitment solely in terms of representation in leadership, office-holding, and public prominence, we overlook women's contributions. The union participation of most wage-earning women was intermittent and unofficial. Within the labour movement, women largely performed devalued and mundane duties, and their contributions confirmed rather than challenged conventional ideas about women's proper place in employment and society. However, the restricted nature of their participation does not indicate that they were insignificant or unsupportive of the labour movement. Commenting on the early UAW, a female union activist said, 'Most of the girls I was close to, they were all in the union, a great percentage, a tremendous percentage. You know we didn't live and breathe and think union, it was all so new ... you just paid your dues and if there was an election [you voted].'[12]

Women auto workers strengthened the union in undramatic and seemingly unexceptional ways. Although their attendance was disproportionately lower than men's, many women frequently went to union meetings. 'We went to all kinds of meetings,' explained GM worker Ann Brisbois. 'We used to go up to the high school to meetings ... And the women always sat at the front – always had the front seats at that time. Don't ask me why. We were there anyways,' she stated with laughter. When several groups of women employees first attended a meeting of 400 McKinnon workers, the men greeted them with an enthusiastic reception.[13] During the union's early years in Oshawa local union leaders even held meetings exclusively for women. These meetings were attended by workers from the sewing room, wire and harness, rod and tubing, and rad room in GM. The rationale behind sex-segregated gatherings is unclear, but one worker believed they were set up because women and men had different wage rates from one another and thereby had some distinct contractual demands.

Rank-and-file women also did their duty as 'foot soldiers' in the early strikes and sit-downs. For this activity they again received a warm reception from male co-workers. During the 1937 strike at GM in Oshawa men cheered 600 women workers as they left the company buildings.[14] Elsie Karn remembered the day the strike began. Said Karn, 'The committee girl came along and told us they hadn't signed the contract and that we were going out – our foreman just sat there looking at us, and we had to wait one minute, because we had all punched the [time] cards.'[15] Shop steward Helen Graham reported that 'there was some that didn't go for it at all. Others that were for it.' Graham noted that there was no strike pay at the time. 'And there was a lot of women that worked in the sewing department that needed that work,' she explained. 'So they weren't in favour of a strike at all. But they all went out.'

Some women backed their locals without hesitation. For example, when asked if she participated in strike activities, Ann Brisbois remarked, 'Oh, definitely! Oh, you bet! We took our turn picketing. I should say.' Helen Graham likewise recollected, 'I walked right at the gate at the end of ... Bond and Mary Street ... We used to have to picket there ... Cutting and sewing was a big department and the men and women used to ... keep walking around the line ... a great big line there. And the foreman and that, they'd all go into the plant, but they'd go down through the parts and service which was down at the end of Mary Street ... We used to holler, 'Scab, scabs!' ... The only ones that went into the plant were the foremen and superintendents and that. All the workers were out.'

When more than 4,000 McKinnon employees staged their first strike over a four-month-old wage demand in 1941 St Catharines women also played a key role.[16] Media reports indicate not only that women workers picketed, but that their participation was newsworthy. Although 4,000 workers were involved in the strike, the St Catharines Standard focused on a small group of women. Apart from office staff, a unit of young women employed in the Delco division by the British government remained in the plant alone and unaffected by the dispute. The newspaper described how the striking women and the 'British supply girls' greeted one another when the former group left the plant during their lunch hour.[17]

UAW leaders also publicized women's involvement on the picket lines. The participation of women workers was notable because many of them had just recently become members of the union. In fact, a sizeable number of women, mainly from the Delco division, signed union cards in the first few days of the strike.[18] As the dispute wore on, they continued to give their support, bolstering the pickets. Even women who had not yet joined the union sympathized and peacefully patrolled the main plant entrances.[19] Union officials claimed that after reporting to work in the morning, twenty-four women walked out of the plant to join the strikers.[20] Promoting the women's commitment, Local 199 organized an 'all girl' picket from three o'clock to six o'clock in the evening.[21] In the first few days of the strike, roughly fifty women workers were on regular duty in the mornings, although the numbers of male and female picketers dropped as the dispute continued.[22]

Like wage work, strike participation was divided along gender lines. Some union men adopted a paternalistic though well-meaning stance towards their striking sisters. Observers explained, 'There were so many that were into leading, that the women didn't seem to have as much in it ... They didn't want the women on the picket lines too much. I think they were just more or less afraid of complications or somebody getting hurt.'[23] According to one worker, the men 'kept saying, "You girls shouldn't be here, we don't really need you. There's no reason for you to go around here in the cold," and all this kind of stuff.' This gesture did not insult the women, however. Ivy Imerson stated, 'Then we began to think well, it does seem kind of silly because I didn't like the idea of being stuck with three or four men and that sort of thing. They mostly stuck it through the days for the women and mostly the main gate.'[24] In the afternoon the women were on the picket line for two shifts, each of which lasted two hours. Women picketed the gate that led to the plant in which they worked.[25]

Before the formation of ladies' auxiliaries (support organizations composed of working men's wives and daughters), women workers also provided refreshments to their striking brothers. According to Ann Brisbois, 'a lot of the women went out ... Used to spend nearly all day making sandwiches and coffee in a little store at the corner of Mary and William Street ... And the men that were on strike, they used to come over there for coffee and sandwiches.' Proud of her contributions, Brisbois declared that she was not a 'free rider.' 'Anything we got, we worked for,' she said. 'It's sad that we always had to go out. And I always felt very, very hurt that the salaried employees would do nothing ... But they were the first ones to try and find out, "What did you get?" ... because they would get the same thing. And that bothered me ... We were the ones who worked for it. But then I'm glad it was me, that I worked for what I got, rather than sitting there and letting somebody else do it.'

Some women also expressed strong opinions about the St Catharines dispute. Reflecting the diverse and resolute viewpoints among the female population on strike at McKinnon Industries, the *St Catharines Standard* featured a series of commentaries by women workers and the wives of male workers. The reactionary stance of a minority of women generated forceful rebuttals from others – responses that revealed a powerful union consciousness. Representing the conservative reaction, the wife of a McKinnon worker wrote that she and her husband were grateful for his earnings of 52 cents an hour. Criticizing UAW representative Robert Stacey for claiming that the workers were inadequately paid, she adamantly declared that McKinnon wages were ample to provide for a well-kept home and a family of three. 'I don't understand how anyone can quibble over a few cents in these times,' this 'McKinnon Worker's Wife' angrily asserted.[26]

These comments generated equally angry replies from female strikers. One woman responded, 'Did that McKinnon's wife ever work in a factory under high speed pressure all day long?' Female employees, she noted, 'work extra hard instead of making a good bonus' only to find that their rates (productivity quotas) have been raised and 'we are working harder for less and less.' Furthermore, this woman underlined the need for extra money in order to pay for medical expenses which mount because of the hardships of work. She stated, 'I want to see this strike settled as much as anyone but not until we get our increase, which we are entitled to, and the company can well afford to pay it.'[27]

Anti-union sentiments also prompted a female auto worker to make the following incisive comments:

I am not so good at composing a letter of this kind, but I believe I can convey my meaning. I am one of the girl employees on strike at McKinnons'. I have worked there a good number of years and every time I have ever asked for a raise, have been told the company could not afford it ... If the so-called big names feel they would like to sacrifice and be patriotic, they can take their own sons and daughters out of college and let them do their share of slaving. McKinnons and the government have their representatives and we picked Bob Stacey as ours. As far as I know I certainly wasn't forced or coerced into joining the union. I joined because it stands for democracy, which is what we are trying to fight for. There are plenty of millionaires being made out of this war and they sure do not care who gives their lives as long as they rake in the money. We don't want Hitler here, but we are being run by a few 'would-be' Hitlers. The working man of McKinnons should be able to live not merely exist and have the right to save a dollar and send their children to college the same as G.M.'s executives do. The workers are the ones that count and should not be treated as ignorant dogs. If I do not have my parents to live with I would have gone short many a day on McKinnon's pay ... Here's hoping the government realizes we have to live, too!

She signed this letter, 'A "live and let live" reader.'[28] Few women spoke about the union with equal passion, but even women who rarely attended meetings and never walked a picket line (either by choice or because of obstacles such as inadequate transportation, conflicting obligations, or long distances to travel)[29] upheld the basic principles of unionism and understood where they were located in the hierarchical class structure. For instance, although GM worker Marion Manning was not a regular at UAW gatherings, she 'felt the union was a good thing' insofar as it ensured that veterans would return to fair working conditions. Manning furthermore believed that the union offered her some security. In her view, 'if you had a problem, the union was there to help you.' Similarly, Celia Wigg never took part in union activities, but she never crossed a picket line either. Having worked in the Motors both before and after the UAW, she recognized the union's positive impact. Wigg declared, 'The union came in then and ... they had to pay us a little bit better and ... you couldn't get away with a lot ... you couldn't get fired just for nothing ...

You always thought, well, you'd have to have a good excuse before they could fire you.'

WOMEN AND EMPOWERMENT

Yet, in spite of their union loyalties, women were peripheral to the administration of the UAW. For intermittent participation in sit-downs, strikes, and standing committees, the union drew heavily on their time and labour, but few women held office or controlled the social and political direction of the union. In short, UAW leaders organized women workers, but women were not empowered. Indeed women were caught in a vicious circle insofar as their restricted participation in the union prevented them from gaining the formal experience considered necessary for entry into influential positions in the labour movement.

The structure of the UAW was made up of various offices that existed at three main levels of administration. The central decision-making body was the UAW International Office in Detroit, Michigan. At this level, there was a president, a vice-president, an International Executive Board, and various staff representatives, each of whom carried out specific duties within separate jurisdictions. While the international staff represented workers throughout Canada and the United States, there were also regional offices and within each region, various UAW locals existed to serve their own membership. Each UAW local would furthermore elect its own executive, as well as set up various union standing committees.

Few women at any level held the position of president or vice-president, and rarely was a woman elected plant chairperson. In 1944 the UAW-CIO reported one female president in all of its locals across the United States and Canada.[30] Women activists were more likely to become recording secretaries – a position that involved traditional secretarial duties – recording and delivering the proceedings of union meetings and handling the local's correspondence.[31] Recording secretaries had a good grasp of local issues and politics, but they lacked power and authority. They could vote and speak on motions that were brought before the local union executive, but they did not have a voice on the bargaining committee.[32]

Insofar as they set the agenda for negotiating contracts, bargaining committee members, conversely, wielded considerable influence. In an exceptional case, a woman sat on the first GM bargaining committee in Oshawa. Indeed Gertrude Edwards, a committeewoman in the cutting and sewing departments, was one of the few women ever to fill this position. George Burt, Canadian UAW director, recalled that 'Gerty' 'represented the girls and ... went all over the place with the guys.' As a steward, she was responsible to approximately 200 women. As a member of the Local Bargaining Committee, she was accountable to a total of about 500 women. Edwards negotiated contracts in Windsor, St Catharines, and Oshawa.[33]

Some women were also elected stewards or committeewomen and, less often, chairwomen in female-dominated departments or plants.[34] In 1937 Florence Smith, possibly the first female member of Local 222, served as a steward for women in GM's wire and harness department.[35] During the war years Isabel Baird also represented the wire and harness women, and in the late 1930s Helen Graham was a steward in GM's sewing room. Also in this department a machine operator named Carrie served as steward, chief steward, and alternate.[36]

UAW regional directors also appointed some women to union standing committees. Committee members offered advice and recommendations to union leaders, but they did not set policy. According to a Report of the International Credentials Committee to the first UAW Women's Conference in 1944, in only five locals represented at the conference were women not involved. A breakdown of the nature of their activities, however, reveals that they were concentrated in recreation, education, political action, social welfare–counselling, and women's committees.

Women's limited place in the union was in many ways rooted in sex-segregated employment. Their confinement to a small number of female-dominated departments and their minority status in the auto plants ensured that few women could rise to executive positions in the UAW. At both the international and the local levels these were elected rather than appointed offices, and few women could mobilize the support necessary to win plant-wide elections. Furthermore, women's marginal status in the auto plants most likely limited their aspirations. Given the nature of their recruitment during the war, many women perceived wage work as temporary or at most a secondary commitment. Consequently, they had a weaker investment in the union than their brothers.

Gendered divisions in society also ensured that few women could sustain ongoing participation in the labour movement. Because of the organization of domestic work as a private undertaking, the inadequacy of community support for families, and a division of labour in which women were primary care-givers in the home, most women found it difficult, if not impossible, to become fully absorbed in union activities. Labour leaders spent countless hours in meetings and conferences in somewhat remote locations. Most of this activity, furthermore, took place after working hours. The level of commitment demanded by the labour movement was unrealistic for most women and explains the intermittent nature of their involvement. One exceptional woman activist remembered that she and her husband were on thirteen different union committees. Explaining how she managed to maintain this level of participation, she stated, 'I go home at night and I do washin on Mon night come home on Tues damp down the clothes, iron on the Wed and I have my whole life just mapped out of what I was going to do ... I said, yeah, but there's just so much that any human being can do and still survive.'[37]

Predictably, most of the small number of women who became labour activists did not have the burdens of child care or care of men in their homes. The majority of pioneering UAW women were either single and childless or married to men who were also highly active in the labour movement. Shop stewards Gertrude Edwards and Isabel Baird never married. And labour organizers Ethel Thomson and Mary Turner were married to men who also played a prominent role in the UAW; these couples centred their lives around labour agitation and political action.

In addition, women's marginal role in the UAW was reinforced by the exclusive attitudes and behaviour of union men themselves. Newly recruited war workers clearly understood that since its origins the UAW was led and defined by men. Female members lacked both the personal and the material resources necessary to make themselves heard. With the exception of a few women-only meetings at the beginning of unionization, UAW sisters in Canada had little opportunity to set their own goals and shape their own struggles without feeling inhibited or intimidated by men, sensitive about their political inexperience or softness.

In comparison, American UAW women made greater gains in this direction. For example, in April 1944, in response to a growing female membership, the UAW-CIO War Policy Division introduced a Women's Bureau,[38] with Mildred Jeffrey as director and Lillian Hatcher as staff representative.[39] The bureau's mandate was to 'develop recommended policy and program affecting ... women members.' It focused on seniority, safety standards, maternity leave, and other problems that affected women's employment. Furthermore, through the bureau, Jeffrey, Hatcher, and others attempted to develop techniques to draw rank-and-file women into union activities and develop their sense of union citizenship.[40] As part of the War Policy Division, however, the Women's Bureau had a temporary status.[41]

Largely owing to the efforts of these women, the UAW held its first International Women Workers' Conference in Detroit, Michigan, on 8–9 December 1944, with 146 delegates representing ninety-nine locals from every region in the union except for Regions 6 and 9A, in attendance. Conference organizers set out to address women's immediate post-war problems.[42] Mirroring the goals of the UAW Women's Bureau, they also addressed full employment, equal pay for equal work, the fair application of seniority rights, the activation of female members, and women's 'special' problems.[43]

These early initiatives successfully highlighted women's unique place in industry,[44] fostered a 'sisterhood' within the UAW, and suggest the emergence of a feminist consciousness.[45] According to Nancy Gabin, women's involvement in these forums gave them political experience, skills, and self-confidence – resources that permitted UAW women to challenge sex discrimination in later years (1984: 57).

UAW-CIO leaders, however, frequently reminded the women of their limited powers to initiate change. Such reminders sometimes revealed both indifference and condescension. For instance, at the union's first (American) women's conference on 7 February 1942, UAW Secretary-Treasurer George Addes claimed that although working men believed that women should be displaced before men, female delegates should not debate the issue at that time. Furthermore, when a woman from Local 174 in the United States recommended that a woman chair the afternoon session, Addes responded, 'I'm not too much interested in chairing this meeting ... because I have a lot of other work I could attend to' (cited in Gabin, 1984: 84–5).

Similarly, in 1944 a newspaper commentary read, 'Women may wear the slacks but the men still wear the pants in the UAW-CIO.' Reporting on the first UAW Women's Conference, the American Dorothy Jones stated, 'Though it may be all right for the woman who slaves over a hot lathe all week to vote in November, it isn't fitting for her to become too global in her political thinking. All the Rosie the Riveters and the Winnie the Welders had their say about such topics as maternity leaves, cockroaches in plant food, whether powdering the nose was an essential activity and the minimum number of minutes required in the rest room [but they were not permitted a voice on more wide ranging political issues].' At the meeting, Pat Telenig of Local 740 in the United States stated that she had sent a telegram to Winston Churchill voicing the women's objection to some of his political statements. As she read her message aloud, the sisters applauded enthusiastically. However, Victor

Reuther, assistant director of the UAW War Policy Division and chair of the conference, reacted differently. Reuther 'rocked back on his heels at the unexpected turn of events.' After the applause died down, he stated, 'Sister Telenig, you have put the chair in a very embarrassing position. I'm afraid that such matters are far removed from the subject matter planned for this conference. You must understand,' he added, 'that such an important action as speaking to heads of foreign governments is the province of the national executive committee.' He then quipped, 'If such a telegram were approved some of the other sisters might want to send one to Stalin to tell him how to run his government or to Chiang Kai-shek.' Ann Lamont, an organizer at Bendix in New York, replied, 'I can't understand why, if we are allowed to have our own conference, we can't take any action we see fit. The executive board says that women workers must participate in the PAC [Political Action Committee] but they think we can't understand what is happening in Greece. If they want us to take part in political and national questions, then now is the time for us to start taking part. The Greek situation requires the attention of everyone – not just the men of the world.' Amidst strong opposition from the women delegates, Reuther eventually convinced the conference to send the telegram for approval to R.J. Thomas, UAW president.[46]

Such tensions resurfaced at the fourth quarterly meeting of the UAW Executive Board in July 1945. At this meeting a delegation of American women demanded stronger female representation within the UAW power structure. They wanted to see, for instance, one woman on staff in each region or a woman on each co-director's staff, a woman in the UAW Education Department, and a separate women's bureau with additional female representatives. They further demanded that women be appointed on staff in the international office and they requested the assurance that there would be close cooperation between women's committees, regional directors, and top union officers, as well as better coordination between departments, with access to information. In response to these requests, R.J. Thomas and a Brother Kerrigan proposed to the other board members that the union place four women on the War Policy Committee. In addition, he and George Addes suggested that they appoint a woman on each board member's staff. The UAW Executive Board, however, rejected both of these proposals.[47]

The limits of women's struggles during this period were especially apparent in Canada. During the war, women in the Southern Ontario plants did not mount equally militant and organized protests for sexual equality. This is partly because women were a much smaller force in

Canadian compared with American war production plants. In 1939 there were 39,500 women in the American auto industry, and by November 1943 this figure had risen to 203,000, boosting the proportion of women in the industry to 26 per cent (cited in Gabin, 1984: 5). In comparison, in 1943 General Motors in Oshawa and McKinnon Industries, the largest employers of women among the Big Three manufacturers in Ontario, employed 400 and 1,200 women, respectively.[48] Women in Canada were thus even more isolated and peripheral than their American sisters. They were a minority within a minority of women.

Furthermore, because the UAW was an international union whose head office and the majority of whose membership were based in the United States, resources were not widely available to Canadian members. The union was highly centralized during these years, conducting most activities from Detroit. As well, the pioneers in the union's struggle for women's rights, Mildred Jeffrey, Lillian Hatcher, and Caroline Davis, were Americans who had a limited understanding of the Canadian context. In turn, women in Canada had little input in the UAW International Women's Department. Phoebe Blair from Local 192 in Tilbury, Ontario, represented Canadians on the nine-woman advisory committee to the women's conference.[49] But given the huge number of American women relative to Canadian, conference organizers concerned themselves primarily with U.S. developments and issues in both the legislative arena and the plants.

The UAW Women's Bureau worked in close contact with American government agencies, such as the Labor Production Office (War Production Board), War Manpower Commission, Federal Security Agency, and Department of Labor.[50] Accordingly, speakers at the first International UAW Women's Conference, typical of others to follow, included Frieda Miller, director of the U.S. Department of Labor, and Frank E. Hook, congressman from the twelfth District of Michigan.[51]

Admittedly, the UAW Women's Bureau attempted to mobilize rank-and-file women throughout Canada as well as the United States.[52] Largely as a result of these efforts, in 1944 the Local 112 Women's Council in Toronto held meetings in which speakers lectured on housing, industrial health, and hygiene. Women from surrounding union locals also participated in these functions, in an attempt 'to make more women active and to intermingle with members of the other locals to further extend their aims.'[53] In addition, the union's general education program included special training for 'girls.'[54] These undertakings, however, were rare and did not show immediate results.

In 1944 Local 127, representing Chrysler and Ontario Steel Products workers in Chatham, Ontario, reported that even though there were 125 women in the plant, they had neither a local union women's committee nor a child-care committee. Local 199 reported the same for the McKinnon plants. Local officials requested that the women's bureau help them increase the participation of women by providing some literature on women workers and sending a woman to speak at union meetings.[55] In spite of their comparatively large female workforce, GM's Oshawa plant was also without such committees.

Thus, although prominent American women were gearing up the machinery to mobilize female members, Canadian women did not benefit from their efforts for several years. Rank-and-file women in Canada were keenly aware of the political realities of the shop floor and the union local. With this in mind, most were hesitant to make any significant moves towards eliminating or redefining the gendered division of labour. They did not have the organizational resources, personal confidence, or sense of efficacy necessary to collectively and openly advocate women's rights. Thus, while some American sisters tried to 'shake up' the UAW International, working women in Canada did not take up the debate with the same sense of purpose and militancy. Canadian sisters therefore lacked a voice of their own. In principle on behalf of the entire union membership, working men defined the issues, set the agenda, and led the struggle for workers' rights.

WORKING MEN'S VISION OF A JUST WORKPLACE AND THE
ENTRENCHMENT OF GENDER DIVISIONS

During the Second World War, male unionists displayed a narrow, gender-biased vision of social justice. Embracing conventional ideas about the unequal market value and different capacities and responsibilities of women and men, they largely took gendered divisions and inequalities in employment for granted. UAW leaders seriously took up only those matters that they could understand on the basis of their own experiences in industry. As a result, they challenged arrangements that obviously threatened working men's position. From a narrow perspective, they addressed sex-based inequalities as one of many contractual issues that arose in their ongoing struggle with management. This approach was part of a gendered strategy.

This strategy, however, unveiled many contradictions. As noted above, the UAW-CIO was a broad-based movement to organize workers by industry rather than by trade or skill. The basic principles of industrial unionism, however, clashed with working men's beliefs in a male bread-winner and women's inferior position in the labour market. One view posited democracy and economic justice for all, while the other promoted a hierarchy among workers, exclusiveness and privilege based on sex. Given these contradictions, union men had to constantly reconcile the philosophy of their union with their patriarchal practices. Principled unionists monitored the actions of their more reactionary brothers, and the workers' struggle was therefore fundamentally fractured – in both ideology and action.

EQUAL PAY FOR EQUAL WORK

The UAW campaign for equal wages for equal work exemplifies the union's partial and ambivalent understanding of social justice. Union leaders had long known that women auto workers received lower rates of pay than men, but they viewed these differentials as legitimate insofar as they were linked to sex-based job classifications. As long as women performed work that was labelled 'female' and had been traditionally performed by women, the lower rates were acceptable.

As sexual divisions became blurred during the war, however, union leaders began to re-evaluate some jobs. Specifically in cases where women were performing 'men's work,' the union demanded equal pay regardless of the sex of the worker. According to some unionists, this policy would enhance the UAW's credibility among unorganized female employees.[56] Upholding this view, in June 1942 George Campbell of Local 199 warned, 'Unless the Union is able to give leadership to the struggle for equal pay for equal work we will remain weak among the women.' An influx of women into McKinnon Industries made it 'doubly important' that they give the issue 'specific attention.' The UAW District Council also warned that thousands of women would soon enter industry and would 'only be forthcoming if they are justly treated.'[57]

Insofar as few women protested their lower rates, however, it is unlikely that this was the union's primary concern. More important, union leaders recognized that if employers could pay women less money than men, the latter's bargaining position would be jeopardized. In some plants, men's fears of female replacement or wage undercutting were realistic, while in others they had little basis. Yet regardless of the plausibility of such outcomes, these anxieties spurred action. Workers discussed equal pay with increasing frequency at District Council 26 and Canadian Region staff meetings throughout the early 1940s. As employers hired women to perform men's work, unionists demanded that they immediately implement UAW equal pay policy.[58]

Typically, auto employers rejected the workers' demands. In January 1943, for example, the GM Shop Committee in Oshawa reported that management was using various means to evade equal pay.[59] According to Al Shultz, Local 222 financial secretary, GM had redistributed work and claimed that job operations that women were performing were never, in fact, done by men.[60]

In Local 200, working men's fears of female substitution were so strong and employers' resistance to equal pay was so steadfast that the issue precipitated a strike. For years, the Ford plant in Windsor employed only men in production work. But in October 1942 the company notified the Local 200 Bargaining Committee that it planned to hire 1,500 women and was requesting permission from the Regional War Labour Board to employ them at a reduced rate of 50 cents per hour. Despite the union's protests, Ford officials proceeded with the application and informed the labour board that the two parties had failed to reach an agreement.[61]

Local 200 officials were confident of their position because their agreement with Ford had stipulated that the company not hire women without first consulting the union.[62] The local thus requested that further action be stalled until they could make proper representations. However, in the interim, the labour board suggested that Ford's request be granted, subject to further inquiry. Although the UAW warned that this action would precipitate serious trouble in the plant and reiterated that they would not accept lower rates for 'female help,' the board did not heed their warnings.

The union thus called a joint meeting of the steward bodies of Local 200 and Amalgamated Local 195, including shop chairmen and stewards from Chrysler, Gar Wood, Backstay Standard, Kelsey Wheel, Canadian Bridge, Border Cities Industries, Gotfredson, Canadian Industries Limited, Champion Spark Plug, and others to discuss Ford's plans. One after the other, these men reaffirmed their full support of Local 200. The unionists agreed that Ford's proposal would jeopardize the position not only of Ford employees, but of workers in other Windsor plants as well. The plant chairmen then formed a committee to take joint action if necessary. Also in response to these developments, District Council 26 reaffirmed its position on equal pay and, in doing so, described the harmful effects of low wages and the need for a decent standard of living among women.[63]

By the end of the month the Ontario War Labour Board had temporarily ruled that Windsor employers be prohibited from employing women in any position or job where men were previously employed at rates in excess of 65 cents per hour.[64] Ford officials, however, were anxious for a permanent ruling. The company claimed that they faced a severe labour shortage, could not hire men through the National Selective Service, and had invested extensively in preparing facilities such as restrooms for women workers. Between August and December 1942 close to 3,000 men had left the company's employment, including those who joined the armed forces.[65]

Growing impatient, Ford hired thirty-seven women to work in its 'stock 7' department. And while men had been paid 85 cents per hour, the company paid these women on a salary basis, from $70 to $100 per month. When questioned, Ford officials boldly confirmed that they had indeed hired these women to perform the men's work and that they would hire as many women as they saw fit. Local 200 leaders stated, 'This meant the possibility of hundreds of our union brothers being likewise replaced by low salaried female help.' Under this threat, UAW members from almost every department in the three Ford plants flooded the union hall and requested that the local take action. The next morning, the workers themselves acted. Men in the three plants walked out in unanimity and established picket lines at all of the gates. Shortly after, Ford officials admitted that they had to discontinue operations.[66]

After many meetings, the labour board was forced to deny Ford's original request of a 50-cent-per-hour hiring rate for women, and by late Sunday the parties reached a settlement. This agreement stated that the company must acknowledge that the Wartime Wage Control Order, P.C. 5963, did not prevent employers from adopting the principle of 'equal pay for equal work.' Ford was also to confirm its policy of employing only males in manufacturing operations with the stipulation that if it became necessary to alter this policy in the future, they would apply the principle of 'equal pay for equal work' and discuss the matter with the union. Furthermore, the employment status of any or all of the thirty-seven women employed in department 'stock 7' would be referred to an umpire. Ford agreed to terminate the employment of women in any positions that the umpire found to be subject to the terms of the existing collective agreement.[67]

On Monday morning Ford workers gathered at the City Market in Windsor in what was then reported to be the largest closed union meeting ever held in Canada. The more than 9,000 male workers in attendance unanimously accepted the settlement. The workers then held a victory parade to the City Hall, where they were congratulated by Windsor Mayor Reaume and other speakers. By midnight the first shifts of Ford workers had returned to work, and within twenty-four hours production had returned to normal.

Controversy, however, continued into the next year. On 3 June 1943, seven months after the strike, W.H. Clark, personnel manager of the Ford Motor Company of Canada, told the Regional War Labour Board that because of a shortage of male labour, the firm would have to immediately employ women throughout its manufacturing plants. Clark requested the board's permission to hire these women at 60 cents per hour. This figure represented 80 per cent of the current (male) hiring rate of 75 cents per hour. Ford officials claimed that they were acting in accordance with the provisions of the agreement between Ford and Local 200 because they had raised their plans with the union committee. Claiming that they faced a 'critical situation,' Ford representatives urged the board to consider their application and render a decision at its meeting that month.[68]

Like many employers, Ford management reasoned that female workers should receive a lower rate than men because women would create an increase in production costs. 'Production costs' typically referred to the expense of constructing additional washroom and changeroom facilities for women. Union leaders believed that such concerns were superfluous and merely obscured the more consequential matter of equal pay. 'These several points to us are not the main issues and we do not intend to fall into the trap the Company is setting for us. We intend to bargain on the one point and one point only that is equal pay for equal work,' said a labour representative. He asserted, 'We welcome the coming of women into our plant, but insist that they have equality.'[69] The union requested that the labour board postpone its decision for two weeks, while they prepared a strong brief. The board ruled a stay of one week. However, in the interim Ford backed down and withdrew their application to the board.[70]

The employers' interests were blatant in the Ford case. As soon as Ford officials realized that they could not hire women at a lower rate than men, they cancelled a lucrative government contract and farmed out work to smaller and lower-paying feeder plants. According to George Burt, after the strike, the company 'never hired one single, solitary girl in their production operations for the whole period of the war.'[71]

Members of the Regional War Labour Board, largely businessmen, also revealed their vested interests. In the 1942 case Ford had originally proposed to hire women at 60 cents per hour. However, it was the labour board that recommended they lower this figure to 50 cents.[72] In addition, Local 200 leaders reported that labour board representatives directly tried to dissuade the unionists from seeking the equal pay clause. According to unionists Roy England and Thomas Muir, 'three members of the Regional War Labour Board spent one whole week-end in Windsor trying to convince our Negotiating Committee that if we established the principle of "equal pay for equal work" we would be causing the disruption of the whole economic system in Canada.'[73] District Council 26 delegates called the board's reasoning 'ridiculous in view of the fact that across the river in Detroit this practice was recognized in the last war and more widely in this one in both the United States and Great Britain.' They were 'unaware of any economic upheaval there.'[74]

Throughout these years UAW leaders openly criticized the Regional and National War Labour Boards. In a brief submitted to the National War Labour Board, District Council 26 argued that nothing in the wage order prevented employers from paying women the same rate as men. Although it was illegal under the order for employers to change the basic rate range of a given job classification without the board's authority, many companies were hiring women at lower wages even though there was no sex differential in productivity. According to the union, this was permissible 'mainly because of the uncertain attitude on the part of the former National War Labour Board in dealing with this problem.' Unionists further stated that even though they had won equal pay for equal work in many cases, these gains had entailed the time-consuming process of considering each case on its own merit and carrying it through the grievance procedure under the collective agreement. Most often the employer referred the cases to the Regional War Labour Board, which was reluctant to take a stand.[75]

The UAW itself, however, also acted expediently. As soon as they won equal pay clauses to protect established male rates, the unionists lost sight of the matter of decent wages and living standards for women. After Local 200 negotiated an equal pay clause, they made no effort to hire women into the relatively high-paying Ford Motor Company. In fact, in 1946, local officials again agreed to the company's policy against the employment of female workers in manufacturing operations in Windsor (including Ojibway). These men accepted a clause that read, 'If the employment of female workers becomes necessary or desirable they shall be paid on the basis of equal pay for equal work.'[76] Ford did not hire women in its production facilities until the late 1970s.

Union men presented the equal pay struggle as an uncomplicated attempt by employers to erode the UAW's power. In 1945 a writer for the Local 222 newspaper, the *Oshaworker*, stated that in the equal pay dispute at Ford, the company's goal was to 'keep the Union from functioning in the plant.' The author said that 'in spite of the tremendous profits the company was making, they still were not satisfied and their policy was to use the girls for cheap labour.'[77] Likewise, in June 1943 District Council 26 delegates contended that Ford's proposal to hire women at a rate less than men for the same work threatened to abrogate the collective agreement and imperilled 'the vital principle involved in enlisting thousands of women in industry.' The council also claimed that it was an attempt 'to impair existing working standards in industry.'[78] Later that year, they added that 'industrial wage standards must be maintained now, not only to prevent a disastrous slump after the war, but in order that men leaving to go into the armed forces will know that the women who carry on in industry are not being forced to undercut established wage standards.'[79] Such remarks were undoubtedly accurate, but they overlook the specific implications of the equal pay issue for women and they fail to address the assumptions about gender that underlay both the company's and the union's actions.

Furthermore, leaving aside the more fundamental issues of sex segregation and comparable worth, UAW leaders continued to negotiate unequal wages based on male and female job classifications.[80] For example, in 1943 Malcolm Smith, chair of the UAW Bargaining Committee in GM, applied to the Regional War Labour Board for adjustments in rates for day workers in the GM plant in Oshawa.[81] One of the union's requests was that the board consider raising the wages of female inspectors, stock clerks, and material handlers. Rather than propose an equalization of wage rates between women and men, however, the union maintained these sex differentials as a base on which to make increases. For instance, noting that male stock clerks earned 75 cents per hour, while females earned 50 cents per hour, the local proposed that it would be 'fair and reasonable' to raise the men's rate to 95 cents and the women's rate to 70 cents.

Union officials again accepted prevailing wage inequities when they applied for a rate increase for female sanders in GM's aircraft division. When the Regional War Labour Board directed GM to raise the range for this classification from 51-to-62-cents per hour, to 55-to-66-cents,[82] the company argued that the work did not justify an increase because the sanding machine used by women was 'not unlike an ordinary electric floor polisher used in a private residence.'[83] GM furthermore warned that the differential created by the regional board's decision would disturb wage rates paid to other female classifications.[84] Union officials contested the company's description of the work, but in their rebuttal they too manipulated cultural assumptions about women's more delicate sensibilities. For instance, the unionists stated that the sanding operation is extremely 'hard' and 'unpleasant' work, 'insofar as being a *female* operation is concerned' [my emphasis]. Like the labour board and the company, UAW leaders furthermore compared this work only to other women's jobs. 'Our contention,' wrote Malcolm Smith, 'is that there is a gross inequality and injustice existing between the rate paid to female sanders and the rate paid to other female workers in the General Motors Aircraft division.'[85]

Admittedly, the ability of unionists to compare and evaluate jobs was limited, given minor differences in the nature of 'women's' and 'men's' work. Moreover, occasionally they at least tried to reduce sex-based differentials in pay. In one instance, GM placed women and men in separate stock rooms and exempted women from lifting 'unduly heavy weights,' in an attempt to justify the wage gap for male and female material handlers. In response to this measure, union leaders argued that regardless of this difference in job location and content, women were still required to lift and handle the material all day. They also stated that females 'do everything the men do except the weights,' and 'this difference in their work does not seem to warrant a differential of 21 cents.'[86]

Rare attempts to break down gender divisions were often met with ambivalence by unionists who viewed desegregation as more trouble than it was worth. For example, when some UAW representatives proposed to GM officials in Oshawa and Windsor that they eliminate certain sex-based job barriers, both the company and their own regional director rejected the proposal. George Burt stated, 'I agree with the Co.' According to Burt, since only the cutting and sewing and wire and harness departments in the Oshawa facilities hired women during peacetime operations, the implementation of this proposal 'would mean that the girls who had always been employed in these depts. on what has been considered girls' jobs would have plant wide seniority and would inject into the plant a condition which ... we have never had to face.' In his view this would only have increased the union's problems with returning veterans. It would not be a problem in GM's Windsor plant as there were no female employees. But he noted that approximately 500 women were employed in the Oshawa facility.[87] Union officials were willing to protect the rights of their female members, but without questioning the gendered division of wage labour.

Furthermore, UAW claims for equal pay for equal work by women and men were remarkably similar to their arguments for equal pay among various other (male) categories of labour. For instance, during the war union leaders complained to the labour board that (male) foundry workers in St Catharines were being paid less than those in Windsor. In addition, they protested similar wage discrepancies in Windsor and Oshawa. In their view, 'The Government cannot justify a policy that pays citizen Jones 15 or 20 cents an hour less than it pays Citizen Smith for doing the same work on the same job on the same gun, tank or aircraft for the same government.' Likewise, District Council 26 called for 'the levelling-off of wage rates in similar classifications within an area.' They argued that job rates should be equalized because most war workers 'feel as they are working for the government,' and the Canadian people 'are paying them while they are contributing to the war effort.' Thus, they argued that 'it should not make a great deal of difference whether a man welds a tank for the Gar Wood Company or the Ford Motor Company. If he is doing the same quantity and quality of work he should receive the same amount of remuneration.'[88]

The paradox is that although these equal pay disputes emerged in a context of unequal gender relations, the debates surrounding them largely circumvented the issue of gender. Indeed, the UAW equal pay campaign in Canada left the theme of gender inequality virtually untouched, and thereby failed to reconstruct the social meaning of gender. Most union leaders, like the population as a whole, took sexual inequalities for granted, and during this time, female members had not developed a specific critique of their oppression as a sex. Consequently, in their demands for equal pay, working men rarely tried to present themselves as defenders of sexual justice. Prompted by the implications of unequal rates for their own agenda, they negotiated equal pay for equal work as a pure and simple wage demand – one of many contract items that had to be sorted out in the ongoing struggle between labour and management.

It is furthermore ironic that women themselves played a minor role in these debates. In a rare case in 1944 approximately thirty women in the gear department filed a grievance against McKinnon Industries for paying them 15 cents per hour less than men who performed the same job. After the general plant foreman and the plant manager denied their claim, a UAW-CIO representative took the case to arbitration. Mabel Larkin, a gear grinder, was one of four women who attended the hearing at Queen's Park in Toronto. She recalled that the general manager claimed that there was nothing to the women's job. 'His wife could do the job,' he stated. 'I'm sure she could have done the job,' Larkin replied. 'Anybody could do the job, really. But that was not the question. The question was the men were getting more than the girls were and we were doing exactly the same job ... especially in my instance and one of the other girls, we set up our own machines.' Nevertheless, the arbitrator ruled that the union did not have a case, and he dismissed the grievance. Larkin blamed her union representative for this outcome. In her view the representative should have argued that at issue was the rate, not the women's capacity to perform the job. However, at the time, Larkin did not voice her opinion because the women were told to speak only in response to direct questions during the proceedings. In addition, given their lack of experience in public speaking, most of the women felt too timid to verbalize their point of view. Larkin explained, 'I'd never been in Queen's Park before ... and you're sort of shaky.'

In another incident later that year two women protested unequal wages when they were temporarily placed in a strictly male department. As there was no female classification or wage scale in this department, the women requested that they be paid the men's rate. One of these women, Margaret Heritz, recalled that management 'hemmed and they hawed' and restated that the transfer was temporary. Yet Heritz maintained her position. 'It's a man's rated job and I'm not doing it on a woman's rate,' she declared. The women eventually won their claim and in doing so, they set a precedent in the plant. 'My argument was that if a man isn't able to do a job and he comes on the women's line, he only gets a women's wage. So if I'm gonna do a healthy man's job, I want his wage,' said Heritz. 'To me it seemed completely logical. I think it was very black and white. It was never in between.'

These cases were exceptional, however. Most women accepted unequal pay because they compared their rates only to those of other women. 'Naturally' women would receive less money if they were on jobs that were never officially classified as a man's, said Mabel Larkin. If women who temporarily performed men's work received a few cents more than those who performed traditional 'female work,' they were content. Thus, when they lost their equal pay cases, the women may have been temporarily disheartened, but they were not surprised. Larkin claimed it did not bother her at all. 'I can't say that I gave it a thought really ... You tried and you lost so what are you gonna do,' she remarked. In any case, after the war, the equal pay campaign began to fizzle within the labour movement, generally. 'We didn't get brought up to the men ... but then the war ended and consequently that was dropped completely.'

THE SENIORITY DILEMMA

As war production declined, the matter of women's seniority rights and job security gained prominence and overshadowed the equal pay challenges. The seniority issue, however, was more problematic for the union. As noted in the preceding chapter, seniority was one of organized labour's most precious gains. Thus, when employers attempted to cheat women of this right, UAW leaders were forced to uphold the principle and back their sisters. At the same time, though, some union members believed that scarce jobs should go to men first. Like equal pay, the seniority issue posed a dilemma for some unionists. On the seniority question, union leaders experienced prolonged internal debates before they could issue clear directives on the matter in discussions with employers.[89]

Auto manufacturers and UAW leaders established sex-based seniority in their first contracts. The 1937 agreement between General Motors and UAW workers in Oshawa, for instance, stated that in any department in which both women and men worked, the sexes should be divided into separate and non-interchangeable occupational groups.[90] In practice this clause meant that during a lay-off, women could move only into 'women's departments.' Since their seniority was specific to their sex, they could not 'bump' any male employees. Thus, a man with three years of service with the firm could potentially retain his job, while a woman with ten years of service would be laid off (and theoretically, vice versa).

For many years both workers and employers took this clause for granted. However, as war production diminished and unemployment grew, women's seniority became a subject of heated discussion. Although these economic trends affected all workers, they touched women most critically. In December 1944 UAW President R.J. Thomas reported that the union's research department found in a survey of UAW plants that women were suffering unduly from lay-offs. In aircraft parts plants in the United States, for example, women made up approximately 42 per cent of total employment, but they comprised 60 per cent of the laid off workers. In aircraft engine plants, they comprised about 40 per cent of the total workforce, but were 86 per cent of those laid off. Similarly, in shell and gun plants, women formed 26 per cent of total employment, but 61 per cent of laid off workers were women.[91]

There were various reasons for the disproportionate effect of lay-offs on the female workforce. Because women had restricted, sex-based seniority rights, they were not permitted to transfer into many departments throughout the plants. Thus, the legal application of the seniority principle resulted in the lay-off of many experienced women workers while newly hired men retained their jobs.

In addition, however, some employers began to dismiss women, regardless of their rights under collective agreements. Union officials reported that these women, many of whom were wives of servicemen or sole providers for their families, had extreme difficulty finding another job, especially because many companies refused to hire females after the war.[92] Putting aside their union principles some working men joined forces with their employers in violating or proposing to violate the restricted seniority rights of female employees, even though UAW policy prohibited such acts. For example, in 1943, when approximately nineteen women were laid off from the Hayes Steel plant in Merritton, Ontario, both labour and management expressed doubts about retaining women while men were unemployed.[93] That same year, the Auto Specialties firm put their feelings into action. The company laid off thirty-five women and hired male farmers in their place.[94]

Viewing these events as precursors of a widespread trend, George Burt called for a full discussion of the union's lay-off policy. He warned that employers' plans to replace senior women with newly hired men would create major problems in Canada. Thomas McLean of the UAW likewise recommended that all Canadian Congress of Labour unions meet with government and industry representatives to discuss the matter, with the auto industry taking the lead.[95]

As plant lay-offs spread women employees continued to face extreme hardship. For example, when the federal government cancelled its war contracts with GM in 1945, extensive lay-offs hit the UAW membership in Oshawa. GM planned to completely close down its aircraft division by the end of June. In addition to smaller layoffs in departments throughout the facility, this would result in the unemployment of approximately 1,800 to 2,000 workers.[96] At a mass meeting in March 1945, attended by 1,300 members of the GM division of Local 222, troubled workers called on Minister of Reconstruction, C.D. Howe, to help provide employment to 1,500 laid off workers in the district. Their prospects looked bleak. Local Selective Service officials claimed that only 500 jobs were available in the district for the roughly 2,000 individuals who faced lay-offs. In an emotional reaction to these developments, the union local approved a plan to lay off married women first, soldiers' wives next, and single women third.[97]

As expected, lay-offs mounted in the summer and fall. By September 1945 the Oshawa plant reportedly employed approximately 2,000 workers compared to a previous labour force of 5,000.[98] Moreover, after Victory in Japan day, only four departments, domestic parts and service, the Dominion truck line, maintenance, and the 'conversion knock down' would run as usual.[99] Because the government had issued GM a new work order, the lay-off would be gradual, however, and it would be completed at the end of October. Furthermore, GM officials claimed that the elimination of all war production from the plant would result in a boost in maintenance work. The company also planned to increase production on the number one truck line from twenty-five per day to 100 per day as materials became available. As this increase would result in the absorption of many men, the union was optimistic that the lay-off would not reach previously anticipated proportions.

Women's job security, however, was more uncertain. Of the women who were laid off during this period, only five had sufficient seniority to be recalled. These women had seniority dating from 1934 to 1941. The remaining 250 women lost their jobs.[100] In October 1945 GM decided to lay off junior women and replace them with women who had higher seniority. Senior women who had transferred to the aircraft division during the war returned to their pre-war jobs in the cutting and sewing departments.[101]

Local 199 also reported a problem of serious unemployment. During its wartime high, McKinnon Industries boasted 4,500 employees. However, by August 1945 this figure had dropped to 3,150. The company predicted that by October 1946 the plant population would reach a low of 1,500.[102] Various restructuring moves contributed to this reduction. For example, in May 1945 the cancellation of a fuse contract and the termination of the manufacture of dynamotors resulted in the displacement of forty-two men and 292 women. Given that the company would not reopen these departments, management permitted the workers to exercise their plant-wide seniority to move into other jobs. With this option to transfer, McKinnon Personnel Director H.W. McArthur claimed that the fuse and dynamotor cutbacks would not adversely affect male workers, as long as they could perform other duties. He believed, however, that the cutbacks would affect women with low seniority, although the firm was trying to provide suitable jobs for high-seniority women.[103]

In an attempt to reinstate the pre-war sex-based division of wage work, both company officials and some unionists further recommended that in cases where high-seniority women had been performing 'men's work' during the war, they be replaced by junior men and newly hired men. In their view, the displaced women should be transferred to jobs that had been classified 'female' prior to the war. This arrangement meant that many women lost their wartime jobs in the reconversion period, even though they remained employed by the firm.[104] In some locations, women faced even harsher measures. For instance, in 1944 the union committee and GM management in Windsor agreed to lay off all women, regardless of seniority, before any men. Approximately sixty women were employed in GM's Windsor plant at this time.[105]

At the war's end such contract violations were reaching serious proportions throughout UAW plants in both Canada and the United States. In 1945 UAW President R.J. Thomas euphemistically admitted that managements had often successfully denied women their contractual rights only because of the 'laxness' of union locals. He cited a case where employees in an entire department stopped working in protest when management placed a woman on a job that she could perform and to which she was entitled. In another case members of a UAW local seriously entertained an employer's proposal to terminate women's seniority through the payment of a bonus in the form of severance pay. Some plant bargaining committees were furthermore failing to protect the seniority rights of female stewards and committeewomen on the same basis as their male counterparts.[106]

How can we explain the actions of working men during this period? Some male unionists were reluctant to defend women's job rights because employers continued to use women as a source of cheap labour. In a May 1944 issue of the *Oshaworker*, an A.J. Turner commented on this response. Turner wrote that when the 'boys' at the 'rest period 'hot stove' sessions' asked about women's fate in peacetime, 'the quickest, shallowest and easiest answer is 'Send 'em back to the kitchen.' But the difficulty is that many women won't want to go back to meals and mops ... Right off the bat most men trade unionists get 'sore.' They figure, and rightly so, that women are underpaid and as such are a threat to the men's rates of pay. Most certainly if a woman can do the same job as a man, get paid 35 c an hour less, she is a threat!'[107]

Yet if unionists had resolved the equal pay dispute in earlier years, women's position in the industry might have been less threatening and less contentious at the war's end. UAW leaders, however, both failed to rectify gender-based pay inequities and revealed extreme ambivalence about protecting women's seniority rights, because they were guided by prevailing domestic ideologies. They assumed that men were breadwinners and women were financial dependents. Moreover, they believed in the legitimacy of this arrangement.

The pervasiveness of these ideas did not rest simply on the force of tradition. The social construction of man as breadwinner bestowed upon men certain privileges – privileges that included material gains, such as higher rates of pay and comforts in the home, but also extended to the subjective. It reinforced in men the perception that the union and the workplace were rightfully masculine domains in which men could affirm their gender identity. As such, women warranted at most a marginal position in these spheres. Thus, when Hayes Steel officials called for the voluntary resignation of women who had some financial means, 'zealous male employees with back-to-the-kitchen complexes' assisted in the women's departure. According to Ruth Thompson, alternate delegate representing Local 676, working men in September 1945 'placed hand made placards on machines operated by married women urging them to quit "and give the single girl a chance."' In response to such practices, approximately fifty women left their jobs.[108]

It was not only men, however, who voiced such attitudes. Also guided by the belief that a woman's place is in the home, some wage-earning women themselves violated the rights of their married sisters. The precarious economic times pitted married women against single women, widows and divorced women against working wives. In February 1944, at a Local 222 meeting, women workers agreed that the company should first lay off married women whose husbands were employed, followed by soldier's wives, and thus leave jobs open for single women. Local unionist Malcolm Smith, however, warned the women that this policy would not work in locations where wages were so low that all women needed jobs regardless of their marital status. UAW Canadian Director George Burt furthermore pointed out the impracticality of the measure, explaining that the union could not have one policy in one area and yet a different arrangement in another.[109]

UPHOLDING THE PRINCIPLES OF INDUSTRIAL UNIONISM

Though they were in the minority, some union men firmly opposed the unfair layoff of women. F. Steeve of Local 199 was one of the most adamant critics of this practice. Like the proponents of equal pay, Steeve grounded his argument in the philosophy of industrial unionism, highlighting the importance of worker solidarity, democracy, and the sanctity of the collective agreement. Calling for an immediate and definite stand on this issue, he reminded unionists that the UAW had guaranteed all workers seniority rights under its contracts with various companies, and he stressed that neither labour nor management should break these agreements. Women, he contended, must retain and be governed by their full seniority. If senior women were laid off, the union would, in effect, be putting union members out of the plants and agreeing to give jobs to non-union employees hired as replacements by management. This would violate one of the underlying tenets of the union, he asserted. Steeve therefore made a motion that the regional union adopt a policy of strict adherence to seniority, regardless of sex. This motion was carried unanimously on the premise that insofar as women accumulated seniority under the union contract, they had the right to a job.[110]

As regional director, George Burt also was forced to take a position on women's seniority. Like Steeve, Burt underscored the obligation of the union to protect the interests of all of its members. Furthermore, he stated that employers' plans to replace women would blatantly undermine the seniority principle. 'If we adopted a policy of laying off women and giving preference to men,' he said, 'it would mean that a girl with 12 years seniority could be laid off in preference to a man with one year's seniority, and the girl would be sacrificing a job which she held prior to the outbreak of war.[111] In another forum, Burt described how the Motor Products Company in Windsor tried to place a lower-seniority returning male veteran in a work group by laying off another male worker. In his view this incident revealed that strict adherence to straight seniority was in the long run as important to ex-servicemen as to anyone else. He then urged UAW international representatives to make this point clear to all members in local union meetings.[112]

The following year R.J. Thomas echoed this argument. Thomas told all union local presidents, regional directors, and international representatives that they must stand behind their seniority contract provisions because failure to do so would weaken the UAW's basic seniority structure. 'If management is successful in disregarding seniority rights of women workers now,' he explained, 'they will be in a stronger position to disregard seniority rights of other workers later on.'[113] In private caucuses UAW leaders also claimed that they must take a fair stand on women's seniority rights because they had based their equal pay cases on this principle. Failure to do so would therefore threaten their legitimacy.[114] Once again, women themselves did not publicly voice their opinions on the issue.[115] Nevertheless, while UAW leaders in Canada eventually recognized the need to uphold contractual seniority rights regardless of sex,[116] they continued to negotiate sex-based seniority systems. General Motors, Chrysler, and smaller plants throughout the province maintained male and female lists through the 1940s and into the late 1960s.[117] Insofar as unionists failed to question the premise of gender segregation, this outcome is not surprising.[118] However, in codifying these inequalities in legal agreements, the UAW officially condoned and legitimated them. This reduced the likelihood that women would or could challenge their separate and unequal position in future years. During this period, the union helped entrench gendered divisions in the auto plants for years to come.

THE UAW AND WOMEN'S LIVES

In developing the union's program of action, UAW leaders showed a limited understanding of the realities of women's lives. They represented women on issues that they were familiar with, but overlooked those concerns that were unique to female employees. Male unionists addressed both equal pay and women's job security largely because of their consequences for the working man and the union as a whole. While equal pay for equal work was a matter of economic expediency with political ramifications for organized labour, women's right to seniority was an issue of political expediency with economic implications. However, policies regarding married women, sexual harassment,[119] pregnancy and maternity leave,[120] child care, and domestic responsibilities – all vital aspects of women's work experience – had little direct bearing on the working man's status. Predictably, unionists paid marginal attention to these issues.

Although UAW-CIO policy statements prohibited discrimination on the basis of marital status, this form of injustice was widespread within the plants. Employers commonly placed married women on work shifts and seniority lists separate from those of other (male and female) employees, and assigned them a temporary status. In addition, before the war auto manufacturers had demanded that women quit their jobs upon marriage. And there is no evidence indicating that workers openly contested this measure. 'It was law,' said a woman who left GM soon after she wed, 'GM law, so you did nothing about it. You were mad ... I said, well why can't I work but the point is who you gonna fight. You can't fight'. She explained that the union, furthermore, failed to challenge this practice. 'They were just trying to get the men back to work and get some decent wages,' she stated.[121]

In the midst of wartime exigencies employers relaxed this longstanding policy, but only temporarily. At the height of the war over half of the employees in GM's aircraft division were married women. However, as the Second World War ended, and jobs again became scarce, the company dismissed many of these women or strongly encouraged them to quit. GM later recalled some married women, but many never returned to the plants. Consistent with their past practices, union leaders did little to challenge these dismissals. According to one auto worker, both 'the union and management tried to get rid of the women after the war.' She recalled that the aircraft department 'just closed down and ... the single girls they were [sic] transferred to cutting and sewing and the wives [sic] places were in the home.'[122] Because most women and men clearly recognized the power of conventional gender ideologies, this practice did not generate discussion between labour and management.

The UAW in Canada furthermore neglected women workers' pressing need for accessible child care. In response to a growing contingent of married women unionists in the United States, the UAW International took some steps to provide child care during the war.[123] For example, in September 1944 the international union advocated a union counselling program to address workers' problems 'outside of the shop,' including child care.[124] Also in this year the UAW Constitutional Convention passed a resolution on nursery schools and the U.S. Lanham Act. Historian Nancy Gabin (1984) notes, however, that we should not inflate the significance of these initiatives because they cost the union very little.

Even these limited efforts were not matched in Canada. In the auto plants, both child care and maternity provisions were new concerns largely because married women had only recently entered the industry. Thus, wage-earning mothers relied heavily on individual and temporary government facilities. In July 1942 the federal and Ontario governments agreed to establish day-care facilities in the province for children whose mothers were employed in war industries. The first day nursery under this agreement in Ontario opened in Brantford on 4 January 1943. In February three additional units opened in St Catharines, Oshawa, and Toronto, and to accommodate the increasing numbers of married women entering employment, six more nurseries were established in Ontario between April and September (Pierson, 1986: 51–2). In 1944, again with the financial support of both levels of government, the Oshawa Board of

Education also set up a day-care unit for five- to seven-year old children of women who were working in 'essential industry.' The UAW encouraged women members to use the service.[125] In St Catharines the Dominion-Provincial day nursery depended largely on the voluntary services of dozens of McKinnon workers' wives who were not themselves employed.[126]

UNIONISM, MASCULINITY, AND FEMININITY

Most women recognized that they were on the margins of the UAW power structure, and they acted accordingly. As noted, women attended union meetings, but they rarely voiced their opinions. Typically, they remained unobtrusive and claimed that they had a limited knowledge of union policies and procedures. According to one woman, 'The men [unlike the women] wouldn't wait until another one was finished before they would want to start speaking.' This made it awfully hard for neophytes to keep track of the issues.[127] Another worker observed that women 'were more afraid to say anything.' In comparison, the men would 'get up on the platform and they'd say, "Well we'll do this and we'll do that and something else,"' and by the end of the evening, she did not know what to think.

Their status as a numerical minority in this unfamiliar milieu further inhibited women. One employee recalled that there was only one other 'girl' at her first union meeting. 'The rest were all men,' she said. 'In those days you just felt the difference.' She recalled thinking, 'Ohhh, what am I doing here.'[128]

Many women were bewildered by the web of bureaucratic rules and procedures that were part of the culture and administrative structure of the labour movement. The contract clauses, multilayered wage demands, payment systems, seniority lists, job classifications, and rhetorical policy statements were puzzling. They were furthermore unfamiliar and uncomfortable with the technical, legalistic language that was widely used in discussions between union, company, and government representatives. Moreover, few Canadian women attended UAW regional and international conferences, the arenas in which delegates and officials debated resolutions and set policies and learned the rules of parliamentary procedure.

Typical of many women, wire and harness worker Ann Brisbois strongly supported the union, but she had a limited understanding of its inner workings. On the one hand, she emphatically declared, 'I was one hundred percent union. And if it hadn't been for the union, a lot of people wouldn't have the privileges they have today. Because we were getting starvation wages and we were working hard and the big company was making the money.' Yet she also confessed that she 'didn't know anything [about the union].' 'I had never heard of a union or anything about unions,' she declared. Brisbois recognized, however, that workers 'had to do something.' In her words, 'we could not work two hours a day and come home ... and come back at four o'clock and work till nine o'clock at night ... We couldn't go on like that.' Another woman explained that when she went in to work, her co-workers would ask what she thought about the previous night's union meeting. Her private response was, ' "Oh God, don't ask me. I don't know.' I didn't know what it was all about.' Presenting herself as an outsider, she remarked, 'They'd have their meetings.'

A smaller number of women channelled their perceived marginality into opposition to the UAW. A sewing room worker proclaimed, 'I was not that much involved. I wasn't against the union. I wouldn't want to have worked without one, but I don't know. I just can't explain it. There was a lot of things that I didn't agree with ... I belong to the union the same as everybody was supposed to belong to the union. But ... to me, at the time, they gave me the impression that ... they were doing all their thinking for you, which I didn't agree with. That made me feel that they thought that I didn't have any brains. That you were to follow the dictates of the union no matter what.'

Some women explicitly linked their sentiments about the labour movement to the cultural construction of the feminine and masculine. Given the sometimes sexually exclusive behaviour of UAW leaders and their failure to address women's unique personal and collective histories, many female auto workers viewed unionism as a distinctly masculine endeavour. 'That was men,' one woman matter of factly said about the UAW. 'It was men that were lookin' after all that. I don't know when they started to get the women to take some jobs, like executive jobs in the union. It must have been way long after ... I just didn't bother with it at all ... They'd say, 'Oh well the union's good.' All this and that. Well, then, that's all there's to it. It was mostly all – like the men. I don't know who they were or how many they were but I imagine they were all for the union. I don't think the women had too much to do with it.

As noted above, women auto workers had neither the resources nor the inclination to restructure the union, however. Many workers, in fact, blamed themselves for their lack of involvement, thereby personalizing a structural problem. Some women were embarrassed by their intermittent participation and/or ignorance of union affairs and attributed their behaviour to individual shortcomings. Dorothea Koch, for example, said, 'I'm not a very good union member. I don't take that interest in things like that ... There were ones that were very active in it ... I just let them get things for me ... I wasn't that involved with anything ... I guess I'm kind of a passive person ... I said, "I'll take what they give me. And just be glad that I get that much ..." They're some people that are grabby. They want so much. They feel that they owe it to them.'

In some ways, labour activism was constructed as antithetical to proper womanhood. By promoting their views in mixed-sex public settings, women activists would be stepping outside of their subordinate position as both wage earners and women. Contentment was an important component of the ideal and proper woman, whereas the labour movement promoted the open expression of discontent and indeed some measure of radicalism. Moreover, and perhaps most important, as she committed herself to the labour movement, a woman revealed an equally serious commitment to the paid labour force. And this commitment defied the ideal of the male breadwinner family. In chapters 5 and 6, we see that when defiant women demanded an equal voice in the union, they faced severe admonition, not only from employers, but also from their union brothers.

A seasoned woman worker in GM explained that during the war years, 'you were looked down on if you worked for the factory or belonged to the union ... the CIO. When we first started ... they were calling us the Communists in Oshawa.' In many ways critical observers condemned women unionists more harshly than men. At that time a woman raised eyebrows when she associated with union men. Female activists were often called 'mouthy' and 'loose' women 'who went off with the men.' They drank and swore and smoked cigarettes. In short, they violated most of the dictates of proper feminine behaviour. One woman stated, 'I can remember a lot of talk about it [the union] ... They'd want things changed, some of the girls. Some of the girls, they were real into the union ... There's always that bunch that have to be into everything ... and think they know it all. That group, sort of, seemed to be the smoking bunch that sat on the stairs ... They'd be talkin' union all the time.' After all, the UAW was a masculine institution, led by men, and shaped according to white working men's vision of justice and equality.

SUMMARY

During the Second World War UAW leaders did not draw women auto workers into the union on equal terms with men. Women engaged in subordinate tasks on an intermittent basis, while men administered the union continuously. Nevertheless, many women strongly supported the principles of unionism. Given this loyalty, labour leaders could mobilize them during crises such as strikes. Without the power of office, however, women could not determine the UAW program. Male union officials gave little attention to matters that exclusively concerned women. Furthermore, they failed to seriously address the link between disputes about equal pay for equal work and seniority rights and sex-based inequality. For the most part, they took gender inequalities for granted.

This episode in the union's history sheds light on the issue of motive in feminist theory. Central to the gender/class debate in the feminist literature is the question, why have male unionists reacted to women workers in narrow, sexually exclusive ways? Some writers contend that male workers' actions were practical responses to employers' use of women as a cheap and expendable source of labour in capitalist economies (see Benenson, 1984; May, 1985; Sen, 1980). Others claim that working men's exclusiveness was part of a uniform working-class scheme to secure the survival of the class and maintain its dignity in capitalist society (see Brenner and Ramas, 1984; Drake, 1984; Humphries, 1977; Hutchins and Harrison, 1903). In this view, working-class resistance was the product of reasoned decision-making by all family members in the face of historical constraints imposed by the capitalist system.

Conversely, a number of feminist theorists argue that patriarchy, in both its material and its ideological forms, accounts for much of men's behaviour (see Hartmann, 1976, 1979; Cockburn, 1986). According to Heidi Hartmann, for instance, working men's actions are rooted in their interests as a sex. Hartmann reasons that if working men were solely concerned about the threat women posed to their labour market position, they would have organized women in unions and fought to establish gender equality in industry.

These writings are important insofar as they introduce the concept of patriarchy to orthodox class analysis and theorize the relation between the capitalist economy and the sphere of social reproduction. Furthermore, they reveal the distinctiveness of women's oppression and thus call for a specific analysis of gender relations. Much of this literature, however, is problematic insofar as it presents working women and men as distinct totalities, each of whom acts according to clearly defined and unchanging motives.[129]

The actions of male unionists during the Second World War indicate that people rarely act according to consistent and unconflicted motives. One of the contradictions in people's lives is that when they face the realities of living, they do not always uphold reasoned principles. While UAW men had clear economic interests in upholding the principle of equal pay for equal work, their failure to advocate women's rights indicates that they also adhered to patriarchal assumptions about 'women's place.'[130] While some male unionists recognized the logic in unionizing female workers and supporting the principles of equal pay and equal application of seniority rights, many continued to exclude women from employment and limit their participation in the union. Given these inconsistencies, it is impossible to identify a single or primary motive on the part of historical actors.

This chapter in the union's history does, however, indicate that gender politics strongly shaped working men's consciousness and mediated their strategy of resistance in the workplace. Furthermore, though there is little evidence that male workers perceived this relation, in practice the link between gender discrimination and the plight of the working class as whole was inextricable. Women's subordinate position as a sex legitimated their inferior industrial position and eroded the powers of wage-earning women and men in the labour market.

In failing to critique employers' exploitation of women as a sex as well as to question their own gender biases, UAW men unleashed many contradictions. Because workers' patriarchal beliefs clashed with the official position and collective interests of organized labour, union men had to continually juggle their loyalties, reconcile principles and practices, and sometimes contain one another's sexist behaviour. Furthermore, working men's narrow and exclusive perspective contributed to the construction of unionism as a masculine pursuit. Although UAW men presented unionism as gender-neutral in principle, they exposed it as a masculine institution in practice. This narrow definition posed many dilemmas for both women and men workers, and it constrained their resistance in significant ways.

In entrenching gender inequalities in collective agreements, unionists also constructed tactical impediments to broader forms of worker resistance. Once codified in membership-approved union contracts, gendered divisions gained a legitimacy and permanence. The elimination of sex-based inequalities herein necessitated a fundamental rewording of contract language and this was a substantial task. Thus, regardless of the perceptions of women and men they were constrained from implementing certain changes. Developments during these early years of union activity, in short, fractured and restricted the working-class struggle for years to come. In the following chapters, I uncover the ways in which these developments shaped future acts of resistance.

3

Femininity and Friendship
on the Shop Floor (1937–1949)

During the war years women workers did not have a strong voice in setting the UAW agenda. The terms and conditions of employment in auto manufacturing were largely negotiated by male unionists and male employers, according to their own interests and understanding of the world. Women workers did, however, informally shape the meaning of gender and the experience of work in day-to-day living on the plant floor. When we listen to their own words and recollections we can clearly see this process.

'We were a very accepting generation,' said one woman about her work group at GM in the 1940s. At first glance this appears to be a straightforward assessment of an uncomplicated time. In many respects women auto workers conformed to social prescriptions of proper feminine behaviour and complied with their employers' demands for high productivity. However, social prescriptions regarding gender are highly complex, far more complex than much of the scholarly literature suggests. Though we can identify hegemonic ideologies, we cannot use them as a sole basis on which to determine behaviour. While most women accepted gender prescriptions in principle, they sometimes challenged them in practice. Moreover, while dominant gender ideologies were highly limiting to women, they were not blinding. Few women were acquiescent. The political implications of gender prescriptions is a highly complicated matter that cannot be fully understood without examining the social-historical milieu.

People may respond to dominant ideologies and structural inequalities in various ways, with one form of response more prominent and consequential than others at given points in time. At times, they may cooperate or comply; on other occasions, they may actively resist. Such actions may be individual or collective. Sometimes, people procrastinate. Usually, they simply carry on with their lives as best they can, without thinking about the larger social processes and the historical consequences of their actions.

While women auto workers strongly supported the UAW, they manifested this support in subtle and socially acceptable forms. Likewise, in the auto plants women were critical of the labour process but they expressed this sentiment in individual, indirect, and distinctly feminized ways. The nature and level of women's shop-floor resistance was strongly shaped by their identification as women, the strength of their emotional ties to one another, and a unity of condition. They expressed their resistance by drawing on a women's culture that was based on a conventional definition of femininity. Moreover, the women responded to their new industrial position in a context of economic hardship, limited options, and a strict sex-based division of labour. In short, their strategies of resistance reflect power relations in the workplace, as well as in the larger society. The women were trying to make sense of their lives within a patriarchal capitalist setting – with limited access to resources for social change. Their strategies were formulated as they lived in a context of unequal relations between women and men, as well as workers and employers.

PERSONAL HISTORIES: OPPORTUNITIES AND CONSTRAINTS

Who were the women who laboured in the auto plants during the war? What kinds of experiences, needs, and resources did they bring to the industry? Moreover, how did their personal histories shape their approach to auto work? Like their male counterparts, women auto workers were raised in working-class families in small towns across Canada. Many of them, in fact, were born in Southern Ontario, not far from the auto plants. Vivid in their memories of growing up in these families was the experience of sacrifice and coping with financial insecurity. The women recalled their families' survival strategies in detail. 'My family, when I was growing up, we were poor. I mean we were on welfare,' explained Marion Manning, a GM employee. 'I grew up the hard way and learned to look after my money as it came through ... [During the Depression] my Dad couldn't get a job ... So my mother ... used to go in and look after young babies and their mothers and their children ... We bought a house and we lost it ... The money just wasn't there.'

Even after the Depression, 'times were tough,' and these hardships touched young girls and boys in memorable ways. Kay Anderson, one of six children, recalled that 'times had been terrible' and being on public 'relief' was 'demeaning.' Anderson's father worked on construction or anything else he could find. He would get a work slip to take to the Relief Office and come 'home with a potato sack filled with rice and wheat, staples, on his back.' It was Kay's job to go to the meat store with the tokens. 'I was just twelve or around and I hated it because everybody ... if they weren't on relief, they knew I was ... The good old days in some ways were, but there were a lot of the good old days that weren't.'

Likewise, sisters Marie Smith, Bea Parkin, and Ann Whyte recalled that their father, like most auto employees of early times, worked in 'the Motors' six months of the year – often only two or three days a week. During the other six months he laboured on a farm 'or did whatever else he could find, anything just to get food' for his seven children. According to Smith, 'Dad could get all the food we needed except meat from this farm.' Parkin added, he 'always had a big garden just up ... the field ... And he was able to use part of an acre of land ... We all worked and all chipped in.'

In addition, most of these women had relatively few (officially recognized) skills, little formal education, and only limited experience in low-paying female job ghettoes. Marion Manning was typical of the female auto worker in the 1940s. Owing to financial hardship, Manning quit school when she was roughly fourteen years old. Her first job was in the Schofield Woolen Mills, an Oshawa underwear factory in which many local women gained experience as sewers. She made low wages, however, and therefore in 1940 she applied for a job at the Motors.[1] In her view, the only other option for women was the munitions plant in Ajax.

Bea Parkin and Marie Smith also entered their first jobs at the age of fourteen in the Schofield Woolen Mills. Parkin worked in the mills for roughly one and a half years, sewing men's plum knit woolen underwear. Smith, who had joined the firm two years before her younger sister, turned and packed the garments. Their GM co-worker Helen Beaugrand had just turned sixteen and played 'hookie' when her father told her to either go to school or find work. To his surprise, in 1941 Beaugrand headed straight for GM. She had sought employment at the firm several times previously, but had been turned away because of her youth.

Ann Brisbois earned five dollars a week as a travelling hairdresser the summer before she started to work at GM. At age nineteen, this wire-and-harness employee 'walked all over Oshawa' with her 'little bottle of lotion,' giving 25-cent 'finger waves' to the local women. However, her father felt that Ann would be more useful helping her mother at home, and he consequently ended this enterprise. Hairdressing had also been Dorothea Koch's aspiration. However, there was no hairdressing school in Oshawa, and her parents could not afford to send her to a school in Toronto. Koch therefore left high school to work in a general store in Port Perry, Ontario. Her starting pay was seven dollars a week and after about eight years she earned ten dollars. 'It was Depression, the end of the Depression,' she explained. 'There weren't a lot of jobs.' Like many women, Koch also did 'a little bit of housework and things like that' before starting at GM. 'I babysat ... And then another man, his wife was pregnant, ended up in the hospital, so I went up and kind of kept house and looked after their little girl.'

Mabel Larkin's first job outside of the home was picking fruit. Later, she too did housework for pay in Welland, Ontario. Larkin and others minimized the value of this type of work. Feeling a need to explain her job history, she added defensively, 'I never took secretarial education.' Similarly, after stating that she had only babysat and performed other domestic jobs that were part of a girl's gendered training, Jane Kelner commented, 'I didn't have any real jobs.'

For most unskilled, relatively uneducated women in small towns across Canada, employment opportunities were few before the Second World War. Celia Wigg, a GM sewing room worker since 1927, explained their situation. 'Oh God. Now, you wouldn't put up with it, you know. You'd say, to heck, I'll go out and get myself another job – but you couldn't in those days because you couldn't get a job.' Prior to the war, few women worked in the auto industry. Indeed, many young women had never previously earned wages or worked outside of their own homes.

New to an industrial setting, these women were unsure of themselves and hesitant to assert their rights in the workplace. In describing their initial impressions of auto work, most women related fear. 'You were quite bewildered,' explained Jane Kelner, 'because ... you'd never seen anything like that before.' 'You have to go in a factory to see how people work ... It was a huge, big room. A monster of a room.' Likewise, Effie Baldwin recalled, 'Everything was so massive to me – just being around my own home ... I had very good parents and I wasn't made to do this and do that.' A massive industrial complex, especially the size of GM, was overwhelming to many women.

Finding work at General Motors, one of the most highly desired employers in the area, was a particular feat. For woman or man, 'the Motors has always been the best place to work as far as wages go.' 'For years and years and years it was the only big industry here,' explained Kay Anderson. 'People just said they ran Oshawa.' In turn, GM's high wages sent workers running to them. 'Around this town, it was all GM ... Everybody liked to get into GM,' commented auto worker Marie Wilson. 'It was the best paying job around.'

Incomes based on piece work were so high that Margaret Heritz and her work group in McKinnon Industries were featured in a local newspaper as the five highest paid women in the Niagara Peninsula. You didn't make that much money working in a store, commented another employee. Even when women performed similar job operations in female-dominated firms, they earned less than they did in the automotive sector. For example, as a sewer in the Schofield Woolen Mills, Bea Parkin earned approximately 14 cents an hour. However, when she sewed materials for army trucks at GM, her starting rate was roughly 97 cents an hour. In fact, many women auto workers earned more money than husbands and fathers who were employed in other industries. When Parkin married in 1946, the company forced her to quit her job at GM. However, given that her employment was more lucrative than her husband's job at the Oshawa Public Utilities, this arrangement was not the most sensible. Parkin's sister, Marie Smith, noted that because she worked many overtime hours, her pay cheque was even higher than her father's, a man with seven children.

These relatively high wages in the face of extremely limited employment options partially allayed the women's shop-floor discontents. For instance, GM employee Celia Wigg remarked, 'I can't complain too much about working there because I couldn't do any better 'cause there wasn't any other place to go.' Indeed, most of the women performed their work diligently and obediently. Marie Smith explained that one 'wanted to do a good job so you could keep your job. Even though jobs were easy to get [during the war] ... we knew how lucky we were to be working at GM.'

Furthermore, even though a wider range of jobs became available to women during the war, sex-based inequalities continued to structure the labour market. Many employers still refused to hire women and those that did tended to undervalue the work they performed and pay them less than men in comparable jobs. Female auto employees overlooked glaring sexual injustices in the industry, as they compared their plight to that of their female friends, sisters, mothers, and neighbours in lower-paying, lower-status, female-dominated industries. Reflecting on past circumstances and potentially worse economic conditions, these women expressed gratitude for their restricted employment in the auto plants, and they did not openly challenge their employers.

The youthfulness of the female workforce also influenced their approach to wage work. We lack exact numbers, but informants agreed that the women who worked in GM's St Catharines and Oshawa plants during the war ranged in age from about fifteen to sixty years.[2] This is because permanent departments such as the cutting and sewing had long employed women, many of whom never married and stayed with the firm for decades. Wartime recruits, however, tended to be young. Indeed, Helen Beaugrand was so young when she started in GM that when her boss saw her coming down the aisle to report to work, he said 'he thought he would go up and ask the matron if she had any baby bottles.'

This youthfulness and inexperience compounded the women's sense of indebtedness and simultaneously injected a zealousness in their approach to wage work. According to Marie Smith, 'We were that young, we were so glad to be working and enjoying it and everything.' Similarly, Smith's cousin, GM employee Elsa Goddard, declared, 'I was thrilled to death to think that here I am just a kid and I can do the same work as what older people can do.' Partly because of this youthful enthusiasm, they tolerated arduous jobs. About standing all day at work, Celia Wigg said, 'Well, you know, they say when you're young you put up with a lot.' Likewise, about time studies, Kay Anderson conceded, 'Oh well, that was just something you put up with. There was no way you were going to change that so you accepted it ... but you didn't accept it gracefully. You moused and crabbed and they always thought that whole system was unfair. But see, at my age I didn't care. I was getting a pay cheque.'

Moreover, many war workers viewed wage labour as temporary. Typical of the young women who were new to the industry, Paterson said, 'I knew that when Pat [her husband] got out of the service, that I was going to quit work. I guess because I thought we were gonna have a family.' Similarly, when Marion Manning started to work in the Motors she thought, 'I got a job. I'm gonna earn some money. I'm getting married.' Like many young women, Manning did not rethink her life plans because of her new employment. Rather, she attempted to integrate employment into her longstanding aspirations of marriage and full-time housekeeping. 'The money was important to save,' she said, 'because at that point we were thinking of getting married ... My thinking was your place is in the home with your family. That was my basic feeling. A lot of us felt that way during the War – to get the job over and get back to normal.'

Notwithstanding the perception that their incomes were merely supplementary, most women made valuable economic contributions to the family household. In fact, financial necessity was the overriding reason they entered auto employment.[3] Helen Beaugrand, one of five children, claimed that she gave more money to her family than any other 'girl' in GM. 'I seemed to get back two dollars out of my pay,' she stated. Similarly, as a teenager, Bea Parkin gave her entire pay packet to her father. Her sister Marie did not keep her own pay until about a year before she married. In turn, most parents amply provided for their daughters' needs and often granted them luxuries as well. Therefore, few women resisted or resented this arrangement. Smith and Parkin respected their financial obligation to their family and claimed that it taught them the value of money. Even after they kept their own incomes, the sisters purchased gifts of furniture and other household goods for their parents.

Few working-class families, even if headed by a relatively well-paid male auto worker, could survive on one wage packet. Economic downfalls, unemployment, and personal misfortunes all required parents and children to pool their resources. Breadwinners came in all ages and genders. At one time, Celia Wigg was the only one in her family who had a job. 'My Dad was sickly and my mother worked,' she explained. 'She had five kids at home ... somebody had to work.' 'Most of the girls had to.' Wigg's burden was not eased until her sisters got a bit older and did housework for pay.

In addition, the social welfare system of the late 1930s and early 1940s in Canada was inadequate to meet their families' needs. Dorothea Koch's father worked in a plating mill, but her mother had several serious operations that ate into their funds. 'In those days,' observed Koch, 'you didn't have hospitalization and medical insurance.' After marriage, Koch again faced huge medical bills when her husband, a cancer patient, was hospitalized. She started to work at GM in 1943, at the age of thirty, about six months after he died. 'I had to get work,' she explained. 'I was married in '39. And my husband died in '42 ... I had no money ... My home wasn't paid for when he died. And I hadn't finished payin' the loan off then ... It was trying to work ... And it was the place that was getting me the most money. And I wasn't happy about having to work, but I needed the money ... because I had nothing.'

Although these hardships sensitized women to economic injustices and instilled in them a keen sense of their precarious position as wage earners in a hierarchical society, feelings of anger and resentment were tempered by youth, inexperience, and a recognition of their oppression as a sex – all of which limited their opportunities in the labour market and internalized in them a sense of subordination.

It is not surprising that few women openly protested working conditions during the war. Kay Anderson observed that the men on GM's Chev

Line perceived an 'us and them' situation – 'the union guys against the supervision and General Motors ... It was distinct,' she noted. However, there was no comparable division in the female-dominated sewing room or aircraft division. Effie Baldwin said that the women generally did not complain about their working conditions because 'everyone was hard up and glad to get what they could.'

Indeed, some women manifested a highly instrumental orientation to wage work. Marie Wilson, for example, stated, 'You did what you were told ... It was a job. You wanted to get good money on pay day. You worked for it.' According to Marie Smith, 'We were just having a good time ... Not like it is today ... You did your job and when you left General Motors that was the end.' For most women, auto work was a means to other ends. Rather than openly struggle for control of the labour process, they coped and resisted in other ways. One strategy was to escape the realities of work through detachment. According to Jane Kelner, 'If somebody said ... "I wish I didn't have to work" or something, I'd say ... "If you don't like it why don't you quit, if you don't have to. Take it which ever way." That would be my answer ... I grew up through Depression years and, you know, you had to make money. You had to work to get by.' With the union in its infancy and times of extreme economic insecurity still vivid in their memories, these workers revealed a strong sense of gratitude for their employment, moderate expectations, cautiousness, and an adherence to hard work.

WOMEN'S CULTURE: WAGE-EARNING WOMEN'S PERSONAL
STRATEGIES OF SHOP-FLOOR SURVIVAL AND RESISTANCE

Regardless of the employee's age, gender, or personal history, however, auto work was alienating (Chinoy, 1955; Beynon, 1973; Wells, 1986). Insofar as the industry was characterized by a highly detailed division of labour, jobs were fragmented and void of intrinsic meaning. Women in particular were likely to perform detailed and repetitive assembly work. Tied to a constantly moving conveyor line, many women also had limited physical mobility. In addition, they were paid according to a bonus efficiency or piece-rate system that forced them to 'put out' with great speed in order to earn a respectable income.

Within this context, many women faced dilemmas. While most of the women were raised to be agreeable and accommodating, if not somewhat deferential, the degradation of factory work fostered in them some resentment and an underlying criticism of factory organization. Furthermore, most women aspired to marry and become full-time wives and mothers. Yet as noted, this arrangement was unrealistic for many working-class families. Only a small number of labouring men earned wages sufficient to comfortably support a wife and children in a growing consumer economy. How did women auto workers reconcile these contradictions? They developed a particular strategy of coping and resistance that brought conventional feminine culture to the industrial shop-floor.[4]

Although women war workers were breaking ground in performing some non-traditional jobs in a male-dominated industry, they clung to highly conventional feminine images. Indeed, during the Second World War the women's departments in the auto plants reflected a traditionally feminine culture. This culture was especially pronounced in the female-dominated sewing room and wire and harness department in GM's Oshawa plant, as well as the commercial motors department in McKinnon Industries. It was more difficult to sustain in work groups that were situated in or near men's departments. Although small groups of women were segregated in the core room and fuel pump departments in the McKinnon plant, for example, their numbers were relatively few, and they were within close physical proximity of working men. These women were less likely to develop intimate bonds and nurture a woman-centred work culture.

GM's sewing room was ideal for the formation of close relationships as it was relatively quiet, workers sat side by side at machines or on benches, and employees could 'stack' production, which permitted them to take occasional breaks from their labour. In addition, men and boys entered the department only on occasion to repair machines or retrieve materials. Since this department reflected the strongest expression of feminine culture, the following discussion focuses on the experiences of sewing room workers.

FASHION, FEMININITY, AND PERSONAL EXPRESSION

Physical appearance, make-up, clothes, and hair styles – all defined by contemporary standards – were central to this culture. During rest periods, 'We'd always be combing our hair and putting on make up,' explained GM worker Jane Kelner. 'What else were you gonna do?' Many women, in fact, arrived at the plant with their hair done up in pin curlers and covered under kerchiefs. Bea Parkin and Marie Smith explained that they did this so that they could style each other's hair at work. If they had special plans for the evening, women came early and sat in a corner of the washroom, while Parkin set their hair. She combed it out for them during their lunch break. Pin curls were the trend during the war.

Company publications both reinforced and reflected these concerns in regular women's columns such as 'The Fair Sex' and 'To the Ladies.' If these columns did not mirror the realities of contemporary femininity, they at least underscored cultural prescriptions for women's behaviour. The January 1945 issue of *McKinnon Doings*, for example, told women how to keep well-groomed while performing their jobs and instructed them in the art of hair styling.[5]

Beautiful hands were the focus of other articles. McKinnon publications regularly highlighted women's need to keep their hands soft and pretty. A 1943 article stated, 'Whether you work in the factory or in the office every girl likes to have smooth white hands.' Its author, Jean Bunker, had discovered 'a very economical and effective way to achieve this result.' She advised, 'Before leaving home in the morning, rub or pat well into the palm and back of your hands a little olive oil or vaseline.'[6] Similarly, in an article entitled 'Beauty Line,' a columnist for *McKinnon Doings* magazine told her readers, 'Girls doing work that soils their fingernails are digging them into a bar of soap before going on the job.' She also offered the women tips on making their lipstick last for hours on end.[7]

Given the importance of fashion and beauty in women's culture, it is no wonder that female auto workers resisted employers' attempts to regulate this dimension of their work lives. In 1944 amendments to the Factory, Shop, and Office Building Act stated that during working hours girls and women employed in factories must wear a 'close-fitting cap or other suitable headgear' to keep their hair from coming into contact with machinery, shafting, belting, or any material.[8] Prior to this time women wore hairnets, but because strands of hair filtered through the open mesh and the mesh itself became entangled, the agency declared them unsafe and unacceptable. Factory inspectors had previously targeted women who worked at machines and among moving parts, but because some accidents involved women who were only occasionally near machines, the government decided to apply the amendment to all female employees.[9]

With strong concerns about their physical appearance in the workplace, some women employees resisted attempts by the provincial government to tighten enforcement of this act. Thus, throughout the war and into the following decades, government agencies, employers, and women workers struggled over the seemingly trivial issues of hair protection, safety shoes, and proper dress for female plant workers. Both auto employers and government representatives repeatedly appealed to women to comply with these broadened regulations. Chief Inspector J.R. Prane, of the Department of Labour warned women of potential 'scalping hazards' and reported extensively on the incidence of workplace accidents. 'Accident records disclose all too clearly that scalpings ... are increasing and most of them mean permanent disfigurement for the victims,' Prane stated. 'Prior to the bobbed hair period,' the department faced a similar problem and then for at least a decade short hairstyles reduced the hazard considerably. However, 'styles for female adornment change quickly' and as the Second World War began, 'the hair was worn longer.' Prane said that women's reluctance to wear safe hair covering was one of the biggest problems of the department.[10]

Prompted by a case in which a woman bent down and got her hair caught in a small machine, Frank Mulvale, a safety columnist for Mc-Kinnon Industries, echoed these appeals. 'A woman's hair is her crown and glory but whether she wears it as a crown or gets crowned because of it depends upon the common sense between her ears,' Mulvale asserted. He graphically described the consequences of inadequate hair protection. 'Static electricity in moving parts of machinery will draw her hair into machinery resulting in painful lifelong and even fatal injuries,' he wrote. He provided examples: A woman who was trying to replace a belt on a pulley when static electricity generated in the line shaft pulled her hair around the shaft. She was completely scalped and died nine weeks later. In addition, a power sewing machine operator put her head under the table to retrieve an object when her hair was caught in the shaft, and the scalp was torn off. According to Mulvale, she never recovered from the shock.[11]

Constant reminders were necessary because women continued to resist the regulations. Why? Their hair 'made them feel feminine,' explained McKinnon worker Amy Swanson. Another McKinnon employee said that women always want to look 'good.' The women's efforts to 'look good' were, in part, attempts to assert some control, maintain dignity, and impart personal style in the workplace. In forcing them to wear unattractive bandanas, management and government were encroaching upon their ability to achieve these ends.[12]

Women workers and employers also clashed over women's attire, though this matter never garnered the controversy of the bandanas. Auto employers enforced few dress regulations, but they did have implicit rules about apparel. The guiding rule was conservatism, no overt displays of female sexuality. These prescriptions seem to have been largely based on the personal preferences of managers and supervisors.

Most women complied with management's preferences and took pride in their clothing. Sewing room workers usually wore a skirt and blouse or a dress. 'We never went sloppy,' said Celia Wigg. 'That's one thing, when we worked our hair was done. And we were dressed nice ... We never had runs in our stockings ... There was nobody sloppy.' Following a Depression-era and wartime custom, Marie Smith and her sisters painted lines on their legs to give the appearance of nylon stockings. Other women had a more casual approach to dress. Marie Wilson, for instance, said that 'women always worry what they look like,' but she was not concerned about her appearance among her workmates in the sewing room. On special occasions, some women wore fancy clothes. For instance, on Friday, pay day, the women celebrated by 'dressing up a bit.' 'It was a great thing to get kind of dressed up on pay day,' explained Kay Anderson. 'I don't know why we did that, but we generally went out for lunch' in a local restaurant.

In GM's aircraft division women wore coveralls made of a strong navy blue fabric with burgundy trim and the initials 'GM' embroidered on the pocket. According to Anderson, every one bought a couple of pairs from the firm's safety office. The women wore coveralls or smocks in order to protect their own clothes as the work in this department was dirty and physically demanding. Marie Wilson, for instance, recalled that her job involved climbing over the fuselage of planes and walking along a scaffold-like structure in the aircraft. Wilson joked, at least this 'solved your problem for working clothes. You didn't have to go in worrying whether you looked alright or not, you know. Everybody looked the same.' The coveralls were also comfortable and easy to get in and out of.

Auto makers tried to increase the appeal of these uniforms by emphasizing their fashionableness and flattering lines. For instance, in 1942 *McKinnon Doings* featured photographs of women workers modelling the newest versions. Dorothy Harris, 'assembly line pretty,' exhibited the 'smarter new coverall.' 'Its trim lines carried out in navy and airforce blue are slenderizing and comfortable,' the caption read. The author of the article furthermore boasted that these outfits, designed specifically for female war workers, were 'worn one hundred per cent by the girls in such large airplane plants as Nordune [sic], Dehavilland and Fairchilds.' These 'girls' said, 'Since donning our new zoot suits we feel smarter, look smarter, and mean business. The dirndl with an apron was alright in a candy factory but now we are really doing a job we want to look the part.'[13]

Even when clad in GM uniforms the women found small ways to assert their femininity and personal style. Everyone wore coveralls, recalled Marie Smith and Bea Parkin, but the 'girls' added their own touch to the outfits. 'We used to wear fancy hankies in it,' they explained with laughter. Some women embroidered butterflies and other pretty and delicate images on the handkerchiefs during their spare time in the plant.

Some workers furthermore refused to wear safety shoes, preferring more fashionable and feminine high heels or open-toed styles of footwear (though this ruling applied only to certain groups of women). 'Remember – when you started to work at the McKinnon Industries Limited, you promised to wear a low heeled sturdy shoe – are you doing it?' company officials rhetorically inquired in their magazine. 'The wearing of high-heeled shoes while at work in the plant is certainly not a safe practice – they create a tripping and a falling hazard. You are asked not to wear them at work,' they reminded women employees.[14] Employers tried to convince the women to buy the regulation footwear by stressing their comfort and highlighting their attractiveness. In 'advertisements,' McKinnon spokespersons stated, 'The safety feature is concealed in the fibre toe-cap which protects the foot from the impact of falling objects. They are so smart and durable – and reasonable ... you will want to own at least one pair for work. In this way you can keep your more expensive shoes in good shape for special occasions!'[15]

Amidst wartime shortages the women also discussed the local availability of commodities such as silk stockings and underwear, both of which were rationed. One woman recalled, 'Somebody'd hear, oh, Zellers, they got a big shipment of underwear in. So we'd all dash down.' Marion Manning stated, 'My goodness, you'd hear there was nylon stockings downtown in some store and everybody would go down and get their nylons.'

Women workers took comfort and pleasure in these interchanges, for they were part of a popular culture that emphasized the personal and the feminine. This culture was important to women because it represented one of the few arenas in which they could affirm their identity as a sex, and highlight the values and sensibilities that emerged from the realities of their gendered lives. Moreover, it was strong because of the homogeneity of women in the auto plants. As noted, most of them were born and raised in small towns across Canada. They were of Anglo-Saxon or Eastern European background. And they grew up in working-class families.

By participating in, and shaping women's culture on the shop-floor, female workers were able to assert their uniqueness in an otherwise masculine milieu and retain important elements of their pre-war existence. Because femininity was a central aspect of their identity, feminine culture allowed the women to express themselves as individuals in a work setting in which the personal and subjective seemed to be foreign and unwelcome, binary opposites of the job. Furthermore, incessant talk of hairstyles and make-up offered them a fun escape from the drudgery of auto work. Although they did not protest unequal wage rates, unfair seniority systems, and the inadequate ventilation of work areas, women auto workers resisted what they perceived to be an unjust encroachment on their dignity – an assault on their femininity and gendered culture.

MARRIAGE AND DOMESTICITY

Talk of marriage and domestic life was another striking feature of work in the women's departments. Indeed, the themes of courtship and marriage were at the core of women's culture in the auto plants. As noted above, most war workers planned to centre their lives around marriage and motherhood. In fact, many women became engaged to be wed during the war years. On the weekend that Marie Smith wed, only six women remained in the sewing room. Smith explained, 'Now that's how many got married out of our department that weekend.' Her sister Bea Parkin added, 'All along people had boyfriends and they'd be engaged before the guys went overseas and this sort of thing. Oh, every Monday you didn't know how many were coming to show you their ring.'

Accordingly, throughout these years, the women threw many bridal showers, served as one another's bridesmaids, and attended co-workers' weddings. At work, furthermore, they took up collections of money for wedding gifts and engaged in pre-marital rituals.[16] 'If anybody was getting married, we'd dress them all up and get one of these skids ... and put a chair or something on there and push them all around the cutting and sewing department, explained Helen Graham. 'We had a belt, a conveyor belt that used to go from department to department. And there were big baskets on it. They used to put the finished work in. And ... we tied somebody up and put them in these conveyor baskets and send them away over to another department.'

As well, both company and union publications regularly featured weddings and engagements. A typical column in the Local 222 newspaper, the *Oshaworker*, read, 'Cupid sure has been doing a great deal in the Sewing Department. We are sorry to say we have lost three union members and one is the Alternate. However, we wish Ann Kushnk and Kay Sheridan the very best of luck. And also Dorothy Milne who left the GMC and was married in some part of England ... Best of luck to Vega, Alice, Muriel, and Noreen.'[17] Similar items appeared weekly. Even the UAW committeeman for the cutting and sewing departments reported on marriages and engagements far more often than grievances and layoffs. Committeeman Pat Meagher's regular column was appropriately and frankly entitled 'Cutting and Sewing Gossip.' 'To the Ladies,' a regular feature in the McKinnon magazine, also read like a social column. In addition to reports on recreational and sporting events, its author listed weddings, engagements, and birth announcements.[18]

Given the strength of conventional domestic ideology, it is not surprising that many women eagerly anticipated entry into the occupation of housewife. Women had long been divided into two categories, single and self-supporting, on the one hand, and married and financially dependent on a husband, on the other (see Pierson, 1990; Tentler, 1979). Workers and employers believed that unmarried women needed to work for wages, though not necessarily in high-paying jobs and industries. As financial dependents, married women were thought to work only for luxuries. Thus, they did not require paid employment. However, in this view, men, as household heads, deserved to be paid a family wage. The comments of some women exemplify the strength and pervasiveness of these ideas.

You went in there knowing that you worked until you got married and when you got married you knew that you couldn't work ... When I went in there that was great and when it come time to get married, okay, I'm going to be finished.

In those days, when you got married you seemed to want to quit work and raise a family ... A lot didn't mind leaving. I was happy to leave the job when the time came to leave ... War work was alright ... It was better than the Depression, I guess, and no work at all. But I was happy to stay home ... I was hoping that the War would be over and we'd get back to normal living.

It was a good thing because it gave jobs to young single girls. GM figured that once you got married, your husband should be able to support you ... I knew right from the day I started there that once I got married that was it.

Women's view of themselves as temporary workers bound for the home was reinforced by patriotic appeals. For instance, Marion Manning recalled, 'As I did these cushions ... I kept thinking, well, this will bring my husband home quicker ... Everything was sort of, all like, to get your guy home. And this was the important part. The war effort was there and you were there to do it. And I felt as if well, I'm doing my bit and the girl next to me's doing her bit to bring the guys home ... I was happy what I was doing ... I think the war was so much in our minds at that time, that with all the fellas overseas and not knowing ... that I'd wake up every day and think, you know, when I was workin' ... I hope he's alright. And that was the main thing that was on my mind.'

These remarks suggest that women had clearly internalized patriarchal ideas, but they do not indicate that women were totally absorbed by them. Women war workers publicly resigned themselves to their place in the gendered division of labour, but they were not happy about their fate, nor did they fully accept it. Out of both economic need and a desire to maintain the companionship of workmates, some women evaded the pre-war rules, without directly challenging them. Manifesting societal contradictions and personal dilemmas, women who openly upheld the restrictive rule against the employment of married women covertly defied it in practice. Women adopted various strategies of resistance.

Kay Anderson and Helen Graham concealed their marital status. Both women were single when they started to work at GM and both intended to quit upon marriage. However, they liked their jobs and after each was wed, she failed to see the logic in quitting. Anderson married in 1942 after a whirlwind courtship. Immediately after her wedding, her husband left for duty in the Royal Canadian Air Force and she returned to work as usual on Monday morning. 'I took off my rings and ... the only person that knew was my bridesmaid and she worked with me.' As soon as GM accepted married women into its aircraft division, Anderson, tired of pretending, transferred from her job in the sewing room.

Helen Graham's circumstances were similar. She also married in 1942 and her husband went overseas the following month. Graham stated, 'I was getting a married allowance from overseas, but I really enjoyed the company so much that I didn't want to leave ... So I thought, well, I'll just keep it [my marriage] quiet ... I never told anybody except a couple of close friends in the cutting and sewing ... I worked there from '42 to about '45.'[19] By 1945 rumours of Graham's marriage had spread, and just after the government had declared the end of war, her supervisor reminded her of the regulation. In response, she quit her job.

In discussing the fate of married women in McKinnon Industries, Margaret Heritz and her workmates quipped, 'Well we're just all going to live together. Nobody's gonna get married.' In spite of strong social censure, some women did adopt this strategy. Celia Wigg recalled a couple of women in GM that lived with men out of wedlock. 'Oh yes! God, yes.

That was quite common,' she remarked. 'A lot of them would say, "well, he's a boarder or he's this or he's that." Well, malarkey.' Marie Wilson had two single friends who lived with men. They married as soon as the company rule was eliminated. Jane Kelner said she knew of six women in such a living arrangement. 'Everybody talked about it,' she said. 'They were older than us.'

Other women delayed marriage. Some never wed. 'I stayed there instead of getting married,' commented sewing room worker Jane McDonald. 'I was engaged to be married and you couldn't work if you got married. So I figured, well, I enjoyed working and I liked having my own money to spend and I figured, well, I'll stay here.' Elsa Goddard explained that the women's reasons for staying single, whether because of company policy or out of personal choice, were seldom clearly defined. 'The money was so good and I think a lot of them just said, "Hell." The job was really good and they could keep themselves and a lot of them just weren't interested in being married.' Joan Jackson added, 'One girl in there ... went with this fella for 25 years ... to this day, she still was never married to him.'

Although on the shop floor the women paid more attention to the romance of dating, engagements, and weddings than to the daily grind of family life, sewing room employees also frequently punctuated their factory duties with conversations about household matters. Rumours would 'go around at work that A&P had butter,' for instance. One observer reported that whenever this happened, 'there'd be a stampede down A&P to get a pound of butter.' During rest periods and slack times, the women crocheted, knitted, and worked on their needlepoint. In company publications, auto employers both mirrored and reinforced women's restricted position in the domestic division of labour. In regular columns, they advised women employees on proper refrigerator maintenance,[20] consumerism, cooking and recipes, extending the life of one's stockings, decorating, sewing, and ironing.[21] In addition, they reported on rations and coupon books for scarce goods such as sugar.[22]

WOMAN-TO-WOMAN RELATIONSHIPS

Some writers have argued that an important feature of women's gendered experience is their greater capacity to form strong social-emotional ties (see Chodorow, 1978; Rubin, 1983). This gender difference, they claim, is rooted in early development. As an integral component of one's psychic make-up, however, it influences women's and men's experiences throughout life. Though they do not all write within a psychoanalytic framework, a number of sociologists and historians have uncovered data that support these claims. Recent feminist research reveals that wage-earning women have drawn on their strong relational capacity as part of a general attempt to humanize the workplace (for example, Rosen, 1987; Westwood, 1985). One can hardly claim that the development of strong friendships was an 'act of resistance' against managerial control (unlike the refusal to comply with dress regulations, for instance). However, these social ties often play a central role in the women's management of the labour process.[23]

In the auto industry, the camaraderie and esprit de corps that typified female departments made wage work tolerable and even enjoyable at times. Life on the plant floor was characterized by frivolity, horseplay, and animated conversation. In the process, many women auto workers formed solid and meaningful friendships with one another, bonds that extended far beyond the plants.

Relationships between women varied in intensity according to the workers' age, marital status, and personality. Single women were more likely to have the time and freedom to associate with co-workers after hours. Young women engaged in more social and recreational pursuits than those who were older. And some women were outgoing and affable, while others kept to themselves. In addition, as noted above, variations in the labour process affected the nature and degree of communication. Many sewing room employees formed close friendships as their work permitted uninterrupted conversations and sororizing. Some machine operators produced their scheduled output before quitting time and so-cialized for the remainder of the day. Moreover, sewing machines and conveyors were set up in long rows, facilitating conversations across the room. In contrast, some areas, such as the fuel pump department, in McKinnon Industries, were noisy and the demands of the line distracting, and the workers' opportunity to chat privately was thus reduced.

The gender composition of departments further reinforced the bonds between employees. As we have shown, gender rituals and gender-spe-cific concerns were important elements of the workers' culture: where many women were concentrated in one department, they were more likely to develop a sense of collegiality than where they mixed with men.[24]

Although many women were acquainted with one another before their employment in the industry, they generally formed close bonds on the shop floor itself. Typically, women who worked on the same line or collectively as a group became 'chums.' On the plant floor, they revealed their camaraderie through various forms of horseplay and joking, not unlike their male co-workers. However, the content of women's escapades clearly reflected their gender. For example, sewing room workers raffled meat pies at work. 'We were trying to make enough money,' recounted Helen Beaugrand, 'to buy this material to go to this dressmaker and get a dress made.' It started out as a joke, but it proved to be effective. One woman made the pie, while the others auctioned the pieces. They received seven cents per slice.

They also customarily collected money to buy one another birthday gifts, threw bridal showers, and on pay days brought food into the plant for small celebrations. Indeed, in some work areas, they placed the food right on the conveyor lines and indulged when it came by their station. More often, however, the women would share food during rest breaks. 'When we had a little bit more money,' Bea Parkin reminisced, 'we used to bring fruit in. And at our rest period in the afternoon, we'd put it all out on a table and everybody'd buy a little bit of something ... we'd have a bunch of grapes or a pear or whatever ... it wouldn't be a feast.' Marie Smith remembered, 'It was the cream puffs that I used to buy at a little bakery.' Dorothea Koch brought in about two dozen doughnuts. 'We always ate Friday afternoon,' she said.

At Christmas the sharing of food took on grander proportions. In both Oshawa and St Catharines each woman would bring a special dish into the plant, and they would eat all day, during working hours. 'We'd have a regular feast that day,' reported Helen Beaugrand. They set up all the food on the tables and work benches.

The women also passed the hours by singing in unison. Most often, they sang war songs. A touch of patriotism went a long way in reinforcing women workers' cohesiveness and dedication to the job. It gave them a sense of common purpose and the songs temporarily released them from the tedium of their labour. One woman stated, 'Three or four of us would all be singin' and workin'.' She immediately added, 'It was a good place to work.' Jane Kelner recounted, ' "Over There" and things like that ... Everybody in your group would be singing that song and maybe another group would be singing a different song. We used to sing a lot to pass the time because especially when you're on the machine and your eyes get tired and your back, sitting there. And so if you sing it sort of takes away from the monotony of the job.' Remembering the collegial atmosphere in their departments, some women likened life in the auto plants during the war years to their days back in school.

The women, however, talked infrequently about the job itself, and some of their best times occurred with workmates outside of the plant. Friendships or 'chumming' also revolved around popular women's culture, involving expressions of conventional femininity – a strong interest in fashion and make-up, shopping, men, dating, marriage, and vacations with the 'girls,' rather than wage work.

In important ways, these concerns could not be divorced from the job. Women's culture was not only fostered within the family or community and imported to the workplace. It was also shaped by their experiences within the plant. Indeed, the nature of women's employment contributed to a particular construction of feminine culture. Furthermore, their shared experiences in wage labour helped to constitute them as a sex. Few women, however, mentioned these connections.

We 'chummed around a lot outside of the plant. We used to chum around together all the time,' reported Jane McDonald. Many single women met regularly after work and on weekends. 'We'd go down to the restaurant maybe at noon hour for our lunch or after work. Maybe we'd have a bet ... or something that one of us would have to take the others out and treat them to a meal ... four or five of us,' recounted Helen Graham. If they had nothing else to do, some women just met down at the Globe Cafe in Oshawa for a Coke, a cherry Coke. Others visited their favourite drugstore on King Street. Trips to the movies, hockey games, bowling, ice skating, and roller skating were also familiar pursuits. 'There wasn't that much to do in Oshawa,' Kelner explained with laughter and humility.

On holidays such as Christmas and Thanksgiving the women revealed a strong sense of family. During the Christmas season they visited one another's homes, and many exchanged gifts. 'We used to have a lot going,' said Marie Smith. Recreational activities were plentiful. In the winter season the 'girls' from one department went on sleigh rides, followed by a visit to an older woman's house for chili or hot soup. In the warmer months they enjoyed hay rides and wiener roasts. Picnics and drives in the country were popular summer pastimes. Effie Baldwin fondly recalled some of these 'wonderful times ... We'd have picnics and outings, dances. We used to have a ball! ... We had a nice big back lawn and we had a badminton court out there. And so often I'd have a group of the girls come down ... and we'd have our supper outside on the lawn and play badminton. Doesn't sound much, but boy, did they all enjoy it.'

Some women even vacationed together. Trips were rarely extravagant, but they offered a release from auto work. For example, groups of sewing room employees often drove to Picton for a getaway, to 'the outlet down on the Lake.' In one incident, Helen Graham borrowed her husband's car, and her workmate Helen Beaugrand was elected to drive. However, none of the women had a driver's licence, nor could they drive. They proceeded nevertheless, with one telling the other when to move the gears. 'If my mother and father ever had of known [sic],' laughed Beaugrand, 'they would have killed me. It took us eight hours ... to go to Picton. While the War was on you couldn't get tires and we had a blowout and three flats.'

After work and on weekends women also went on shopping trips together. Usually they shopped at local stores such as Woolworth's or Kresge's. 'We didn't go to any expensive stores,' declared Celia Wigg. On occasion they also travelled to Toronto, the 'big city.' Marie Smith recalled with amusement that on every pay day she and her friends went down to Fox's or Black's where they always had a dress put away. In those days, she explained, women had to own a pair of shoes to match every outfit, and they carefully reserved a small portion of their pay cheques for such extravagances. When Ann Brisbois was working in the wire and harness department she defied her usual frugality, ignored the limits of her budget, and bought a 'beautiful winter coat with a big lynx collar.' This was an extravagance. 'It was 55 dollars. Well,' she said, 'that was a tremendous price then. Tremendous price. And I had saved for it ... That coat was very, very expensive for the wages that I was getting.'

Friday was a special day. The shopping and talk and planning through-out the week were largely geared towards the events of a Friday evening. 'Friday night was the night we went to the dances,' explained Kay Anderson. 'All the women went. And all the men went. Live music. We had an orchestra ... There was one called the Avalon and one called the Top Hat, and then there was the Jubilee Pavilion ... In those days, it was so much a dance ... They had a velvet rope and they had a ticket taker, and a fella come up and asked you to dance and you went ... And then the dance floor was cleared after the three numbers ... I think most of the women that worked in the Motors went, and the fellas.'

Back at work on Monday the 'girls' talked enthusiastically about the weekend's events, the letters they had received from overseas, family, their flirtations, and their more serious romantic entanglements. 'You know. Just women talk,' said Helen Graham. During these years, 'women talk' involved a sharing of personal concerns far more often than a dis-cussion of wage work, politics, and the union. Indeed, auto work was almost a taboo subject for these women. According to Jane McDonald, 'If somebody started talkin' about work, we'd walk away. Say, "leave it where it belongs."' Another employee claimed that 'unless something had come up during the day ... [her group of friends] never normally talked about work.' Another woman astutely noted that her brothers 'used to say that when they went to the beverage room in Oshawa, that all they talked about was their work and the union. When they went to the beverage room down in Trenton, all they talked about was the farms and the crops and how the tomatoes were doing ... But girls never talked about it very much ... We just enjoyed ourselves. We forgot about the shop.'

These social ties and recreational pursuits clearly provided the women with an escape from the drudgery of their jobs. The relationships not only made auto work bearable, they made the employment experience enjoyable at times. Thinking about her workmates, Marie Smith stated, 'It didn't bother me gettin' up in the morning going to work.' Another woman claimed that she and her co-worker friend 'were happy ... We'd be so glad Monday morning we were going back to work with the gang,' she said. Another employee remarked, 'At that time, we looked so forward to going to work because we enjoyed ourselves.'

Accordingly, the women's most outstanding recollections of auto employment involved their co-workers. Marie Wilson claimed that she enjoyed working in GM mainly because of the people she worked with. Jane McDonald similarly stated, 'I liked the people I met. I liked any job I did, really. But it's mostly the people. You meet so many nice people and you form friendships and that's more or less what you think about when you look back.' Likewise, Marie Smith's most striking memory of the Motors was 'the family atmosphere.' Other women referred to 'the laughs' they had. Helen Graham recounted, 'I think of the girls I worked with a lot ... the girls that were really close.'

Relationships among women auto workers were enduring, far surpassing their tenure in the plant. Celia Wigg quit her job in the Motors in 1947, but in 1990 she still spoke to three of her former workmates at least once a week. Although Marion Manning worked at GM only during the war, she remained close to the woman who worked next to her, and she continued to correspond with another who had moved to a different town. Moreover, two women who met in the plant eventually shared a house and became intimate companions.[25] Undoubtedly, the relatively small size of auto manufacturing communities and the dominance of the auto makers as employers in these towns also contributed to the maintenance of close social-emotional ties among the workforce.

On the shop floor and in the union women auto workers conformed to dominant gender prescriptions. Indeed, they not only accepted sexual divisions and inequalities, they celebrated conventional roles and images of womanhood. Given the strong public consensus on proper gender behaviour and the absence of an ideological challenge to these conventions during the war years, the world that women constructed is understandable. To some degree, the very act of working in an auto manufacturing plant was in itself a radical departure for women. Participating in conventional feminine pursuits and sustaining a familiar gender identity therefore offered some comfort to women in this unfamiliar setting. Through their gendered behaviour, however, some women also coped with their work and resisted management. The harsh realities and contradictions of the workplace and society made it difficult for women to remain entirely passive and consenting. They therefore protested some aspects of their employment in covert, gender-specific ways. Women's life-long learning in a patriarchal capitalist society influenced the specific nature of their resistance. Aspirations of marriage and care-giving offered the women an illusory escape from the drudgery of industrial wage labour. Intimate talks, 'dressing up,' and dating were fun, satisfying forms of self-expression that women learned long ago. They represented a consistent thread in women's lives.

SISTERS AND BROTHERS IN A GENDERED SETTING

The gendered division of auto work also shaped relationships between male and female employees. While the public negotiation of women's official place in the industry suggests that there was friction between the sexes (see chapter 2), tensions were rarely manifested in the face-to-face encounters of women and men on the shop floor. As noted, male unionists and employers bargained sex-based terms of employment, while women played a marginal role in the debate. Similarly, on a day-to-day basis women were so tightly segregated in their own departments that they had little contact with men. Because of the strength of sex segregation, the limited relations between male and female employees were for the most part harmonious, without serious antagonism or resentment.

'We knew the men,' explained Bea Parkin, 'but we didn't associate with the men that much.' In GM's Oshawa plant men worked as cutters down the aisle from the sewers. And apart from supervisors, some men entered women's departments to inspect, deliver stock, and set up and repair machines. However, few men worked permanently in these areas. Thus, although the auto industry itself was highly male-dominated, women often formed a majority in departments or work areas within departments. Men behaved themselves, explained Joan Jackson facetiously, 'because ... the women outnumbered the guys. If they wanted to get on you ... we had a lot of women that would stand right up to them.'

Furthermore, in the auto industry, sex-based contract clauses protected most working men from the threat of cheaper female labour. In the absence of a direct threat, rank-and-file men were less concerned than union officials about the possibility that employers would try to reclassify women's and men's work. While women worked in the male-dominated core room in McKinnon Industries, the collective agreement ensured that they remained in female classifications. Women and men accepted one another's different, unequal positions in the industry and engaged in similarly friendly, though unegalitarian, relations in their day-to-day living.

But while there was little sexual conflict in the auto plants, there were strong heterosexual tensions.[26] Romances between male and female workers were not rampant, but those that flourished generated enthusiastic commentary. Bud Manning, a retired GM worker, laughed as he stated that women and men in the Motors not only 'got along well.' They got along 'too well.' 'There was a little bit of fraternizing going on – sort of undercurrent talk,' added Marion Manning. Joan Jackson and Elsa Goddard similarly recalled with humour, 'You could see them in the cutting room ... having their little smooching time ... You couldn't help but know about ... "Where's so and so?" ... Oh, lots of gossip.'

Occasionally this 'fraternizing' led to marriage. There was one 'really sweet romance going on in the sewing room' that resulted in marriage, explained Kay Anderson. 'We were thrilled ... He was from another department actually, but brought a lot of jobs and work into our area.' Effie Baldwin recalled that at least four couples who worked in the cutting and sewing departments eventually wed. In McKinnon Industries, Margaret Heritz and her husband met in a car pool of auto workers. After about three years, they married and both remained employees of the firm. 'I'd see him [in the plant] at lunch break or you'd come by,' said Heritz, 'somebody'd go by and pass on messages and things like that.' Likewise, Marion and Bud Manning, both GM employees, met outside of the Motors. Bud was apprenticing as a skilled tradesman, while Marion worked in the aircraft division. As they could not take breaks together, Marion stood at the window and watched Bud work. 'That was quite a thrill for me that I could look out and see him over there standing out too, having his break,' she said.

The scandalous sexual relationships, however, were extra-marital.

These relationships were commonplace and involved both married women and married men. Reflecting a societal double standard of sexuality, though, controversy centred around the women's behaviour. In the McKinnon plant, 'you'd see some of the married women running around and you knew they were married,' exclaimed Mabel Larkin. Likewise, Helen Graham reported that 'there were different little affairs going on ... I know of two or three men in the cutting room, they were single fellas. [They] had a romance going [with] ... married girls that worked in the sewing room.' Controversy heightened when some women became pregnant while their husbands were overseas.

For young single women, relations between women and men were 'just super.' 'I was young and blonde and not bad to look at,' said Kay Anderson. 'And I was the youngest woman up there.' Most men in the industry were either very young or at least middle-aged; the others had gone off to war. The young men, recalled Anderson, sometimes wandered in from other departments in the plant. 'They'd come up on pretense of picking up some stock or something,' and 'they'd have maybe a little visit.' When the 'Oshawa Generals' hockey team played for GM, the company gave the players jobs delivering mail and the like. In the eyes of these young women, 'they were the thing.' 'If you went out with an Oshawa General you just had it made. You were big time,' said Anderson. She and a co-worker would linger by the water fountain in the cutting and sewing room, until they heard the elevator. 'And sure enough, off would come two or three Oshawa Generals – all good-looking devils, you know.'

Given the sensitive nature of the topic, it is difficult to ascertain the extent of sexual harassment in the auto plants. In addition, definitions and perceptions of acceptable sexual behaviour vary widely.[27] Some women reported cases in which foremen used their authority to elicit sex with women whom the company had recruited from abroad for the duration of the war. Another employee alleged that some men threatened to dismiss immigrant male workers if their wives did not give them sexual access. The line between coercion and consent was a fine one.

Few women, however, reported that they had personally experienced even a 'mild' form of harassment such as an offensive joke.[28] A wire and harness employee, for instance, stated with hindsight, 'Sometimes I think that we have regressed instead of progressed in many things because we were respected, really. I always felt very respected in there ... If you were a woman ... most of the men that we worked with were nice men and there was no silliness about them ... I never had any problems with them and I'm sure most of them didn't. They wouldn't be coming up and pinching me and that kind of silliness that they seem to have problems with now. Anywhere, I never heard of anybody having too much of a problem unless they asked for it ... I couldn't work in there now, with the way things are now.

Moreover, some women viewed the middle-aged and older men who remained in the plants as 'fatherly types.' They described their relationships with such men as typically good-natured. Groups of women and men sometimes held bowling competitions against one another, with the losers treating the winners to a steak supper. They also had banquets and parties to which the men brought their wives. 'I think we all had a real good relationship,' said one employee. Another woman remarked, 'The fellas were good.' 'One of the men, he raised pheasants and he lived out in the country. And there were three of us girls, that he and his wife wanted out for dinner ... Just social evenings ... there was no conflict really.'

The limited communication between the sexes often entailed teasing and joke-telling by the men, and amusement and nurturance on the part of the women. Some men regularly dropped by the women's departments, requesting free food and snacks. Helen Beaugrand and her workmate often passed food down from a hole in the sewing room floor to a man who worked below them in the aircraft division. Even when men behaved foolishly, they were tolerated by many of their female co-workers. Beaugrand described one man as 'terrible.' 'He'd get these rubber hoses and if you was walkin' up the aisle, you never knew what was going to hit you,' she said. Nevertheless, she added, 'you couldn't help but like him ... he'd get back and shoot it almost like a bow and arrow ... He was always up to something and yet nobody got mad at him.'

These amicable relations were reinforced by family ties. In the small communities of Oshawa and St Catharines, workers lived together as husbands and wives, brothers and sisters, and fathers and daughters. Given the dominance of General Motors as an employer in these towns, family relationships extended beyond the home and into the workplace. Marion Manning's sister, brother, husband, sister-in-law, brother-in-law, and father-in-law all worked for the company at various times. Jane McDonald's father was a trimmer on car upholstery in GM for forty-five years. Eventually, everyone in her family except one worked for the firm. Between them, they had 'over 300 and some years accumulated.' In addition, Joan Jackson and Elsa Goddard, sisters, worked in GM. 'With my Dad,' said Goddard, 'we were all in there.' Their other sister Barbara worked on the door lines, and their youngest sister, Bubbles, came into the Motors after Barbara. Their cousins, Marie Smith, Bea Parkin, and Anne Whyte, were also GM employees, along with their father, a sweeper who started with the firm in 1920. Marie rattled off the list of names, 'Oh yes, Uncle Joe. And Uncle John. And Uncle [inaudible] and Uncle Hank.' Bea added, 'I don't think there was hardly anybody in all our family that didn't work in GM some time.' In explaining her relations in the firm, Marie Wilson stated, 'This is a GM town, let's put it that way.'

Apart from those based on family connections, however, relationships between women and men were not as intimate as the bonds that were forged among the women themselves. Women and men were on good terms, but they were not close companions. Social restrictions, gender-specific experiences, and the different relational capacities of the sexes, as well as physical barriers in the plants, impeded the development of such a level of intimacy.

Like some male workers, foremen tended to regard the women with mild amusement. 'He thought I was such a kid,' said Helen Beaugrand about the foreman in her department. 'I used to always try to get 13 pieces of Christmas cake for New Year's. It would bring me good luck ... He'd come along one day and ask how many I had collected ... I says, 'I'd lack five or six yet.' That evening the foreman telephoned Beaugrand at home, stating that his wife had gone around to the neighbors and collected extra pieces of cake for her. This man also taught Beaugrand to do the 'two-step' on roller skates, and he invited the 'sewing room girls' to his house after a GM roller skating party at Christmas. Another time, when the women got up from their sewing machines in the middle of a work day and danced a Highland jig, he came out of his office, looked, merely shook his head, and walked back in.

The relationship between female workers and male supervisors was complicated. For women there is usually no clear separation between family and work roles, in both a material and an ideological sense (see Tentler, 1979). In the auto plants, women's relationship with male supervisors was similar to their relationships with older male workers.[29] In both cases, they acted as daughters. Indeed, many women affectionately referred to their general foreman as 'father' and described male supervisors as 'real fatherly types,' 'old and comical.'

As daughters and/or employees, the women feared and often resented the foreman's authority, but they did not directly challenge it. At most, they would 'horse around a bit' or visit another operator when they should have been at their own machines. Women usually had someone watch out for supervision. When a supervisor came into the room, they would utter, 'Ninety-nine, ninety-nine,' their warning code. Sewing room workers described their foreman as someone 'everybody was scared of ... Everybody thought he was cranky all the time ... [but] nothing like, you know, mean and nasty.' According to Marion Manning, 'Our foreman he'd be a very hard fast person – fast rule ... he figured you should be not wandering around too much ... You had to look busy whether you weren't. When we'd see him coming we would look very busy. We were quite afraid of him ... Nobody would ... more or less defy him ... They would respect him, I guess you could say ... The boss was the boss.'

Others agreed with this characterization, but they added that the supervisor usually did not have to 'push the women too hard' because most women regulated themselves. This self-regulation rested on a powerful economic incentive, as well as the women's express attempt to sustain positive relationships within the work setting. During the war years most women were paid according to a group bonus efficiency system. This scheme required them to 'put out' a quota of work per day in order to receive a 'bonus on the dollar.' 'We knew we had to put out ... and we did it,' explained one worker. 'If you didn't keep up on the machines, then your efficiency suffered and so did your pay.' In addition, because they worked in groups, the women tended to police one another. If one person worked inefficiently, they all suffered. 'So everybody did their bit,' explained Kay Anderson. 'I couldn't see where you'd have any room to chastise them [women] about anything because in those days you did a good day's work for your money. And that was just part of your bringing up or what you thought. There was no slacking off or – everybody tried to do their fair share and – even the older ladies ... It was just an understood fact that everybody was doing their bit to keep up the amount.'

Both because and in spite of the strength and nature of sex-segregated work, conflict and competition between women and men remained at a legal-contractual level and was not strongly manifested in face-to-face relations on the shop floor. Women and men seldom acted as rivals or adversaries. Rather, there was a striking harmony between the sexes – a relation that was reinforced by men's paternalistic attitudes towards women workers and neutralized by sexual/romantic tensions. Family ties between female and male auto workers also encouraged this amicability. In addition, men treated women favourably because women did not contest their subordinate position in the gendered division of labour. Many women perceived their relationships with men as based on respect, a form of recognition that served as an important source of their dignity as workers. In chapters 5 and 6 we will see that disrespect on the part of men, and, indeed, serious conflicts between the sexes, emerged, however, when women became a more viable, visible, and equal force in the industry.

UPHOLDING GENDERED DIVISIONS AND INEQUALITIES

When an auto employer suddenly, without explanation, replaced an experienced female group leader with a man, the displaced woman was highly distressed. However, she did nothing about it. She protested neither to the union nor to management. 'That was discrimination really,' observed a co-worker, 'but we didn't know what discrimination was. No. We didn't know what it was!'

Gender divisions and ideologies were so firmly entrenched in the 1940s that the women did not openly question their subordinate position as a sex. 'The women were not geared up and demanding ... That all came later on,' reflected Kay Anderson. 'I don't remember anybody ever sayin' ... ' I could do that job as well as him,' you know, and 'I'm a woman.' I don't remember any of that." Marion Manning perceptively stated, 'There was no women's rights then.'

Notwithstanding, female auto workers were keenly aware of the rigid separation of women's and men's wage labour. 'I never figured that I was doing a woman's job or a man's job,' said Jane McDonald. 'I was doing a job ... We were never asked to do it [men's work] and we never thought of asking to do it. That was his job and that was my job.' The sex-based division of labour itself prevented cross-sex comparisons. Kay Anderson frankly remarked, 'I don't even remember what else went on in that room – except our own little department where we did the drilling.'

To some degree the women also had an emotional investment in prevailing arrangements. Sex-segregated jobs and gendered work culture offered women and men the security and comfort of the familiar and the social validation of 'womanhood' and 'manhood' through involvement in 'women's work' and 'men's work.' In addition, female workers had a material stake in upholding the sexual division of auto work. Sociologists and economists have long discussed the ways in which workers carve out for themselves labour markets in order to protect their exclusive interests (see Rubery, 1980). Although women auto workers did not themselves establish the sex-based job classification system, they defended it in order to maintain their restricted position in the industry. Many women viewed female departments as 'shelters' from the intrusion of more powerful male labour. In the process, they drew on dominant cultural beliefs about women's and men's proper place.

Although women could not enter the myriad job classifications in GM's huge Oshawa complex, they found comfort in knowing that men would not invade their sewing room. According to Joan Jackson, 'I just figured, hey, I had a great job and ... this man couldn't come in and do my job ... You don't find too many men that know nothing about sewing, so you knew that they weren't gonna come in and try and take your job ... That was one thing they never ever did.' Similarly, Margaret Heritz noted the short-term benefits of unequal wage rates in McKinnon Industries. Returning war veterans would not take women's jobs because they would get only the women's wage. In regular times, healthy men did not take women's jobs because 'they were pretty well defined,' she reasoned. Only disabled men sometimes moved into the female classifications.

As noted earlier, women utilized gender ideologies and highlighted socially constructed gender differences to cope with the harmful effects of the labour process, but they also wove these beliefs into a more active strategy to improve their conditions of work. For example, in defending her support of the 1941 strike at McKinnon Industries, a woman employee publicly stated that 'longer hours [of work] mean more lost time through illness, especially among the girls. Therefore, we need extra pay in order to be able to pay our doctors and dentists.' Furthermore, in arguing for a definite rest period for women, she stated, 'Everyone should know that girls are not as physically strong as men and should have this privilege.'

Echoing management's view that men's work was always more arduous than women's, another female employee stated, 'But the women didn't have to slug on the line then like they do now. We were given jobs off the line preparing stuff for them, that the men used. So I don't know whether they [women in GM] progressed or not.' Expressing concerns about congestion and the intermingling of the sexes, GM management furthermore permitted women to 'punch out' at ten minutes before the final hour of work, while men had to wait an additional five minutes. Most women did not know the rationale behind this rule, but they accepted it nevertheless. The women justified the policy by claiming that they needed more time to wash-up, must be cleaner than men, and must fix their hair and make-up. Women auto workers recognized that they could extract from management some limited entitlement based on their different needs as a sex, even if they did not have equal rights with the male workforce.

Taking into account the opportunities and constraints in their lives, as well as ideological and cultural influences and resources, women and men developed gendered strategies of coping and resistance. These strategies entailed a recognition that women and men occupied very different and unequal positions in work and society.

SUMMARY: THE IMPLICATIONS OF WOMEN WORKERS' STRATEGY

The position of workers in the gendered division of wage labour strongly shaped their responses to the rapid changes that were occurring in the auto industry during the Second World War. Both women and men drew upon familiar gender ideologies and gendered culture as part of their strategies in dealing with the industrial context. In the last chapter, we saw that working men upheld notions of a male breadwinner and a female housewife, and pursued a family wage through their most effective ve- hicle, the UAW. Noting that women had a weak voice in the union, in this chapter we have explored women's informal responses to auto employment by examining their experiences on the shop floor.

Most women war workers grew up believing that they would become full-time homemakers, economically dependent on a man. Yet over time, many of these same women realized that this type of family arrangement was unrealistic for the majority of working people. A male breadwinner alone could not supply the family's financial needs, and this family form did not fulfil the social and emotional desires of women at home. Female auto workers reconciled these contradictions by upholding a conventional definition of womanhood in the workplace. By drawing on elements of conventional feminine culture, these workers expressed their womanhood in a male-dominated industry. The shop-floor life they created accommodated their long-term plans of marriage and child rearing. Because conventional femininity was an important aspect of women's identity, it provided them with an outlet for self-expression in what could otherwise be an impersonal context.

Women also drew upon familiar gendered ways of thinking and behaving in response to the labour process itself. Both their perception of workplace injustices and the nature of their shop-floor coping and resistance were gendered. The women did not directly challenge sex segregation, unequal wage rates, separate seniority lists, or the exclusion of married women from employment. The concepts of sexual discrimination and gender inequality were not in the popular discourse during these years. However, many women did resist managements' attempts to dictate their style of dress and inhibit their shop-floor interaction, and they developed private strategies for evading company policies against the employment of married women.

The women not only used conventional gender ideologies passively and defensively, but also integrated them into active strategies to improve their position in the workplace. Recognizing that they had limited resources and few formal rights, they sometimes upheld prevailing gender divisions in order to preserve their restricted position in the industry. Unafraid of highlighting gender difference, they even drew on cultural assumptions about women's limited capacities in employment, in an effort to better their shop-floor existence.

Throughout the war, these women also drew upon and nurtured a strong gender identity and developed a female camaraderie. Because of these bonds, the women often enjoyed their work, despite its hardships. However, women's loyalty to familiar gender relations left many unfair aspects of their employment untouched. Women used gender ideologies to cope with the tedium and degradation of work, but this form of resistance was covert, and passive, and thus largely concealed their underlying discontent. Furthermore, it reinforced the separation of women from the union and the popular notion of females as politically reactionary.

This strategy was useful only in the short term. In the long term, it reinforced a structure that ultimately threatened to leave women workers without any place in the industry. Women's departments may have provided a sense of security and insulation from the harsh industrial environment, but this protection was illusory. Women abruptly learned this lesson in the post-war years – when they no longer faced a labour shortage, auto employers reinforced old policies against the employment of married women.

During the Second World War McKinnon Industries sponsored many labourers from the Canadian West and the East. But when war production ceased in 1944 the company laid them off. Furthermore, with the exception of tool room employees, women who had been performing men's work were immediately transferred to other jobs. Supervision made the placements, and if a woman disliked her new job, she had no option but to quit. 'You had no just [cause] to protest it,' said Mabel Larkin, 'because you were on a man's job ... There was no question, no question on it.' 'It was just the general feeling of the guys are coming back to get their jobs.'

Because the company began to expand some female departments soon after war's end, however, McKinnon Industries retained many women, and recalled others. As well, during the war the firm had expanded the female-dominated ball bearing department and enlarged the spark plug line and commercial motors. When it reconverted to domestic manufacturing, the company was also in high production and thus was able to absorb many female employees. McKinnon even hired some women during this period of growth.

In Oshawa, conversely, GM laid off married women in massive numbers. So weak was the women's protest, their position so marginal, that few women or men even knew what had happened to them when the war ended. According to a sewing room worker who retained her job, 'I don't know, things just went back to what they were before. I don't remember anybody ever being laid off. [So all those women who were hired were kept on?] Most of them, I think, were kept on.' Another woman was aware of the lay-offs, but admitted, 'It was done and we were just on the sidelines listening.'

Helen Graham was one of the many women who were displaced. She recollected that in 1945 Stan Hutson, a general foreman, came over and said, 'Helen, I have a question to ask ya.' He said, 'I've been hearing rumours that you are married. Is it true?' And of course, anybody come right out and ask me a question like that, I couldn't tell a lie. I couldn't say no I wasn't. I said, 'Yes I am.' And he said, 'Well, I'm sorry, but Friday will be your last day at work.' I felt terrible ... My husband was still overseas and I enjoyed the work. I enjoyed the girls ... I didn't want to lose my job and I knew that as soon as they found out I was married, I would lose my job.' Bea Parkin also recalled, 'One day ... several of us called into the office and the boss ... said, 'You got married, and you got married. You're all married.' And they said, 'We can't keep you any longer because once you're married now you have to quit.' And you had no say in the matter. You were married so you just had to.'

Indeed, as war production ceased the entire GM aircraft division was closed down. Stated Dorothea Koch, 'About three days after the War was declared over, they just come on and said, "We're closin' the place up." The woman next door where I boarded, said she never saw anything more forlorn looking than me comin' home with all my bits and pieces. It gives you an awful let down feeling 'cause you're wondering now, what happens, where do you – what do you do next? I didn't really know.' GM eventually recalled Koch only because she was a widow. Married women disappeared as quietly and unassumingly as they had appeared in the auto plants.

4

Becoming 'Union-Wise' (1950–1963)

For the first hour when you're comin' in, you're laughing and joking ... and all of a sudden, there's a quiet for a couple of hours. And everybody's got their own thoughts. I used to write letters. I used to build houses – in my mind ... You never thought of that job because if you did, you'd go nuts. Very monotonous kind of work to do ... it wasn't very fulfilling, at all.

Bev McCloskey, auto worker

You might as well take a shackle and put it on your ankle and give you four or five foot of chain and leave it there.

Betty Murray, auto worker

When auto manufacturers reconverted their operations to domestic production in the mid-to-late 1940s, many women lost their jobs. However, with bursts of economic growth in the early 1950s and renewed prosperity in the early 1960s, employers recalled some war workers and hired additional women. What were the experiences of this new cohort of female workers in times of relative social and economic stability?

Predictably, women's responses to auto work were similar before, during, and immediately after the Second World War. In each of these periods, women's gender identity and subordinate position in society strongly shaped their relation to auto work. Newly hired workers in the industry upheld conventional beliefs about the sexes and did not challenge sex-segregated work arrangements. Like the cohort that preceded them, these women made strong investments in friendships and family.

After the war, however, as the UAW gained strength and legitimacy, and as women secured a more permanent position in the industry, they developed a stronger self-identification as wage earners and as unionists. By the 1950s many women recognized that they were in the plants to stay. Consequently, they paid greater attention to the terms of their employment, and they formally protested a number of shop-floor conditions.

Shop-floor resistance among women workers grew noticeably during the post-war years. Sometimes this resistance took the form of an individual grievance. At other times it was expressed through group action. Collective, organized struggles often grew out of an accumulation of complaints by individual workers. Significantly, throughout the 1950s, women tended to draw increasingly on the tools of resistance that working-class men had constructed years ago – the UAW grievance procedure and the collective agreement.

While women tried to reshape some unfair aspects of their employment, they left others unchallenged. Notably, they still did not openly contest their subordination as a sex. Indeed, in their protests women often drew upon conservative gender ideologies. There is strong evidence, though, that working-class women's oppression in industry was forcefully mediated by their sex. Furthermore, there is some indication that a number of women perceived this relationship. How, then, can we explain the absence of a direct challenge to sexual oppression and exploitation during this period?

In this chapter we will see that the resistance strategies of women auto workers were largely shaped by the gendered politics of earlier times – a politics that led to the dominance of a masculine agenda and male discourse in the union. The UAW, the women's most viable resource for change at this time, embraced working men's vision of social justice – a vision that upheld conventional gender ideologies, accepted sex-based inequalities, and was premised on the unquestioned assumption that because women were different from men, it was reasonable to treat them differently (less well). At the same time, however, unionists continued to promote the ethos of worker solidarity and unity, and the universal pursuit of social justice. Guided by this contradictory outlook, male union leaders entrenched and legitimated blatant gender inequalities in collective agreements, while they simultaneously championed female workers' rights as dues-paying unionists.

These contradictions resulted in a fractured workers' struggle. Yet this fracture only constrained the *nature* of struggle. It did not obstruct *struggle per se*. Throughout these years, women auto workers became increasingly 'union-wise' and with their knowledge of unionism, they lodged battles that would ultimately have great consequence for the organization, and experience, of wage labour.

A NEW COHORT OF WORKERS IN A CHANGING CONTEXT

By the late 1940s and early 1950s, auto manufacturers were again expanding their operations and recalling some of the women they had laid off at the war's end. In addition, they were hiring women who had never before worked in the industry. In 1948 350 women were employed out of a total of 4,850 plant workers in GM's Oshawa complex (representing 7 per cent of the total workforce). Local union officials reported that all of these employees were white.[1] By 1955 this figure had risen to at least 433.[2] And in 1961 GM reported that there were approximately 280 women in the sewing department and 140 women in the wire and harness department.[3] Women constituted a higher proportion of the workforce in GM's McKinnon Industries, though their numbers were still low overall. In 1948 the plant employed 400 white women (16 per cent of the total), 1,965 white men, and 35 black men out of a total workforce of 2,400.[4] By the spring of 1950 the number of women employees had risen above 500, thus marking their highest peace-time total to date.[5]

Women's relation to wage work after the war was consistent with the past in many ways. Notably, close friendships and social ties continued to be an important feature of their shopfloor life. Echoing the themes of earlier years, Pat Creighton, a GM employee since 1955, said about the sewing room, 'It was just like a sisterhood in there ... Oh, it was wonderful ... Oh the friendship! Friendships [sic] goes back 34 years. And it was all started in there ... We used to party together, drink together, go dancing together, go to each other's weddings, and you know, baby showers ... The kinsmanship ... It was just the best times of my life.' In addition, the women continued to express a strong identification with their sex. Daily, they conversed about various aspects of their experiences as women – in families, marriage, and other intimate relationships.

Yet the women's talk also reflected subtle changes in their lives and in their outlook on life. They revealed, for instance, greater candour about female sexuality than in the past. Creighton remarked, 'Some of the girls were having babies out of wedlock and at that time you didn't keep it. Very rarely they kept their babies ... And then there was no unemployment [insurance] ... You had six weeks sick leave ... I've seen them work till Friday night and have the baby on Saturday because they only had six weeks ... If they were having a rough time at home or if they were single, it was just like a bunch of mother hens around you ... There was like family. We took care of them ... Kind of a nice time then.' She further commented, 'I can remember ... when birth control came out ... Before the birth control pill came out, the only thing you used to do is pray to God, you know, "Please send me you know what." But when the birth control pill come out, one of the girls ... [would say], "Oh my God, I forgot to take my pill today. Does anybody have any?" ... [Another woman would respond] "Okay bring it back to me tomorrow" ... [We talked about] everything from sex to men to who was running with the foreman, who the baby was – just the whole gamut ... Somebody had read in a book about doing a vaginal exercise. So Alice decided we all needed to tighten up. So she had us – things like that. And we'd laugh and laugh.'

More striking, however, is that women began to vent their discontents about wage work. While they consciously avoided the topic of auto work during the war, it became an important part of their conversations in the post-war years. Auto employee Doris Lepitsky said, 'When we got mad, we'd be talking about work ... at our lunch hour. [In the lunch room, the women would] bitch at that girl that gets away and doesn't do nothing and that one has to work harder and all that stuff ... They'd bitch about the foreman too, but not so that he could hear.'

Women's growing shop-floor protest can be linked to some intersecting developments. First, the structural framework in which they were living had changed significantly. In spite of recessionary periods and growing foreign competition, the employment of women became more stable than in the past. Simultaneously, the UAW was growing in strength and legitimacy. With the lifting of wartime controls, unionists could make greater demands on employers, the grievance procedure became increasingly effective, and in 1945, organized labour won the union 'check-off,' known as the Rand formula. With the check-off in place, the company's payroll department automatically deducted union dues from the paycheque of every worker in the bargaining unit. All of these developments fuelled the labour movement and contributed to a more economically secure working class.

In addition, a parallel change was occurring in the workforce itself. After the war, women auto workers could be divided into three main groups. Unmarried, high-seniority employees who had worked in the industry prior to the Second World War comprised one cohort. By the post-war years, many of these women were thirty-five to forty years old. They recognized that they would most likely remain single, and they strongly valued their work for both its material and its social rewards.

Another group included women who entered auto employment as war workers. These women married either during the war or immediately after. Because of company restrictions on the employment of married women, most of these workers lost their jobs when war production ceased. Manufacturers eventually recalled some of these women when companies faced labour shortages in the 1950s. Third, and most important, a new cohort of women entered the auto plants during the late 1940s and throughout the 1950s. According to one observer, GM periodically hired large groups of women during these years. When they entered the industry, most of these women were between twenty and thirty years old. Some were married, while others were single, divorced, or widowed.

The female workforce was thus far more diverse than it had been in the past. Women auto workers had always varied widely in age, and both married and unmarried women had worked in the plants during the war. However, in the post-war years, the women had more diverse employment experiences and perspectives on wage work. In addition, since GM hired greater numbers of Eastern European and some Dutch immigrants after the war, the labour force became more ethnically heterogeneous.[6]

Importantly, much of the post-war female workforce was familiar with industrial employment. Women in the first two categories had experience in the auto industry itself, and many of the new employees had previously worked in some sort of factory setting. These women were not bewildered by a huge industrial complex. Although many of them still feared their supervisors and were hesitant to openly assert their rights, others were bold and defiant. The bold and defiant frequently stood up for their more timid sisters. GM employee Fay Bender explained, 'There was a few of us that would stand up to them [supervisors]. But then a few of them, they would sit back and they would talk among themselves but they wouldn't do anything. They'd say, "Oh, what's the use of complaining. They won't do anything."' Bender's workmate, Laura Saunders, likewise commented, 'If someone saw that somebody else was being picked on a little bit and we felt that it was unwarranted, why, we'd all stick together and a bunch of us would – if that person wasn't a very strong person and was more of a meek and mild person – then we'd fight them. Some of us stronger ones that could stand up and speak for ourselves would fight for that person, stick up for that person.'

While they continued to work out of economic need, few women expressed an overwhelming sense of gratitude for their employment. Furthermore, while many women planned to leave employment upon marriage, others viewed wage work as a lifetime endeavour. Over time most of the women adjusted their aspirations to the material realities of their lives. These realities forced them to recognize that they were permanently tied to the labour force. And as they accumulated seniority and pension rights, they were less inclined to quit their jobs.

A brief description of some women who made up this new cohort of workers reveals their diversity in outlook and experience. In 1953, at the age of twenty-five, Phyllis Yurkowski (Holman) joined the GM sewing room, and she stayed with the firm until 1985. Yurkowski moved to Oshawa from Belleville, Ontario, after she heard that GM needed 'female help.' She was single at the time and was enticed by the high wages in the industry. Before she worked at GM Yurkowski had been employed in a grocery store and in a restaurant. She was also an experienced sewing machine operator. She explained, 'I already worked in Belleville so I knew what plant work was ... I liked it ... I liked sewing. I thought it was really great.'

Rose Taylor joined McKinnon Industries in 1952. Taylor had previously worked on wiring at Comstock Industries, a manufacturer of bathroom parts. She had also made earrings in a jewellery factory in Quebec and had been employed as a cashier in Woolworths', Zeller's, and Wallace's retail stores. After hearing that McKinnon Industries was hiring married women, she decided to temporarily supplement her husband's income with the relatively high wages of auto work. In her words, 'When I started there ... we all had the same thought. [Our] husbands weren't making that much at that time ... Everybody ... wanted drapes or a new chester-field ... Every year I was going to [quit]. I thought, "Oh, I'll just get this and I'll quit" ... I never thought I'd be there that long, to tell you the truth. And then of course my husband took sick and he didn't work for quite a few years. So by then there was a necessity ... I always figured too, when we'd have our first baby ... But we never had any children so I just kept working.' Elsa Goddard started to work at GM in 1947. She too planned to work until she wed. However, because her husband was employed out of town, she decided to stay in the labour force. 'I thought ... I might just as well go back to work and it helped save for a home ... And I figured if I'm gonna work I might just as well go back there as take a job with half the money ... I really hadn't intended to go back after I got married, but the way things turned out, I figured I might just as well.'

Similarly, in 1955 Pat Creighton (Kress) began work as a bench hand in GM's cutting and sewing room. 'I was only going to work till I got married,' she explained. 'Two marriages later, and a 32 year-old son, I finally retired. That's how we used to think – that I'm going to quit when I get married. It didn't work that way then, it doesn't work that way now.' Betty Murray joined the GM workforce in 1956. Murray, who had been a pilot since the age of seventeen, had just left the Royal Canadian Air Force and was heading for work in a steel plant in Hamilton, Ontario. 'I had read that the highest-paying job was steel in Hamilton and the second highest was General Motors in Oshawa. And I said, 'Well, I'm going down to Hamilton to see if I can't get a job there' because the money was what I was after.' Unlike most women of her generation, Murray never viewed wage work as temporary. 'I always thought, "Oh, gee, there's too many things out there' ... I never planned my life around marriage ... I always planned my life around fun.' Martha Cox started to work in the sewing room in 1956. 'I didn't want the job and I got it,' she recalled with laughter. Roughly three weeks before her wedding, she heard that GM was hiring and her fiancé encouraged her to apply. Cox performed the work easily. She had experience as a dressmaker in Scotland and in assembling condensors for radios in a Toronto factory. 'I had worked in factories before so it was no [problem],' she stated. 'After a while it was just like falling off a bicycle. You can get back on again.'

As the industry expanded and the economy prospered, as the union gained might and legitimacy, and as women's lives unfolded, they gained a stronger sense of themselves as permanent workers and unionists. Large-scale structural trends converged with women's personal histories to produce an altered response to auto work.

DEVELOPING A UNION CONSCIOUSNESS

After the war, women remained peripheral to the union administration. Few women held an elected office and consequently they still had little input in the union's agenda. Similarly, their attendance at membership meetings, representation on union standing committees, and participation in conferences remained disproportionately lower than men's. By 1961, there were 3,612 female members in the UAW Canadian Region; however, only twenty-two women held office in a UAW local. They included two presidents, six recording secretaries, three financial secretaries, ten trustees, and one sergeant-at-arms.[7]

Nevertheless, women workers continued to firmly support the philosophy and goals of industrial unionism. While the figures on women office holders hint at the extent of their access to the UAW power structure, they do not, in turn, tell us about women's allegiance to the union. Bev McCloskey, committeewoman in the cutting and sewing departments, pondered the complex, contradictory relationship between women and the UAW. About the female sewing room workers she said, 'They'd call you up – the boss would give them hell and they'd be cryin'. It took me years to get them to stop cryin', you know, because their feelings would be hurt ... But I don't know ... Women – when we had strikes, they were right there. They were the best people going. Right out on that picket line. And they had to fight just as hard as anybody.'

In 1954, when UAW committeeman, Pat Meagher, thanked workers for supporting him in a union election, he specifically congratulated the women members for their enthusiasm.[8] During the local zone elections in 1957 union officials noted that sewing room workers cast a larger vote than ever.[9] Women workers also played a vital role in the 1949 and 1955 strikes at GM in Oshawa. Maurie Shorten, recording secretary of Local 222, recalled that during the 1955 strike the women workers issued the strike pay in the union hall. 'We played cards every night ... drank a lot of wine, went on plant gate collections in the middle of winter,' she stated.[10] According to Pat Creighton, 'the men run the show' but women 'participated in lots and lots of ways.' Reflecting the sentiments of many women, Elsa Goddard commented, 'We didn't go [to union meetings] as often as we should ... but we did [go]. And when there was something that really came up, that you knew you should go for, you did go ... There was a good turnout of women because they knew that ... they had to stand behind the union.'

As these statements illustrate, women's weak formal participation in the UAW was rooted in the social organization of the union, industry, and society, not in women's ideological stance. As noted, female members had trouble getting elected to office and attending meetings and conferences because of inadequate child care and transportation, as well as their confinement to women's departments in the plants. The masculine culture of the labour movement also hampered their involvement.[11] These obstacles explain women's seeming indifference to the union in normal times, but active commitment during periods of crisis.

Some women recognized that (male) union leaders treated them differently from their brothers. Phyllis Yurkowski believed that her UAW committeewoman Bev McCloskey was a good representative. 'She made sure everything was right,' said Yurkowski. 'There was no givin' to a man or takin' away from a woman.' Conversely, Yurkowski complained that the committeeman did nothing for her. She stated in frustration, 'If the foreman picked on you and didn't like you and you couldn't jump when they hollered, why you had to put up with it. I used to have to get the committeeman all the time ... and you might as well call nothing. I walked out of there crying because you just get ... With women, see, if you called a committeeman, it was a man. Well, unless you was a favourite or something.' However, the women were not critical of all union men. According to McKinnon worker Jean Cormier, 'The union guy was good! Gordon. He was a good guy! ... Gordon Lambert ... He didn't go in the office and laugh. If the foreman come out, he came up on the line and he seen how we were workin' and he told the foreman to change our break-down ... Everybody liked him. He helped a lot of people.'

Furthermore, despite their criticism of some men, the women turned to their union representatives for support in conflicts with supervision. If you needed a committeeman you called him, explained a female auto worker. 'If they give you a job that was too much and sometimes they changed the time on it ... you'd just know very well that you couldn't do it so you'd call a committeeman ... There wasn't too many women that got really involved [in the union] ... They didn't want to get involved and get in there arguing and stuff like that, but ... they liked the protection from the union.'

Like their male co-workers many women placed their trust and confidence in their union leaders. For example, Martha Cox explained that few workers thoroughly understood the collective agreement. 'You'd actually have to be a Philadelphia lawyer to read them,' she said. Like her work-mates she relied on union officials to tell her right from wrong. 'You'd get a paper from the union tellin' you what you were getting and what you weren't gettin. Other than what the union told you, you didn't understand.'

These loyalties grew largely through workers' experiences on the shop floor. Perceiving injustices in the daily relations between bosses and work-ers, most women believed that a union was essential to defend their rights. Betty Murray stated that union leaders were 'fairly good' because 'they'll fight for the underdog.' She explained, 'Union was here and management was here. And there was no gettin' together. They were just at loggerheads all the time ... When I first went to General Motors, right away I was always very strong because ... management were doing a lot of things that weren't right ... So I thought well, you know, it's best that I start looking after my own interests because if I don't who's going to do it? The union is there, but if you don't work with them – so that's how I got involved with the union. I started going to union meetings.' Another senior GM employee explained that 'the company was very, very domi-nating ... back then ... and you really had to have some protection ... from the union ... You belong to a union and you are paying union dues so you had to have that support.'

Women also learned about the labour movement from male relatives. In the last chapter, I noted that many women had fathers, brothers, and uncles in the auto plants. Some of these men were actively involved in the union and they frequently extolled its benefits. 'My dad was a union man in General Motors [said Elsa Goddard] ... We learned lots from my father ... We knew our rights and you knew that there was always a good union man there to back you up and if you had a complaint you knew who to go to.' Her sister, Joan Jackson, added, 'Oh we lived union. Father was always away at conventions ... being so involved with the union ... He'd come home ... and we'd say what ever was goin' on and he'd tell us ... you can do this, you can do that. And then he went to union meetings ... Every night it was something to do about somebody that put in a grievance.' 'It was just a family of talk about GM,' said Goddard.

In turn, UAW leaders consciously and often aggressively attempted to foster union loyalties in women.[12] For example, an article on women and organized labour in a 1955 issue of the *Oshaworker* stated, 'You can't expect the men to busy themselves trying to get justice and equality for a bunch of females who can't be bothered to pull their own weight, who just sag when they're asked to take responsibility ... It's time for them to move in and add their strength, for their own sake as well as for the sake of the men and women in industry all over the country. And we have just the gals who can do it!'[13]

WOMEN'S GRIEVANCES AND PERCEPTIONS OF GENDER ON THE SHOP FLOOR

The women most clearly revealed their growing union citizenship by taking full advantage of the strengthened UAW grievance procedure. Throughout the 1950s and early 1960s workers filed grievances on a wide range of issues. 'Everything you could ever think of that's a grievance, we had them,' said Bev McCloskey. On the basis of fragmentary archival data we cannot make a conclusive statement about the number of grievances filed by women. However, the records and interview data available indicate that some women used the grievance procedure extensively and that during these years there was a notable increase in their formal complaints compared with earlier times.[14]

Although it was not overwhelming, women's use of this form of protest is striking given the historical context. After the war organized labour was stronger than ever, but it was still attempting to establish itself in a highly conservative era. This was an era in which legislators, private individuals, and even some labour leaders themselves were attempting to purge unions of a 'Communist threat' (see Yates, 1988). In addition, conservative voices strongly enforced the view that woman's proper place was in the home. Through both the experience of wage work and participation in the union, however, women auto workers adopted values and expectations that in a contradictory way overshadowed, as well as highlighted, gender prescriptions. Throughout these years, union officials encouraged all workers to use the grievance procedure to uphold their contractual rights.[15] Notably, they directed this recommendation at women as a distinct group.[16]

During the 1950s, employers in mass production industries increasingly relied on the intensification of work or 'speed-up,' as part of a classic Fordist/Taylorist strategy to increase productivity and assert control of the shop floor.[17] Indeed, the production standard was one of the most contentious issues facing workers. Given the sex-segregated nature of auto work, women could not compare their production quotas with those of men. Nevertheless, they did evaluate their work requirements by their physical capacity to keep up, and on this basis they believed the quotas were unjust. According to Phyllis Yurkowski, supervisors in all the women's departments made excessive demands on the workforce. In the cutting and sewing room in Oshawa, for instance, 'some foremen ... just wanted women to keep their nose to their sewing machine. They just wanted so much work done ... But some jobs were heavy and harder and that made them slower ... You got so many pieces off of that job when you were doing it and that was that. But then if they come along and speeded something up ... then that's when you'd call the union in.' About the wire and harness department, she stated, 'I had everything to complain about there. Speedups and putting terminals in fuse boxes ... oh, your fingers would be bleeding. And the ... foreman and the group leader would get their heads together and go and speed up lines and ... you were just going like this and here you're trying to get those terminals in the fuse boxes to work. And oh, your fingers were so sore! Oh! ... It would get on your nerves.' Similarly Elsa Goddard recalled, 'You had to produce or they let you know that you weren't producing ... They used to come around every so often and time the job ... We'd always hope that the person that was the fast one never got timed because if that's the time they chose everybody had to work at that speed. And there could be a lot of problems because there was a lot of women that just couldn't do it at that speed.'

Women's gendered learning heightened their susceptibility to supervisors' demands. Like many women, these workers took pride in their diligence, efficiency, and high productivity. In addition, some of the older workers placed an emotional stake in securing the bosses' approval. In order to prove that they were reliable workers and good women, they pushed themselves hard. This hard work took its toll on many individuals. Indeed, in 1950 a Local 199 representative in McKinnon Industries reported that in trying so desperately to keep up with the demands of the line, 'the girls were breaking down.'[18]

Wire and harness worker Ann Brisbois described her experience.

I worried terrible, just awful, about it. I got very nervous when I was being timed. They'd tell us the day before. And I would be almost sick to my stomach to think that I was going to be timed ... They all knew that we didn't like it.

When you're being timed you either work too fast or too slow because you're nervous. [A friend] was being timed by this fellow ... She'd put these rubber insulators on and then she'd use her foot to open it and then put a wire in to put the insulator on. So he had timed ... her hands, and I looked over and he was on his haunches timing her feet. And I thought, well why would he time her feet? Of course, [she] felt like kicking him in the chin ... It really got on my nerves and I went to my doctor on my way home from work one night. And I said, 'That place is driving me crazy!'

Sewing room worker Effie Baldwin related a similar experience when her foreman put her to work on a machine that was obviously too big for her. 'I have exceptionally short arms and exceptionally short legs ... But he gave me these big floor mats and ... I was binding them and ... they were timed for seven an hour. And the best I could do no matter how I tried was five because they were so big ... And I'd go home a nervous wreck at night trying to do seven an hour and I couldn't make it ... I struggled away and struggled away till I had to come home. I took sick one day there and sent me over to the plant hospital ... I had a nervous breakdown. And that was just through trying so hard to give them what they wanted.'

Each of these women had each devoted over twenty-five years of her life to GM. They therefore resented foremen who entered their departments without a practical understanding of their work. Effie Baldwin was highly dedicated to the company and seldom criticized anyone. Yet she stated that her foreman 'didn't know one side of the material from the other. He didn't know the right side from the left. And as far as the machine goes, he didn't know which end of it was up. He just didn't know beans.' Feeling the same way, Ann Brisbois declared that the foreman who timed her workmate 'didn't know anything ... These were things that used to annoy us,' she said. 'Somebody like him who come in there after the War, didn't know anything about a department, but because he was maybe good at ... making you do more work than what you actually could do [he got the job].'

Such working conditions forced some women to leave their jobs for work in lower-paying but less demanding industries. Others resisted the labour process through small acts of sabotage. For instance, when GM management increased their quota from ten pieces to fifteen pieces per hour, a group of angry women in the Oshawa plant 'beat' the time study men by putting a block of wood under the machine so that it could work only at a limited pace.[19] Likewise, on a Valentine's Day, Maurie Shorten and eight other women in the wire and harness department were suspended for one day when they sabotaged the line. Shorten explained that the women taped harnesses and a special kind of tape 'went on the first job.' When the tape machine ran out of tape they would shut the line down until the group leader replaced it. However, eventually the company decided that they could no longer shut the line down. In retaliation, when they ran out of tape the women built the harnesses without it. Shorten, an active unionist, knew the contract well and said to the foreman, 'Well, we'll get paid so don't worry about it.' She was correct. They did get paid.

Encouraged by their union leaders some women also protested unfair work standards through formal channels. 'The dictionary defines the word Intimidation to mean, inspire with fear; to overawe, cow, making afraid. This seems to be the practice lately in the Sewing Department,' declared union representative Bev McCloskey. 'The foreman's idea of a "Fair Day's Work" is to stand behind the employees with the Standard Men for a period of 8 hours, 2 or 3 days a week. The employees in this department are well aware of the tactics the Company used to get increased production out of the workers, without increasing manpower. This situation will not be allowed to prevail. The dignity of the workers means something to the Union, even if it doesn't to the Company. I'm requesting all the affected employees, to call their committeeman.'[20]

Women responded to such requests by filing a series of individual and group grievances against GM.[21] 'I ... protest the action of my foreman in asking me to do more than a fair day's work,' read one of many such complaints.[22] 'We feel we are definitely performing to the best of our ability and every time we manage to produce more he [the foreman] reprimands us for ... not performing a fair day's work and we request that this practice cease immediately,' declared four women from the McKinnon plant.[23] In May 1951 twenty-seven women in the Delco division protested a rate change without a time study of their work operations.[24] In April 1957 fifteen women protested speed-ups in department 63.[25] And in March 1959 ten women in department 64 grieved management's use of a light to monitor the work output of the first operator on their line.[26]

Reflecting the humour as well as the emotion of these disputes, the chair of the McKinnon Shop Committee likened a foreman in the Delco division to an insect. 'You might describe ... [this] bug as a scavenger because it thrives on the efforts of others,' Gordon Lambert wrote in a union leaflet addressed to McKinnon women. 'The mating of the ... bug sounds something like "morwork." The ... bug is very ambitious to become a big ... bug, but to become a big bug, and scavenger that it is, the efforts of others must increase ... Science has discovered that the only way to exterminate [this] ... bug is for a union bug to step on this foul insect and "squish." ' Lambert called on the workers to inform the union of further speed-ups.[27]

One of the most extensive disputes over production standards occurred in GM's sewing department. Prior to January 1957 the company placed 300-Watt sewing machines in the department. Because these machines were faster and more efficient than those used in the past, management simultaneously set new work quotas for the operators. The sewing room women strongly resisted this decision, however, and they filed forty-three grievances in protest. Eleven of these complaints were against supervision's reprimands and thirty-one claimed that GM had violated a clause in the master agreement. This issue generated such fervour that UAW committeeman Pat McCloskey 'was engaged almost constantly in discussions' with the foreman and the workers. In November 1957 an arbitrator dismissed the grievances on the grounds that the company was entitled to 'receive an honest work effort for the wage it pays ... and the employee ... is obligated to give honest work effort.' Nevertheless, the magnitude of this case reveals the women's steadfast defence of their rights under the collective agreement.[28]

Underlying women's attempts to assert control over the labour process was an effort to maintain some personal dignity in the workplace. Some women understood that the exercise of power and dominance on the shop floor was inextricably tied to gender relations within society as a whole. Many women, for instance, claimed that foremen harshly disciplined them specifically because of their sex. As well, some women were reluctant to assert themselves because their bosses were men. GM employee Laura Saunders stated that 'because you had ... men bosses ... through the chains, from supervisors to general foremen to superintendents ... and it was all men you were dealing with ... you didn't talk back to your bosses, and a lot of people were very frightened of the bosses back then. And when you were trained and taught to do a job, you did your job ... Men were treated the same way, but I suppose it seemed to be more back then, a little more, I thought, domination towards the women.'

Another GM employee, Fay Bender, claimed that supervision was unjustly 'hard' on women for absenteeism. 'We didn't have any more absenteeism than men,' she stated, 'but it was just the point that they could hassle the women. And a great number of them wouldn't say anything back to them ... it was just their continual hassle of us. It even got to the point that if you took a day off, so that you wouldn't get too much of a hassle even for a headache – you went to the doctor and said I have to have a doctor's note.'

Women also resented the sometimes flagrant favouritism of supervisors. According to McKinnon worker Rose Taylor, 'There was an awful lot of favouritism, so I wouldn't want to work in a place like that without a union.' Helen Beaugrand, formerly of GM and later a Chrysler employee, served as a union steward in Local 1090 for six years. In deciding to run for this position, she said to herself, 'Why should some get this and others turned down all the time? And you seen different little things that you didn't like and I thought well, I'll run.'

Some women believed that favouritism had a basis in men's attitudes towards female sexuality. 'If you had hair colour that might be right, could be blonde, could be brunette, you know, or a red head ... they could do no wrong and other girls weren't favoured, said Laura Saunders. 'And they would get the dirty jobs. ' McKinnon employee Doris Lepitsky believed that the middle-aged and older females paid for the foremen's preference for young women. She explained, 'Say you're 17, 18, and I'm 40. And I got 20 years seniority and you only got 5, but because the foreman likes you because you're young and everything else, he gives you soft jobs and he gives the older women harder jobs. Then you gotta call the union and fight it out 'cause you got more seniority. You shouldn't be pushed around ... And then the foreman will go along with the union. A couple of weeks later, he does the same thing. You gotta fight again with the union ... It's like that all the time ... Once the foremen hit 40 years, he's lookin' for young girls, lookin' for someone to go out drinkin' with.'

In February 1951 a woman quit her job in GM's wire and harness department in reaction to her foreman's behaviour. Shortly after, she related her feelings about the nature of GM supervision in the *Oshaworker*. For the benefit of other women in the department, she wrote: 'A foreman in a factory can quite easily be the straw that breaks the camel's back. It is within his power, if he has any feelings of compassion in him, to make an unbearable job bearable. But when to the monotony of mass production methods is added a domineering foreman, it would be only a man chained by economic necessity or one devoid of any sense of right and decency who would continue to endure his surroundings. I quit General Motors on February 6th because of such a foreman ... I could no longer stand by and watch my fellow workers being subjected to indignities.'

The incident that forced this worker to resign was a typical one. On her way to the washroom, the woman was approached by the foreman for stopping and speaking to a friend. His eyes, she stated, were 'fixed in glazed indignation at us standing there brazenly talking on G.M. time.' He allegedly said something to make the woman blush. When she asked him if there was a problem in talking to someone for a moment, he became furious. 'Like an enraged bull he turned on me,' she declared. ' "There certainly is,' he said. 'This is General Motors and we don't pay you to stand out there in the aisle and talk. Do you want to make something out of it?" I don't remember what I said. My head was nearly busting in anger – but I do know I quit.' This woman regretted her actions because, she later admitted, 'by quitting I have helped no one. The girls are still being bullied.' She added, however, that her co-workers in the wire and harness department would be pleased to see her letter in print.[29]

In lodging such complaints, most workers were simply attempting to secure a measure of human dignity. However, both male and female employees, on the whole, believed that women deserved special respect (albeit not equality) because of their sex. Workers were particularly critical of male bosses who verbally abused female employees. And in their confrontations with supervisors on this issue, they often drew on cultural beliefs that women are extremely sensitive, far more vulnerable than men.[30] Revealing that a strong gender identity and adherence to conventional images of femininity and masculinity do not automatically lead to complacency and conservatism, some women angrily contested profane language, threats, and intimidation by their foremen.[31] In August 1961 a woman in McKinnon Industries complained that her foreman had allowed a male employee to 'conduct profane language' towards her. She was indignant at his behaviour and demanded that it cease immediately.[32] Similarly, in November 1962 a female employee protested the foreman's 'snide remarks' about her.[33] And the following year, several women in department 64 filed separate complaints that their foreman was 'hollering' and 'yelling' at them.[34]

With chivalry, male unionists also defended their sisters against the sometimes boorish behaviour of management. For example, in May 1952, when the Local 199 Shop Committee met with McKinnon representatives to discuss the transfer grievance of a woman, union officials protested the company's conduct towards the griever. According to the unionists, the employee went to the restroom 'white as a ghost' as soon as she left the management office. When her foreman asked her what was wrong, she burst into tears. According to the union, she did not want to give management the satisfaction of seeing her in this state. UAW chairman Gordon Lambert stated to H.W. McArthur, McKinnon personnel director, 'The manner you treated Letta in the office, I wouldn't talk to a lady in that manner. The union feel you have no right bringing a lady in the office and treating her in the manner you did.' Lambert claimed that the griever was home sick because of this episode. 'I can't use the language you used because there's a lady present,' he remarked.[35]

The following year Pat Meagher reported that many foremen in the sewing department were unreasonable and uncooperative when workers approached them with complaints. 'I refer to the one who is bellyaching all the time about everything and doesn't know how to address *female* employees,' he stated (my emphasis).[36] Also in defence of his sisters, a male worker, Alex Grazewki, protested the foreman's use of coarse language while female employees were in the vicinity.[37] Similarly, when some women confronted their union leaders with complaints about sexual harassment, the McKinnon shop committee angrily warned management that the foreman better 'keep his paws off the girls or get his mouth slapped.'[38]

THE DIFFERENTIAL TREATMENT OF WOMEN WORKERS

Women auto workers did not resent the somewhat protective actions of their union brothers. Indeed, the women themselves continued to promote differential treatment on the basis of their distinct position in the industry and their unique needs as a sex.[39] These women were not acting manipulatively, nor were they blind to the political dangers of this strategy when taken out of its social-historical context. Rather, they drew on familiar, widely accepted, and 'comfortable' ideas about the sexes, in the absence of an alternative strategy. Insofar as cultural prescriptions of femininity and masculinity were sharply defined in this period, and sex segregation and inequalities were deeply entrenched in the collective agreement, women auto workers had nothing to lose by demanding to be treated differently than men. They could only gain by it.[40]

With this understanding, women in McKinnon's commercial motors department filed a group grievance when the company refused to grant them their sex-based privilege of leaving work at five minutes to the hour. Women had historically received the extra five minutes before lunch breaks and quitting time when they were working a regular shift. Company officials explained that they had given women this privilege to avoid congestion in the clock house, the area in which employees punched their time cards. In their view it was 'undesirable for the girls' to be in a crowded area with men. However, management refused to grant women this extra time when they were working the evening shift or overtime. According to company spokespersons, if women exited with only a few male employees, there was no reason to maintain the sex-based difference.[41] In response, union representatives asked, 'Why is it that the girls on nights are not allowed to quit 5 minutes before the lunch period as the girls on days do? They have to come from one side of the road to the other and then stand 10 or 15 minutes in line with a lot of smart alecks.'[42]

Relying on a similar logic, women workers demanded special transportation to and from work,[43] complained about walking to the parking lot when they worked the night shift,[44] and hesitated to work the evening shift with men only.[45] Undoubtedly, women's fears for their safety in a male-dominated environment were legitimate. And at this time they were not reluctant to express their unique needs as a sex.

In a further attempt to preserve dignity and secure some degree of control, women workers struggled with their supervisors over the issue of 'personal relief' time. This seemingly minor issue generated considerable conflict throughout the decade. In GM and McKinnon plants women received one ten-minute break for 'personal relief' in the morning and one in the afternoon. In addition, management usually assigned an operator to relieve women on the continuously moving line. According to Betty Murray, the relief operator went from person to person all the way around the line. When she came around, said Murray, 'you better hope that you're ready to go 'cause if you're not,' you lost your chance. Supervisors overlooked occasional emergencies but they frowned upon frequent, unscheduled trips to the washroom.

The requirement of seeking permission to go to the washroom was not unique to women. All workers who were tied to a moving line in the industry faced this degradation. Supervisors, however, deepened the humiliation of women workers by applying stringent disciplinary measures to ensure that they obey the company's rules. In the women's departments, management imposed strict controls that involved monitoring workers in the washroom and interrogating them about the frequency and duration of their visits.[46] According to Murray, if a worker had to take an unscheduled washroom break, the supervisor asked, 'Can't you control your kidneys?' or 'Can't you control your bowels?'

Insofar as they did not work on a line, sewing machine operators had more autonomy than the other women. Yet sewers also had restricted mobility. Supervision 'felt that once you had that break you should have gone to the washroom then, and they were complaining that too many women were spending time up in the bathroom,' explained Elsa Goddard. To observe sewing room workers, management placed a matron and a former supervisor in the washroom. In some cases an instructress or group leader on the floor also acted as a watch dog. One worker recalled that the group leader would reprimand them: 'You were up there five minutes or eight minutes ... You're not supposed to be going up there and spending that kind of time up there.'[47] Phyllis Yurkowski reported that the women had to provide an explanation if they spent more than five or six minutes in the washroom. 'Then you had to let her know if you had your periods or whatever,' she added. 'And she put that down her little book. Well they didn't want you stayin' in the washroom too long, but if ... you had your periods you could stay longer.' Pat Creighton explained, 'We were sure that she could tell when you were having your period 'cause everything went down in this little black book of hers.'

In April 1960 GM imposed a crackdown on the sewing room workers. According to union officials, some supervisors were in fact 'browbeating' female employees. Malcolm Smith, president of Local 222, claimed that supervision 'called down' some of the women 'so roughly that they were reduced to tears.' One male supervisor, for instance, said to a woman, 'You should ... control yourself and go to the washroom at rest period.' Smith declared that 'maybe some of these ... supervisory experts on human needs would like to see a medieval system [of pails] installed on the production lines in the Cutting and Sewing department.' After meetings with labour, the company agreed to ' "call off the Hounds of the Baskervilles" for one month, and put the women on their honour.' If production figures rose, management would curtail these disciplinary measures. However, if there was no improvement they planned to impose further penalties.[48]

GM management furthermore frowned on women smoking cigarettes in the washroom. 'Sometimes there'd be two in a toilet smoking like crazy,' recalled Pat Creighton. The matron would come in and yell out that she knew what they were doing. If you were 'in her good books,' said Elsa Goddard, 'she just didn't bother. But she often reported them.' When this happened, the women would all run down and face repri-mands. At times they even stood on toilet seats so that the matron could not identify them. They were treated 'like little kids,' observed Bev Mc-Closkey.[49]

In fact, in 1951 a UAW committeeman complained to the McKinnon Personnel Director, 'It's getting just like school; it's getting so they have to stick up their hand. This girl put up her hand, and the foreman wanted to know why she wanted to leave the room, and she said 'Nature's call-ing.' It's getting to the point where they'll explode if that keeps on.'[50] The women viewed these disciplinary measures as insulting, humiliating, and an invasion of their privacy. 'It's very embarrassing,' said Martha Cox. 'You're going to the washroom and somebody's sittin' there marking the time you go in and the time you come out. And if you're too long they want to know what you're doing.'

Despite their resentment, many women held back their anger. 'At that time, you just did what you were told and there was no talkin' back,' said Phyllis Yurkowski. 'You just got your job, and if they told you was five minutes too long and the next time don't stay so long, you'd say, "Okay." ' Others, however, clashed with supervisors. For instance, when the foreman in the sewing room questioned Pat Creighton's request for personal relief, she said, 'I'm sorry, this is an emergency.' He said, 'Well, how bad an emergency can it be?' Turning management's own tactics against them, Creighton responded bluntly, 'Well, I don't really like to have blood running down my legs.' He was exasperated, she recalled. 'His face – I'll never forget it. My period had come early. He just went so red ... he couldn't even bear to say the words.'

In another incident, Creighton sat on the washroom floor smoking a cigarette, while the group leader went from toilet to toilet checking on the women. She looked at Creighton and said in exasperation, 'Well?' Creighton defiantly responded, 'Well, what? ... You caught me. My name's in the book. And I ain't buttin' this cigarette.' In the meantime, the group leader had caught another woman and was waiting for her to exit from the cubicle. 'They made a big deal of it,' she noted. On one occasion, Creighton and roughly fifty of her workmates were so annoyed by these measures that they marched to the union hall in protest. It was 'just like being in prison,' said Martha Cox, one of the participants.

Like speed-ups, the 'personal relief' issue generated several official grievances, as well as informal complaints.[51] In January 1957, on behalf of all the workers in her department, a female employee in McKinnon's spark plug division protested when her supervisor refused to allow her to leave the job for 'personal reasons.' The griever requested 'the right of all employees, and *especially female employees* to "personal time" ' of their own choice (my emphasis).[52] Similarly, in June 1963 two women in McKinnon's department 89 complained that their foreman threatened to discipline them whenever they went to the washroom or got a drink of water.[53] In the same year, eight women from the radio department protested that there was an insufficient number of relief operators on their lines.[54]

Indeed, between February and March 1960 four women bench hands in GM filed eleven separate grievances contesting their discipline for allegedly wasting time going to and from the washroom with excessive frequency. The company issued numerous verbal and written reprimands and one- to five-day suspensions to the grievers for this behaviour. On behalf of these workers, the union argued that they usually allow three minutes per hour for male employees, but women must climb up and down two flights of stairs to reach the washroom. In addition, they stated that women 'find it necessary on occasion to wash off the dirt acquired on the job.' Unionist Bev (Gibson) McCloskey added that given the inadequate facilities, not all women could use the washrooms during the rest periods. The union officials further declared that a woman should not be required to provide an elaborate explanation of her need to temporarily leave her work station. It was unreasonable, in their view, to expect a woman to give a detailed account to a male supervisor. Moreover, they maintained, two or three trips to the washroom in one day is not excessive for women.

According to a UAW official, 'if the foremen in the Wire and Harness department concentrated more on the schedule and not on the girls going to restrooms, this would rectify the conditions of unnecessary lay-offs and recall in the department.'[55] Similarly, when a foreman in this department tried to cut a woman's pay for allegedly spending too much time in the washroom, a union brother remarked, 'This foreman would be well advised to get a few facts of life from his wife ... or even better still go over and see the company doctor and have the facts of the birds and bees explained to him.'[56]

In all these cases management's concerns about maintaining control of the workforce and, to a lesser extent, maximizing efficiency and profits, were undisguised. Employers believed that in spending time in the washroom, the women were lowering productivity. GM claimed that in the latter case, the women almost invariably left their jobs three times a day. They further estimated that the most frequent duration of the women's absences was ten minutes, and the most frequent total daily absence from work was twenty-five minutes.[57] These absences forced supervision to use extra labour power on relief operations. 'We have to tighten down sometimes if a few employees take advantage of a situation,' company officials said to union leaders.[58] H.W. McArthur, McKinnon personnel director, admitted that supervisory controls were 'extreme,' but he added that the women 'brought it on themselves' because when one goes to the washroom, about fifteen follow.[59] According to Bev McCloskey, this was GM's way of keeping 'the people stirred up ... You keep control that way ... You get everybody mad and frightened among themselves and they're not going to be fightin' the company.'[60]

Women's struggle with supervision over headgear was another nagging item that revolved around the themes of control and discipline.[61] Since the Second World War women auto workers had resisted wearing bandanas both because they were uncomfortable and because they were unflattering. Occasionally management let this safety rule lapse, but it never died. When it resurfaced in the early 1950s, however, women openly complained to their foremen and their union representatives. In April 1951 women in McKinnon's fuel pump and ball bearing departments told their committeeman that they preferred to wear a hair covering made of a light, mosquito netting instead of a heavy bandana. The bandanas, they said, kept perspiration soaking on their head all day and contributed to headaches. The union, however, was unsuccessful in resolving the issue. The company forcefully responded that they used hairnets in the past and found that they quickly fell apart, leaving a woman with just a string around her head.[62]

In the early 1960s the women complied with the safety regulation, but they began to let a few strands of hair peek out and rest on their foreheads. McKinnon employee Rose Taylor explained, 'We just didn't want to look like nuns.' Women, she said, always want to look their best. Staying pretty in an ugly job was important. Co-worker Jean Cormier agreed. She stated, 'We'd think it was ugly. It *was* ugly!' This tactic, however, was short-lived. In 1962 supervisors reprimanded the women for 'improperly wearing' their bandanas. While most of the women obeyed the order and again fully covered their hair, one woman in the radio department resisted. After she refused to comply with management's requests on four separate occasions, the company suspended her. This action led her to file a grievance with the union, protesting her suspension and requesting compensation for lost earnings. The UAW committeeman argued that her discipline was inappropriate because she revealed no more hair than 95 per cent of the women in the plant.[63]

Although only one woman officially grieved this measure, the dispute over bandanas concerned many others.[64] Revealing the extent of its impact, Local 199 leaders distributed a leaflet calling all women in the radio department to a union meeting. The leaflet featured a satirical cartoon of two male supervisors wearing bandanas above the caption 'The Bandana Kids.' The union shop committee wrote, 'The girls in the Radio Dept. are to be congratulated in their beginning to stand up to the boss and demanding their union representatives be called on their problems. Supervision ... like little children, are resorting – in order to get even – to childish action – such as the bandana incident ... Is it because supervision have faces that only a mother could love, they are jealous of the good looking girls in Radio, thus creating the bandana incident.'[65]

Throughout the 1950s women also tried in various ways to make their shop-floor environment more comfortable. Reasonable temperature and ventilation, adequate restroom and lunchroom facilities, and the provision of gloves and hand cream were seemingly petty items, but they had important implications for the experience of work and for relations of dominance and subordination.

During her thirty years of service to GM, Martha Cox filed only two grievances. One complaint was about the temperature in the wire and harness department. 'It was so cold,' recalled Cox, 'we had our winter boots on.' Conversely, it was unbearably hot during the summer. Elsa Goddard and Joan Jackson explained that the heat and ventilation problems in GM's sewing room were severe because the machines were constantly running and the abundance of material generated a great deal of dust. In McKinnon Industries, Margaret Heritz likewise recalled that the temperature in the core room was sometimes 100 degrees by 10:00 a.m. The heat was also excessive on the spark plug lines. You 'would have towels around your neck, you're sweating,' explained Rose Taylor. 'It must have been in the 90s because you had the heat from the machinery besides the heat from outside.' In both these departments, conditions at times were so unbearable that the women had to go home at noon. 'I guess [this was] because they all complained so much,' said Taylor.

During the summer of 1956 the women's complaints prompted the Local 199 Shop Committee to request adequate ventilation in the women's lunch room. Female employees proposed various techniques for deflecting the heat. For example, in January 1956 the union committeeman reported to management that 'the girls would like the windows painted green.'[66]. In January 1957 the women walked off the job in a dispute about air-conditioning.[67] In the early 1960s they also demanded an electric fan to help solve the heat problem.[68] This group of McKinnon workers, however, did not get the benefits of air-conditioning until the 1970s.

Women also filed grievances about the air and odour in their work area.[69] They furthermore refused to pick up their chairs at quitting time[70] and they protested their proximity to the men's washroom.[71] Throughout the decade and a half female employees demanded a buzzer on the clock in their department, a handrail on the stairs that led to their washroom, the use of stools while working, their own coatrack, sufficient time to clean up, a women's lounge, larger washrooms, a matron on every shift, soap containers, hot water, and hand cream.[72]

Women workers and their supervisors periodically fought over the provision of work gloves throughout the decade.[73] In March 1959 a woman who operated a welder in the A.C. division requested gloves to protect her hands because the shell part of the spark plug became hot after it was welded. Although she picked up the plugs by the porcelain, she occasionally missed this area and got burned. None of the other women in her department had asked for gloves and according to the union, this item would have cost the company only 25 cents. Yet management steadfastly refused to provide them. Even when the griever borrowed gloves from workers on another line, her supervisor stopped her from wearing them. Thus, on one occasion the union official suggested that she bring in gloves from home. Initially management argued that this would constitute a safety hazard, and when the union representative contested this argument, the foreman claimed that if he permitted her to wear gloves, all the other 'girls' would want them, as well. 'Gloves have never been used on this job, and the nature of the operation does not require gloves or lend itself to the use of gloves,' declared the superintendent of the division.[74]

Over time, the resolution of such demands in the women's favour resulted in a significant improvement in their working lives. The conflict over work gloves epitomizes a larger struggle between women workers and their supervisors over dignity and discipline. For both labour and management, these disputes were seldom based exclusively on considerations of material gain. In many cases the grievers requested only an apology and an end to offensive practices.[75] Throughout her thirty-four years at GM, Marie Wilson filed one grievance, in protest of a man swearing at her. Wilson recalled, 'He was a bit of a smart aleck. And I just said to myself, he's not gettin' away with that. If he does with me, he's going to do it with somebody else. He had to apologize to me ... and everybody in the place knew that he had to do that. So that kind of took him down a notch or two.' Supervisors, in turn, claimed that their actions were necessary to assert control and set a precedent in the discipline of workers. Some foremen claimed that they were merely reprimanding employees for misconduct and/or failure to perform their jobs in a satisfactory manner.

These disputes furthermore indicate that the workers' class and gender strongly shaped the articulation of these power relations. The discipline of female workers to some extent reflected employers' conceptions of proper womanhood. Elsa Goddard stated that GM supervision 'just wanted you to be proper women, really.' Similarly, Pat Creighton noted that the general foreman of the cutting and sewing departments 'liked his ladies to look like ladies.' Appearance was one manifestation of proper 'lady-like' behaviour. From these conflicts, we get the sense that proper womanhood also involved deference, compliance, and a childlike obedience.[76]

WORKING WITHIN THE PARAMETERS OF THE COLLECTIVE
AGREEMENT

During the 1950s and early 1960s, however, women auto workers left unchallenged the two most outstanding and fundamental instances of sex-based discrimination – sex-based job classifications and wage rates, and separate seniority systems based on sex and (women's) marital status. This strategy needs to be understood in light of the women's protests regarding other aspects of their employment.

Gender Segregation and Sex-Based Wage Rates

In the 1950s, despite increased hiring, women were still confined to a few departments. For example, in GM's Oshawa facility, women remained in the radiator room, the wire and harness, and the cutting and sewing departments.[77] At one time, a small group of women also worked in the parts and service department.[78] Within these departments, they continued to occupy a narrow range of jobs. For example, in 1955, there were approximately nineteen female and twenty-five boys' job classifications in the Oshawa plant, compared with roughly 393 adult male classifications.[79]

Women in McKinnon Industries were also segregated in a narrow range of jobs, although, as in the past, they had more options than women in Oshawa. Throughout the 1950s women were concentrated in six departments at the McKinnon plant: the foundry, fuel pump, bearing, axle, commercial motors, and Delco departments.[80]

Sex-based job classifications furthermore provided the foundation for unequal wage rates for women and men. Without a thorough analysis of work content, it is difficult to equate women's and men's jobs; however, a few classifications permit comparison. In 1953 in GM's Oshawa plant, an adult male assembler received between $1.49 and $1.60 per hour, while a female general assembler earned between $1.24 and $1.31. In comparison, general assemblers in the boys' group received $1.24 to 1.39 per hour.[81] In 1956 the job rate for male bench hands was $1.69, while the rate for female bench hands was $1.45. Male clerks were hired at a rate of $1.56, while boy clerks and female clerks started at $1.26. The job rate for male material handlers was $1.66, while boys received $1.44 and women earned $1.45. In addition, male tag writers in the salvage, repair, and inspection department earned $1.74, whereas female tag writers in the cutting and sewing departments earned $1.45.[82]

McKinnon workers faced similar inequities. In 1956, female general assemblers were paid $1.34 per hour, while male general assemblers earned $1.63. Despite across-the-board increases in rates from one set of contract negotiations to the next, the parties maintained this 29 cent per hour gap. Similarly, all male piece workers received 75 cents above their day rate, while female coil winders (who were piece workers) received an increase of 5 cents above their day rate and 4 cents to their objective rate, and female core makers (also piece workers) received an additional 6 cents to their day rate and 4 cents to their objective rate.[83]

Insofar as the gendered division of labour and sex-based wage rates were sanctified in the collective agreement, women rarely challenged them. Such a challenge would be considerable. Without sufficient resources women instead sought fair rates for jobs they performed within female classifications and work groups.[84] Admittedly, some women attempted to reduce sex-based differentials in pay. For instance, in January 1951 four female core makers in McKinnon's foundry complained that the differential between male and female core makers was 24 cents, whereas the differential between male and female production workers was only 12.5 cents. They did not, however, challenge gender segregation, the basis of these differences in pay.[85]

Foreshadowing emerging feminist debates, many women did forcefully protect their restricted contractual rights, though. When management gave them work that officially fell within a man's classification, some women demanded that they be paid the appropriate *male* rate.[86] Employers paid men the 'male rate' when they temporarily performed a woman's job,[87] and they continued to pay women a 'female rate' when they performed a man's job. In 1956, on behalf of women employees, the union demanded that McKinnon Industries pay the adult male rate to women who assembled glove-box doors, a job which the local wage agreement defined as 'properly belonging to an adult male.' Upholding the contract, a UAW official declared 'that where a job is allocated seniority wise to adult males then the rate for that job should certainly be that of adult males.'[88]

Some women also protested management's violations of the local seniority agreement. Again, however, insofar as they occupied non-interchangeable sex-based seniority groups, they directed most of these grievances against other women.[89] For example, in March 1950 a UAW committeeman reported that GM junior supervisors were acting like 'nasty little brats' in violating the seniority rights of sewing room workers. The union official claimed that because the general foreman selected the twenty-fourth woman on the seniority list for a highly rated job, he had twenty-three 'wild women on his hands, every one of them with a grievance.'[90]

Management infrequently replaced women with male workers. However, when this happened women upheld gendered divisions with equal resolve.[91] For instance, in March 1957 a female inspector in McKinnon Industries wrote, 'I ... protest being transferred from my group when an employee from a Male Seniority Group is employed on work normally performed by female employees.'[92] In December 1961 twenty-four women from one department formally protested the lead-man working overtime on their job, and they demanded that this practice cease.[93] Similarly, McKinnon worker Doris Lepitsky grieved on two separate occasions when her foreman performed work that should have been done by employees in her classification.[94] According to the company, the foreman spent five minutes at most on this job. Nevertheless Lepitsky declared, 'I request management put a stop to this.'[95]

In 1954 several women from GM's radiator department also upheld the contract when the company replaced them with boys (males under the age of eighteen). At the time approximately twenty women were working in this department, and for over thirty years (prior to 1950) women had exclusively performed the operation in question – 'fold and form and centre machine operator – female.' The exception was during the Second World War (1939–40 to 1944–5) when boys alone did the work. On 20 June 1950, however, GM again placed a boy on the job. The following month the company instituted a second (night) shift in the department, and because provincial legislation prohibited night work for women, they hired additional boys for this shift. The boys worked steady nights and the women worked steady days. In an attempt to increase productivity, management informed the boys that if they heightened their efficiency, they could move onto the day shift. Responding to this incentive, the boys began to outperform the women and consequently by 1953 they had entered the day shift, labouring alongside the very same women who had trained them in their jobs.

When management eliminated the night shift the following year, they laid off seven women but retained the boys. Maurie Shorten, one of the displaced women, recalled that management gave the women their lay-off notice roughly five minutes before the plant shut down for the day. 'They didn't even let us back into other departments,' she said. This prompted her to go the women's homes and convince them to file grievances.[96]

The women formally complained that in laying them off while retaining the boys, GM had violated their seniority rights. In November 1954 their cases went to arbitration. While labour and management agreed that it was 'management's right' to hire boys or adult males instead of or in addition to women, the union noted that the women had acquired seniority status in a non-interchangeable group and that 'only females could exercise seniority rights in that classification.' They therefore contended that males should be laid off first, regardless of their length of service with the firm. Company officials, however, stated that boys had formerly performed this job and that even though the group was labelled 'female,' women had not worked as centre machine operators. They further claimed that the union's proposal was unfair to male employees who might have invested many years on the job and who would be replaced by women with less seniority. They suggested that the boys constituted a temporary seniority group – 'separate and distinct from the female seniority group,' with males and females subject to lay-off according to their seniority in their respective categories.

The arbitrator, however, found no evidence to support this claim. He noted that by 1945 at the latest, women had taken over the job and that it had remained an exclusively female operation until June 1950. He further acknowledged that boys worked on the night shift only because the law forbid women to work these hours. In addition, he declared that the company's interpretation of the agreement meant that it 'has it in its power to destroy completely the seniority rights of all female employees who presently enjoy such rights. The Company would not only be entitled to retain at work male employees with greater "seniority" than the female doing identical work ... but, since there could be no limitation upon the Company's authority in this regard, it would also be entitled to establish such new groups to parallel every female classification and staff them with low "seniority" male employees whom it could retain at work while long-service female employees could be laid off ... It could scarcely be said that in such a state of affairs female employees would be given 'an equitable measure of security based on their length of service with the Company.' The arbitrator upheld the women's complaint and directed GM to rectify the situation. The grievers each received $200 from the company in back pay, but women ultimately left this department.[97]

As this example indicates, women auto workers relentlessly protected their restricted position in the industry, yet they were bound by a collective agreement that institutionalized sex-based job classifications, wage rates, and seniority systems. Their efforts were therefore limited. A struggle to change the collective agreement would be formidable because of the nature of the undertaking and thus the effort that would be involved. A change in contract language required direct input in the bodies that set the UAW agenda, the resources to launch an organized campaign, and considerable bargaining leverage over management. Moreover, because of the give-and-take nature of collective bargaining in North America, eliminating sex-based contract clauses necessitated that UAW leaders place priority on this demand and relinquish another item on their agenda. However, we have seen that women had restricted powers in the union, their resistance was largely confined to isolated and sporadic acts, and management strongly opposed changes in the division of labour. Furthermore, dominant gender ideologies powerfully legitimated gender segregation in the workplace. Bev McCloskey aptly described the consequent limitations on women's workplace resistance. 'We used to fight like hell about different things ... but not really ... because we were in a mould. We'd been socialized, you know, to think, well this is the status quo, so therefore that's where you stay. That's your job ... And there wasn't any arguments or fights about well, we want that job and we want that job. We did try to transfer [into men's jobs] – which we couldn't do. Nobody could transfer at that time. It wasn't in our contract.'

MARRIED WOMEN AND THE 'VICTORY SHIFT'

During this period a few pioneering women did, however, successfully contest the unfair treatment of pregnant women and married women. Yet these struggles were also inspired by a growing union citizenship, not a critique of women's specific subordination as a sex in industry. The grievers left intact beliefs that married women were financial dependents, and they did not openly challenge the premise of gender discrimination. Again, women were limited by a masculine discourse.

Both union men and employers treated the job-related rights of married and pregnant women with far more ambivalence than the other concerns of female employees. Nevertheless, women were able to successfully challenge the unfair treatment of married women because the collective agreement categorized workers by sex only, not by marital status or pregnancy status.

For example, in March 1953 an unmarried woman applied for employment at GM. On the job application, she answered 'no' to the question 'Any known physical defects?' At the time, she was over three months pregnant, but the company was unaware of this. They hired her and she worked for slightly under six months, until the day before she gave birth. Roughly two weeks later, the company dismissed this woman on the grounds that she had provided false information on her employment application. Desperately in need of the job, this woman protested the company's actions through the UAW grievance procedure.[98] During the arbitration hearing of this case, company representatives clearly indicated that if they had known about the worker's pregnancy, they would not have employed her. They further argued that this decision was their prerogative given that, under the collective agreement, management had the right to hire and fire as it saw fit. Consequently, the union's representatives fought this case around the issue of the worker's honesty and integrity rather than the more general and fundamental matter of the firm's policy against pregnant women. In reviewing the case, the arbitrator stated, 'Admittedly, the aggrieved employee failed to disclose that she was pregnant. On the other hand, she was not asked specifically whether she was pregnant; she was asked whether she suffered any physical defects.' Taking a strategic and unprecedented stance, the union argued that the term 'physical defect' refers to 'an incapacity accompanying or resulting from illness or injury, and that pregnancy is not looked upon as a physical defect but rather as a natural and normal physiological condition.' On this premise, they claimed, the employee properly answered the question on the application form. The arbitrator accepted this view and concluded that management had improperly discharged the griever and must reinstate her.[99]

Throughout this period the question of marital status as grounds for discharge also came to the fore as a few married women, too, tried to protect their right to employment. During the war, married women in McKinnon Industries had worked the 'victory shift,' a six o'clock to eleven o'clock evening shift.[100] Due to the expansion of some departments at the war's end, McKinnon management retained many victory shift workers in the reconversion period. Blatantly using them as a reserve labour force, the company placed these women in work areas that were subject to rapid fluctuations in demand. Furthermore, they continued to define married women as 'temporary employees' and denied them full seniority rights.[101]

Because the GM plants in Oshawa did not immediately expand production after the war, they reinstated their restrictions on the employment of married women, and, as noted in the last chapter, many women consequently lost their jobs. However, when GM increased production in the 1950s, they again relaxed their policy and recalled and hired married women.[102] Although the Oshawa plants did not have a victory shift comparable to that at McKinnon, married women in this location had a similarly restricted, temporary status. 'It was an understanding when they came back they just worked in this busy season and then they were automatically off again,' explained GM employee Jane McDonald. 'During the busy season, they didn't acquire seniority ... They come back just for that. It might have been maybe three months, two months ... and that was it.' Without seniority rights, married women could be easily 'let go' when production declined. Furthermore, given the vulnerability of these employees, supervisors had tremendous power to overwork them. According to a married woman in GM, 'If you're not going to sit in there, boy, and push out your quota, they get rid of you. And they can get rid of you in three months.'

Married women had long resented this arrangement, yet it went unchallenged for many years. It was not until September 1953 that a worker named Rosina Saxby decided to openly contest it.[103] Saxby, a married sewing machine operator in GM, had been laid off because of a shortage of work. While on lay-off, however, she discovered that the company had recalled an unmarried woman who was junior to her.[104] She thought, 'I don't get this ... I don't like this idea ... I don't know why they would call her back and not me ... I had been in there approximately nine months.'[105] Perplexed, Saxby asked questions. Rosina's husband, Bill Saxby, a UAW shop steward at Houdaille Industries, informed her that insofar as married women were paying union dues, they should have some seniority protection. 'This is why I come out and fight,' said Rosina. 'When I went into General Motors, they started to take money [union dues] out of my paycheque.' She said to Bill, 'I can't see the point in this. If we're not in the union, why are they taking money out of us?' He suggested that she speak to her union committeeman.[106]

The committeeman said that he would do what he could, but he added that Saxby was a married woman, as though this fact in itself justified her treatment by the company. Most local unionists were indifferent to her concerns. Nevertheless, Saxby persisted, stating, 'I want to go on a seniority list where, along the line, I've got protection.' In a private meeting, local union officials discussed her concerns with management, and in January 1954 they cleverly sidestepped her complaint by establishing a separate seniority group for married women. This measure gave married women the right to accumulate seniority among themselves, but it did not give them the seniority rights enjoyed by other workers either male or unmarried female. Pleased with this course of action, the chairman of the Local 222 bargaining committee wrote, 'Your Committee has tackled this very ticklish problem and we are attempting to negotiate with Management a satisfactory settlement.'[107]

This measure, however, was also in violation of UAW International policy. In June 1954 the UAW International Office had issued an administrative letter in which they advocated the fair treatment of married women and upheld the union's seniority principle. In addition, a recent UAW Convention had resolved to protect married women's employment rights.[108] When Caroline Davis, director of the UAW Women's Bureau, heard about the local's actions she immediately requested an explanation. Echoing arguments that were typical among solid unionists at the war's end, she asked, 'How long will it be before they will suggest separate seniority lists for single men, who have less home responsibility than married men, and then older men, whose children have married and left home. And what about the person who has a small farm, filling station or store? Do we in turn put them on separate seniority lists – and what, then, happens to our unity? ... Our safest position,' she concluded, 'is to not vary from established seniority.'[109]

While the local wavered, Bill Saxby appealed directly to Walter Reuther, the UAW President, for a just resolution. Saxby also sought the help of his friend Doug Sutton, a UAW committeeman at GM. On 10 December 1953 Rosina filed a grievance with Sutton, but in the meantime the company discharged her. GM also issued 'removal notices' to twenty-seven other married women, declaring that none of them had seniority rights.[110] On 26 January 1954 Saxby sent a telegram to Reuther stating, 'Contrary to International Policy and GM contract I have been dismissed because of married status please advise.'[111] Days later, Douglas Fraser, assistant to Reuther, directed George Burt, the UAW Canadian director, to investigate the case.[112] The following week Burt requested that the local provide him with a report.[113]

Unionists up the ranks, including George Burt, had long known that married women were treated unfairly. However, they did not contest this treatment. In February 1954, acting on Fraser's directive, Burt told Sutton that even though UAW policy on women workers had been clearly established for many years, the union and management colluded in denying women their rights. He wrote, 'I have known for some time there have been violations of this policy by an understanding with the management of General Motors. In many cases we have been unable to negotiate a policy which would give interchangeable seniority and equal pay to women workers ... However there are very few plants in the Region which discriminate against women workers because of getting married.' Burt admitted that the union did not condone this form of discrimination, but he added, 'However, we had received no complaint from the Oshawa local or its members until this serious situation developed. As far as I am aware, the contract does not allow the company to discriminate against women employees because of marital status, although I believe an arrangement was made with the Company agreeing to give such employees a voluntary quit slip.'[114]

He further told Sutton that the local union 'must realize' that under the UAW constitution, Saxby could 'successfully appeal to the [UAW] International Executive Board' and he warned him that they must therefore deal with the case properly in accordance with the constitution.[115] Yet in June 1954 Saxby was still awaiting a response from the union. She appealed to Burt, 'As this matter has been negotiated for approximately nine months, I would appreciate your help in getting an early settlement.'[116] This prompted Burt to write Sutton once again: 'I understand this is a very difficult case, particularly after so many months have elapsed, but the trouble is that she has an appeal through the appeal procedure under Article 30 of the [UAW] Constitution which makes it rather embarrassing to say the least ... In order to dispose of this case, I would suggest it either be processed through the grievance procedure, or taken to the membership and disposed of by them. In this way you would have a record of the disposition either way, and if Sister Saxby wants to appeal to the International Union, then it will be disposed of in that way.'[117] After much stalling by the union, Saxby's grievance made its way through the various stages of the procedure, and in December 1954 it went to arbitration.

'I can remember sittin' at this long, long table,' said Rosina Saxby, recalling the arbitration hearing. 'There was my foreman there. And then there was Doug Sutton ... Cliff Pilkey and ... the other guys from General Motors. And they still would not give me a chance [to speak for myself] and [they] swore up and down.'

At the hearing UAW International Representative John Eldon argued that GM both failed to recall Saxby in accordance with her seniority rights and had improperly discharged her. In turn, the company claimed that as a married woman Saxby had no seniority rights under the contract. GM spokespersons also stated that they had recalled another woman before Saxby because the former was better trained to perform the work required. J. Finkelman, arbitrator in this case, confirmed the information that Burt had privately given Sutton. He stated, 'The agreement itself does not, either by express words or by implication, indicate that married women are to be treated thereunder in any way different from unmarried women.' However, the company countered that long before unionization, GM acted on 'the premise that married women did not acquire seniority rights and that, immediately upon marriage, females forfeited whatever seniority rights they had acquired during their unmarried state.' Company representatives added that because the union had never in the history of their bargaining relationship opposed this practice, one must view them as consenting to it.

The arbitrator contended that where a provision in an agreement is 'vague or ambiguous,' the interpretation should concur with past practice. However, he did not see any vagueness or ambiguity in this case. Furthermore he did not hear 'any suggestion that the Company would have refused to agree to the terms of the Section as it stands if the Union had insisted that it apply to married women as to other employees. Nowhere in the Section is there so much as a word or a phrase from which it could be inferred that the parties intended to deprive married women, solely by reason of their marital status, of the rights to which employees are entitled under the Section.' On this basis, he reasoned that Saxby acquired seniority rights in the same way as unmarried women and that GM should have recalled her in line with her seniority. He therefore directed the company to compensate the griever for lost time.[118] Saxby received $1,200 in back pay, yet the company refused to reinstate her. Regardless of the validity of her protest, because the union had failed to take her grievance to the third stage of the procedure within the established time limit, they lost their chance to dispute this matter.[119]

The following month another married woman in the plant protested her dismissal. Like Saxby, she fought her grievance within the technical bounds of the collective agreement. This case clearly revolved around the issue of gender, yet both labour and management made scarce reference to the griever's sex or the social implications of her gender. Again, the company defended their actions by drawing on past practice. 'For over twenty years it has been the policy and practice of the Company to dismiss female employees upon marriage and to replace them with single employees,' argued GM officials. Over time, 'hundreds of married female employees have been dismissed' with 'the full knowledge of the Union, and ... the union has never protested such discharges.' Union representatives admitted that they had never contested this policy, but they claimed that it was nevertheless contrary to the provisions of the agreement and was therefore invalid.

The arbitrator upheld the union's case of improper dismissal, stating that the 'marriage of a female employee can hardly be characterized as having a discreditable connotation or meriting discipline.' However, like Saxby, this woman paid for the union's prior inaction. In view of the UAW's previous compliance, the arbitrator exempted the company from financially compensating the griever.[120]

These two women won their cases largely by drawing on their legal-technical rights under the union contract. However, women workers were less successful in winning their claim when these claims fell outside the boundaries of the collective agreement. For example, in September 1962 a female assembly operator protested her dismissal on the basis of marital status.[121] This woman went to work for McKinnon Industries in 1960. She was then laid off and rehired in May 1962. Owing to a reduction in schedule, she again faced a lay-off in July 1962 and while on lay-off she married. In September 1962 a McKinnon personnel officer called the woman to discuss her return to the firm. But when she reported her marital status the hiring officer said that it was against company policy to employ married women and he sent her away.[122] In fact, the company had posted a notice in its waiting room, stating that they did not accept job applications from married women.[123]

Company officials argued that the griever was not a current employee and that under the master and local agreement, management had the right to hire as they pleased. In turn, the union claimed that if management did not wish to rehire this woman they should have previously notified her that re-employment after marriage would not be possible.[124] However, insofar as management had not violated her seniority rights, and had refused to negotiate contractual provisions regarding hiring discrimination, the griever's claims were weak.[125]

These cases all had significant implications for women's perceptions of their rights as wage earners, as well as for their structural position in the industry. Although they were rare and isolated, these grievances set precedents and generated important debates among the union membership. Rosina Saxby recalled that her case 'was brought up on the floor at a big union meeting with General Motors. And of course there was men that were for, there was men that was against married women. And I got up and I did my thing and I can remember being extremely nervous about it ... I can recall one man gettin' up and telling me I had no business being in General Motors. He felt that ... married women should not work ... There was a lot of that way back in the '50s ... They figured you're married you should be at home with the kids and all that kind of stuff.' Witnessing these struggles, some women began to think about the larger questions they raised. For example, Maurie Shorten, who later became a strong feminist in the union, was on the Local 222 executive board during the controversy. Like most of her workmates, Shorten believed that a married woman did not require an independent income. 'That was tradition,' she said. Yet she pondered the matter. Shorten recalled: 'I argued with John Eldon [UAW Representative] ... not totally against it, but just trying to figure out in my mind what really should happen. And he said that marital status had no place in union agreements because if there was a big layoff, would they lay off single men first? And then would they go to the married man with one child? And then would they go to the married man with two children? And then what would you do with the married man who'd worked there 40 years and then all his children were gone?' Ann Brisbois similarly remarked that the Saxby case gave her 'a lot of food for thought.' She recalled, 'We thought, well now, they've been getting away with that for years and years.'

Yet despite these outcomes, the women who initiated the complaints did not directly contest the gendered division of wage labour. Indeed, both workers and employers tended to uphold the belief that married women were essentially financial dependents and therefore less deserving in the sphere of employment. What then prompted these women to file their complaints? Fundamentally, they felt that management had violated their rights as unionists. As dues-paying UAW members they believed that they were entitled to seniority protection. Although they did not demand equality with men, they felt that they should have the same contractual privileges as other women.

Rosina Saxby did not refer to her rights as a woman nor did she criticize the company's assumptions about the female sex. Likewise, Bill Saxby, a solid trade unionist, stated, 'I agree in principle with the argument that if two people want a job, two women, I think the ... single woman should get preference because they need the money more. But the fact is if the company hired the married woman and ... and they took ... union dues out of her paycheque, she has the right. She should have the same rights as everybody, as a single woman.'

These views were consistent with those held by many union members and leaders alike. Addressing such sentiments at the fifteenth UAW Constitutional Convention, Walter Reuther declared that apart from the pros and cons of women's employment, the union should recognize that many women are currently employed and must work in order to survive. The union was therefore responsible for protecting their rights against management's exploitation. Failure to do so, he exclaimed, would undermine UAW standards.[126]

Nevertheless, some male unionists could not reconcile these principles with their patriarchal beliefs. They consequently used their authority and knowledge of the union and industry to circumvent the contract and deny their sisters' rights. Ultimately, however, these men were challenged by the very system (industrial unionism and its tool, the collective agreement) that they themselves instituted. In many ways, the union contract 'froze' the gender inequalities that existed in the workplace and society. Yet it also granted women workers limited rights to protect themselves against management and encouraged them to regularly exercise these rights. The union therefore pushed women forward and drew them back. The agreement shaped worker resistance. It both embodied and contained workers' struggles.

SUMMARY

As economic conditions stabilized in the early 1950s and again prospered in the early 1960s, auto manufacturers both recalled women who were displaced at the war's end and hired new female workers. In comparison to the wartime workforce, this new cohort of women employees had diverse experiences and perspectives, they were more likely to view themselves as permanent wage earners, and they had a stronger sense of union citizenship. Their growing understanding of unionism paralleled the increasing strength and development of the UAW.

A notable outcome of these converging trends was women's greater attention to shop-floor conditions and increasingly frequent use of the union grievance procedure to voice their complaints. Admittedly, many women continued to defer to supervision, did not participate in a daily militancy, and did not always view their world in 'us versus them' terms. As in earlier times, several women workers in fact spoke fondly of their supervisors. Yet they also recognized that foremen sometimes acted unfairly. And for every one grievance they filed in protest of such injustices, there were several complaints that never became public. Workers often solved problems in a 'wait and see' fashion, with the most bold and vocal individuals taking a public stand while others observed (and benefited from) their struggles. Insofar as groups of three or more women often signed the same grievance, they had also developed some level of collective mobilization. In addition, many individual women filed only a few grievances in all their years of employment, but as a whole the female workforce protested often.

The women complained about many shop-floor conditions, mostly in an effort to secure some measure of dignity and control, and resist managerial discipline. Some women workers also began to recognize that their gender strongly shaped their relationship with supervision. GM employee Martha Cox observed that until the 1950s the company 'pretty well did as they liked with women. Really, women were actually second class citizens as far as the male gender was concerned.'

Despite this understanding, however, women did not directly challenge many of the sexually discriminatory practices in the industry. Indeed many women upheld patriarchal attitudes and practices, and advocated differential, sometimes protectionist, treatment on the basis of their sex. This resistance strategy was framed within the sexual division of wage labour. It may appear that women auto workers participated in their own exploitation. But they were not blindly absorbed by dominant gender ideologies nor did they shrewdly manipulate these ideas to suit their material ends.

Although the women did not openly challenge sex-based inequalities, they attempted to better their conditions of work with the recognition that, as women, they held a different, albeit unequal, place in society. By no means acquiescent, they protested particular aspects of their sexual subordination by management. Insofar as classes are gendered, any attempt to improve their working life indirectly affected their treatment as a sex. These protests, however, were not couched in a feminist critique, nor did they openly challenge contemporary gender ideologies and prescriptions of masculinity and femininity.

Women's shop-floor protest was primarily guided by a narrow union perspective, a masculine discourse. Female employees waged their struggles within the parameters of a collective agreement that working men negotiated according to their gender-biased vision of social justice. Within this framework, there was only a weak link between gender-based difference and equal rights. Thus, it was predominately by drawing on longstanding union principles and their rights as dues-paying unionists that women were able to win many grievances.

This strategy was based on ideological concerns and practical considerations. The degree as well as the nature of the struggle determined women auto workers' partial resistance. Insofar as sex-based job classifications and seniority systems were entrenched in the collective agreement, they were far more difficult to challenge than workplace issues such as speed-ups and washroom facilities, matters that could be negotiated directly and immediately by workers on the shop floor and in meetings between local union committeemen and first-line managers. Given women's lack of power in the union, and their hesitancy to directly participate in this masculine domain, movement on these issues was more within their reach. In the absence of an alternative ideology and social movement, women's strong gender identity was not channelled into a fully developed feminist consciousness. Rather, like men's gender identity, it was channelled into a union consciousness that presented the workforce as uniform in need.

Through both the experience of wage work and their participation in the union, however, women adopted certain values and expectations that overshadowed, as well as highlighted, their gender prescriptions. According to GM worker Betty Murray, 'I think that if you didn't have a union, I'm not too sure how a shop would operate. Let's say a couple of hundred women would they get together to discuss their problems? I don't know. It starts with your union and with your union hall.' In the following chapter, we see how these isolated acts of resistance that grew out of women's union loyalties were eventually transformed into a more concerted and organized campaign for gender equality.

The UAW was built on the strong support and enthusiasm of both women and men. Auto workers marched victoriously through the streets of Oshawa, Ontario, to mark the end of the 1937 strike.

So that they would always remember their times together in department 32, the GM sewing room, a group of women workers had their portrait taken after work at a local photo studio in Oshawa in 1944. *Top row, left to right:* Lena Clarke (Kowaluchuk), Helen Forestall (Beaugrand), Eileen Sandford (Riseborough), Freda Shields (Saxby), Connie (Leighton), Eleanor Terrell (Ransberry), Marie Smith (Taillon). *Bottom row, left to right:* Joan Bino (Gyare), Edna Bowers (Baxter), Margarite McGrath, Helen Graham (Lott), Kay Robinson (Murdoch), Bea Parkin (Taillon).

Woman auto workers spoke often about how they loved to dance. The formation of UAW Local 222 in Oshawa in 1937 was an important occasion for celebration. General Motors workers held a victory dance at the end of the day.

Woman war worker at GM, 1940s.

During the Second World War women would often arrive at work with their hair in pin curlers. During breaks they would comb out and style one another's hair in preparation for an evening out dancing.

Women members of UAW Local 199 joined the 1944 Labour Day parade and marched through the streets of St Catharines, Ontario.

Upholding a dominant belief in a family with a male breadwinner, UAW men long fought for a family wage. This strategy, however, did not take into account the needs and concerns of women members.

As growing numbers of women entered industrial employment, UAW leaders made some attempts to draw them into union activity.

A lone woman delegate among many men representing Local 199 at a UAW International conference.

Every three months over 125 delegates, from every UAW local in Canada, debated union policy at a District Council meeting. Women members described these gatherings as highly masculine.

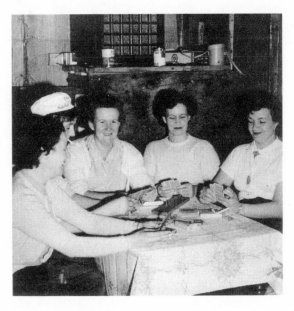

Women employees of an auto parts warehouse playing cards at strike headquarters in Ajax, Ontario.

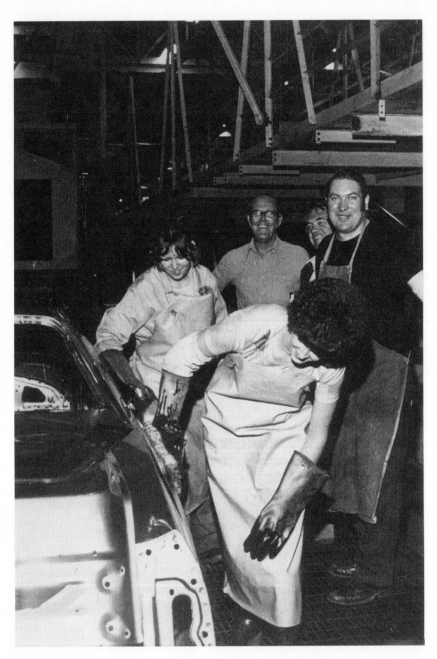

After the women of UAW Local 222 won their campaign to amend the Ontario Human Rights Act to include the word 'sex,' women auto workers proudly entered jobs that previously had been exclusive to men.

5

'That Wall's Comin' Down!': Industrial Restructuring and UAW Women's Struggle for Gender Equality (1964–1970)

The restructuring of the auto industry in the 1960s had dramatic effects on the sex-based division of wage labour. As auto manufacturers consolidated their operations across North America, many workers lost their jobs. However, because women were confined to a narrow range of classifications and could not exercise their seniority rights throughout the plants, they suffered especially harsh consequences. Hence, this period witnessed a massive retrenchment of the female workforce.

This structural upheaval prompted a core group of women to challenge their subordinate status in the industry. As we have seen, women auto workers had been experiencing subtle changes since the end of the Second World War. The most striking dimension of this transformation was a growing adherence to the principles of industrial unionism and familiarity with union procedures. In the years to follow women supplemented this understanding with some of the ideas of the emerging women's rights movement in the wider society. The economic developments of the 1960s joined and heightened the influence of these two movements – unionism and feminism – in shaping women's lives.

In short, these trends inspired women auto workers to revise their strategy of coping and resistance. In the past most women had upheld gendered ideas and practices in order to protect their restricted position in employment. By the mid-1960s, however, they could no longer sustain this strategy. In order to retain even a limited place in the industry women were forced to challenge sex segregation. Unlike past efforts, this challenge was collective, organized, and publicly led and defined by women workers themselves. Furthermore, UAW women began to view gender equality as a specific goal, rather than a residual gain in a universal working-class struggle. Their vision of equality encompassed the same rights for women and men specifically in the workplace and more broadly in society.

INDUSTRIAL RESTRUCTURING, THE AUTO PACT, AND JOB LOSSES FOR WOMEN

In 1963 GM of Canada transferred the production of motors and machining on head and engine blocks from its Windsor plant to McKinnon Industries in St Catharines. From McKinnon, it moved the commercial motors (also known as the fractional horsepower motor job) to its diesel plant in London, Ontario. The company also relocated the transmission department, and the balance of machining to Walkerville, Ontario.[1] In the following year GM announced plans to build a new trim plant in the Windsor area. It would consequently eliminate the cutting and sewing departments in Oshawa.

Company officials assured UAW leaders that these transfers would not severely affect male workers, most of whom could move into jobs created by the expansion of other departments in the plants. Women, however, posed a problem. According to a GM spokesperson, displaced cutting and sewing room employees (most of whom were female) had three options. One, roughly twenty to thirty workers could move into a small department that manufactured truck trim. Two, the expanding wiring department (the only remaining section in which women could exercise seniority) would absorb 100 to 130 employees. Three, they could follow their work to the Windsor area. George Morris, a GM official, predicted that roughly 360 jobs would go from Oshawa to Windsor.[2] Claiming that company figures were conservative, the women themselves estimated that over 400 jobs were in question – with implications for an overwhelming proportion of the female workforce in the Oshawa plants.[3]

These numbers, however, indicate only one facet of the job losses. May Partridge, a sewing room worker since 1962, wrote a poem that poignantly conveys the women's feelings about this move. It was entitled 'The End of Old "32",' and it appeared in a 1967 issue of the *Oshaworker*.

As you sit here at your sewing
machine,
Does the thought occur to you?
The days within these walls, with
friends, are
Numbered in the few?

We've had our share of problems,
when
The schedule fell behind
But when the season ended we
finished
Up on time.

We've done our share of griping
as we
Complained about our lot.
But being women, that's our pri-
vilege,
And the only one we've got.

We felt no obligation to show up
every day,
But when a short week was on
schedule,
There was hell to pay.

We grieved against the foreman,
We thought he was a jerk,
They paid him for doing nothing,
But still he liked to work.

We don't know where we're going,
or what job
We'll get to do.
But when we think of season's
end,
We can't help feeling blue.

We hope when we're recalled,
though it be in
A different place,
We can look over our shoulder
and see a
Familiar face.

We'll only have our memories, of
the times
We spent in here
We hate to face the parting

Of this, our final year.

We'd take all the headaches,
We'd even ask for more,
To have our old department re-
main as it was before.[4]

Although they had heard rumours of a transfer for many years, the cutting and sewing room women were ill prepared for the close of their department. Many of the 'girls' refused to believe that it would happen, reported Martha Cox, a sewing machine operator for eleven years. Like the others, Cox felt 'let down.' 'When it did happen,' she remarked, 'you get a sinking feeling because you know there's only one place to go – the wire and harness. If the wire and harness goes, you've got no job.' Cox had sufficient seniority to transfer into this department, but she worried about the fate of her more junior workmates. 'There were lots of girls who worked there, had no husbands ... What are they going to do?' she thought. Both these comments and Partridge's poem indicate that most women were primarily concerned about job security, but they also mourned the loss of their niche in the corporation, its safety, family atmosphere, and strong worker bonds.

Sewing room employees also felt as though GM had acted too abruptly in closing the department, even though they knew that the union and company had long debated the move. GM just 'up and ... pulled out,' commented one woman. 'Once they made up their minds to go, that was it.' The women furthermore perceived this act as callous. Pat Creighton sympathetically described its effect on a workmate. 'I can't remember her name but I can still see her. She was walking out the gate crying because she thought she was so lucky to get into General Motors. She'd been widowed with five kids. And she'd been in there for about two years and there was no way, there wasn't much seniority to hold in that north plant.'

The women workers' powerlessness and marginality in the decision-making process and preceding debates intensified these sentiments. Over two decades after the transfer, few of them even knew why the company had relocated.[5] According to union activist Bev McCloskey the Oshawa facility was competitive, but GM moved the work because Windsor was a depressed area. She thought that there were political motives behind the decision. GM bosses felt they could get the work done cheaper in Windsor, speculated Phyllis Yurkowski. They got a grant from the government. Maurie Shorten, another strong unionist, thought that this arrangement was more convenient for the firm because the new trim plant was the sole supplier of arm rests for all North American–manufactured GM cars. In fact, the chairperson and GM bargaining committee in Local 222 estimated that 75 to 85 per cent of the plant's output was shipped across the border. For every package of trim to outfit one car shipped to Oshawa and Ste-Thérèse in Quebec, six went to the United States.[6]

As the move became imminent, women workers desperately sought information from both the union and the company, but neither party seriously addressed their appeals. Revealing either ignorance or a lack of concern, a few UAW officials drastically underestimated the magnitude of the problem. In September 1965, for example, UAW Representative Richard Courtney informed UAW Canadian Director George Burt that only thirty or fourty girls might be temporarily affected by the dislocation in Oshawa.[7]

Company officials were similarly unresponsive. Expressing her coworkers' frustration, May Partridge published a poem in the form of a letter on their behalf to a Mr Walker of General Motors:

A mystery is prevailing, clouding our whole room.
Is our future really settled, or will Windsor spell our doom?
We've been reading all the papers, just looking for the facts.
Now Windsor is forgotten, the news is auto pacts.
It's favourable to Canada, the borders open wide.
The next edition tells, we wait, we wait on congress to decide.
We signed a contract in December, the strike was in the past.
What good are all the benefits if our jobs aren't going to last?
We sit here and ponder what our future has to hold
Should we order that new car or keep the one that's getting old?
We work the extra hours to get production off the line
Will our loyalty be remembered when it comes to moving time?
We know that supervision likes to keep things hush-hush,
We don't think this policy is exactly fair to us.
You've had all kinds of meetings by this time it's agreed
Which ones will be moving, which ones you won't need.
We're tired of hearing rumours, each one bigger than the last,
We'd appreciate straight answers to the questions we have asked.
We're not trying to be presumptuous, we think it's only fair
Next year, if we're working, we'd like to know just
'WHERE.'[8]

General Motors gradually removed workers from the cutting and sewing room between 1965 and 1967. During an early phase in this process 139 women from the department petitioned George Burt to investigate their problems. They were not contesting the decision; they merely wanted to know more about their fate. Fifty to sixty bench hands were being laid off, and they feared that if they did not immediately transfer to Windsor, they would lose the opportunity. Yet the workers hesitated because they preferred to stay in Oshawa until they had no other option. 'Many have homes and families here and do not want to make a hurried decision to move now if it is not necessary,' they wrote. 'We do not look forward to becoming one of the many unemployed in this country of ours.'[9]

Fear and doubt pervaded the sewing room. The women 'didn't know what they were gonna do,' explained Martha Cox. 'If it had been open to flow through the Motors – right through – the girls in the sewing room, none of them would have lost their jobs because they all had at least three, maybe four years [seniority].' But with restricted rights, they worried. 'Did we have enough seniority to bump over there? Would they allow us to bump? ... It was quite a trial on a lot of them,' she recalled. In 1965, noting that machine operators were not yet permitted to transfer to Windsor, the women asked their union representatives, 'What will become of them?' The workers repeatedly requested to see a master seniority list for the wire and harness department so that they could assess where they stood in seniority among the entire female plant workforce.[10]

When confronted with these concerns, George Burt flippantly remarked that despite job losses, 'we must remember that employment has been provided ... for 900 employees in the Windsor plant.' This, he claimed, was 'an indication that the balance is certainly in favour of additional job opportunities being provided as a result of these moves.'[11] Acting on this belief, labour and management canvassed laid-off workers to determine how many planned to move to Windsor. The first company survey indicated that thirty-six employees definitely wished to go and sixteen would go only if they could not stay in Oshawa.[12] On 16 June 1967 GM and UAW officials agreed to permit applicable employees to transfer (with their seniority) to the new trim plant within a little over a month, no later than 31 July 1967.[13]

Although some workers took advantage of this agreement, such a move was unrealistic for most.[14] Pat Creighton and three workmates considered the prospect and went to the area to explore. They found that the new GM plant was located far from housing and was somewhat inaccessible. 'It's one thing for a single woman to move into a strange area with no car,' said Creighton, but with children it could be 'frightening ... We all were given the opportunity to go to Windsor, but that's not easy when you have children.' Most of the women who moved with their jobs were single and without dependents.

Furthermore, the women feared that union representation in the new trim plant would be weak. They explained, 'Many of the foremen working in Windsor where [sic] at the Oshawa plant and know that the Oshawa girls are very union wise and are quick to call for there [sic] union if necessary. What protection have we from them if they wish to take past petty grievances out on us and go to the extend [sic] of firing us.' In fact, the UAW master agreement was functioning in Windsor, the union committee was active, and the local agreement covering Windsor employees was almost complete, but the women were unaware of these developments.[15]

Ultimately, many women lost their jobs even though they had accumulated numerous years of seniority. In 1967 all remaining trim work in the Oshawa plant moved to Windsor. At this time UAW leaders also feared that GM had overestimated its projected requirements for female workers in 1968, and that the company would consequently lay off women with seniority from October 1961 or earlier without immediate prospect of recall.[16]

Some of these laid-off workers received minimal financial assistance through the government's Transitional Assistance Benefit (TAB) plan. Others found work in surrounding plants, such as the Chrysler Trim plant in Ajax, Ontario. In fact, many of the women who currently work at the Ajax plant lost their jobs at GM during the 1965 move.[17] Insofar as most women worked out of financial necessity, only a minority stayed at home as full-time housewives and mothers. Most women hoped to be recalled.

At about the same time that women were laid off in Oshawa, female employees in McKinnon Industries met a similar fate. The illusory protection of gender-segregated work was collapsing before them as well. There is widespread agreement that women at McKinnon were displaced by moves stemming from the 1965 Auto Pact between Canada and the United States. According to the trade agreement, manufacturers in Canada could import American cars and parts duty free, while Canadian-made cars and parts could, in turn, enter the United States without a tariff. American auto makers were required to raise Canadian car production by $240 million annually.

Overall, the Auto Pact generated much employment.[18] Even its creators and most staunch supporters, however, recognized that the restructuring would displace certain groups of workers. And there were early indications that the trade agreement would affect McKinnon employees most severely. Of this workforce, women again suffered unduly because of non-interchangeable sex-based seniority.

By the mid-1960s, figures on plant lay-offs came rolling in at union meetings. In March 1966 GM spokespersons told UAW officials that the firm's plans under the Auto Pact involved the lay-off of 108 men and seventy women from the Delco division, ninety-seven men and ten women from the front end, seventy-three men from the bearing, and twenty-four men from the gear divisions.[19] Except for the prop shaft line, which would move to GM's Frigidaire plant in Toronto, these operations would disappear into American production. The company, however, assured the union that it would take care of all the displaced men, but again, it said nothing about the women.[20] With greater frankness than GM officials, UAW leaders stated that male workers might be absorbed in other parts of the plant, but at least 100 women would lose their jobs.[21]

By August 1966 George Burt reported that 500 women in St Catharines had lost their jobs as a result of the Auto Pact.[22] In the fall McKinnon laid off an additional 375 employees, bringing the total number of permanently separated workers in this plant to over 1,000. In November 1966 the situation worsened as McKinnon planned to move its bearing division (another department that employed many women) as well as manual and power steering. The relocation would affect approximately 150 jobs. Union officials noted that any woman involved would be laid off.[23]

Between June and December of 1966 the female workforce at McKinnon had dropped from 326 to approximately 170, with the only women's lines remaining in the firm in Plant 1.[24] This figure stands in stark contrast to the more than 1,200 women employed during the Second World War. By March 1967 McKinnon had laid off 900 employees, 244 of whom were women, revealing a disproportionate effect. Furthermore, the company did not disclose plans to recall many of these workers.[25]

Recognizing that they could not prevent lay-offs through collective bargaining, UAW leaders proposed that the government at least make Transitional Assistance Benefits available.[26] However, this remedy was extremely limited insofar as administrative stipulations prevented many workers from receiving the benefit. For example, the Transitional Assistance Board had to determine that the lay-off was caused by the Auto Pact, that fifty employees or 10 per cent of the workforce must have been laid off for at least four weeks, and that eligible workers must have been employed in the industry at least thirty weeks immediately preceding the lay-off. In 1967 out of roughly 660 men laid off from McKinnon Industries, the Transitional Assistance Board had certified only 255 as eligible for TAB. And of the 240 women on lay-off, they had certified only 140. The board claimed that the balance of workers were not victims of the Auto Pact.[27] In comparison, by September 1967 150 women at GM in Oshawa had been officially certified to receive TAB as a result of job loss from the Canada-U.S. Agreement.[28]

After the TAB review board had denied benefits to twelve women from Local 199, the UAW Research Department in Canada took up this issue and claimed that the board's regulations compounded past discrimination against married women who had recently been on maternity leave. In addition, union leaders argued that the stipulations discriminated against women who were on sick leave, since the TAB Board refused to regard these women as attached to the industry.[29]

The government also offered retraining programs for women, but these too were of limited value.[30] Indeed, displaced women from McKinnon Industries stated that government-sponsored commercial and stenography and basic upgrading, courses were useless. 'What good will office jobs be to me?' one woman asked rhetorically. 'I've a young sister with two years university and commercial experience behind her and she hasn't been able to land a job in two months.' Another worker for whom English was a second language noted that insofar as women with four-year diplomas were not finding work, she had little chance. Furthermore, the women recognized that clerical employment did not pay nearly as well as auto work.[31] Like their sisters in Oshawa, McKinnon workers were paying dearly for the sex-based contract clauses that labour and management had negotiated many years ago.

Even while they witnessed the harmful effects of gender segregation for women at GM and McKinnon Industries, UAW officials did not attempt to redefine the sexual division of labour in newly constructed and expanding firms and departments. Rather, through the restructuring, labour and management replicated the sex composition of existing plant workforces and duplicated sex-specific seniority lists and wage scales. For example, when commercial motors jobs moved from McKinnon Industries to the GM Diesel plant in London, the company and union set sex-based quotas for the transfer of seniority employees. GM officially agreed to hire no more than forty-three men and twenty-two women. After the application period, the diesel plant offered employment at the rate of fewer than three men and two women per week until all applications were processed in order of seniority. These quotas were based on sex ratios in the original location.[32] In addition, the parties agreed to create four female and nine male job classifications under the new contract. The women's starting rates would range from $1.81 to $1.96 per hour, while the men's starting rates were between $2.19 and $2.28.

GM also established male and female jobs in its new Windsor trim plant, although company publicists highlighted the plant's large female workforce. 'Nowhere at GM will the woman's rightful place in industry be more evident in the months to come than at the new trim fabrication plant,' read an article in the magazine *GM Topics*. Its author stated that 400 men and women would be employed by the summer, and by the middle of the 1966 production year over 800 women would be working in the plant.[33]

Even before the plant was built labour and management had negotiated a contract for Windsor trim workers. 'They got exactly what the Oshawa workers were receiving. Everything was to be the same,' reported Bev McCloskey. Union representatives believed that this was in the best interests of workers as there were reports that companies had attempted to reduce wages as jobs were being transferred. GM management had also predetermined the sexual division of labour. 'The women will operate sewing machines and do door and trim panel fabrication. Men will carry out dielectric [*sic*] embossing, material handling, cutting of upholstery material and departmental maintenance.'[34] In the new plant's cutting department, there were seven male jobs and only one female job, though there were more female classifications in the sewing department. Even unskilled maintenance was divided along gender lines, with separate janitor and janitress classifications.[35] In addition, local seniority provisions specified non-interchangeable occupational seniority groups by sex.[36]

IMMEDIATE REACTIONS TO INDUSTRIAL RESTRUCTURING

Women's immediate reaction to industrial restructuring and its consequences reflects elements of their past strategies, but it also reveals important modifications. In the mid-1960s female auto workers largely drew on conventional gender ideologies and shaped their responses within the context of the sexual division of wage labour. However, compared with women workers who were displaced during the war reconversion period, the female workforce of the 1960s tended to be more aggressive, organized, and vocal in their protests. Their initial reactions to the upheaval caused by restructuring forewarned of dramatically different strategies of control and resistance in the following years.

As they were beginning to feel the effects of job displacement, some female workers clung to scarce employment and restated old claims that married women should be laid off before single women, regardless of seniority. In the mid-1960s, Anne Thomson, a McKinnon employee, was one of the more vocal advocates of this policy. With this goal, Thomson organized and led a group of thirty-eight female employees who called themselves the 'committee for self-supporting women.' In 1966 the committee wrote to Prime Minister Lester Pearson about the lay-offs in McKinnon Industries. Rather than direct their protest at the company or the government, however, they blamed women workers themselves for their misfortune. According to this group, the company was using the free trade pact to eliminate women who had long misused sick leaves, complained about 'unpleasant jobs,' and loitered in the washrooms. 'The girls have been the architects of their own misfortune in many cases,' claimed a widow with fourteen years seniority. Drawing on a family wage argument, Thomson's group asserted that if married women need to take time off from work, they should simply stay at home. 'This makes it bad for the company and for the deserving women who need the work,' they asserted. 'We feel the innocent are suffering because of the guilty.'[37] Local media widely publicized these views, beliefs that married women worked for '$50,000 homes, trips to Europe and Florida, Cadillacs and color TV[s],' while others laboured for necessities.[38]

Recognizing that union leaders were bound by the collective agreement, these 'self-supporting women' suggested that the UAW amend the contract to place financially independent women, especially those who support families, in a separate category. 'Our union stress [sic] Race, Colour and Creed and the right to work, but are these women really working?' they asked. 'Our union is against discrimination, but when self-supporting women are denied the right to work because of others, then we believe this is discrimination.' 'We want to stress that we believe in unions but we feel an injustice is being done in this case ... To women who have to work this thing seems so unfair and so heartless.'[39]

Though steadfast in their protests, the committee for self-supporting women did not receive much attention from UAW leaders. George Burt ignored their petition calling him to St Catharines to discuss this matter.[40] And James Connell, president of Local 199, called the proposal nonsense. 'I'm sure that not one of the group complaining would have given up her job and seniority to another woman out of sympathy alone. It would be laughable to ask her,' remarked Connell.[41]

Nevertheless, frustrated by further lay-offs as well as the union's inaction, this small group of single, divorced, and widowed women intensified their campaign. They were particularly upset with the UAW. According to these women, company officials were sympathetic to their plight, 'but with the union calling the shots on who's kept on, nothing can be done.'[42] 'The union's inflexible attitude ... is the root of the problem,' a group of women exclaimed.[43] Bypassing local and regional union leaders, Anne Thomson sent a telegram directly to Walter Reuther of the UAW International. It stated that women with up to nine years of seniority were being laid off, while hundreds of men were newly hired. She demanded that the union act on the matter.[44]

In making their case Thomson's group drew largely on maternal images that appealed to the media and garnered further publicity. 'All is not well for the mother of four, separated, and out of her $100-a-week job on the spark plug line,' read an article in the *St Catharines Standard*. 'Losing the medical and drug benefits that have kept two chronically sick youngsters in $25 worth of drugs each month is a catastrophic prospect.' 'All is not well for the widowed mother of five children facing a bleak Christmas.' 'All is not well for the lone mother supporting three teenagers, one of them a nervous wreck needing hospital care as a result of the family's financial situation,' they continued with melodrama.[45]

In the GM plant competition for scarce female jobs took a different form than in McKinnon. In Oshawa single women did not blame married women for their plight. Rather, tensions arose between the 'west plant girls' of the sewing room and the 'north plant girls' who were employed in the wire and harness department. There had been implicit rivalries between the two groups of workers even before the war, but contracting employment opportunities made them more pronounced. Sewing machine operators were 'sort of the elite' of the women, explained Bev McCloskey, although they were never officially recognized as skilled workers. Most wire and harness workers, however, performed light assembly work that was highly detailed, but was not deemed to require technical know-how.[46]

Compounding these distinctions were insinuations about the sexual behaviour and virtue of the women in the two departments. Some women in the sewing room referred to the wire and harness women as 'tough' and 'loose,' the type that smoked and swore and went drinking. The 'west plant girls' defined *themselves* as more naive and gentle. Not everyone was aware of these distinctions. Moreover, it is questionable if there was any real basis to the rumours. Nevertheless, the undercurrents were significant in furthering the perception among some workers that there was a fundamental difference between the two groups of women.

When some sewing room workers bumped wire and harness employees in the 1960s, these tensions soared. Because cutting and sewing workers generally had higher seniority than those in the wiring room, the displacement of the latter group by the former occurred on a large scale. In fact, some observers noted that the north plant women were more angry at the west plant women for coming in and taking their jobs than they were at the company or union for instituting the sex-based clauses that were at the root of the problem. Initially, the wire and harness girls were hostile, noted Martha Cox, who was bumped into the department. 'I can't really blame them. We were taking their jobs and they got put out on the street. There was nowhere for them to go.' Cox recalled that of the fifteen women with whom she worked on a conveyor line, all were from the sewing department. This meant that 'the fifteen girls that had worked there before were gone.'

Though it is highly unlikely that the company conspired to politically divide groups of female employees, some supervisors exacerbated the friction that was growing between them. 'One foreman used to refer to "our girls" and "them,"' recalled Pat Creighton, ' "them" meaning us in the west plant.' In her words, 'They've always been able to divide women in half. They would always do it. If it wasn't the union, it was the management ... [The foreman] would say, "God damn women are coming from the west plant ... I don't know how many of you girls I'm going to use." ... So of course, he'd have them [the wire and harness women] all geared up and by the time we showed up ... well, the kind of tone was that.'

After this initial period, however, the women from the two departments, now concentrated in one, got to know each other, and as they struggled over the same conditions of work, day after day, they began to reflect on their common situation. They decided that they had better unite. Creighton explained, 'It was us and them, but then once the women got to know each other ... they realized, "Hey, I bleed red and you bleed red, and you got children and I got children." And then somehow somebody said one day, "You know, if they ever shut this place down, we'll all be out on the damn street." And that's when it started. There was no place for us to go but that wire and harness.' 'Women have great strength in numbers,' she reflected. 'It's when you divide them that they don't have the strength.'

GENDER IDEOLOGIES IN TRANSITION

The gendered division of labour had long pitted women against each other as competitors for scarce resources in this male-dominated industry.

It is paradoxical that when competition was most intense, when opportunities were most narrow, and when women were fewest in number, they began to realize their common predicament and unite. Their experiences of the worst effects of sex segregation pushed women together to challenge their subordinate position in the industry.

As we have seen, employers similarly had displaced a large portion of the female workforce in the 1940s, when war production ceased. During the Second World War, however, there was a strong consensus about women's and men's proper place and these beliefs legitimated the massive dismissal of female employees. The women themselves even upheld, albeit partially, the idea of a male breadwinner. Women were strongly aware of their sex and formed close bonds with one another, but they did not channel this identity and cohesiveness into formal protest. The gendered division of labour permitted the surviving female workforce to rely on alternative strategies of coping and resistance. As noted in the last chapter, small acts of resistance were ongoing among the women. During the war, they were covert and private. As long as women did not marry, they could remain in the female departments and continue to cope in this way. However, displaced female war workers had few resources for mobilization and formal protest. Thus, although they were unhappy with their situation, they resigned themselves to it and quietly left the auto plants.

By the 1960s women auto workers still had limited powers in the union and restricted opportunities in the labour market, but there were key differences. The female workforce itself had undergone changes, gender ideologies were in transition, the larger women's rights movement offered working-class women access to political and organizational resources, and significantly, women auto workers could no longer sustain established workplace strategies. Because of the industrial reorganization in the 1960s, they had little recourse but to challenge existing arrangements if they wished to remain employed in the plants.

Many of the young women who were newly hired during the Second World War had left the industry in the reconversion period to marry and raise families. However, long-term employees, women who either were widowed, had never married, or married relatively late in life remained in auto employment after the war. By the 1960s these women had accumulated several decades of seniority. Wage work was at the centre of their lives and some of their most important relationships were forged on the shop floor. A new cohort of women also entered the auto plants during the industrial expansion of the 1950s. Because of the time and terms of their entry these women were more likely to view themselves as permanent workers and dues-paying union members who deserved some rights in the industry. They entered the plants with some employment experience, and they were not new to industrial labour. A small segment of this group, moreover, became highly active in the union. While the majority of women were not similarly committed, they were aware of their rights as union members.

Furthermore, although conventional gender prescriptions remained strong throughout this decade, they slowly came into question with the resurgence of feminism in the wider society. A core group of women with years of active involvement in the UAW fervently threw itself into the contemporary feminist debate. These women became the driving force behind the fight for women's rights in the auto plants. During the mid-to-late 1960s, this cadre of women began to critically assess their position as a sex in the industry. According to a GM employee, female auto workers began to question sex-based seniority rights at the same time that 'the women were marchin' all over for their rights.' It was 'after Betty Freidan's book came out [in 1963] and everything,' that 'we realized, look it, this is it. We've got to start fightin' if we want something.'

When pushed by the economic developments of the 1960s, some women stood up and said, 'Enough is enough. Don't push me any longer.' Bev McCloskey, a GM worker, explained the changing attitudes during this period: 'You really don't get into a fight until it affects you ... and then all of these things start coming out ... what's right and what's wrong. But our big fight started ... in the '60s. We were always fightin' for different things before that, but in the '60s when our people were being laid off and they were hiring people and this is when we really got organized and mobilized and got going for these different rights.' 'This is when we decided,' exclaimed activist Pat Creighton, 'hey this has gotta stop ... And what the hell, why shouldn't we be allowed to go into the other plants!'

Some women vividly described how they began to reassess longstanding beliefs – beliefs in a family wage, a male breadwinner, and women's subordinate position in society. Their criticism and defiance, however, must be understood in historical context. These challenges did not occur spontaneously. Rather, they grew slowly over the years – years on the shop floor and in the union. The events of the 1960s merely shook up and pushed along enduring tensions, doubts, and growing discontents in the female workforce. In the words of GM employee Betty Murray, by the 1960s 'I think we were ripe. I think we were ready for something.'

At the forefront of this movement for change was a small group of approximately seven women from Local 222 in Oshawa. In the early-to-mid 1960s these women decided to collectively confront sex discrimination in both the industry and their union. Observers note that the general level of union organization and militancy of workers was comparable in Locals 199 and 222. However, the Oshawa local, the largest in the union, had some unique and particularly outspoken and politically astute female members. Most of these women had long been active in the labour movement and firmly believed in the principles of industrial unionism. These loyalties strongly influenced their campaign for equal rights. The union offered them a strong vision of social justice, a vehicle to express their views, and a practical training ground – all of which were necessary for the success of their campaign.

Bev McCloskey, the key figure in the women's campaign for equality, had been fighting for social justice since she was a child. Her beliefs grew largely out of her hardship during these years. Born and raised in Oshawa, she first worked for pay at the age of twelve, peeling potatoes. Her mother, a single parent to five children, scrubbed floors. 'When you come from my background,' said McCloskey, 'you're always fightin' ... We just had a history of struggling ... You had to fight for anything you wanted.'

McCloskey became active in the UAW during her first year at GM in 1949. During the 1949 strike she registered workers at the union hall. Throughout the following decades she garnered experience as a committeewoman, alternate committeewoman, steward, chief steward, and member of various union standing committees. In addition, she was an Oshawa and District Labour Council delegate and a Canadian UAW Council delegate. She also served as recording secretary on the Local 222 Executive Board for seventeen years.[47] According to a co-worker, 'Bev, when she started, she just pushed and pushed and pushed.'

Maurie Shorten, chair of the original Local 222 Women's Committee, also had strong union loyalties and deeply grounded political insights. Shorten stated that she 'became aware of some extreme examples of poverty' and saw the need for 'group action in resolving individual problems' when she was first employed as a clerk in the Gray Coach bus terminal located in an economically depressed area of Toronto. Upholding these beliefs, she joined the Co-operative Commonwealth Federation at the age of twenty. In 1946 she became active in unionism first as a local representative and later as an area representative at Bell Telephone.[48] In December 1950 she began to work at GM, and from 1953 to 1956 she served as recording secretary on the Local 222 executive. In 1956 the head of her union caucus offered to run her for first vice-president, but, for personal reasons, she declined – a decision that she later regretted.

Bev McCloskey described union activity as 'the greatest education you'll ever get.' 'You have to be on top of everything ... You have to know the laws, how they affect your people, compensation, health and safety, every law going,' she explained. Union work gave her personal confidence, and it endowed her with a strong sense of right and wrong. It is wrong, she declared, that 'people should have so much over on one hand, where they can control the life of other people.' We've gotta have a fair society for everyone. This is what I've learned from the labour movement ... You could never buy that. You could go to university. You could read all the books you want to. But for practical experience, you're never gonna get it. You have to be there and live through it.'

Few women expressed such strong sentiments, but many were keenly aware of their basic rights as workers and dues-paying union members. Notably, women workers supported the seniority principle, the cornerstone of the labour movement. A strong belief in this principle inspired women to assert their employment rights even though they continued to believe in the legitimacy of a family with a male breadwinner. GM employee Martha Cox, for example, stated that even though married women may not need a job as much as other workers, they should be entitled to one as long as they had seniority. Likewise, Maurie Shorten reminded workers that it was unfair to lay off women with seniority, while the company hired new male employees. She declared, 'We want to have the right to a job in the plant on the same basis as any union member in any UAW plant. Seniority and the ability to do the job should be the only restrictions placed on any worker. The question of sex, race, creed, colour, and marital status must be eliminated, if we are to have a true Democratic Union.'[49]

Also drawing strongly on the union ethos auto worker May Partridge argued that gender 'discrimination merely helps the employer to divide union members who ought to be united in the battle against employer exploitation.' This, she stated, 'is the purpose of trade unions.'[50] Likewise, at a Local 222 meeting Dorothy Meehan, UAW representative, identified seniority as the most valued possession of the 'working man.' She added, however, 'It is just as highly cherished and valued by every woman member of the U.A.W.' Meehan warned, 'Employers will continue in their efforts to destroy our seniority structure by sowing seeds of dissension and disunity among workers, hoping to pit group against group, worker against worker, until finally they can pick and choose as they please between men and women workers.'[51] However, as women drew on UAW philosophies, they recognized that many of their union brothers did not practice the theories they preached and that industrial unionism was not sufficient to ensure their particular rights and needs as a sex. With sadness, but without resignation, in 1968 Bev McCloskey wrote to Caroline Davis, head of the UAW International Women's Department, 'I never realized in all the years I have been active in our union, the discrimination against the female employees in our own union that is prevalent today.'[52]

As in the past, male union leaders were ambivalent about women's rights and made few attempts to eliminate gender inequalities. Since women had a marginal standing in both the industry and the union, it was not expedient to support their protests. According to one woman, 'We're all paying the same [union dues] ... but it didn't matter because you were a female so therefore you were a second-class citizen.'

In 1968 women with seniority dating back to 1962 had been laid off, 'on the street' for fifteen months, while General Motors continued to hire male employees.[53] Such practices angered the women. 'We kept fightin' this and saying that this isn't right,' reported McCloskey. However, most union officials were deaf to their protests. In fact, one local president abruptly responded, 'Why don't they go to Toronto and get a job.' Insensitive to the constraints in women's lives, union leaders took seriously the company's proposal to move displaced women from Oshawa and St Catharines to new jobs in GM's Frigidaire plant in Scarborough, Ontario.[54] Furthermore, when McCloskey proposed that women bump lower seniority men on the assembly line, the chairman of the plant bargaining committee quipped that 'he wouldn't want his wife hanging off a welder in the body shop.' The women retorted that maybe she herself should make the decision.[55]

Women did not view their brothers as a monolithic block of opposition. 'A certain bunch of men were helping the women and were standing beside you,' said Laura Saunders. Fay Bender also claimed that there were some supportive union men, though she emphasized that they were 'very few in number. They all kind of laughed at us and thought that we were crazy. We got no resources from the union whatsoever,' she stated bluntly. On one occasion the chair of the GM bargaining committee said that if women ever won the right to move into men's jobs, he would put them all to work in the pit. 'This is a pit that's in the floor and you have to work on the car above you,' explained Bender. 'Now at that time there was probably ... between 300 and 400 women working in the plant.' She retorted, 'Well, if you can get us all in there, that's fine. We'll have the prettiest pit that you ever wanted to see. And we'll have it all pink, fur-lined.'

Bev McCloskey recalled, 'Oh we'd write to the International. We'd write a letter off and say this is happening, that's happening. No matter what happened we'd just send a copy up to Caroline Davis up in the UAW Women's Committee and we'd say, "This is happening and what do we do on this?" And we'd squeal on them. Everything that ever happened, we'd just squeal on 'em. We'd say, "To hell with you! We'll go to the papers! We don't give a shit about you guys" ... We'll tell 'em what the UAW's all about.' Every time an incident arose, the women were right there asking questions, said May Partridge, 'we were there and there was nothing they [the men] could do about it. Whether they liked it or they didn't, you know, we knew that we had to keep fighting.' The women regularly got up at union meetings and aggressively asked, ' "What about our women?!" and "How come they're laid off?!" ... Oh it was terrible for a while there.'

One woman conveyed the group's growing frustration with their union brothers in a poem that appeared in the Local 222 newspaper.

I get my Oshaworker, I read each and every line
Though I may be in a hurry, for this I find the time;
I feel an obligation to keep up on the news
Not always in agreement with all the written views.
They report on all conventions and what they're going to do
On price control and rent control and what it means to you.
The talk is of amendments and what they're going to ask –
Not even a postscript am I added at the last.
I read that whole darn paper and never make the grade;
Do they just count the females when union dues are paid?
We wait on recognition and it better show up soon
I feel more isolated than the men that walked the Moon.
So all you fancy journalists, here's one thing to remember:
I'm classed as just a female but I'm still a Union member.[56]

NEW STRATEGIES OF COPING, RESISTANCE, AND CONTROL

These lessons prompted women activists to look beyond the established perspective of their union. While they based their struggle for gender equality on the basic tenets of industrial unionism – the seniority principle and the right to grieve discriminatory treatment as dues-paying members – they also drew on ideas about women's rights in society. They began to expand their vision of social justice and revealed a greater sense of effi-

cacy. In redefining patriarchal unionism with a sensitivity to gender politics, women workers began to theorize the links between the various
bases of social inequality.

Contrary to the popular belief that the North American women's movement was an exclusively middle-class development, the experiences of
female auto workers suggest that a distinct 'feminist trade unionism'
emerged in the 1960s (see Maroney, 1986). Indeed, in some ways, the
relationship between women of different classes was unproblematic. In
their pursuit of such gains as equal rights in employment, working-class
women drew on the resources of middle-class feminists largely academics
and artists. Apart from these concerns, however, wage-earning women
tended to take themselves out of the movement. Consequently, there were
few notable tensions between the two groups. Though the movement was
dominated by middle-class women, others played an active and important part in defining feminism.[57]

As they mobilized, UAW women from Oshawa and surrounding areas
frequently attended women's rights rallies and demonstrations in Toronto. At these events they met women from various backgrounds and
discovered that they shared problems and goals across economic boundaries. Although they forged an especially strong bond with women who
were active in the left-leaning New Democratic Party, more broad-based
and non-partisan groups such as the Voice of Women also became part
of their network.[58] We 'hooked up with' middle-class, academic women
who were waging the struggle for sexual justice, noted Bev McCloskey.
These women included feminist activists Kay Macpherson, Bonnie Kreps,
and Mary Ann Kantaroff. 'We were just all sort of together fightin' for
the same thing – the rights of women – that we have our right to stand
up and be equal. And we got a lot of strength from them and a lot of
support.' In the mid-to-late 1960s the Local 222 women even invited
speakers from Toronto-based women's liberation groups to activate plant
workers. They enthusiastically described these years as one big celebration. 'It was just all of us goin' whenever we heard there was a meeting
... You'd meet the same people all the time.'

The rank-and-file activists also turned for support to women unionists
on staff at the international office across the border. Caroline Davis, director of the UAW International Women's Department, and UAW Representatives Dorothy Haener, Dorothy Meehan, Cecelia Carrigan, and
Lillian Hatcher were among those who provided some direction. 'This is
where it started – the American women,' McCloskey explained. At times,
the Local 222 women felt that the Americans should have been more

radical in their politics and outspoken on women's rights. Nevertheless, they gave them credit. 'They were here all the time to help us organize ... They were pioneers ... Any time we wanted them to come up for a meeting they come up.'

As noted earlier, whereas UAW women in Canada were only beginning to mobilize in the 1960s, their American sisters had been organizing around the issue of sex discrimination since the Second World War (Gabin, 1984; Meyerowitz, 1985; Milkman, 1987). By the late 1960s they had achieved unprecedented legislative gains (such as Title VII) and established effective women's agencies at the national and regional levels in the union. For instance, the UAW Women's Department was set up in 1955. It conducted audits on female membership and employment, advised regional directors and the UAW executive board on women's concerns, advocated stronger female representation in the union, and issued policy statements against sexual discrimination.[59] These gains did not always directly and immediately affect women in the Southern Ontario plants, but they gave legitimacy to the efforts of Canadian women and inspired them to pursue their own struggle.

The annual UAW International Women's Conference was also an important forum for female unionists. Though only a small number of delegates from Canada attended these meetings, their benefits were far-ranging. Participants 'role-played' in mock union locals, assessed shop-floor strategies for confronting discrimination, and learned about the UAW grievance procedure, policies, and legislation affecting women employees.[60] These gatherings were important in highlighting the specific status of wage-earning women. At these conferences working-class women articulated the links between the labour movement and the women's movement.

Inspired by the American sisters they met at union conferences, on 18 September 1968 the women from Local 222 established an official women's committee.[61] This was one of the first of its kind in Ontario, as neither GM employees in St Catharines nor Chrysler workers in Ajax had yet mobilized around the issue of gender. At best, the locals sent one or two delegates to annual international women's conferences in the United States.

On the first Local 222 Women's Committee, Maurie Shorten and Betty Murray, both GM employees, served as chair and vice-chair respectively, and Mary Rutter, a Coulters worker, acted as secretary. The committee also included GM workers Helen MacInally and Bev McCloskey, and Duplate employee Doris Wallace.[62] McCloskey hand-picked the first members to ensure a cross-representation from the various plants under UAW contract. She wished to avoid the nepotism and sectarian politics that plagued the men's dealings. 'You'd have to spread out with everyone if you want to be effective,' McCloskey asserted.

In 1968 the women's committee was such a novelty that the local union 'pretty well just let us go,' recalled Pat Creighton. Union leaders, however, did not foresee women's potential. Creighton recounted with laughter, 'Oh God. It was funny. We went to the chairman of the plant ... We asked him if we could use the union hall to explain to the sisters what would happen if that North Plant went down ... Well he said, 'You're gonna have about as much interest – why don't you go get yourself a telephone booth?' ... But that wasn't so.' One hundred and thirty-five women attended the first meeting, and they loudly voiced their complaints.[63]

The committee's official mandate was to identify the problems that women workers faced as a sex and, on this knowledge, make recommendations for action to the local union executive board. In order to accomplish these aims committee members had to familiarize themselves with both UAW policy and the local contract. As well, they were expected to facilitate discussions and coordinate programs with other groups in the labour movement. Education, community fund-raising, social events, and current legislation were all within their jurisdiction. In this sense they carried out the goals of the UAW International Women's Department, though on a more frequent basis. Both bodies promoted women's union citizenship and furthered their understanding of UAW technical procedures.[64] Some women, in fact, saw the committee as 'a training ground for future jobs' in the union. 'We used to discuss the Constitution and have speakers in on it and stuff like that so that everybody was educated on the whole aspect of the union,' stated May Partridge.

Significantly, the committee provided women workers with an arena in which they could identify issues, air frustrations, and recognize their common predicament. Although they feared ghettoization, the women saw the need for a separate forum. Betty Murray, vice-chair of the original Local 222 committee, explained that 'there didn't seem to be any place that the women could move to.' They could not 'get their foot in' the union. 'We were there participating,' she said, 'but we were not making ... anything that really showed, anything that really counted.' Bev McCloskey similarly declared, 'As I've told a lot of our fellas ... 'I want to see the day when we never need it. But ... as long as we got those inequalities around ... we're going to have to have it. You've got to have that pressure group until everything straightens out." ' The committees were essential to the women's personal growth and political development.

As noted in the preceding chapters, close bonds, woman-centred talk, female-exclusive gatherings, and small acts of resistance were not new to women auto workers. In the late 1960s, however, female activists attempted to transform the 'chumming' and 'companionship' of the past into a sense of 'sisterhood' and 'solidarity.' They tried to channel the 'rumblings' and individual grievances into open and collective protest. According to some workers they had to turn 'bitching and whining sessions' into a concerted struggle for change. In short, the women's committee set out to politicize the average woman worker. Betty Murray vividly described this process. Sometimes a group of strong union women would

pass the word around right at the plant. 'Let's meet down at the Genosha Hotel for a beer. Pass the word down the line there.' Maybe you might get 25, 30 of those women coming down the Genosha Hotel. 'Let's go in there and have a beer and talk about this problem that we're having here.' But you'd only talk about five minutes about that problem, and run into another problem, and run into another.

What was nice about the women's movement and the way the women got together, it gave them a chance to let their hair down and complain and then go home happy because they had somebody to talk to. [It was important to get women together] away from the home and sit down for an hour ... over coffee or tea or beer or whatever it is. To sit down and just let your hair down and say how you feel and what you think ... You let her go, you know. You say, 'There, I told 'em where it was all at, boy!'

Yet most women were still hesitant to channel their discontents into public protest. A primary obstacle to their radicalization was fear – not fear of empowerment or success, but fear of reprisal by those (men) in authority. Female activists explained that 'it was alright for the women to stand back in little groups and talk, but then for them to come up front to back you up when you went in the office for anything, then they would back down.' 'They wanted to, but they were just too hesitant.' Some workers apologetically said to the more militant women, ' "No, I can't." A lot of them were afraid,' explained Murray. 'Scared. That's the big word. They were scared. They would whisper, "Ya. I'm with you." They were with you about three steps and they were gone.'

Over the years, women auto workers had developed various strategies for coping within a restrictive context. The women's committee members tried to abolish these ways of thinking and behaving and replace them with new strategies. 'It was a process of education,' said McCloskey, a process that necessitated various tactics and seemingly inconsistent messages.

Central to their campaign was the message that women have a place in the UAW and that they should therefore use the union as a vehicle to achieve gender equality. Barriers that had been established since the UAW's formation undermined this equation, however. Most women still viewed the union as a masculine domain, a working man's organization, to which women were marginal. Frustrated by these perceptions, women's committee members sometimes reprimanded rank-and-file women for their inactivity and threatened them with the potential consequences of their seeming inertia. For example, May Partridge, chair of the Local 222 Women's Committee, wrote the following poem to her workmates:

We're the ones that are guilty, excuses we can find,
We can't attend a meeting, we haven't got the time.
We only find the Union Hall when our pay cheque's on the line,
WE forget we are a member every day of every year.
We don't show our loyalty unless it's contract year,
The daily paper tells you a strike will last so long,
Then Parliament will send you back to work even if it's wrong.
Enforced arbitration the new anti-union name,
Will rob you of your rights, the ones you fought to gain.
So make sure every meeting is crowded to the door,
Find out what the news is, bring your 'beefs' up on the floor.
You're part of the largest union, that's why you pay your dues,
You'll never get the story straight, by buying washroom views.
You can build a better union, the strongest of them all,
By giving up a little time and being present at the Hall.[65]

Similarly after very few women had attended a union meeting, Hazel Cotton, a GM steward, unsympathetically commented on their explanations. 'What were their excuses?,' she asked 'One girl said she walked by and all she saw was a lot of men. Another said she was expecting company on the weekend, and she must start preparing for their arrival ... We pay our dues so we are members, and we are to be active and loyal. Does it hurt to devote just two hours one night a month to come to a meeting? ... Don't you think members that it's high time you got up on your feet and started attending something worthwhile?'[66]

Female activists also attempted to discredit conventional gender ideologies by confronting women with the material realities of their lives. In an issue of the *Oshaworker* the chair of the local women's committee reproached her female co-workers, 'Instead of spending hours talking about the views of socialites with pictures in the Star, think for yourselves ... These people are not workers. Work, to them, is modelling at $70.00 an hour. We could all be "Loved instead of liberated" if our husbands were stockbrokers ... We have been invited to Toronto ... to speak to female union members. This is your kind of people.'[67]

The committee frequently reminded women of their precarious position in the industry and the need to stand up for themselves in order to protect their jobs. 'There is always one department in any industry labelled a loss for income tax purposes,' read a women's committee report. 'You have a little island of 278 women, a loss to the Company and a forgotten minority by the Union. You pay to belong to a Union ... and if they never see or hear of you, they won't worry about you ... If you cannot find the time to stand up for yourself, you may end up with all kinds of time and no one to care.'[68] Likewise, May Partridge stated, 'Don't let the word "equality" scare you. During the working year your seniority seems to disappear but when it comes down to the final move it's the only thing you have left.'[69] Bev McCloskey similarly warned, 'If there's a layoff and you're only in a so-called female department, then you're laid off out on the street ... You only have this certain little woman's department you gotta stay in. And you gotta be a good little girl and stay there no matter ... They weren't gonna give you the opportunity in this because you're a female.'

The committee furthermore attempted to erode the pervasive belief that women's place is first and foremost in the home. One month after the Local 222 Women's Committee was formed, Maurie Shorten identified this process of relearning as one of their primary goals.[70] 'Most women work for the same reasons men do, because they need to,' she wrote in the *Oshaworker*. 'Of all women workers in March 1968, 70 percent were single, widowed, separated or married to men whose income was less than $5,000 a year. Whether women should or should not work is no longer a question for debate.'[71]

Shorten's ideas, however, did not have widespread appeal. 'Oh! They thought we were nuts,' explained Bev McCloskey. 'Some of them were on our side, certainly, but no, the majority weren't.' Clinging to old strategies, many women who had high seniority stated that they were happy with the way things were and did not want to enter men's jobs because such jobs, in their view, were more difficult to perform. 'I could never figure out why women wanted to be equal with men, really,' remarked long-term employee Jane McDonald. 'You see some men slugging away on a job and you want equal rights and then they ask you, 'Would you do that job?' ... If you want to be equal with the men, you should be able to do anything that they can do, which I don't believe women can in a lot of instances.' 'But of course,' added Maurie Shorten, the women who made such comments 'weren't the ones out [laid-off] on the street ... [They] never had much contact with the [unemployed] people out on the street.'

It is paradoxical that in attacking these myths, the women's committee found it necessary to rely on domestic images, and employ traditional woman-centred techniques for mobilizing and politicizing workers.[72] While they reprimanded their workmates for inactivity in union affairs and collusion in a middle-class ideal of womanhood, female activists were also attuned to the realities of working women's lives. They knew that women did not juxtapose home and work and that their various responsibilities in life overlapped. They knew that child care and housework competed with union activism for women's time and energies. They also saw that many women workers still found security in conventional domestic images and themes. Unlike male unionists, they shaped their recruitment strategies accordingly.

'You just couldn't get them to come to meetings. So you would think of everything you could, to try to get them down there,' explained McCloskey. In 1968 the women's committee first drew women out for a potluck supper. A potluck supper with female workmates was far more inviting and less threatening to regular working women and their families than a formal meeting to discuss women's rights. Riding on the success of this event, the committee then held a 'social bingo' in the UAW hall and 140 women from the local attended. It was the first of many 'social nights.'[73] In November 1969 they planned a Christmas bingo and an open house. They also had a fudge table and auction.[74] In 1970 they waived their regular meeting for a fashion show and education seminar.[75]

Women's committee leaders did not strongly advocate this method of mobilization – a method that largely reinforced conventional images of womanhood. Indeed some of them thought it was 'a stupid, bloody thing for women to do' in a union hall.[76] However, they were interested in the collective gain, and this proved to be the most effective means. 'If that's how we can get them out is to run a bingo, let's run a bloody bingo,' McCloskey reasoned. 'And we'll get a few words in on the side.' These events also included seminars on women's employment rights, lectures on time study, unemployment insurance, supplementary unemployment benefits, and other related topics.[77]

Although some women never learned the difference between the worker-based women's committee and the UAW ladies' auxiliary (an organization made up of male worker's wives and daughters), many came out, listened, and became aware of the specific concerns of female wage earners. 'We were hopin' that maybe one of them would get the idea in their head and it wouldn't go away. Oh, it worked, ya ... something sank in,' McCloskey reported. The committee measured their success during the summer of 1970 when they set up a booth at the local's annual picnic. Female workers inundated them with inquiries and consumed literature on women's rights. Although the committee planned to work only half the day, four women had to stay on duty all day to answer questions.[78]

SEX SEGREGATION AND THE COLLECTIVE AGREEMENT

These initiatives fostered some individual protests. At first a small group of women zealously denounced all conditions that they felt were unfair. 'Anything we seen that we didn't agree with, we would write to the Ministers, raise it at the Executive Board, raise it on the membership floor ... we had letters going all the time,' recalled Bev McCloskey. The local sent a man to sit as the liaison officer to the women's committee, but he got thrown out 'if he opened his mouth.' The women were intent on setting their own agenda. However, women were still restricted by a collective agreement that upheld sex-based job classifications and seniority lists. Consequently, the complainants were seldom successful. For example, in November 1968 Maurie Shorten filed a grievance protesting male stock supply and machine set-up men performing the work of female repair operators. Shorten requested that this practice be discontinued, or that the female repair operators be paid the highest of the three rates. The company, however, argued that historically machine set-up men had performed this work and that it was not the exclusive work of female repair operators. They therefore dismissed the grievance.[79] The following month, May Partridge filed a related grievance regarding male operators in the body shop at GM. In defence of its actions the company claimed that there were no seniority groups in this department for female employees. Again, the union dropped the grievance.[80]

That same year another female employee protested the seniority rule itself. On the griever's behalf, a UAW representative argued that if women could perform jobs within the male seniority classification, they should be recalled to such work before junior male employees. Company officials, however, upheld the separate seniority lists as specified in the contract.[81] The local agreement had stated that 'the seniority rights of male employees and female employees shall be exercised only in separate seniority classifications and shall not be interchangeable.'[82]

The following year a laid-off bench hand in GM filed yet another seniority grievance on behalf of a group of women on lay-off. According to the griever, the women should have been placed on jobs in line with their seniority before newly hired men. The union argued that the lay-off represented a violation of a section of the master agreement, which stated the contract should apply 'to all employees ... without regard to race, colour, creed, age, sex or national origin.' In their view this provision superseded the local seniority agreement. Company officials, however, pointed to another paragraph in the agreement that stated that supplemental local agreements are 'made a part of' the master contract. Thus, once more, the union dropped the grievance.[83]

According to UAW procedure in the GM chain grievances could go through four stages, at which point a UAW International representative would meet with local unionists before taking the case to arbitration. When the union repeatedly dropped the women's complaints at the fourth stage, female activists complained to American Dorothy Meehan of the UAW International Women's Department. After concluding that local committeemen had refused to file the women's grievances 'on the grounds that women have no business in the plant,' Meehan requested that Canadian Director Dennis McDermott, look into the matter.[84]

Angered by this request, the women's union representative defensively stated that from the beginning all the agreements in Local 222 provided for the separate seniority rights of males and females, and women had never (until recently) tried to amend this provision. He claimed that he could find no evidence that a committeeman had refused to file a grievance on the grounds stated by the women. The union official was acting legitimately, but narrowly. Thus, while the women acknowledged the limits set by the local seniority clause, they protested the attitude of their committeeman. Bev McCloskey had warned him that if the grievance was going to be dropped before going to arbitration, they may as well 'forget about it. "The Company must think we are all a bunch of nuts," she stated. 'And then lo and behold the Committee dropped it at the 4th Step.' McCloskey remarked, 'What have we got to lose, we have no security now because of our seniority. I have always been under the impression that the Master [Agreement] supercedes the Local.' Distressed, she wrote to Dennis McDermott, 'I do not like to be told that we will have to form a pressure group to get our rights as UAW Members in our own Local Union.'[85]

Remembering this period, McCloskey emphatically declared, 'Hell! I fought just as hard with the union as I did with the company ... When we had our women laid off ... every meeting I'd get up and [ask] "When are they gonna bring our women back?" ... And they'd skirt all around it – even in the caucuses.' Like company spokespersons, male union leaders typically argued that they were bound by the contract. Yet they did not fight to change this contract. 'We didn't get any backin' from our union so I don't want anybody thinkin' they did,' said McCloskey. 'I've said this before ... Our big fight was with our union people, like along with the company, but with our union people to take the case up.'

CREATING A BASE FOR GENDER EQUALITY: THE LEGISLATIVE ARENA

In order to achieve meaningful change, the women were forced to extend their demands beyond the union and the workplace and utilize another tactic that union men had long relied on – the lobby for legislative rights. Legal rights, they believed, would provide a foundation for more effective struggles in the future. 'You had to ... get your rights first,' explained McCloskey. 'You could yap all you wanted, but it didn't mean nothing.' At the same time, the women's committee members began to address the concerns of a wider range of women, not only those who were employed in high-paying unionized sectors of the economy. Moreover, they demanded women's rights throughout society, rather than in the workplace alone. 'We wanted the right to go into a hotel if we wanted to and sit and have a beer without male and female places,' said McCloskey. 'We used to do that all the time over here – try to get that wall knocked down, you know. We'd say, "That wall's comin' down!" And so after our women's committee meeting, we'd all head over to the men's [drinking] room and sit there.'

The committee's most consequential struggle, however, involved a revision of provincial legislation. Recognizing that the Ontario Human Rights Code, 1961–2, prohibited discrimination on the basis of colour, race, creed, and national origin, but not sex, the women launched an organized campaign to amend the act. ' "Sex" in the Human Rights Code is not a dirty word,' a unionist advised women members. 'It is the right of every working woman to earn a decent living. It won't end discrimination, but with the law behind them ... [women] can get better wages and opportunities in every field.'[86] Securing the legislative amendment in fact became the committee's central and defining goal.

In June 1969 the Oshawa women convinced their parliamentary representative, Cliff Pilkey, a New Democrat back-bencher, to present Bill

36, a private members' bill to amend the law before the provincial legislature. Three members of the women's committee took time off from work
and drove to Toronto to attend the session in parliament. This was only
the beginning of a long endeavour. The government eventually adopted
the premise of this legislative proposal in Bill 83, 'An Act to Prevent
Discrimination in Employment because of Sex or Marital Status.'
Throughout the following year and a half, the women participated in an
intense lobbying campaign for the amendment.

'We hooked up with the feminists in Toronto. We wrote Briefs ... We
used to go up and lobby the Labour Minister. We would go up and we
would sit in the gallery,' recalled one activist. They also wrote letters to
300 women's groups asking them to declare their support of the bill to
Labour Minister Dalton Bales. Apparently, the mail poured in.[87] On their
days off, the women also held demonstrations to draw public attention
to the issue. Activist Pat Creighton noted, 'We used to have marches on
Queen's Park ... then other women joined in. Oh, other workers from
Toronto and London ... By this time it wasn't just General Motors' workers, right, or auto workers. It was some people in the banks, and different
groups. We met wonderful, wonderful women from any age. Very young
to very old ... All those things that happened in the sixties we did – and
this was all part of it.'[88]

When the bill was delayed at the second reading committee members
even sought the support of Coretta King, wife of United States civil rights
leader Martin Luther King, Jr, Creighton recalled.

It was coming closer to June. And if you don't have a final reading, it dies when
they sit for summer holidays. That's it and then you have to start the nonsense
all over again ... Somebody come up with the bright idea that I should write to
Coretta King, and let's stage a march that them bastards never seen before. And
I wrote her and explained to her ... what was happening. It kept stalling and
stalling. So she wrote back and said that, yes, she would be willing to come to
Canada. So then I wrote Mr Davis' office and the Minister of Labour, Elgie ... I
would have loved to seen the face. We oft laugh about it because could you
imagine having Coretta King, wife of Martin Luther King, in Toronto, leading a
parade of women? ... The Tories must have haemorrhaged.

I can still see Bev McCloskey – we were up at Queen's Park then. [The Labour
Minister's] walking down the hall and she's asking him or begging him when
they're going to have the final reading of this Bill. Well, he kind of ignored it ...
and she wouldn't let him in the door.

'We fought really hard and really long. And there was no money,' recalled

Creighton. 'Every time we had to go to Toronto, money was always out of our own pocket ... some weeks two or three times a week [to Toronto]. And then on weekends, sometimes there'd be parades and demonstrations.'

Ultimately, the women were successful. In the spring of 1970 the superintendent in GM's wire and harness department called Creighton into his office. She said, 'What for? Do I need the union?' She was thinking, "What the hell did I do now?" But he said, "The Minister of Labour is on the phone and he wants to talk to you." And he was. And he said the Bill was to have its final reading. He gave me the day.' In December 1970 the bill became law.[89]

In the same year that the legislation was passed the GM contract came up for renegotiation. When questioned about the implications of the new law for collective bargaining, the women's union representative confidently stated, ' "Well, it won't affect our contract." And we just all laughed at him,' recalled Creighton. 'We said, "Obviously you're ignorant of the law. Any law, change in law, supersedes the contract." ' Consequently, both parties were required to remove the word 'female' from the collective agreement and amalgamate the seniority lists. 'And then it dawned on me that we had really won,' said Creighton, 'that we could really go anywhere in General Motors. And the first place we all – most of us – transferred to parts and service. We thought we died and gone to heaven.'[90]

Revealing the meaning and power of both social unionism and feminism, UAW women significantly altered the gendered division of wage labour. Their struggle was momentous. They played a key role in amending the Human Rights Code in the province of Ontario which in turn, eliminated all sex-based language from union contracts. 'It was because of the legislation,' stated Maurie Shorten. 'I mean I'd like to say it was because of the union, but it wasn't.' Primarily, it was because of the efforts of this core group of UAW women.

'THAT WALL'S COMIN' DOWN': THE COLLAPSE OF GENDERED DIVISIONS IN THE AUTO PLANTS

When GM eliminated sex-based job classifications, eight women were still laid off, 'out on the street,' but they had not yet lost their seniority. These were the first women to enter the exclusively male south plant in General Motors.[91] Under the new plant-wide seniority system, the company also hired an additional forty-five women. Like their male co-workers, these women worked a two-shift week and received an equal $4.12

minimum wage per hour.[92] In February 1971 UAW committeeman Tommy Thompson reported that all of the ' "girls" who were laid off' had returned to work. GM agreed to permit women with sufficient seniority to 'flow through her division' (in the north plant), while the remaining women who lacked the seniority were placed on jobs where and when there were openings.[93] May Partridge, then chair of the women's committee, declared that after thirteen weeks and two years of effort, women were on the lines 'down South,' in the rad room and stamping plant in GM's Oshawa complex. Many of the 'girls' called Partridge to express their happiness to be employed once again.[94]

High-seniority women who were never laid off also took advantage of their new rights. 'It was a slow trickle at first,' explained Pat Creighton. 'If you only used to play in one little playground, it kind of becomes a security blanket.' But 'from there, they all started goin' all over the place in the plant.'[95] For instance, Phyllis Yurkowski was the first woman to transfer into the plastics department. After carefully observing Yurkowski, another woman transferred in behind her. Another woman followed her, and then more women came after them. In June 1971 approximately 100 women were working along with men, under the same terms of employment.[96]

While many women had previously refused to take a man's job, they changed their minds shortly after the opportunity arose. 'They were the first ones that applied for it. They didn't care if it was men's job or whose it was because it was more money than what they were making in the [wire and harness] department,' observed May Partridge. 'I don't know what they were thinking of because once the door is open ... They don't think nothing about it ... There was women that said, "I will never work with men. Never,"' reported Pat Creighton. But when the law was passed, 'you gotta put your fanny up against the wall because you'd get run over as they're running to the south plant.' As they entered men's jobs, 'they were proud.'[97]

SUMMARY

The restructuring of the Southern Ontario auto industry had important implications for the gendered division of wage labour. When auto makers consolidated their operations, they created opportunities for many workers while they dislocated others. Because union contracts upheld sex-based job classifications and seniority systems, laid-off women could not transfer into jobs throughout the plants, and thus a large segment of the female workforce was eliminated.

Women faced similar lay-offs at the end of the Second World War. However, in the 1940s, they lacked the resources to challenge their treatment. Furthermore, these dismissals were legitimated by a strong ideological consensus about women's and men's proper place in the division of labour. Thus, women workers either coped and resisted in individual, clandestine ways or quietly left the industry. In the 1960s, however, they responded differently.

In the preceding decade, years of some industrial expansion and periodic economic prosperity, a new cohort of women entered the auto plants. These women viewed themselves as permanent workers and dues-paying unionists, and they frequently used the union grievance procedure in an attempt to improve shop floor conditions. Some of these women also became active in the UAW. These developments coincided with the second-wave women's rights movement in the wider society. And a core group within this cohort fervently grasped the emerging ideas and extended the feminist debate to the shop floor and the union.

Women auto workers were ripe for a confrontation and the consolidation of work operations pushed these trends with vigour and force. The job losses made glaring the inequalities that had long characterized auto employment. They also forced women to recognize the ways in which employers used gender to legitimate inequalities in industry. As the 'sheltering' effect of the gendered division of labour wore thin, women recognized that past strategies were no longer viable. With these developments, the historical (and artificial) dichotomization of gender and class inequalities began to collapse.

As their struggle unfolded, female activists recognized that industrial unionism, as practiced by UAW men, was not sufficient to achieve gender equality. Male union leaders had long juggled the democratic principles of industrial unionism, on the one hand, and exclusive notions of a male breadwinner and family wage, on the other. These were inherently contradictory philosophies, however, and male unionists therefore displayed ambivalence and sometimes resistance towards women workers. Thus, while their union loyalties strongly influenced their critique of, and assault on, gender inequalities, UAW women drew on the support of feminists across class lines, and mobilized separately from working-class men. Through local union women's committees, female workers could link their loyalties to both movements. Unlike working men, the women did not face a contradiction between their union principles and their gender ideologies. Indeed, these philosophies converged. In this sense, unionism and feminism reinforced one another, pushed one another along.

Women unionists, however, were not a homogeneous group. A cadre of women who had long been involved in the labour movement led the struggle for gender equality, sometimes in spite of resistance on the part of their sisters. Indeed, central to the women's struggle was the radicalization and politicization of the female workforce. In attempting to mobilize others, women's committee members built on the social bonds that female workers had forged on the shop floor long ago. They also tried to channel women's growing discontents and isolated acts of resistance into concerted and open protest. In short, they attempted to eliminate old ways of thinking and behaving, as most women clung to familiar shop floor strategies.

Unlike their UAW brothers, however, women activists understood the predicaments and dilemmas of the typical female wage earner. They recognized that for most women there was no neat separation between the domestic sphere and the workplace, between their responsibilities as workers, activists, and wives and mothers. Sensitive to the realities of women's lives, the activists utilized woman-centred mobilizing techniques. They mixed elements of domestic life and conventional feminine culture with masculine union strategies. This approach was effective in the long term. After women won the right to exercise their seniority throughout the plants in 1970, they purposefully entered jobs that had, in the past, been exclusive to men.

This episode in the long struggle over the gendered division of labour shows that wage-earning women relied strongly on the UAW as a vehicle for change. Yet despite this connection, women unionists do not always adopt the same mobilization techniques, methods of protest, goals, and visions as their brothers. Female unionists employed gendered strategies of coping and resistance – strategies that stemmed from their unique experiences in wage labour, the union, and family. Their particular approach was developed in a context of limited options and many restrictions. Primarily, the women's campaign for gender equality was shaped by their distinct, subordinate position in the division of labour. In turn, however, through this campaign UAW women dramatically redefined these divisions. In the next chapter we examine the informal negotiation of these new arrangements on the shop floor, the implications of the unionism-feminism alliance, and the limits of legal-contractual equality rights within a patriarchal setting.

6

Social Change in a Complex Milieu (1970–1979)

Women's gains during the late 1960s significantly influenced gender relations throughout the following decade. Equal seniority rights permitted women to directly compare their shop-floor experiences with those of their male co-workers, and the knowledge they drew from these comparisons gave them the confidence and grounds to assert their discontents more boldly than in the past. The material and ideological outcomes of their struggle also inspired women to broaden their agenda and address their experiences as mothers and wives, as well as wage-earners. Throughout the 1970s challenges to gender divisions and inequalities moved from isolated and individual protests to organized and collective campaigns.

Social change, however, occurs gradually and unevenly. In the midst of change, people experience dilemmas and act in contradictory ways. Predictably, sexual desegregation forced the workers to alter their relationships, but it did not automatically lead to greater egalitarianism. In their day-to-day dealings, both women and men sometimes resisted the legal-contractual changes. Indeed, conventional gender ideologies and familiar gendered strategies proved to be most resilient in face-to-face relations, in everyday behaviour. Contract clauses, policy resolutions, and principled debates thus take on varied meanings in lived experience. In this chapter we will explore the ways in which legal-contractual changes touch individual lives, and we will look at the strategies that people adopt in order to deal with the disruption of long-standing arrangements.

One of the central contradictions that emerged for women auto workers during the rapidly changing 1970s revolved around the dichotomization of equality and sexual difference. While women had won equal contract rights, sexual differences persisted. In some ways, they acquired heightened meaning in the workplace. Sex-based differences are not inherently antithetical to sexually egalitarian relations. However, because male workers and employers tended to view the 'female' as subordinate, the concept become harmful to women. Women workers thus faced a dilemma. They acted in a context in which equality and sexual difference were presented as 'binary opposites' – one in which they had to choose to behave just like men or risk losing their newly won equal rights.[1]

GENDER AND THE LABOUR PROCESS

After GM amalgamated its seniority lists, employee Betty Murray immediately transferred from the wire and harness department to parts and service. She confided, 'When I went into parts and service, I thought I had died and went to heaven. There is no other way I can tell you ... I'd say to the guy – he was training me ... "Stop there. Could you give me a little pinch? That's pretty good. Pinch a little harder." "Why?" he says. "Just want to make sure that I haven't died and gone to heaven." '

Murray explained that work in the north plant was more desirable than the female-dominated west plant because of the male environment. 'The more you got around the male environment, your environment wasn't as bad,' she stated. 'It's always said ... you get a group of women working together, they're bitchy ... but I think they work hard. Women work hard. It's just something in them. They can't just go along like the men can. "Well, when I get it done, I'll get it done" ... If they're sitting at a sewing machine and they're thinking of maybe something at home. They're just taking it out on the machine ... I observed them and said, "Gee, what a difference." That's why ... when I went to warehousing, I thought I'd died and gone to heaven, because of the way the work went.'

As women entered men's jobs they saw more clearly than ever the relationship between their shop-floor experiences and their treatment as a sex. Notably, they realized that supervision placed greater demands on women than men. Male union leaders agreed that the 'women's jobs' were among the most difficult. 'There's no doubt in my mind,' stated former Local 222 president Ted Murphy. 'You had to be fast.' The speed of the conveyor lines in the wire and harness department was 'unbelievable.' Pat Creighton similarly observed that in this department women's hands moved rapidly and continuously. When they entered the 'men's departments,' their new male co-workers warned them to slow down. We were 'killing the job ... We were working too fast ... We were making them look bad. See, we had never worked in a man's department,' she explained. Women, Creighton reasoned, were more assiduous than men because of their experiences as *women*. '[Women] were always regimented ... You have to have a schedule ... if you've got children and a home to run and you're working outside. You just can't throw it to the wind.'

Because of the excessive production standards, few men in turn attempted to transfer into 'women's jobs.'[2] Most of the men who entered the 'women's department' were newly hired and therefore had limited options. Those few who chose to transfer into the wire and harness from other areas of the plant quickly left.[3] By 1973 all of the fifty men who were sent to work in this department had moved out.[4] 'They said it was too hard,' recalled Martha Cox. 'They said that the jobs in the south plant were a lot easier than the jobs we were doin' there.' Workers had three days in which they could transfer, but some men withstood only one.

In addition, 'women's jobs' were undesirable because they generally paid lower rates and had a lower status than men's.[5] Men resented working on the conveyor lines beside women, said Bev McCloskey. 'Oh did they ever! You know why? 'Cause they were comin' in at women's wages.' In addition, they disliked the humiliating work rules that women had long endured. For example, men who worked near machinery were required to wear hairnets or bandanas, just as the women did. Amused by this gender twist, some women spitefully 'laughed like hell' at men in bandanas. 'The guys hated that,' recalled McCloskey. 'We had a lot of fun with them.'

Women marvelled at the range of jobs to which they could now move, and they fully exercised their plant-wide seniority. Bev McCloskey moved from the wire and harness department to a fork-lift truck. 'I loved my lift truck,' she asserted. 'I fought like hell to get that lift truck ... I was in charge and I was in control of what I was doing. And I used to take a lot of pride in that. And I was mobile. I was moving. I wasn't stuck in one spot or anything.' Betty Murray thought she had 'died and gone to heaven' in the parts and service department because of the greater autonomy. A desire for variation prompted Phyllis Yurkowski to transfer to the plastics department and then from plastics to quality control. 'I used to just work for a little while and then I'd get sick of it, and then I'd transfer someplace else,' she noted with satisfaction. 'This is the thing,' said McCloskey, 'seniority rights.' 'Once you got seniority, you just put a transfer in to the jobs you felt you could do ... Use your seniority.' With greater autonomy, mobility, and diversity, and higher wages, and without the severe discipline and strict production standards of the women's departments, women who moved into previously male jobs emphatically stated that they would not look back.[6]

As full participants in the industry, and with a deeper understanding of their treatment as a sex, women workers intensified their efforts to shape the workplace. Putting women alongside men was one of the biggest mistakes GM ever made, according to Pat Creighton. It spawned a new wave of protest around longstanding shop-floor discontents. Betty Murray similarly observed that women's legal-contractual gains inspired them to act on nagging problems. 'I saw the changes,' she noted. Just as important, 'I saw the changes in the people that wanted the changes.'

As a UAW committeewoman representing female employees, Bev McCloskey also witnessed these trends. McCloskey claimed that when women 'got mad' and 'got pushed too far,' 'they would really go after something.' Personal transformations were sometimes expressed in small ways. For example, by the 1970s women stopped crying on the job. 'That was the thing that used to bug me,' she said. In the past, 'they'd cry when somebody would turn and look at 'em sideways ... that was just a natural reaction to them. But it got to the point [where] they toughened up and they just quit cryin' because they got a little bit of self-confidence.' These personal, individual developments inspired further open and collective struggles for social change.

Encouraged by the local women's committees, women continued to use the union grievance procedure.[7] Observers stated that in the past men tended to file more grievances than women, but they did not notice a significant gender difference in the 1970s and 1980s. Like men, women typically contested violations of their seniority rights[8] and unfair production standards.[9] They also protested job classifications and rates, job placement,[10] violations of the local wage agreement,[11] health and safety standards,[12] overtime rights,[13] work shifts,[14] transfer rights[15], relief time,[16] and rights regarding call-in pay.[17] In addition, grievances centred around foremen's actions,[18] discipline for improper behaviour, absenteeism and lateness,[19] insubordination,[20] poor quality work,[21] and illegal work stoppages.[22] Women 'weren't afraid to stand up and tell the foreman that he was wrong,' recalled May Partridge. 'They knew their rights under the contract.'

PUTTING SEX DISCRIMINATION ON THE UAW AGENDA

Women did not, however, confine their protests to general and traditional shop-floor issues. Throughout these years, they continued to fight against sexual discrimination. Changing the Human Rights Code was only the first step in a long struggle. Legislation provided women with a base on which to make further claims. 'Once we had that in,' remarked Bev Mc-Closkey, 'we would go after different things ... newspapers where it had male or female ... language in schools, in textbooks ... all of the things that affected women at that time.'

Admittedly, like men, most women auto workers were not radical. Many women held on to conventional gender ideologies, and most remained marginal to activism of any kind. Once they gained an equal status under the contract and a legal recourse for action, however, they defended their rights more frequently and more vigorously than in the past. Women's committee members repeatedly warned their sisters not to become complacent after achieving their initial goals. 'You could have all kinds of change, but if you don't take advantage of it, change is not going to be beneficial to you,' declared Betty Murray. 'You may look and see it in the book and see it in the contract and say, "Oh, that's nice." But if you don't start to question it and say, "Okay, well I want to put that into force," ' it will be worthless. Seasoned union negotiators maintain that they can bargain anything. Implementation is the key to change.[23]

In September 1971 a female conveyor operator and harness builder in GM drew on her new contract rights and filed one of the first 'sex discrimination' grievances in the industry. She alleged that her foreman had made offensive remarks to her and failed to call her committeeman upon request. 'None of the male employees that worked with me have ever been treated this way,' she contended. 'I am the only female employee working on that conveyor and I am also the only employee that receives discipline. I think supervision ... apply the provisions of the agreement in two different ways – one way for male employees and one for female employee [sic].' Company officials stated that the griever was 'obviously a very sensitive individual,' and they argued that male workers, too, were asked to explain their conduct. Predictably, they denied the grievance.[24]

This case was not isolated. After a member of GM's personnel department visited her home to investigate her absenteeism, another employee in the wire and harness department also filed a protest of sex discrimination. On her behalf, union officials again complained that foremen treated women differently than men. The 'same supervision,' they claimed, never requested such an investigation of men who were absent from work.[25] While some unionists admitted that GM policed both women and men,[26] the woman perceived this action as sex discrimination, and her union representatives contested it on this ground.

Some women also filed charges of sex discrimination with the provincial Human Rights Commission. Typically, workers launched discrimination complaints through both the union and the government agency. In the early 1970s Fay Bender was one of the first auto workers to draw on the amended Human Rights Code. For roughly one year she was the only woman in GM's battery plant, and during this time she competently performed the job of stacker. However, when other women entered the department they refused to perform this job, claiming that it was too heavy. Consequently, in 1972 supervision decided to 'red-circle' or 'exempt' women from the stacker, break apart, trucking, and cleaning jobs in the plant.[27]

Company representatives based their decision on the argument that few females could perform these jobs because of women's 'nature.' Given this, they believed that it would be a waste of time and money to teach them. Bender, however, contested this reasoning on the grounds that she, a woman, was already competently performing one of the jobs in question. 'Hey, I do it!,' she exclaimed. 'Some men can do it and some men can't. Some women can do it and some women can't.' Angered by the company's actions, Bender called in a Human Rights Officer to investigate. After looking into the case, Investigating Officer Colm Caffrey, of the Ontario Department of Labour concluded that GM had no right to exempt jobs. Only the Department of Labour could grant an exemption, he noted. He further stated that although the jobs were undesirable with regard to shifts and working conditions, this was not sufficient reason to grant an exemption as it would deny access to qualified and interested women.[28]

In 1975 the new GM battery plant became the site of an even more contentious sex discrimination case. The plant employed 258 workers and supervisors, including ten women. It had been operating at 65 per cent capacity for about one month. In November GM closed the plant for two days in order to conduct a 'lead-oxide clean-up.' According to Jim Hamilton, GM director of public relations, lead-oxide readings outside the plant were satisfactory, but inside they were unacceptable.[29] Paul Larkin, Local 222 health and safety representative, also confirmed high lead readings in twenty-nine workers, ranging 'from borderline to ... dangerously high.' Steve Nimigon, Local 222 secretary-treasurer, called this 'a scary situation, not only for the men inside the plant but for their families.'[30]

The industrial processing of lead in the battery plant had long been a health and safety concern because of the potential accumulation of lead in workers' bodies. Such an accumulation could result in lead poisoning and various related disorders. Disturbance and damage to the blood, digestive system, nervous system, cardiovascular system (heart and circulatory system), and urinary system were among the potential health problems. There was also evidence that exposure to lead could cause damage to a fetus.[31]

In November 1975 GM suddenly acted on the latter finding. Without warning, a company spokesperson announced that 'any woman of child-bearing capabilities shall no longer be employed on jobs which continually expose them to lead oxide.'[32] Company officials then produced a letter that offered medical evidence to support their decision, and they notified the union that they would shortly transfer the women out of the plant. As well, a GM spokesperson claimed that recent research at Johns Hopkins University confirmed that continued exposure to lead oxide could be harmful to a human fetus.[33]

GM stipulated that women who wished to remain in the plant must present a medical certificate verifying they could not bear children. Few of the women, however, could provide such evidence. As a result, seven of the ten women were forced to move to other departments. All but one of these workers received a pay increase in their new jobs, and one woman's rate was unchanged. After proving to the company that they were not fertile, three women were permitted to remain in the plant.[34]

Fay Bender and May Partridge retained their jobs because they were past childbearing age. Yet along with their female co-workers, Bender and Partridge were angered by the company's actions. Bender had been employed in the battery plant for five years prior to this incident, and she claimed that GM had never before acted on this medical evidence.[35] Furthermore, she had proof that the letter advising the company not to employ women in the plant was dated 16 June 1969. Bender wanted to know why GM did not heed this warning until 1975, when ten women were working in the department. In her view the company was reacting primarily to the increased number of females in the plant rather than to a general concern about the women's reproductive health.[36]

Bender's suspicions were fuelled when supervisors later requested that she too transfer out of the plant after a high lead count was found in her urine.[37] Her count had not been high in the past, and this sudden change confused her. She was especially puzzled because the test was conducted immediately after a ten-day Christmas break, during which she had been out of the plant. The company agreed to test her once more, but Bender also went to a laboratory for an independent test. The independent test showed her usual count, while GM's test again indicated an unacceptably high reading. This discrepancy prompted Bender to approach the GM superintendent and threaten to relate the incident to television stations across Canada. After this encounter, her lead count suddenly 'went down and there was no more talk of moving her out of the plant ... It was just another ploy to get a female out of the battery plant,' she maintained.[38]

With growing concern about GM's actions, Bender, Partridge, and others also did some research on their own and learned that lead oxide was hazardous to men as well as women. Indeed, after hearing about these findings, some men chose to leave the department because of the possible health risks to themselves and their families.[39] The women felt that by singling them out, GM was practicing sex discrimination. 'It means equal rights,' one battery plant worker asserted.[40]

By December six women had requested a transfer from the plant, though they did not all go willingly. Some women liked their jobs and, for various reasons, did not wish to leave. For example, Norma James, a thirty-four-year-old separated mother of four, recognized that she was on 'the filthiest job in the place,' but she preferred the 11:00 p.m. to 7:00 a.m. shift in the plant because it enabled her to spend time with her children.[41] Revealing her strong desire to remain on the job, in December 1975 James underwent a tubal ligation.[42] The company had transferred her to a daytime job in the north plant, but she was unhappy with this arrangement.[43] 'If you want your job badly enough you'll do anything,' she commented.[44]

Some union leaders argued that a woman should have the right to decide for herself, if she wished to bear children. Local 222 president Abe Taylor, claimed that women should even exercise the right to take a risk.[45] The implications of these arguments roused much media attention and public commentary.[46] Labour Minister, Bette Stephenson, publicly declared that, as a physician, she recommended that the women leave the plant. Stephenson added that this 'very well could turn into a case concerning the rights of the unborn,' and she praised GM for being 'reasonably astute and medically responsible.' Similarly, Attorney General, Roy McMurtry claimed that although GM's actions 'could be [considered] paternalistic ... an employer has a responsibility to protect its employees.' 'It's not an answer for a woman to say she's prepared to take that risk. It's up to the employer to protect them from such foolishness,' McMurtry declared. 'They may say they aren't going to have children, but they could change their mind. Then what?'[47]

On behalf of the women Local 222 leaders launched a policy grievance against General Motors, charging the company with violating the workers' transfer rights, seniority rights, and wage rights under the local and master agreements. Two women workers also filed personal grievances against GM, claiming discrimination with regard to their seniority rights. In December 1975 Abe Taylor stated that the union would proceed with the grievance until the company could prove that lead oxide is dangerous to the fetus. Until this time they would maintain that GM was wrong to transfer the women.[48]

Seven women from the battery plant also filed charges of sex discrimination against the firm with the Ontario Human Rights Commission,[49] and on 2 December 1975 the commission began its official investigation into the company's possible contravention of Section 4(1) (C) (e), (f), and (g) of the Ontario Human Rights Code, R.S.O. 1970, c.318, as amended. The women rested their complaint on the company's application of this requirement to women only.[50] In November 1976 the commission made its ruling. The commissioner concluded that the issues 'appeared to be medical in nature' and therefore 'do not embrace discrimination within the meaning of the provisions' of the Ontario Human Rights Code. On this basis he advised the Minister of Labour not to appoint a board of inquiry and closed the files on this case. However, he added that insofar as medical evidence indicates that injury to the fetus may result when either mother or father is exposed to these conditions, 'either directly or indirectly,' both sexes 'should be protected against the possibility of exposure.'[51]

In December 1979, four years after the women filed their grievances, an arbitrator, E.E. Palmer, ruled on the union's complaints. Palmer claimed that discrimination must be made on the basis of sex in relation to matters that are not relevant to employers' legitimate interests. And on the basis of medical evidence, he believed that the company's policy was 'clearly reasonable.' In his view,, 'the mere fact that such a policy merely affects females *per se* does not make such a step "discriminatory."' 'In some areas,' he stated, 'there are distinctions between the sexes and one can think of no more obvious such difference than in relation to the procreative function.' He furthermore believed that the lead exposure posed a greater danger to fertile women than to men who are capable of procreation. On these grounds he dismissed the grievances. However, he too added that men should be permitted to refuse such work without fear of discipline as it is reasonable to believe that the work is unsafe.[52] After these disputes were 'resolved,' only a few women worked in the battery plant. In 1991 only one woman was employed in this department.[53]

At issue in these cases is not the validity of the workers' or company's arguments.[54] The politics of the debate itself are informative. Women's use of the concept of sex discrimination and their mobilization of feminist ideologies reveal a revised strategy of workplace resistance. These protests stand in contrast to those launched by women during the Second World War. During the war, wage-earning women addressed perceived injustices in covert ways, and the form of their resistance was strongly shaped by conventional feminine culture and patriarchal ideologies. In comparison, throughout the 1970s, the women used legislative means to directly challenge discriminatory treatment on the basis of sex. Significantly, they defined sexual discrimination as a failure on the part of management to treat women and men in identical ways.

The union's support, albeit cautious, of the women's claims is also telling.[55] The battery plant incident marked the first time in the union's history that union representatives incorporated 'sex discrimination' and 'gender equality' in their shop-floor (bargaining) vocabulary. As seen in the last chapter, early collective agreements contained a 'no-discrimination' clause, but in practice sex-based seniority rights and job classifications nullified it. Thus, beliefs and convictions aside, union representatives had little chance of winning a sex discrimination case. With the elimination of the word 'female' from contracts, sex discrimination became a legitimate ground for complaint. Union leaders were therefore more receptive to utilizing the concept in bargaining for shop-floor gains. In this sense, women's new legal-contractual rights reshaped the framework of labour's struggle.

Though less dramatically, women also drew on these new rights and arguments to resolve nagging day-to-day disputes. For example, when GM supervisors forbade them to wear shorts or pedal-pushers in spite of unbearably hot temperatures in the plant, twenty-five women in the wire and harness department went home, rolled up their pants (few of them owned a pair of genuine pedal-pushers) and returned the following day in the prohibited attire. 'We phoned the press and the TV and radio, and we all came together at the gate,' recalled Maurie Shorten, an organizer of this protest.[56] Some union men even joined in their picket,[57] and when the GM security guard turned the protesting workers away from the plant, they 'all went down to the union hall and played cards.' At one o'clock in the afternoon the company called and asked them to return to work. 'They never put another clothing restriction on us from then,' said Shorten.[58]

In the 1970s women auto workers similarly resolved the enduring conflict over headgear. Betty Murray proudly proclaimed that she never wore a hairnet when she worked at GM. When management declared that all women must wear hairnets, the outspoken Murray retorted, 'Oh is that right?! Well, this is interesting.' Aware of her equal rights under both the union contract and the law, she stated, 'I want this man here to put one on, I want him to put one on, and I want him to put one on, and I want all these other guys ... ' Her supervisor responded, 'Oh no, it's only women.' Murray replied, ' "Oh? Is there something different about my hair and that guy?" "Oh ya. It's longer." "Only for the next three hours it's gonna be longer. I'll see you tomorrow morning." By geez, my hair was just like it is right now [short]. I said, "Now, who's gonna wear the hairnets?!" The introduction of bandanas caused men to dash to look up the Industrial Safety Act, reported May Partridge. Partridge told them, 'Sorry boys, hair is hair no matter who is wearing it.'[59]

At roughly the same time GM employee Dora Hildebrand raised this issue in St Catharines. Hildebrand steadfastly refused to wear a bandana. Every time she came without a bandana the foreman sent her home, recalled co-worker Doris Lepitsky.

She'd come back the next day without a bandana, he'd send her home again. He'd send her home four days in a row. And she fought and she fought ... [The other women] were kind of laughing at her. And I said, 'Well, what are you laughing at her for?' I said, 'She's good. She can fight for us.' ... She always used to say ... 'Look at that man, he's got hair up to here and he hasn't got a bandana. Why should I?' And we were all even then. Men and women got the same wages. And that's where it all started. Till a man put a bandana on, she wouldn't put a bandana on ... She was suspended for two weeks without pay, but she still fought. And then the girls used to say, 'Oh, I don't know why she always wants to call the union man, she knows she can't win.' But then when she won, the first day when she won ... everybody came without a bandana.

WOMEN AS WORKERS, WIVES, AND MOTHERS

Reflecting the continually changing nature of feminist demands, in the 1970s women's struggles also became broader in scope. Female unionists advocated equal pay for work of equal value,[60] access to the male-dominated skilled trades,[61] establishment of a UAW women's scholarship program,[62] the elimination of protective legislation for women,[63] policies regarding sexual harassment,[64] fair pensions for women,[65] and improved maternity leave provisions.[66]

At the April 1970 UAW Constitutional Convention union women called for 'full equality now.'[67] These few words accurately describe their agenda throughout this decade. Recognizing that they were affected not only by what happened on the shop floor, but also by the social organization of private households and the wider society, women unionists moved towards a critique of gender inequality in its various forms and in different sites of social relations.

Like feminists in the broader women's movement, union women identified their multiple and intersecting roles and responsibilities[68] (see Adamson, Briskin, and McPhail, 1988). For example, at the Canadian UAW Women's Conference in 1971 a sister Peggy Buchanan declared, 'If we could bring equality into the home where men would share the housework and care of the children, it would allow women to fulfill career potentials and make the men something besides just breadwinners to their children.'[69] Similarly, Betty Murray stated, women 'had trouble at work, but they had trouble at home too. One went with the other.' 'A man works eight to ten hours a day. A woman works 24 hours a day.' According to Pat Creighton, 'Nothing changed when the woman came home. She still got to keep all the housework. The only thing that changed was that she was bringing money home. So therefore he had more money to go out doing a little bit of partying, doing a little bit more fishing. Because I'm sure maybe ten percent of the population of men helped around the house, but the other 90 per cent nothing changed for them, except they got liberated in the pocket book ... It's no damn fun to come home and do it all. And this is after you put eight hour shift in and there he is slugging back beer or watchin' TV, sayin' "That's your job." '

'Women all over the world are experiencing a new consciousness of their rights, status, and of themselves as persons,' declared Director Caroline Davis of the UAW-CIO Women's Department, before the Ninth Annual Canadian Women's Conference in 1972. She cited women's efforts to establish paid child care as a prime example of this change.[70] In addition to promoting the child's welfare, union women advocated child care for women's own well-being. Furthermore, they criticized day-care schemes that overlooked the needs of factory employees who worked rotating shifts.[71] These women long 'fought for babysitting in the workplace,' recalled Betty Murray. 'They wanted some kind of a system where they could bring their kids to work and not be worried. They could go down there at lunch time and see how they are ... They fought and fought for that.'

Some UAW women also put birth control and women's reproductive rights on their agenda.[72] Pat Creighton recalled sitting in Ottawa in a committee room during their campaign for equal rights. A female physician got up and 'said if that Pill was meant for men, it still wouldn't be on the market. They'd still be testing it ... That was another side effect from the Women's Committee ... It just branched out! And the women started thinking, it wasn't just in the workplace that they were abusing us. All the young women we knew were taking these birth control pills.' Creighton celebrated this process of expansion. 'It's like you open one door and then another door opens and somebody remembers another group of women and it just kind of snowballs and that's exactly what happened.'

In May 1970 the Local 222 Women's Committee publicized the 'abortion caravan' that was travelling across Canada, advocating the legalization of abortion.[73] Maurie Shorten, chair of the original Local 222 Women's Committee, even established an abortion referral service. For fifteen years she ran an advertisement in the local union newspaper for a doctor in Buffalo who ran a legal clinic. Abortions were then illegal in Canada. 'I used to get all kinds of calls, she said. 'We had to get it [the ad] through the [union] executive board. Well, it wasn't easy, but we got it in. And then the "Right to Life" ... came ... and they got their ad in the Oshaworker too ... There were [GM] guys calling about their girlfriends. And women. The Oshaworker goes into the homes, so there'd be married women who got the Oshaworker. I had people call me a murderer.'

Union leaders furthermore called on union women to involve themselves in party politics. 'How much power do you women have in the New Democratic Party?,' American UAW Representative Olga Madar asked a delegation of sisters in Canada. 'The NDP is not going to be successful unless it does involve women to a greater extent,' she stated. 'We have to give leadership in the political processes of the government and the union.'[74] The UAW also stepped up its campaign for women's legal rights.[75] In addition to employment standards, women promoted more egalitarian marriage and divorce legislation[76] and more stringent laws regarding the abuse of women and children.[77] Some members of the Local 222 Women's Committee were personally involved in efforts to aid battered women. They also helped establish a local rape crisis centre and drug and alcohol treatment programs for women.[78]

'The women's revolution will be a mistake, if we just make it from our own standpoint,' declared Olga Madar. 'We must open doors of opportunity for families to participate.'[79] 'We do not agree with every tenet of different women's groups, but we must work together on basic principles.'[80] GM employee Laura Saunders stated, 'As time kept going, you know, the women started getting more open and stronger. And they would stick together more and pay attention to a lot of what was going on around them. And I think just everything in general. The women were changing, the world outside around you was changing, the work was changing, and things in life got to be where a lot more women had to stay working and go to work, that the women had to start to stand up for what they wanted to do and make them known – make themselves heard.'

Though these changes seemed explosive in the 1970s, their emergence was gradual, occurring over the course of many decades. Women's consciousness of their oppression as a sex came out of a shared history of struggle, a struggle that began years ago, and was shaped by developments both within and beyond the plant. The development of a feminist consciousness is an ongoing process. By the 1970s groups of female auto workers not only recognized their sexual subordination, but also came to share a vision and a strategy for collectively ending their oppression.

While only a minority of women were activists, others were not untouched by the politics of the women's movement. 'Union-wise' feminists had educated their sisters in various ways and degrees. Even women who clung to conventional beliefs and arrangements modified their strategies and filtered them through new ideas. In many women, elements of feminism coexisted (uneasily) with patriarchal ideologies.

THE SECOND STAGE OF STRUGGLE

This uneasy coexistence of feminism and patriarchy is most clearly reflected in women's and men's daily interactions. Just as women formally negotiated gender equality through the grievance procedure and the legislative process, they had to informally bargain their relationships with men on the shop floor. However, in spite of legal-contractual changes and bolder assertions of women's rights, conventional gender ideologies and gendered strategies continued to define these relationships. Equal contractual rights were necessary, but not sufficient to redress inequalities. Friendships and acquaintances were especially resistant to change. Both women and men frequently resorted to old and familiar responses in day-to-day living. Moreover, guided by the union ethos of solidarity and uniformity UAW women bargained equal (identical) rights with male workers, but they did not restructure the workplace and union to accommodate gender difference.

When women entered the men's departments after roughly seventy years of strict gender segregation, 'it was a novelty.' 'Men had ruled the roost for so many years. It was an absolute novelty,' commented Pat

Creighton. Not all men welcomed this change. As women joined them at work, many men clung strongly to exclusive gender ideologies. In contrast to their bemused indifference and respectful paternalism towards women workers during the war years, in the 1970s some men were strongly disrespectful, if not blatantly hostile. After struggling for equal contract rights, 'you got a men's attitude,' said Martha Cox, 'that is something else again.'

Some men supported women and helped them adapt to the new jobs. For example, in 1971 GM employee Louise Urie stated, 'The fellows are really nice guys. By the time I got here, they were used to the women.'[81] Most women, however, recalled that many men strongly resisted their entry into 'male departments.' As Cox's remark implies, the lines of conflict were clearly drawn by sex. Men whose wives worked in the plant tended to avoid debates about the appropriateness of females in men's jobs, but on the whole, men's attitudes on this issue did not vary by class, race, ethnicity, age, or marital status. The only significant difference was that male supervisors had greater resources than workers to control women's experience of work.

Supervisors 'tried everything possible' to resist the movement of women into men's departments, recalled May Partridge. Initially, they placed women on 'preferred jobs' on the motor line in the chassis plant, rather than take the low seniority person out. According to union representative Ted Murphy, management knew that this would upset the male workers, and he firmly believed that they did this to obstruct the smooth integration of women through the plant. The women themselves understood it was wrong, said Murphy, and eventually they straightened it out with the company.

Much of management's resistance to women, however, was more directly punitive. Auto workers were highly aware of the 'good' and 'bad' jobs in the plant, evaluations that were largely based on light/heavy, dirty/clean, and fast/slow dichotomies (see Game and Pringle, 1983: chapter 1). In what the women perceived as a retaliatory act, GM supervisors placed women on excessively heavy or dirty jobs that few men themselves could or would perform.[82] Phyllis Yurkowski called these 'the nasty jobs.' According to Yurkowski, men were 'upset that equal rights had come in and ... that was their revenge.' When she moved to the plastics department in GM, her boss put her to work on a machine lifting great big grills. 'Oh, I'm telling you,' she exclaimed, 'they wouldn't allow you to stop the machine ... They put you right on and these grills, oh my God! When you're used to doing small stuff, these grills, they might be ten pounds!' Her husband, also a GM employee, believed that they weighed fifteen or twenty pounds.

Similarly, Margaret Heritz recalled that the company hired three new workers in one department. These included a six-foot-two-inch man weighing about 200 pounds, a sturdy five-foot-eight-inch man, and a petite, five-foot, 100-pound woman. In Heritz's view the foreman spitefully placed the woman on a job in which she had to dip objects that weighed roughly twenty-one pounds. At the same time, he placed the burly man in a corner on a stool doing detailed work. Although he criticized the woman for dropping the heavy items, the foreman insisted that she remain on it. The next morning he put her on the same job. The third day she was on it again. In the meantime, the large man on the stool was extremely dissatisfied with his job in the corner.

Some foremen also increased the pace on women's machines even when they were already working harder than the men. 'They didn't do that to the men, but to me they did it,' recalled one worker. 'And they knew they could get away with it.' This woman furthermore believed that some union representatives colluded with management in these schemes. 'I called the committeeman but they didn't do nothing,' she said. 'He knew that they were speeding the machine up and they were doing it to me because I was a woman. But he wouldn't come and fight the case.'

Union women were especially dismayed that many of their UAW brothers participated in these acts of sabotage. 'That's your fellow workman that's doing that to you. It's not management,' Betty Murray exclaimed. Working men did not have the authority to place women on undesirable jobs, but they could make shop-floor life difficult for women in other ways. For instance, a union representative agreed with the company's decision to place Fay Bender, a high-seniority employee, in the exclusively male and undesirable battery plant. Bender criticized the union more harshly than management for this decision. 'I still blame the chairman of the bargaining committee,' she stated. 'When he told me where I was going, he laughed.' Although she grew to like the work, Bender was displeased with the manner in which she was placed on the job.

In the battery plant Bender was required to lift boxes of small parts onto a table. A male workmate, however, overfilled the boxes so that she would have trouble carrying them. She tolerated the situation until two other men in the department complained that the boxes were so overloaded that *they* too could not lift them. Like other women, Bender felt that as a pioneer in the department, she had to prove her competence.

'I wouldn't complain,' she said, 'because he was doing this because of *me.'*

Many men punished women by applying equality to the letter. Rose Taylor encountered the same tactic of overloading boxes at the GM plant in St Catharines. 'When they first come out with this idea of equal rights and equal pay, there was a little bit of friction,' she explained. Men's antagonism even extended to those women who remained in traditional female jobs. On one work operation for example the men had always helped the women by lifting big boxes onto the conveyor line. But after the law changed, they said sardonically to their female co-workers, 'Well, you can lift them yourself ... well, equal rights.'

Some male workers also deliberately taught women to perform jobs incorrectly, neglected to give them vital information about work operations, and were generally uncooperative and aloof. 'Some of the guys were pretty good,' noted Laura Saunders, 'but others, they weren't very easy to get to know and they weren't all that friendly. They stuck together kind of in their own clan.' 'We had some fellas in the shop who used to make it rough for us,' recalled Bev McCloskey. 'They used to put signs all over. They'd be over fightin' with us all the time. That women can't do our job. "You can't do this." And they had signs up like, "Mafia" and "lesbians." And they would wreck our machines. They would pull some real dirty ones. And we had some awful fights with them, you know, some really bad fights with some of the men in the shop. They'd yell, "That feminist! Get away from that feminist."'

Women responded to this treatment in various ways. Some women resorted to old strategies, rather than prove their worth on equal terms. 'There's always some people that'll play the game,' McCloskey explained. In the past women often had had to 'play up to the foreman' in order to survive on the shop floor, and they continued to use this tactic because certain men favoured it.[83] Using gender and sexuality as a strategic resource, they would utter, 'I can't do this. I can't do that,' until surrounding men performed the more arduous tasks for them. 'Well that's a lot of crap,' said McCloskey. Female union activists frowned on this behaviour and implored the women to avoid it. May Partridge recalled, 'We said to them, "You can't have preferential treatment. If they put you on a job and you honestly can't do it then they have to offer you two more jobs ... Don't injure yourself trying to lift or do anything ... but you can't expect to do half of the job with some man running and picking stuff up for you and doing half of the job for you." ' 'Sometimes you had to give them a good talking to,' claimed Margaret Heritz.

Other women, however, stoically proved their competence on difficult tasks, even when there was no immediate need to do so. For example, when the supervisor in the battery plant placed May Partridge on a strenuous job on a large machine she was determined to succeed. One well-meaning observer said to her, 'Why don't you ask the boss to take you off this job? It's too hard for you.' She replied, 'I'll never ask to be off it.' When he said, 'You're going to make a good lookin' corpse,' she stated, 'Well, I'm gonna stick it out.' She 'stuck it out' for about three weeks until the supervisor decided to move her. At the time he assured her that she was 'doing fine,' but he later admitted that he could not stand to watch the way she was 'running to do the job.' In any case, shortly after this incident GM automated the work operation.

In the process of demonstrating their competence to men, many women also proved something to themselves as they grew accustomed to the physical demands of the jobs. 'You can do lots of things that you think you can't do,' stated Bev McCloskey. 'The first job they gave me was the heaviest, dirtiest job you could find. I'm this tall and there's a guy six foot something and he's puttin' little screws in the bag and I'm lifting the big bumpers, fenders. And I had to do it otherwise the other women couldn't follow me ... Every night I would just get in the car and I thought I would be [too] tired even to drive home. And it kept up like this for about the first month. And then my muscles got tightened up. And I started using the muscles I've never used before. And hell! I could do it like nothin'. And it was funny that we all found this out after, eh. It's just that we were usin' different muscles.'

In the women's view, men resisted sexual integration for various reasons. Some working men viewed women as competitors for desirable jobs. A woman who worked in McKinnon Industries during the 1940s and early 1950s encountered this idea when she returned to the plant in the mid-1970s. Margaret Heritz stated that male workers resented her when she came back, though they did not display such feelings before she left. Someone had spread a rumour that she had high seniority, and because women and men were equal under the contract, they believed that she would be replacing a more junior man.

Many working men, furthermore, disapproved of women's diligent work habits.[84] According to Betty Murray, some men said, 'We've got it pretty good and we want to keep it that way. That's why we're not in a hurry to have too many women come in here. When they come in, they're ruined. They go like hell.'

Insofar as male supervisors as well as workers attempted to exclude women from their departments, however, men's fears of labour market competition only partly explain the gender dynamics of this period. Socialist-feminists argue that working men and employing men both have an interest in maintaining a traditional breadwinner family, though often for different reasons (see Hartmann, 1979, 1976; Rose, 1986). As women became a more viable force in the industry, men advocated this family model more strongly and loudly than in the past. 'They were in that male attitude, the women's place is in the home, the man is the boss ... and all this kind of crap,' said Bev McCloskey. Although some men contested this ideology, they were drowned out by those who supported it. 'You need more men taking a look and saying, "Geez, they don't just give birth to children. They're breadwinners too," remarked another woman. Women commented extensively on the pervasiveness of these beliefs after 1970.

All you could hear was, 'Don't know why these women don't stay home. They don't need the jobs. They're coming in here and taking men's jobs.' I'd say fifty per cent of the men had that attitude ... If their wives worked in the Motors, they didn't.

Men were mad that they got equal pay for equal work! Oh, they were mad! They didn't like that. They were mostly complaining on the women's lib. They said, 'This women's lib is going to ruin the world' ... a woman's place is in the home.'

Men were geared to think that women had a place at home in the kitchen, cooking and baking and cleaning house and washing and ironing ... And a lot of men didn't feel that the women should be working outside the home ... And so with that atmosphere in the mind of the ordinary workers ... that same idea was in the mind of the bosses ... They felt that women didn't belong.

Undoubtedly, the idea of a male breadwinner figured prominently in men's desire to exclude women. Yet, despite its strength and persistence, this ideology was not necessarily rooted in a single and uniform logic. Rather, men often drew on culturally dominant beliefs selectively, in order to legitimize their different interests over time. We can thus observe variations in the degree of men's resistance to women, as well as in their adherence to conventional domestic ideology.

By the 1950s male workers and supervisors tended to accept married women in the industry as long as they remained in 'women's departments.' Even when women auto workers secured high pay rates through the piece work system, few men were antagonistic towards them. Men's attitudes notwithstanding, by the 1970s economic conditions ensured that few workers could exist on the wages of one breadwinner. It was an impractical arrangement even for relatively highly-paid auto workers.

If a desire to preserve the male-breadwinner family was the exclusive or primary motive of men, we should observe stronger and more consistent male opposition to the employment of married women in the industry as a whole. Moreover, if men's actions were inspired by a genuine desire to keep wives in the home, they should have directed their hostility towards married women specifically. During this period, however, men rarely distinguished between different categories of women in practice. When foremen placed women on excessively heavy jobs and when working men sabotaged women's machines, they did not separate women who were married from those who were widowed, divorced, or single. They were hostile to all women.

Men's beliefs in a male-breadwinner family and a family wage strategy, and their fears of female competition for scarce jobs do not fully explain their reactions. A contextual analysis of their behaviour suggests that these responses were shaped by another dimension of patriarchy – the subjective (see Fox, 1987). Gendered subjectivity is an important element of both women's and men's emotional composition. In particular, it shapes their consciousness as workers and mediates their experience of the labour process. Just as femininity and feminine culture had important implications for the gendered division of wage labour and women's experience of auto work, masculinity, too, played an important part in shaping men's workplace experiences.

Numerous researchers have discussed the links between masculine subjectivity and wage labour (for example, Baron, 1991; Blewett, 1991; Cockburn, 1983; Dunk, 1991; Game and Pringle, 1983; Lewchuk, 1993; Willis, 1979). The breadwinner function, they claim, is an integral component of the cultural construction of a 'masculine' man. Reflecting male privilege and exclusiveness, it represents a means by which a man can secure dignity, worth, and a gender identity. Yet, for most men, the alienating nature of work undermines this equation. As a result, men attempt to maintain at least a limited sense of power and control by reinforcing the gendered division of employment (Game and Pringle, 1983: 22–3). Segregated work arrangements in this sense meet an emotional need in men. In the auto industry, men drew on the widely accepted and familiar ideology of the male breadwinner to express a general disdain for women's entry into their domain. Many women recognized this. Rose Taylor, for instance, explained that after 1970 the men were 'frightened because ... they had always had their place ... and the women couldn't touch it.' Similarly, Laura Saunders stated, 'They made it very, very difficult for some of the girls to do the work ... They felt like we were intruding on their territory, I guess. And it took a long time for them to get used to us.'

Men furthermore used sexuality in an effort to maintain a sense of masculine dominance in the workplace. Sexuality became a tool of masculine aggression against women. It provided the cultural content of men's gendered strategy. While the expression of heterosexuality had long been a part of the culture of auto plants, in the 1970s, it was conveyed with hostility, in ways that highlighted the sexual subordination of both female supervisors and workers. When higher management placed three female supervisors in GM's north plant, male workers and supervisors resisted violently. 'The men just did not want them. That's all there was to it,' related Jane McDonald. Angered, they went to a higher authority in the firm and said, 'You get that woman out of this department or we'll throw her out the window.' Men 'really gave them a rough run,' recalled Pat Creighton. 'Not just the company, but the union guys, too. Oh, they used to make fun of Alice's boobs ... They used to call her Miss Titsy and just general crap like that.' After four or five weeks, one of the women had had enough of their insolence and quit. 'She just said, "Fine, I'll go back on the floor."'

As noted, in the 1970s men seldom distinguished between different categories of women. In all women, they viewed sexuality as a salient feature. When two women joined a male workforce in GM's plant 2 in St Catharines, the men said they welcomed this change because a 'whiff of perfume ... makes the shift seem lighter.'[85] Likewise, in featuring a woman who worked beside men on the line in the Oshawa plant, a local newspaper stated that she remained 'very womanly,' in spite of her job.[86] Men also frequently commented on the women's physical appearance, observing fluctuations in weight, assessing the size of breasts, fetishizing the female body.

The objectification of women was not new. In the 1940s and 1950s, men brought sexualized images to the shop floor in an effort to cope with the inhumanity of the labour process and affirm sexual identity. 'They'd have all kinds of pictures in their toolboxes. Whole toolboxes lined with it,' explained Margaret Heritz. However, 'they didn't leave them open or anything.' Someone might, for instance, 'pass a deck of cards around that had all, you know, everything on them ... [But] you didn't have to look at 'em.' In those years, the women 'didn't really find any pin-ups and that.' In the 1960s the men pinned up posters of Marilyn Monroe in the plants. A 1961 issue of the company publication GM Topics featured men's toolbox lids. 'Most toolbox owners jealously guard their tool chest lids,' the article read. 'The reason why some toolbox owners guard their lids is because lids betray them. A glance inside and you know their families, sports, hobbies, heroes, enemies – women. Young men and those who like to think they are young go in for femmes fatales in all kinds of poses ... Middle-aged men had snap shots of their experiences ranging from the Second World War to their last moose hunting trip. Some family men had photographs of their wives and children ... No matter how greasy a toolbox may get, familiar faces pasted to it seem to make the job more pleasant.' Some men who had lockers plastered them with life-size pin-ups.[87]

After women entered their departments men's representation of women became increasingly narrow and nasty. Some men plastered their work areas with pictures of naked women or women in g-strings,[88] images that women workers found far more offensive than the swimsuit-clad starlets of the 1940s, 1950s, and 1960s. In comparing the old GM cutting room with the 'men's' departments in the 1970s, Phyllis Yurkowski said, before 'everybody was a big happy group. Everything was so respectful. [But] now, oh, I'm telling ya, it's wicked.' Some men also brought in pornographic magazines and ensured that the women viewed them. 'You'd go up to check their work and [they would say], "Hey, look at this,"' Yurkowski recollected.

'ROLLING WITH THE PUNCHES': MASCULINITY ON THE SHOP FLOOR

Despite the legal-contractual changes, the shop-floor culture in the auto plants was not radically transformed. Instead, women tried to adapt to the masculine work setting. Most women pretended to ignore men's sexist comments and horseplay by 'laughing them off,' and they hoped that the hostility 'would just go away.'[89] According to May Partridge, 'If you just let it slide by, well, it lost something, so they didn't bother ... you had to roll with the punches. You couldn't be a parson's daughter because they would swear twice as much if they knew it bothered you ... They used to say it – the four letter word – and then apologize. I'd say don't apologize. I hear that every half hour ... They're not gonna change because there's a woman workin' amongst them. If you can't bury your head and say, well, I'm turning them off, let on it doesn't bother you even if it does, it's a lot better than trying to fight them because you'll never change them.' Laura

Saunders held the same philosophy: 'The guys would say smart things to you ... Some of it wouldn't even be repeatable. And you had to just, you know, prove yourself to some of these guys. And you had to be able to handle them in certain ways ... You had to do a lot of shop talk just like the guys ... You had to handle yourself.'

Although they did not genuinely accept this culture, many women tried to prove that they could be 'tough' in dealing with men. Some women placed great value on quick-wittedness and boasted about their individual acts of bravado. To some extent this strategy was necessary if they were to survive the shop floor. Fay Bender, for instance, stated, 'A lot of women have complained that the men used coarse language in front of them. They got a hassle. I blame a lot of it on the women themselves because they let them get away with it. If somebody started to hassle me, I would come back with some remark.'

Ridicule and mockery pervaded many of their verbal exchanges. For instance, Maurie Shorten remarked, 'I transferred down to Parts and Service into a male dominated job, and this one guy says to me, gode [*sic*] we're gettin some nice lookin women in here, I said, too god damn bad there weren't some nice lookin men.'[90] Dedicated union women such as Shorten were accustomed to this manner of exchange because they had long been involved in the labour movement. Shorten recalled, 'I never got too much flack as a woman going into a male job because most of these people knew me from being active in the union. I always answered them. If some guy says he wants to go to bed with you, you say you have ten times better at home. You can't let them get on to you. I have a foul mouth anyways, same as they do.'[91]

Other women, however, felt that they could not engage in such banter. Older and middle-aged women, in particular, resisted this style of inter-action. It was contrary to their gendered learning and cultural experience. Doris Lepitsky described these conversations as though she were an out-sider looking in. Both her observations and her analysis are telling. She stated that when women won equal rights with men, 'they figured, they [would] even talk like men. They use the four-letter word in there ... Not until they got equality, that's when they started being just as rough as men.

Phyllis Yurkowski also felt uneasy in her new work milieu. When one man continually swore at her and told her to 'get the heck out of there,' she complained to her foreman. But he merely remarked, 'This is equal rights. If you don't like it, be like the rest of the men. When the man swears, well, then just swear back.' However, Yurkowski could not employ this strategy. She stated in frustration and with resignation, 'I don't talk like that so I didn't. I had to just take it.' Women's complaints to management about the pin-ups and other offensive images rarely generated change. Management often forced the men to take them down, but in about a month they reappeared.[92] One worker recalled, 'Many high-seniority women remained in the wire and harness department and therefore did not have to adjust to this new shop-floor culture, but a lot of women back then ... didn't survive that pressure and they ended up quitting and going home – and staying at home.'

There is a tendency to assume that as women and men performed the same work side by side and sexual conflicts lessened in intensity, gender no longer defined the workplace. In the 1970s the shop floor did not become gender-neutral, however. Rather, women tried to conform to a masculine model. Bev McCloskey commented on this. 'We should have went for affirmative action and insisted, "We want our quota on every damn thing!" ... 'Cause we've got a different way of looking at things. Women look differently at things than men do ... different experiences, different feelings, we're the care-givers ... And I like thinkin' that we're like that, too.'

Over time, male resistance to female employees subsided somewhat. However, the women did not regain a sense of camaraderie at work. Consequently, many claimed that work in the men's departments was less enjoyable than in the past. Various trends resulting from changing labour-management relations and technical restructuring have influenced the experience of work over time but a number of women linked shop-floor experience to the gender composition of their work group. Pat Creighton, for example, stated:

It wasn't the same. The money was up ... It was gigantic, the difference in pay. But you lost that closeness. Like I say, it was a rare pregnancy and it was a rare shower, and it was a rare wedding. The family atmosphere left. Well, just before I retired in the battery, there was only three women. Fay retired and then I retired, and now there's only one woman ... After a while, you hunger for female conversation.

It's not a happy place. It's not a family place ... It died in the mid '70s ... When we worked the west plant [sewing room] and north plant [wire and harness], we had so much fun. There was days that you just hated to get home. And towards the end of my time at General Motors, I hated to go to work. I just hated it.

Rose Taylor similarly noted, 'The men were pretty good to work with ...

They were different ... I guess it's just that you didn't form the same friendships as you did with another girl. With a man, you'd be friendly with him, but it just wasn't the same, you know. You can't talk to a man like you would to a woman – more or less personal things. Where with a man you have to be more about the work ... There just wasn't that closeness ... It wasn't as easy going ... as when I first started there. It was more aggressive ... The atmosphere wasn't the same.' Thus, although women preferred the greater autonomy and relative laxity of men's departments, they could draw on fewer social rewards. In the past women's gender identity had fostered a cohesiveness. Their celebration of femininity and close bonds helped make work more tolerable and even enjoyable at times. Most importantly, it was the base on which they forged a particular, women-centred resistance.

AN ALLIANCE OF FEMINISM AND UNIONISM

Women fought long and hard for gender equality in both the union and industry. Throughout the 1970s, however, they felt the limits of change in both arenas. While UAW women drew on some of the resources of the larger women's rights movement, feminism and unionism emerged autonomously. At times, they even came into conflict and competed for people's loyalties and the material contributions of society. Because the UAW remained a patriarchal union whose leaders and members did not respect gender difference, female workers continued to face barriers. Just as they were constrained by the masculine environment in the plants, women auto workers encountered many restrictions in the union.

What was women's position in the official union structure? Throughout the 1960s and 1970s the UAW International and, on a lesser scale, the Canadian Regional office publicized the union's prominent stand in the fight for women's rights.[93] Indeed, the union's record is impressive. The UAW Canadian Region held its first women workers' conference in 1964, long before the Ontario Federation of Labour or the Canadian Labour Congress had established women's agencies. In addition, the UAW-CIO women's department testified at the U.S. Senate Hearings on equal pay legislation.[94] In 1970, furthermore, the union created a Canadian Women's Department to coordinate activities for the promotion of gender equality.

These policy statements and demands, however, must be contexualized. While impressive, they were often inconsistent with the practices and sentiments of many (male) union leaders at both the national and the local levels, as well as of the majority of the rank-and-file membership.[95]

Furthermore, even after they won equal contract rights and legal recourse to challenge sex discrimination, women remained on the periphery of union affairs.

Numbers are not always reliable indicators of political might, but they give a rough indication of the status of women in the union. In the 1970s there were still proportionately few women in union office, and, despite attempts to redress this imbalance, the union leadership moved little on this issue. Pressured by American UAW Executive Board member Olga Madar, in 1968 George Burt, UAW director in Canada, recommended that the union improve female representation on staff and hire a woman researcher in Canada.[96] However, later in the year, Dennis McDermott, Burt's successor, maintained that he would not appoint staff on the basis of gender, religion, or ethnic background. 'In my view,' he stated, 'there should be no essential difference in the treatment or the aspirations or the activity of a person in the labour movement because of sex differences ... I do not believe a strictly female suffragette-type movement within the trade union structure is the answer.' In defending his decision McDermott drew on liberal-democratic ideology, promoting equal opportunity and individual merit, ignoring the systemic nature of sexual inequality.[97]

Not to be deterred, female members repeatedly lobbied UAW leaders to appoint women to the UAW-CIO staff,[98] the regional office,[99] the International Executive Board, and the District Council. Some women even suggested that the union implement affirmative action to ensure female representation on local union executive boards.[100] Between 1970 and 1977 the number of women in the UAW Canadian Region rose from roughly 10,000 to 14,500.[101] Yet during these years delegates to women's conferences and meetings observed that most instructors were men,[102] there were no female 'Local Union Discussion Leaders,'[103] UAW leader Dennis McDermott was often absent from these forums, and his substitute speakers seldom discussed women workers' specific concerns.[104]

In 1973 less than 5 per cent of the female membership in Canada (60 out of 13,153) held office in their local union, there were ten women out of roughly 200 District Council delegates, and in the Toronto area there were only fourteen women out of a total of 274 persons on collective bargaining committees. In addition, out of a total of 900 UAW representatives, only seventeen were women.[105] Some women participated in union standing committees, but they were concentrated in consumer affairs, recreation, and women's committees. And while two women were appointed to the Canadian UAW staff in 1976, few had assumed decision-making positions.[106]

Some women claimed that they did not encounter resistance from men in their union locals,[107] but seasoned activists also warned delegates against being 'too optimistic.' 'Some locals don't even tell the members about the Women's Department Conference,' reported one woman.[108] Moreover, a delegate to the 1974 Canadian Women's Conference called the UAW a 'highly male organized group who generally like the status quo' and find women to be 'unacceptable speakers at their meetings.' A number of women also claimed that despite their best efforts, it was impossible for them to win union office. According to GM worker Pat Creighton, 'There's always been one or two women on the slate, but they're never up there in the position of power ... That's the way it's been. That's why you don't see women in the union hall ... It's an old boys' club.' Bev McCloskey echoed this sentiment, noting that there are 'not enough jobs to go around so the guys have got to keep them.' In her view, the only way women can achieve proportionate representation in elected union office is through affirmative action.

Local 222, she explained, was divided into two caucuses, each of which ran candidates on their slate. In order to stand a fair chance of being elected, individuals had to be supported by a caucus. Independent candidates had weak prospects. Though McCloskey was elected through the caucus system, she was an exception. She was an extremely dedicated unionist, long active in the union, and highly outspoken. McCloskey was a pioneer. Relatively few women have been elected since her cohort left the plant. 'We haven't had anyone – maybe on the recreation committee or something – but not in any decision making [positions] ... They won't give it to you,' she contended.

In short, because the legal-contractual changes of 1970 did not fundamentally alter the union, women workers had to continue to wage their struggles in a masculinized setting. This strategy involved many contradictions, and women activists handled the resulting tensions in three central ways. They tended to promote strict 'equality' as opposed to differential treatment based on sex. Many women rejected the label 'feminist' and denied any affiliation with the women's rights movement. Some women expressed ambivalence about separate organizing through local union women's committees.

'That was the concept back in those days – equal rather than preferential,' explained a CAW national representative. This was the philosophy of the old industrial unionism. Although they undoubtedly recognized that there were sex-based conflicts within the union membership and acknowledged women's distinct problems and interests, most union leaders and members maintained that the tenets of industrial unionism alone would eliminate gender-based inequalities. Women's experiences, however, had demonstrated that the general principles of equity and democracy could not achieve this end in a framework of systemic inequality. The seniority principle, democratic rule, and equal application of the collective agreement did not take into account women's subordinate position in society and their historically restricted status in industry.

Yet, when presented with a choice between workplace equality and gender-specific treatment based on difference in situation, most women accepted the dichotomy and strongly advocated the former. The women's gender consciousness was tempered by a keen awareness that their union brothers distrusted and resented the distinct status of a minority group. Auto worker Rose Taylor accurately captured this philosophy in stating, 'The union's more for equality. They won't split up men and women's issues. They're all union issues.' Union members were reluctant to say, 'The women have this issue and the men have that issue.' They preferred to say, 'We all have this issue.'

Consequently, throughout the 1970s just as they tried to demonstrate equal competence on the assembly lines, many women tried to prove that their goals were identical to those of men in the labour movement. This concern likely prompted a UAW member to tell women's conference delegates in 1973 that in order to get women on the Canadian UAW staff, they must form a coalition with men. 'Women's problems are men's problems,' the member stated emphatically. 'You should have specifically invited men here so you could show them that women's problems are men's problems.'[109] At a 1977 women's conference, a group of delegates similarly stated that women had taken on too many 'symbolic issues,' such as changing the name of the 'Workmen's' Compensation Board in British Columbia to 'Workers' Compensation. 'We should consider men allies, not antagonize them,' these women argued.[110] Conference delegates furthermore opposed the rare affirmative action proposal, stating that such a measure would endanger the union's seniority provisions. Why should other workers be penalized because of the companies' discriminatory hiring? was a question asked by American UAW representative Dorothy Meehan.[111]

This perspective also led women to accept the same terms of employment as men, and abandon all references to sex-based differences. For example, when women gained equal seniority rights, GM management decided to remove the stove and refrigerator from their lunch room. Managers reasoned that because the sexes had equal rights under the contract, women should receive identical treatment as men with respect to breaks and facilities. Local 222 Women's Committee chair May Partridge agreed with this view, stating, 'If this is in the interests of equality then I say we have a half-hour lunch break as the rest of GM.'[112] Likewise, in reference to legislation that forced companies to either let women leave work five minutes before midnight or provide them with transportation, Partridge argued that such a 'privilege' was undesirable if women wanted to achieve sexual equality and the respect of their brothers.

Most UAW leaders upheld the notion that 'differential' treatment was 'preferential' treatment or 'privilege.' If women want to 'lead' in the workplace and the union, they had better 'take off the gloves and lace,' advised a prominent union official. Gordon Wilson, then UAW Education Director in Canada, told a delegation of women unionists that they must 'assert' themselves. 'Don't look to be patronized, get in there and fight,' he advised.[113] Conference delegates repeatedly stated that women 'aren't aggressive enough.' 'If women respected themselves as much as men respect themselves, they wouldn't have any problems,' said one worker. Similarly, the American Caroline Davis told the Canadian women that 'timidity' shows a lack of self-respect. She added that 'men don't lack this respect toward themselves or other men.'[114] These comments were part of a pragmatic response to the women's situation, but they were also gender-biased. They championed an approach, a cultural style, that white men had long used in their struggles with management.

In March 1971 the Local 222 Women's Committee reported that although the 'general feeling ... is that Bill 83 [to amend the Ontario Human Rights Act] protects only females ... this is not the case. It is legislated to encompass both sexes ... As one of the girls ... stated, "We are not trying to beat you, just join you."'[115] Throughout these years, women repeated old ideas that they must be accepted as 'UAW members instead of female members' (my emphasis). Women hold office not because they are women, they said, but because they are qualified.[116] One worker explained, 'The problems for a man who is widowed with children, is [sic] the same problems a woman widowed or divorced or left with children. It's the same problem for a man or a woman ... Any problem that arises in the shop – it will be a problem for men and women.' American Dorothy Meehan of the UAW International Women's Department advised female unionists in Canada, 'Know your men, your contracts and then run for office.'[117]

In this restrictive context, most women furthermore denied that they held 'feminist' ideas and loyalties. While they had drawn on some of the principles and strategies of the women's movement and allied themselves with self-proclaimed feminists in the community, many women activists in the UAW declared that they were not feminists. 'You had a couple on there that were feminists, [said a former member of the Women's Committee.] But other than that, no. It was just that we wanted equal rights ... The only involvement I ever had was through the union, trying to get the women in ... Other women's movements, no. I'd never been active in them. Some of them I don't believe in.' Another outspoken committee member asserted, 'That word feminist doesn't sit with me the way it should. I believe that every human being has a right to choices. But nothing to do with male or female. Every human being has a right to choice. And it doesn't matter that one time ... it could be a female and another day it could be a male.' Another female unionist stated that women's liberation was 'a stupid title and it turned off a lot of people.' According to this worker, 'It would have been better to have women's opportunity ... When you put liberation up, men have ... all these nightmares. Bev McCloskey and Maurie Shorten were among the few women to firmly and openly claim that they were feminists.

Given feminism's bad name, these denials at first seem unimportant, especially because they blatantly contradict the women's actions. However, on close inspection, their need to dissociate themselves with the popular concept of 'feminism' and espouse an alternative ideology is telling. Throughout the 1970s, and less noticeably in the late 1960s, women auto workers distinguished between 'equal rights' and 'feminism.' They furthermore promoted a goal of 'equality' as opposed to 'liberation.' May Partridge skilfully explained this distinction in a poem entitled 'Liberation – No ... Equality – Yes.'

We elected a committee
With one aim in mind
To equalize the contract
The solution we must find
In all the daily papers
Others worked toward the end
Of 'Liberating' women
By Eliminating men
This was not the purpose
WE gave up leisure time
By 'Eliminating' language
That kept us in a bind

In this 'JUST' society
It's a rarity to find
A deep concern for others
They haven't got the time
We accepted all the insults
And the apathy within
For our laid-off sisters
We had to fight to win
With the signing of the contract
One list upon the wall
All the laid-off females
Were first to get the call
In a strange environment
Receiving only praise
From a darkened corner
A protest's being made
They're getting all the cushy jobs
The easy ones to master
They are working slow
We are working faster
They hoped that in the morning
They wouldn't show again
For all those 'CUSHY' jobs,
for years,
Had been the lot of men
We're 'dubbed' a liberation group
We've heard it all before
At least without an escort
We can find the wash-room door
They made an observation
For they have eyes to see
They noticed there's a difference
Between a he and she
With Trudeau fighting labour
Employment on decline
A more constructive issue
Should occupy their mind
The law's been passed, accepted,
by this giant called G.M.
Our fight is far from over

Till we educate the men
We know our design is different
On this point we'll agree
We're not asking 'LIBERATION'
Just 'EQUALITY.'[118]

Female auto workers moved carefully and somewhat ambivalently between conventional womanhood, patriarchal unionism, and a working-
class feminism or feminist unionism.[119]

Just as they openly disaffiliated themselves from the feminism of the
women's rights movement, women unionists questioned the future of
local women's committees. This skepticism was rooted in both a lingering
fear that they would be penalized for waging a separate struggle from
their 'brothers' and an understanding that they might become ghettoized
within the union structure. Without secure access to UAW resources
women's concerns could easily be subsumed in the general labour struggle.[120] Thus, some women argued that they should become active in main-
stream union affairs and not isolate themselves in their own group.[121]

Upholding this belief, GM worker Pat Creighton firmly contended that,
after 1970, the Local Women's Committee 'should have died.' According
to Creighton, 'It should have been put to rest ... Then you would sit as
equal partners. But by givin' them the women's committee we were never
an equal partner ... Just take a little jaunt in the [union] hall and ask them
... When was the last time a female sat on the Executive?' Creighton
believed that women were vocal about issues that concerned them, but
'things pertaining to women didn't come up' at the general membership
meetings because they were left to the women's committee. Indeed, some
women unionists suggested renaming the committees 'workers' councils'
and calling the women's conference the 'labour equality conference.'[122]
After much debate, however, delegates to the 1977 UAW Women's Conference decided that such a change would defeat their original purpose.
Members of the Canadian UAW Women's Advisory Committee felt that
women should use the women's committee as a 'vehicle' to sustain their
'own identity' and that by renaming it they would be 'letting down' the
female membership.[123] In defence of the women's committee, an Ann
Bailey wrote,

You want to know what we do
We are trying not to wear a man's shoe
We are standing up for women's rights
To bring your problems to the light

No longer shall we sit back –
To feel that as women we all lack –
The ability to work and take a stand –
Shoulder to shoulder with a man –
All we want is an even share
You may find we make a good pair.[124]

Furthermore, shortly after their success in 1970 many original members resigned from the Local 222 Women's Committee. These women believed that they had achieved their most important goal, equality of opportunity under the contract. Pat Creighton recalled, 'I said, "Uh uh, not this girl." It's like General Motors and the union saying, "Now you girls, you've got the Women's Committee. Now be content with that." Auto worker Fay Bender also left the women's committee after the legislation was passed. Like Creighton, Bender felt that her job on the committee was done. 'What I was interested in at the time, was to change that law ... because there's jobs in the plant that some men are not capable of doing that job where another man is. So it would be the same thing. A female would go in, she might be capable of doing one particular job and another one she wouldn't be.' She was not sure what women's committee members did after 1970. Betty Murray was on the committee for approximately two years and then she became a supervisor in the GM parts plant in Woodstock, Ontario. One union man reported that the women's committee became more of a t-shirt selling collective than a viable political force. In 1972 there were reports that the members met every month but it was 'totally stagnant.'[125]

With equal seniority rights, some long-term women auto workers have been able to retain their jobs in a rapidly contracting labour market. In addition, the manufacturers hired a small number of women. In Bev McCloskey's view this is because women were good workers. She explained, 'The women could really do a job and they weren't goofin' off like the guys do ... [Management] could see that [they] were very good [lift truck] drivers, too. Very conscientious where guys are reckless.' Nevertheless, the sex ratio in the industry was not dramatically altered over the following two decades. There was more lateral movement within GM in Oshawa and St Catharines, the two plants that had always employed women, than female entry into the industry as a whole. In 1971 a Chrysler Canada official stated, 'We haven't had any applications by gals to work on the assembly line.' He claimed that Chrysler would comply with the new legislation, but added, 'You have to be half ape to do some of these jobs.' '[126] Similarly, a Ford representative stated that while the firm had not yet hired hourly rated women, it did not have a written policy against placing women on the assembly lines.[127] In 1976 Ford's Windsor plant employed 129 women (office workers) out of a total of 4,735 employees. By 1977 the company had still not hired women to work on the line. In 1979 GM's transmission plant in the Windsor area also remained male-dominated. There were only twenty-one female employees in this plant out of a total workforce of 1,166. In the GM chain the largest number of women worked in the relocated sewing and trim plant in Windsor. Here, 900 women employees out of a total workforce of 1,600 performed the work that women had long done in the Oshawa sewing room.[128]

Currently, small pockets of women work in departments that remain male-dominated. Dispersed in these masculine work settings, women have lost their own distinctive work culture of past years. The unity that existed among women who were concentrated in female departments, such as the sewing room and the wire and harness, has disappeared at General Motors. In some ways, job desegregation eroded the strong gender identity, women's culture, and sense of sisterhood that grew in exclusively female departments. These feelings had provided a base for women's political mobilization. Consequently, it is not surprising that after the original women's committee members stepped down, a new group of women did not enthusiastically take up where the early activists left off. After 1970 the local union women's committees lacked a clear vision and program. The next issue on the women's agenda should have been affirmative action in both the industry and the union, said Bev McCloskey. McCloskey, the mother of 'women's rights' in the Canadian UAW, maintained, 'You can't let your guard down. You let your guard down, you're forgotten. We used to say if you leave the room, you're forgotten.'

SUMMARY

By the 1970s the concept of gender had moved from a dividing principle to a basis for mobilization. The issue of sexual equality was on the union agenda, and most officials were at least aware of the political dangers of publicly opposing or mocking the specific concerns of female members. Workers and employers had always negotiated employment terms around the concept of 'workplace equality.' However, the UAW's position had long been based on working men's vision of a just workplace. By the 1970s UAW women had begun to alter this vision. As women began to express their interests as a sex, the masculine biases of the union became increasingly evident.

Over time, in response to the demands of women and other minority groups in the labour movement, auto workers broadened their program from one that identified workers' right to organize, no-discrimination on the basis of union activity, seniority rule, and minimum work hours, to one that highlighted the importance of equal pay for equal work, and equal employment for racial minorities. Subsequently, the UAW vision came to embrace equal opportunities for all workers, regardless of race, religion, age, sex, or marital status, adequate child care, abortion access, and fair divorce legislation in society. The challenge to sexual segregation in the auto industry became distinct and legitimate. Furthermore, the legitimacy of women's complaints and the extent of their demands reveal an unprecedented confidence and awareness of their rights.

The 1960s and 1970s, however, were years of heightened contradictions. While individual women often forcefully defended their rights, only a small group saw themselves as part of a collective political movement for sexual equality. In their fight against sex discrimination in the industry and union, UAW women selectively drew on the resources of the women's rights movement in society, yet they declared their opposition to feminists and popular feminist ideology. Many women claimed that they were seeking strict equality as workers, not 'liberation' as a sex.

When they were concentrated in a few female departments, women auto employees celebrated feminine culture with enthusiasm, but as they entered the men's departments and attempted to play a larger role in the union, they downplayed their femininity and colluded in a masculine culture and perspective. Moreover, in the workplace, they faced the disrespect, even hostility, of many of their male co-workers. Women unionists tried to 'roll with the punches.'

Female unionists experienced meaningful personal transformations and effected dramatic societal changes during the 1960s and 1970s. Yet change does not occur evenly. It often takes place gradually and is resisted by many. It creates conflicts even within its strongest advocates. Legal-contractual changes must be negotiated in informal, personal relationships. Large-scale structural trends shake up smaller developments in people's lives. Sometimes the two lines of development converge, sometimes they coexist uneasily. In any case, they necessitate adjustment. Furthermore, intellectual growth and understanding and reasoned strategies are usually mediated by persisting gender ideologies and learned emotional responses. Old and familiar (and sometimes illogical) ways of thinking and behaving pervade our lives.

Women were forever reconstituting their strategies in response to the continually changing society in which they lived. During the 1970s their strategic response embraced these contradictions. Women were trying to assert their rights as female wage-earners in a patriarchal industry and union. Neither the auto plants nor the labour movement was a milieu totally receptive to fundamental changes in gender relations, however. In fact, in these settings, women were often penalized for advocating popular feminism. Thus, women union members sometimes clung to familiar gender ideologies and behaviour. One of the members of the original Local 222 Women's Committee admitted that since 1970 there have been few trail-blazers. 'Very few women are making moves ... They feel that it's not very feminine to make waves or to move into a man's field. We are starting to move, but we are still not moving very fast.'[129] When we consider the experiences of women in industry, we see that securing dignity and respect can be a complicated, if not contradictory, process.

7

Conclusion: Constructing Gender and Equality

When a subject is highly controversial – and any question about sex is that – one cannot hope to tell the truth. One can only show how one came to hold whatever opinion one does hold. One can only give one's audience the chance of drawing their own conclusions.

Virginia Woolf, *A Room of One's Own*, 1928

AGENCY AND RESISTANCE

How do people interpret, respond to, and change the society in which they live? In a context of glaring divisions and injustices, how can people hope to secure dignity, respect, and rights? While women auto workers largely coped with the conditions of their employment, they also engaged in numerous acts of resistance – acts that resulted in a transformation of the workplace, as well as important changes in society. Admittedly, few workers sought control of the means of production or promoted a fundamental restructuring of the political and economic order. However, the concept of resistance need not rest on such dramatic goals and outcomes. Workers resisted insofar as they defied their employers in the pursuit of social and economic justice in everyday life. Through the collective strength of their union and informally, often individually, on the shop floor, women workers attempted to maintain a small measure of dignity for themselves and better their immediate environment. For the most part, these acts were small-scale and undramatic. Nevertheless, they represented direct challenges to managerial authority. These acts largely revolved around the issue of control.

Initially, women engaged in isolated and individual acts of resistance concerning bandanas, relief time, and work gloves. Later, they launched a campaign for change in human rights legislation. 'Bitching' sessions at the bar room in a local hotel led to organized demonstrations in the provincial legislature. Over time, the women stopped crying when their foreman 'looked at them sideways.' By the 1970s these women had begun to file complaints of sex discrimination with the Ontario Human Rights Commission.

To understand these developments we need to be sensitive to the wholeness of people's lives. We need to be aware of workers' identities and loyalties within and beyond the factory gates. Furthermore, in order to understand worker agency, in its diverse and complex forms, we must consider people not only as members of neat-fitting social categories, acting on logical motives and intellectual reason. We have to consider the interplay of the various components of their world, and the contradictions and dilemmas that are often produced by this interplay of forces.

Sociologists have long recognized the importance of analysing both *subjectivity* and *structure*. However, the relationship between these concepts needs to be demonstrated empirically. Materialist analyses have tended to focus on a uniform logic, reasoned motives, and their relation to social structural constraints and imperatives. Socialization and sex role theories, alternately, have tended to ignore the structural framework in which people act, and they have failed to adequately theorize the dynamics of individual and collective social change (Livingstone and Luxton, 1989: 243; Mackie, 1991). In people's experience, however, subjectivity and structure do not merely coexist and cannot be neatly compartmentalized. The conditions in which we find ourselves and the ways in which we perceive and respond to these conditions are indeed inseparable. For example, during the Second World War, women auto workers upheld conventional gender ideologies and sex-segregated work arrangements. They were not, however, blindly absorbed by these beliefs. These women also covertly resisted company policies that prohibited the employment of married women. Many of them in fact concealed their marital status or delayed marriage in order to retain their jobs. The women's strong 'public' support of a male breadwinner and female dependent was in many ways shaped by their limited options during this period. Without viable resources for change, these women were unlikely to contest their subordinate position and challenge prevailing assumptions about the sexes.

In the mid-to-late 1960s, many women auto workers continued to defend sex-segregation. However, again, this attitude was shaped by their perception of feasible alternatives. Most women believed that it would not be possible to break down the gendered division of wage labour. Thus, when a small group of women sought this goal, others ridiculed their efforts. Yet, immediately after the women won equal rights under the union contact, the sceptics themselves entered 'men's jobs' without hesitation. Subjectivity, ideology, and structure continually reconstitute one another.

When we acknowledge the interplay of the subjective and the material, we add complexity to sociological analysis. Reasoned motives cannot always be translated into desired outcomes. Workers rapidly shift their ideological positions in response to changing opportunities. Furthermore, they sometimes forego reasoned decision-making and intellectual assertions, and draw on emotional responses, learned behaviours, and indeed act contrary to the 'logic' assumed by social theorists.

As worker's lives unfold, they experience dilemmas and contradictions. For instance, women auto workers believed in the union principles of social justice, democracy, and egalitarianism, yet in both the union and industry, they experienced outright exclusion and sexism. Furthermore, while they supported a male breadwinner family in principle, they continued to engage in wage work in a male-dominated industry. Over time, many women realized that their need for money, personal fulfillment, and the social ties of a work group, conflicted with, and overpowered, conventional gender ideologies. At times, these contradictions become explosive and force people to sort through them, to challenge prevailing arrangements (see Cockburn, 1983). They become most volatile when small-scale cumulative changes within individuals coincide with large-scale, structural upheavals. Throughout the 1950s and early 1960s the female workforce experienced many changes. Significantly, they were becoming 'union-wise.' They were also developing confidence as permanent wage-earners. These personal transformations coincided with two major developments in Canadian society: the growth of the women's rights movement and the restructuring of the auto industry. The job losses that resulted from economic restructuring forced women auto workers to draw on emerging feminist ideologies, along with unionist beliefs, and challenge gender divisions in the plants. In the words of GM worker Betty Murray, 'We were ripe. We were ready for a change.'

Change, however, does not occur evenly nor does it develop in a unilinear fashion. Like unionization itself, changes in the sexual division of wage labour occurred largely through the initiatives of a core group of individuals. The small number of UAW women who led the struggle for equal rights were left-leaning, politically conscious workers, many of whom had long been active in the labour movement. In addition, these women were noticeably forceful and outspoken. At times, they exhibited qualities that are considered to be typically masculine. In men these traits are positively valued in Western societies. Both publicly and in their personal lives the women defied many of the conventional dictates of proper feminine behaviour. As these 'trail-blazers' made change, opportunities developed and 'walls came down.' As the walls came down, greater numbers of women entered new domains.

THE SOCIAL CONSTRUCTION OF GENDER: GENDERED POLITICS AND RESISTANCE

Not only do gender divisions shape workers' resistance strategies, but through their struggles, workers and employers construct and reconstruct social divisions. When we remove the sex blinders, we see that the history of the UAW has largely been about the formulation and reformulation of gender difference in both the union and the workplace.

Long before unionization, auto manufacturers had segregated the industry by race and sex. They furthermore engaged in many sexually discriminatory practices. Yet union leaders never seriously challenged these arrangements. From the UAW's earliest years working men and company men participated in gendered politics. While the philosophy of industrial unionism rested on the concepts of impartiality and worker solidarity, union policies were not gender-neutral nor was the labour movement without internal fractions. In their quest for social and economic justice, working men incorporated their biases about women's and men's proper places in the division of labour. Guided by these assumptions, they adopted a narrow view of justice – justice within a context of sexual inequality. Thus, in collective agreements, they sanctioned sex-based seniority rights, wage rates, and job classifications. The labour movement itself was male-dominated and reflected a masculine culture, in spite of growing numbers of female members.

Indeed, gender strongly informed the definition of an industrial wage labourer. Female auto workers represented a separate class of worker. They were slightly different from boys, comparable in some ways to disabled men, and clearly distinct from able-bodied black, Armenian, and Chinese men. None of these groups, however, was equivalent to a white, able-bodied prime-age male. The white able-bodied man represented the typical auto worker – the auto worker that both employers and union leaders envisioned in their negotiations over wages, rights, and working conditions. As a marginal group, women received inferior rewards and had limited contractual rights.

The social meaning of gender was so strong that it mediated, compounded, and often overshadowed other traits, such as marital status, age, and class. Employers categorized women according to marital status (married women faced the most severe and blatant discrimination), but they did not treat men in the same way. While men had long claimed a privileged position in the workplace as breadwinners, women were penalized for their family status. Moreover, while married and single women, young and old, were distinct from one another in important ways, their gender threw them together in other respects. Male workers and supervisors rarely distinguished between female employees, female group leaders and supervisors, in their acts of sabotage and informal opposition to desegregation in the 1970s.

Women workers' consciousness and struggles were likewise gendered. Indeed, female auto workers eventually drew on their collective identity and position as women, and challenged the meaning of gender in employment and in society as a whole. We tend to overlook much of women's resistance, however, because it was expressly feminized. During the Second World War women's involvement in the union was intermittent, and they carried out many mundane and devalued duties, such as making coffee and sandwiches and administering strike pay. These differences, however, reflect cultural and ideological prescriptions, as well as power relations within the labour movement. They are not evidence of women's presumed political passivity or a lack of union consciousness.

Over time, female auto workers moved from a woman-centred cohesiveness within a context of sexual inequality – indeed a celebration of gender difference – to a demand for equal (identical) rights with men. By the late 1960s small groups of women explicitly equated womanhood with strength and self-determination. In short, they came to view themselves as legitimate actors in the political process. Nevertheless, to mobilize the majority of female workers, the small cadre of women activists had to draw on a gendered culture, a feminine culture that paradoxically reinforced conventional images of womanhood.

Throughout the 1960s the Local 222 Women's Committee invited female employees to a number of social-recreational events. This was a typical and time-honoured union strategy, but the content of these events has always been masculine and feminine. During the early days of labour organizing, for example, union leaders mobilized members by establishing an exclusively male UAW Rod and Gun Club. By the 1960s such activities had become diversified (including golf and baseball tournaments) and sexually integrated. Yet they retained their masculine content. Women participated in these events, but not as fully as their brothers. Women workers, in turn, held potluck dinners, fudge tables, and fashion shows – functions that their union brothers did not attend. In this sense, workers drew on masculine and feminine culture as a resource. In Ann Swidler's (1986: 273) words, these cultural events and rituals represent a 'tool kit,' 'components' that individuals could use to construct 'strategies of action.' In promoting new ideas and arrangements during these traditional gatherings, workers were also reshaping gendered culture and gendered subjectivity.

THE SOCIAL CONSTRUCTION OF WORKPLACE EQUALITY AND JUSTICE: THE DILEMMA OF GENDER DIFFERENCE

A further outcome of the workers' struggles was the social construction of workplace justice itself. Ironically, the workers' pursuit of justice and equality embraced sexual divisions and power differentials within and between classes. While male union leaders promoted worker solidarity and impartiality on the one hand, on the other they constructed gender difference and accepted what Joan Scott (1988) has termed equality and gender difference as 'binary opposites.'[1] In this view, equality cannot be achieved without forsaking difference.

When women attempted to redefine the union's vision of justice in the late 1960s and throughout the 1970s, they did not question this dichotomy. Thus, while female workers celebrated gender difference (albeit in a context of sexual inequality) in the 1940s, most women denied their distinctiveness as a sex in their pursuit of equality in the 1970s. Female unionists shaped their struggles for social justice within a masculine discourse. In part, this was a strategy shaped by practical considerations. These women had to work within the limits set by a collective agreement that was negotiated by men. In addition, the tenets of industrial unionism, especially the seniority principle, were central to their political education. Within this framework, however, wage-earning women could pursue only a narrowly defined equality. Ultimately through their struggle for equal rights, the women altered the UAW vision somewhat. Yet their resistance was constrained by the gendered politics of earlier times.[2]

While women achieved legal-contractual equality in 1970, the workplace and union remain unaltered in many ways. In the mid-1990s, over twenty years later, workers have yet to achieve fundamental changes in workplace culture and proportionate representation of women. Despite the impressive efforts of a few individuals to promote meaningful change,[3] the labour movement has been more receptive to adding various 'women's issues,' such as child care and sexual harassment, to their agenda. Notwithstanding the importance of these issues, this strategy does not in itself challenge the patriarchal foundations of the union movement.

In order to transform the union, workers and labour leaders will have to question the notion that equality and difference stand at opposite ends of a political spectrum. While employers are largely responsible for implementing sexual divisions in the auto plants, working men participated in the construction of gender differences – differences that were reflected in the division of labour, reward structures, ideology, and union and shop-floor culture. Yet, in their present-day attempts to redress sexual inequalities, union leaders have tended to draw on the old ethos of uniformity and impartiality. Neutral measures, however, have limited effects in a gendered context. If they are serious in their pursuit of equality in the workplace and union, workers and their leaders must overcome the denial of difference. In a stratified world, it is essential to recognize differences based on sex, as well as race, ethnicity, and language. An understanding of such differences may, moreover, lead to a convergence of the historically separated struggles for women's rights, human rights, and the fuller involvement of workers of colour in the labour movement.

A feminist agenda furthermore requires that unionists rethink the concept of democracy. In the past the UAW prided itself on being a highly democratic union. However, it has long promoted a liberal democratic definition of justice – with a focus on equitable process rather than egalitarian outcomes. In a context of systemic inequality, a liberal democratic process will not secure the representation of the broad and diverse groups of workers who form a minority, nor will it guarantee the pursuit of dignity and respect for all. If we measure democracy by majority rule only, we will continue to neglect the unique concerns and interests of white women and all workers of colour. Thus, gender and racial inequalities will persist.

In addition, a feminist challenge requires that workers reorder their priorities and consequently redistribute the union's resources. Currently, labour leaders in Canada tend to view the eradication of sexual and racial inequalities as a legitimate yet peripheral, if not impractical, goal. Strategies to secure gender and racial equality are therefore put on hold. They are reserved for an easier, more prosperous future – a future that may never arrive.

We must remember, however, that our understanding of what is reasonable, fair, and realistic has been shaped by historical struggles. Over time, UAW members have altered their definition of what is acceptable and just. During the Second World War, unionists accepted sex-based differences and took gender inequalities for granted. In the 1950s and early 1960s women workers began to challenge sexually discriminatory measures, and they demanded the fair application of their restricted contract rights. By the late 1960s and throughout the 1970s, however, working women insisted on equal (identical) rights with their brothers. Today, few male or female workers would seriously consider reinstating sex-based job classifications and sex-based seniority rights. Most people would view such an act as an outright violation of the union's moral agenda. At present organized labour must once again redefine its conception of justice and equality – and its vision of what is possible.

Well-intentioned unionists have been able to put equality issues on hold in recent years because of the tendency to dichotomize labour's agenda, with economic imperatives and reason at one end, and a 'moral economy' or the pursuit of social justice on the other. This binary, too, has been socially constructed.[4] Social justice is not necessarily antithetical to economic and political 'realities.' Struggles for dignity and respect were certainly not counterposed to political reason, nor eclipsed by economic imperatives, when the key actors in the fights were white working-class men.

Structure moulds and constrains, but it does not prohibit agency, in either thought or action. Though our definition of what is possible has been limited by structure, people sometimes think in unprecedented ways and push the structure to its limits. In the 1993 round of negotiations with the Big Three, Canadian Auto Workers won the right of employees to walk off the job with pay in the event of sexual or racial harassment. Today, when a woman walks past the assembly lines in GM's Oshawa plant, one hears few men jeer and howl as they did in the 1970s. These recent developments have emerged from past struggles. They signify redefined boundaries. Given the power of capital, especially at a time when employers are continually refashioning the labour process and eliminating jobs, unionists will face considerable difficulties in pushing the limits of structure further. However, the process has a history. To the women and men of the labour movement, this task has represented a formidable challenge – a long-standing dilemma.

Notes

1 See, for example, Balser, 1987; Baron, 1991; Briskin and McDermott, 1993; Cobble, 1993; Cook, Lorwin, and Daniels, 1992; Drake, 1984; Eisenstein, 1983; Frager, 1992; Gabin, 1990; Gannage, 1986; Milkman, 1987; 1985; White, 1993; 1990.

2 The UAW officially known as the International Union of Automobile, Aeorspace and Agricultural Workers, was an international union whose central offices were located in the United States. In addition, several regional UAW offices were established throughout the U.S. and one regional office was set up in Canada. Initially the Canadian jurisdiction was called District Council 26. Later, it was referred to as Region 12, and subsequently it was renamed Region 7 (also known as the Canadian Region). The UAW in Canada remained Region 7 until the mid-1980s. For the sake of historical accuracy, I use the terms Region 7 and UAW Canadian Region interchangeably throughout this book. In September 1985 the Canadian Regional Office broke away from the UAW International and formed an independent union called the Canadian Auto Workers (CAW). I use the term CAW only in reference to the union after the breakaway in 1985.

3 The United Electrical Workers Union (UE) was also known as a highly progressive union, with Communist Party leadership in both Canada and the United States. For a comprehensive discussion of the union's position on women workers see Milkman, 1987; Schatz, 1983, chapter 5.

Milkman offers a detailed comparison of the treatment of women workers by the union and management in the auto and electrical industries during the Second World War period. In her view, the two unions adopted distinct approaches to female employees largely because of differences in the industrial structure of auto and electrical manufacturing. Prior to the war the majority of jobs in the auto industry were performed by men. Thus, during the war the union demanded equal pay for equal work, claiming that the jobs women were performing in wartime were essentially 'men's jobs.' In comparison, the electrical industry had always employed large numbers of women. Consequently, the UE questioned the basis for the differential evaluation of female and male labour and argued for equal pay for jobs of comparable worth.

Schatz notes that in the United States electrical industry, the UE demanded that management end its practice of keeping separate sex-based wage rates and seniority lists. Yet, given management's right to hire and fire, female employees were once again concentrated in the lowest paying jobs, after the Second World War. In 1942, union leaders at Westinghouse also demanded and won larger wage increases for women workers than men. This move represented an attack on sexual discrimination that was unprecedented in American labour history (Schatz, 1983: 124). Subsequently, the UE made 'equal pay for equal work' one of their chief demands. Schatz notes, however, that in practice, the demand for equal pay for equal work contained contradictions. Given that companies were trying to place lower paid women on men's jobs, the call for equal pay for equal work essentially ensured that male preserves in employment would be protected, and sexual segregation and sexual discrimination would be perpetuated.

4 For data on auto workers in the United States, see Gabin (1990, 1984); Meyerowitz (1985); Meier and Rudwick (1979); Milkman (1987).

5 This study was initially a comparison of gender and racial/ethnic divisions in the southern Ontario auto industry and the UAW Canadian Region. Over the course of my research, however, I found that while these two issues are theoretically linked, they were empirically separate in this historical setting. Management segregated both white women and men of colour from white men. Generally, these two groups of workers were subject to comparatively inferior terms of employment. However, employers did not use white women and minority men interchangeably. These groups therefore represented distinct pools of labour. In addition, the union addressed gender inequalities through its Women's Department, while it handled racial discrimination through its Fair Practices and Anti-Discrimination Department. Also, at the local level the unionists established separate women's committees (comprised of white women) and fair-practices and anti-discrimination committees (dominated by men). The latter eventually became known as human rights committees. In contrast, during the Second

World War, one department, the UAW-CIO War Policy Division, addressed both gender and racial inequalities. In ultimately separating these phenomena, both the union and management largely negated the existence (and particular concerns) of minority women. In Canada few women of colour worked in the industry until the late 1960s. By the 1970s they still represented a tiny group within the total automotive workforce. They were furthermore concentrated in the Windsor trim plant and never gained significant representation in the huge Oshawa and St Catharines plants.

The findings presented in this study represent part one of an ongoing research project. In an effort to fully explore their dynamics, I address race/ ethnic relations in the industry and in the union, in part two. On the basis of these findings, I will attempt to theorize the relation between gender and race.

6 See, for example, Cockburn (1986), Hartmann (1976, 1979), Humphries (1977), Hunt (1980), Pollert (1981), Gannage (1986), Westwood (1985).

7 In a critique of this approach, Rick Fantasia observes that whether or not the researcher ' "finds" class consciousness is akin to the problem of whether the glass is half-empty of half-full; it may reveal more about the relative optimism or pessimism of the sociologist than about the existence of class consciousness.' A limitation of attitudinal measures is that they require that a worker's response be recorded as her or his fixed views about an issue. Fantasia notes that in historical and ethnographic accounts, 'discontinuities and paradoxes in consciousness emerge frequently, offering the most difficult, as well as the most potentially rewarding, problems for solution. The sociological survey, in contrast, largely precludes one from discovering contradictory lines of thought, as well as from exploring the methods by which individuals synthesize constradictions' (1988: 5).

8 I thank Joyce Avotri for the way in which she articulated this point to me.

9 In *The History of Sexuality*, Michel Foucault states that although a clear logic may characterize historical power relations, with obvious aims and objectives, it is often the case that no one invented these aims and strategies according to a rational plan. While individuals may consciously pursue goals that advance their own positions, they are not necessarily directing the 'overall movement of relations, or engineering their shape. They may not even know what that shape is' (cited in Bordo, 1992: 93).

10 Arlie Hochschild (1989) employs the concept of a 'gender strategy' in her study of married couples and the domestic division of labour. She bases this concept on Ann Swidler's (1986) notion of 'strategies in action.' Swidler argues that culture ('symbolic vehicles of meaning, including beliefs, ritual practices, art forms, and ceremonies, as well as informal cultural practices

such as language, gossip, stories, and rituals of daily life') influences individuals' actions. In Swidler's view, culture does not influence action by providing ultimate values. Rather, it shapes a 'tool kit' of 'habits, skills, and styles' from which people develop 'strategies of action' (Swidler, 1986: 273).

11 The term 'gendered' refers to the political process by which the female and male sexes have acquired a social meaning that extends far beyond biological differences. I use the word gendered as an adjective and a verb, in an effort to explain this social process. The noun gender, in comparison, tends to merely describe the masculine and feminine.

CHAPTER 1

1 Archives of Labour and Urban Affairs (hereafter ALUA), UAW Canadian Region – Series III Collection, Box 70, File 6, 'District Council, 1939 Minutes,' Report of C.H. Millard, 25 June 1938.

2 CAW National Office Private Papers (hereafter CAW), George Burt Papers: Interview on the History of the UAW in Canada, Interviews by George Burt, unpublished, pp. 12–13.

3 *Guardian*, 14 February 1979, p. 1.

4 CAW, George Burt Papers: Interview on the History of the UAW in Canada, Interviews by George Burt, p. 5.

5 Conde and Beveridge Interviews: Ethel Thomson, 1/9/82, UAW p. 2.

6 In comparison, in 1934, female needleworkers in Toronto reportedly earned at least $21 a week and women instructresses earned between $17 and $28. However, by 1935, these figures dropped considerably to $12.50 and $8 to $11 (Light and Pierson, 1990: 278). There were also reports that female domestic servants in British Columbia were earning as little as $5.00 per month, while working 10 hours or more per day. According to a memorandum submitted to the government in 1937, an experienced cook-general earned $25, a mother's help received $15, and a cook earned $35 per month, for a 54-hour week (Light and Pierson, 1990: 282–3). Given the auto workers' seasonal employment, and sporadic work hours, it is difficult to make accurate comparisons with these groups of workers. However, these figures indicate that in the early-to-mid 1930s, women auto workers could not be described as all that well paid among the female workforce. Their wages did, however, rise considerably after unionization.

7 CAW, George Burt Papers, Oral History Interview of George Burt. Interviewed by Jack W. Skeels, 23 April 1963, p. 11.

8 ALUA, UAW Canadian Region – Companies Collection, Box 155, File 1, 'McKinnon Industries Limited, St Catharines, 1937–72,' Memorandum of Agreement, 27 April 1937; ibid., Memorandum of Conference, 20 May 1937.

9 CAW, George Burt Papers: Oral History Interview of George Burt. Institute of Labour and Industrial Relations, 23 April 1963, p. 5.
10 *Guardian*, 14 February 1979, p. 1.
11 Conde and Beveridge Interviews: Olive Farnell/Doug Clark, 20/8/82, UAW 222/15, pp. 12–13.
12 Ibid.: Harry Benson, W. Grant/ Ted Nichols/ Jack Johnson/ Doug Clark/ Nip Tucker, UAW 222, p. 7.
13 CAW, George Burt Papers, Oral History Interview of George Burt, 23 April 1963, p. 5.
14 Ibid.: untitled, unpublished essay, anonymous, p. 1; *Exhibit 19: What Workers Thought of the Auto Industry 40 Years Ago*, UAW-CIO, 1975.
15 Public Archives of Canada (hereafter PAC), MG 28, I 119, Accession No. 88/324, Vol. 26, File 'Local 222 76–79,' 'Abbreviated History of Local 222.'
16 'Local 199 UAW-CIO St Catharines, Ontario, General Motors,' *Local 199 News*, Vol. 24, No. 6, September 1989, pp. 1, 6.
17 CAW Local 199 Private Papers (hereafter Local 199), 'Local 199 UAW: A History,' p. 1, n.d., unsigned document.
18 Ibid., p. 17.
19 PAC, MG 28, I 119, Accession No. 88/324, Box 26, File 'Local 222 76–79,' 'Abbreviated History of Local 222.'
20 Likewise, in his study of electrical workers in the United States, Ronald Schatz argues that strict application of the seniority principle was important in providing a means by which union leaders could challenge management's arbitrary power to reward their favourites, yet avoid taking on this difficult task themselves. Aside from representing an 'impersonal, impartial, and objective' rule, the seniority principle was advantageous in permitting workers to acquire a form of 'ownership' of their jobs (Schatz, 1983: 113). For a detailed discussion of the relationship between job security and the concept of job ownership, see Storey, 1994.
21 *Exhibit 19: What Workers Thought of the Auto Industry 40 Years Ago*, UAW-CIO, 1975, p. 14.
22 This point was brought to my attention by Leroy Bell and Richard Nicholson, both of whom were long-term GM workers in St Catharines.
23 ALUA, UAW Research Department Collection, Box 11, File 11-11, 'Employment, Women and Negroes, UAW Regions 4-9a,' April 1943, 'Questionnaire on Employment in UAW-CIO Plants.'
24 *Windsor Daily Star*, 31 December 1942.
25 *Ford Times*, Vol. 2, No. 3, January 1943, pp. 7–8.
26 Windsor Public Library, Local History Scrapbook, 'Windsor War Industries and Public Utilities,' Vol. 16, n.d., pp. 17–19.
27 *Ford Times*, Vol. 1, No. 4, May–June 1942, p. 1. By 1944 there were no

women members in the Ford plant in Windsor. ALUA, UAW War Policy Division – Women's Bureau Collection, Box 5, File 5-12. It is likely that there were some women employed in cafeteria and cleaning work in the Ford plant. However, I am not aware of any official data on these workers.

In contrast, Ruth Milkman has noted that in the United States, women represented a significant proportion of the automotive workforce during the Second World War. In 1939, for example, women comprised 6.6 per cent of the total automotive workforce. By 1944 this figure had risen to 24.8 per cent, and in 1945 women represented 22.4 per cent of workers in the industry (Milkman, 1987: 13). While Ford in Canada attempted to introduce women in its manufacturing operations in Windsor, at lower rates than men, male unionists insisted that they only enter the plant at equal rates with men. Given this stipulation, Ford management decided not to hire women. They argued that women must be paid lower rates because their employment involved various expenditures such as the building of women's washrooms. See chapter 2 for a fuller discussion of this incident.

28 ALUA, UAW War Policy Division – Women's Bureau Collection, Box 5, File 5-12.
29 '750 Women Being Trained for Machine Gun Plant Jobs,' *Windsor Daily Star*, 3 October 1941, p. 3.
30 T.R. Elliott, 'The Motor Car Industry Makes Victory Its Business,' *Canadian Geographical Journal*, December 1942.
31 ALUA, UAW Research Department Collection, Box 11, File 11-11, 'Employment, Women and Negroes, UAW Regions 4-9a,' April 1943, 'Questionnaire on Employment in UAW-CIO Plants.'
32 'Canada Organizes Her Resources for the War,' *McKinnon People*, undated wartime issue, pp. 8–9, 18–19, 22–4, 57.
33 ALUA, UAW Research Department Collection, Box 11, File 11-11, 'Employment, Women and Negroes, UAW Regions 4-9a,' April 1943, 'Questionnaire on Employment in UAW-CIO Plants.'
34 'Canada Organizes Her Resources for the War,' *McKinnon People*, undated wartime issue, pp. 8–9, 18–19, 22–4, 57.
35 *Oshaworker*, Vol. 3, No. 19, 17 October 1945, p. 3.
36 'To the Ladies,' *McKinnon Doings*, Vol. 7, No. 4, July 1943.
37 *McKinnon Doings*, Vol. 7, No. 3, June 1943, cover and p. 8.
38 'The Fair Sex,' *McKinnon Doings*, n.d., mid-1940s, p. 5.
39 Likewise, from a content analysis of advertisements appearing in the popular women's magazine, *Ladies Home Journal*, between 1909–10 and 1980, Bonnie Fox concludes that during the Second World War advertisements

highlighted women's contribution to the war effort as an extension of their mothering duties in particular, and their domestic responsibility, in general.

40 Many researchers have found that women's wartime experiences increased their sense of competence, yet these feelings were not paralleled by a breakdown of traditional gender relations nor did they result in the elimination of sex segregation (for example, Anderson, 1981; Kesselman, 1990; Milkman, 1987; Pierson, 1983, 1986). In the auto industry the gendered division of labour took on a resiliency largely because employers recruited women with extreme reservation and continually reminded them in both material and ideological terms that they had a temporary and marginal status in the factories.

41 Economists frequently refer to this practice as 'statistical discrimination.' Statistical discrimination refers to a situation in which employers base their decisions about individual workers on group-derived probabilities. For example, they may view women workers as having less physical strength than men. On the basis of this assessment, regardless of its validity, they will exclude individual women from jobs that require the display of physical strength. See Phelps (1972); Piore (1972).

42 Manning; Nicholson Interviews; personal communication, Leroy Bell.

43 'Those Were the Days,' *Progress*, special edition, 17 September 1983.

44 In the 1930s, women were confined to five departments in this plant. Small groups of roughly six women each worked in the radiator room, the glass and hardware, and the rods and tubing departments. However, by the end of the decade, the company replaced women in the latter two departments with boys. The women transferred to the cutting and sewing.

45 There is evidence, however, that men worked as sewing machine operators in the upholstery department of the Ford Highland Park plant in the United States, in the 1920s and even during the Second World War (see Lewchuk, 1993).

46 In the foundry, there were seven female core makers, two boys, and an unspecified number of female and boy core assemblers out of a total of approximately 753 employees. Small groups of women could also be found in the shipping and receiving area. In this department, there were three female general packers, one female packer, and one female key operator out of a total workforce of 68. Similarly, in the gear division, the female workforce included eight special inspectors and three general inspectors. As well, three boys worked as gear cutters out of a total of 556 workers. In inspection, there were no women's jobs, while there were three special boy operators out of a total of 178 workers. Likewise, there were no women in

drills, the service department, or the forge and die room. The latter employed three trim boys (males under 18 years of age).

Female representation was notably high in the commercial motors department. This department employed approximately 50 women as special operators, 50 women as general operators, two women as instructresses, 25 women in special worker, assembly and machining, and 108 women in general assembly and machining. In comparison, 61 men worked as set-up men and 22 men were employed in various jobs such as tool trouble man, tool grinder, armature repairer, production hand, welder, machine and welding worker, and armature repairer. The Delco division was also female-dominated, as well as an area of female concentration. In 1944 80 per cent of the women employed by McKinnon worked in the Delco on starting motors, generators, voltage regulators, ignition coils, and distributors. In addition, the wartime dynamotor division employed over 350 women during the early years of the war. Source: ALUA, UAW Canadian Region – Companies Collection, Box 155, File 2, 'McKinnon Industries Limited, St Catharines, 1943–44'; 'Canada Organizes Her Resources for the War,' *Mc-Kinnon People*, undated wartime issue, pp. 8–9, 18–19, 22–24, 57; 'The Four Way Machine for Army Truck Differential Trunions,' *McKinnon Doings*, Vol. 6, No. 1, 24 April 1942, p. 8.

47 ALUA, UAW Local 199 Collection, Box 1, File 'Agreement, 1943,' Memorandum of Agreement between McKinnon Industries and UAW Local 199, 13 April 1943.

48 Conde and Beveridge Interviews: Elsie Karn, 27/9/82, UAW 222/21, p. 9.

49 'Delco Delicacy,' *McKinnon Doings*, Vol. 7, No. 9, Christmas 1943, p. 6.

50 For a detailed discussion of this theme, see for example, Ruth Roach Pierson, *'They're Still Women After All': The Second World War and Canadian Womanhood* (Toronto: McClelland and Stewart, 1986); Maureen Honey, *Creating Rosie the Riveter: Class, Gender, and Propaganda during World War II* (Amherst: University of Massachusetts Press, 1984).

51 'From Sea to Sea,' *McKinnon Doings*, Vol. 8, No. 12, May 1945, p. 10.

52 'The Fair Sex,' *McKinnon Doings*, Vol. 5, No. 12, 20 March 1942, p. 6.

CHAPTER 2

1 Nancy Gabin (1990, 1984) and Ruth Milkman (1987) reach similar conclusions in studies of the UAW in the United States.

2 *St Catharines Standard*, 17 April 1940, p. 9.

3 ALUA, UAW Region 7 Toronto Sub-Regional Office Collection, Box 11, File 'Meeting, June 1942, Minutes and Report,' 'District Council 26 Meeting,

Minutes,' 27, 28 June 1942. Out of a total of 4,500 plant workers, only about 500 were paying dues on a regular basis. Ibid., File 'Meeting, August 1942, Minutes and Reports.'

4 ALUA, UAW Women's Department, Lillian Hatcher Collection, Box 20, File 20–2, 'Employing Women Organizers,' 3–9 August 1942.

5 Conde and Beveridge Interviews: Ethel Thomson, 1/9/82, UAW 222/19, pp. 14–15.

6 Ibid.: Mary Turner, 2/3/83, UAW 222/29, p. 2.

7 ALUA, UAW Region 7 Toronto Sub-Regional Office Collection, Box 11, File 'Meeting, August 1943, Minutes and Report.'

8 ALUA, UAW Local 199 Collection, Box 23, File 'Executive Minutes; 1944–45,'; UAW Local 199 Collection, Minutes, Bargaining Committee Report, Local 199 Executive Meeting, 31 April 1944.

9 ALUA, UAW Canadian Region, Locals Collection, Box 87, File 4, 'Local 199, St Catharines, 1945–49,' George Addes to Charles Williamson, 27 July 1945.

10 ALUA, UAW Region 7 Toronto Sub-Regional Office Collection, Box 14, File 'Miscellaneous Material, 1942.'

11 ALUA, UAW Research Department Collection, Box 32, File 'Women and the Labor Movement, 1943–4, 2 of 2,' press clipping, *Detroit Times*, 'Thomas Visions Peril to Union in Girl Workers,' 2 November 1943.

12 Conde and Beveridge Interviews: Ivy Imerson (Bartlett) and Bill Imerson, UAW 222/16, p. 7.

13 Local 199, UAW Local 199 Fiftieth Anniversary Files, Private Research Notes of R. Olling, '1937 St Catharines Organizing Effort,' 1937.

14 'Refusal to Adopt an Agreement,' *St Catharines Standard*, 8 April 1937, p. 1.

15 Conde and Beveridge Interviews: Elsie Karn, 27/9/82, UAW 222/21, pp. 9–10.

16 The UAW had requested a 10 cent per hour increase for hourly workers and a 15 per cent increase for bonus and piece workers. However, the company claimed that it could not increase wages because of a dominion government order-in-council. McKinnon officials also stated that wages were currently as high as, or higher than in any period between 1926 and December 1940. Both parties therefore referred the matter to a board of conciliation appointed under the Industrial Disputes Investigation Act. Nevertheless, the union rejected the board's recommendation and reiterated their demands for a wage increase. *St Catharines Standard*, 11 September 1941, 'Halts Production of War Materials,' pp. 1, 8.

17 'Halts Production of War Materials,' 'Follows Wage Policy.' *St Catharines Standard*, 11 September 1941, pp. 1, 8.

18 'Women Join the Union,' *St Catharines Standard*, 12 September 1941, pp. 1, 10.
19 'Halts Production of War Materials,' *St Catharines Standard*, 11 September 1941, p. 1.
20 *St Catharines Standard*, 13 September 1941, pp. 1, 3.
21 Ibid., 19 September 1941, p. 10.
22 'Withdraw Pickets for Weekend   No Sign of Settlement in McKinnon Strike   Will Resume on Monday   Effective Shutdown Becoming More Widespread.' *St Catharines Standard*, 13 September 1941, p. 1.
23 Conde and Beveridge Interviews: Olive Farnell/Doug Clark, 20/8/82, UAW 222/15, pp. 5–6.
24 Ibid.: Ivy Imerson (Bartlett) and Bill Imerson, UAW 222/16, pp. 4–5.
25 Ibid.: Elsie Karn, 27/9/82, UAW 222/21, pp. 9–10.
26 'Letters to the Editor,' *St Catharines Standard*, 18 September 1941, p. 4.
27 'Views Expressed,' *St Catharines Standard*, 23 September 1941, p. 4.
28 'Letters to the Editor,' *St Catharines Standard*, 27 September 1941, p. 4.
29 Paterson interview, Wigg interview, Koch interview.
30 This was Caroline Davis, who later became head of the UAW Women's Department.
31 ALUA, UAW Canadian Region – Series III Collection, Box 70, File 5, 'District Council, '39,' Recording Secretaries List; Larkin Interview.
32 However, Nancy Gabin found that in the United States female representation increased over the years of the Second World War. In August 1944 women served as shop stewards in 73 per cent of the locals surveyed by the UAW Education Department, and women were members of executive boards in 60 per cent of the locals. Fewer locals had women on plant bargaining committees. By the war's end the union estimated that 300 women were officers in local unions and at least 1,000 served on local union committees (Gabin, 1984: 96).
33 Conde and Beveridge Interviews: George Burt, UAW 222/4, pp. 12–13. As a member of the Local Bargaining Committee, this woman would represent all the women who were employed in plants across southern Ontario, not only GM employees in Oshawa.
34 To a limited degree, then, sex segregation benefited women who wished to run for the job of shop steward. Union locals that faced extreme organizing problems made special efforts to recruit women to fill these positions in female-dominated departments. Yet, women did not hold office in proportion to their numbers at the local or international levels of the union (Gabin, 1984: 28–9).
35 *Oshaworker*, Vol. 6, No. 27, 3 November 1948, p. 2.

36 Ibid. *Oshaworker*, Vol. 7, No. 10, 1 June 1949, p. 4. In addition, Phoebe Blair
    was a committeewoman at Canada Top and Body Corporation in Tilbury,
    Ontario. Blair was also chair of the Bargaining Committee, a District Coun-
    cil delegate, and representative of Region 7 to the National Women's Con-
    ference Committee. ALUA, UAW War Policy Division, Victor Reuther Col-
    lection, Box 27, File 'War Policy, Women's Bureau, November 1944 –
    January 1944.' Also, in 1937, a Margaret Chauvin was on the Executive
    Board of Local 195 in Windsor as Trustee. *Guardian*, April 1956, p. 27.
37 Conde and Beveridge Interviews: Mary Turner, 2/3/83, UAW 222/29,
    pp. 2–3.
38 By 1944 the UAW. International had 250,000 female members. ALUA, UAW
    War Policy Division, Victor Reuther Collection, Box 27, File 'War Policy
    Women's Bureau, October 1942 – October 1944,' 'Women's Bureau Report,'
    1 May 1944.
39 ALUA, UAW Women's Department: Lillian Hatcher Collection, Box 1, File
    1–8, 'Correspondence and Materials, 1957,' Lillian Hatcher to William Oli-
    ver, 24 April 1957.
40 ALUA, Emil Mazey Collection, Box 13, File 13–5, 'Women's Division,
    1941–47, 1,' R.J. Thomas to All Regional Directors and Local Union Presi-
    dents, 22 April 1944.
41 In June 1946 the UAW Women's Bureau became a permanent body within
    the UAW's new Fair Practices and Anti-Discrimination Department. The
    UAW Fair Practices and Anti-Discrimination Department was co-directed
    by William Oliver. Oliver stated that the department's primary concern
    was the black workforce, however, it would also pay special attention to
    women in the industry as they made up the largest minority group in the
    UAW (Gabin, 1984: 154).
42 ALUA, UAW War Policy Division, Victor Reuther Collection, Box 27, File
    'War Policy Women's Bureau, November 1944 – January 1945,' R.J. Thomas
    to All Local Union Presidents, 31 October 1944.
43 Ibid., and File 'War Policy, Women's Bureau, November 1944 – January
    1944,' 'Report of R.J. Thomas.'
44 American delegates focused on seniority rights for women workers, the
    elimination of discriminatory contract clauses, sex-based job classifications,
    laxness on the part of union committeemen, equal pay for equal work,
    lunch periods and rest periods, in-plant eating facilities, health and safety
    practices, child care programs, unemployment compensation laws, price
    controls, and the Equal Rights Amendment. In addition, they resolved that
    the UAW International Executive Board make staff appointments on 'the
    basis of qualifications and competence and that women be considered on a

fair and equal basis without prejudice with men.' Furthermore, they demanded that when additional women be added to the staff, they be given
assignments comparable to those of other staff members. Ibid.
45 An emerging feminist consciousness was manifested in rebuttals to the
sometimes insensitive remarks of male delegates. For example, when a man
stated that women workers who want equal rights should relinquish privileges such as free uniforms, many women unabashedly expressed their indignation. One woman retorted, 'A man worker would not expect his wife
or sister to do heavy lifting.' Another woman stated, 'My job is one that a
man would throw across the room if he worked on it an hour.' Yet another
female delegate asserted, 'I know plenty of men workers who have more
time off the floor than the women do.' Several other heated replies flooded
the room. 'Equal Pay Issue Sets off UAW Battle of the Sexes,' *Detroit News*,
10 December 1944.
46 ALUA, UAW Research Department Collection, Box 32, File 'Women and
the Labor Movement, 1943–44, 2 of 2,' newspaper clipping, 'Men Put Rosie
the Riveter in Her Place on Home Front,' source unknown, 9 December
1944.
47 ALUA, George Addes – UAW Secretary-Treasurer Collection, Box 24, File
24-11, 'Minutes, Board Meeting, July 16–23, 1945,' Minutes, Fourth Quarterly International Executive Board Meeting, 16–23 July 1945, pp. 139–40.
48 ALUA, UAW Research Department, Acc. 350, Box 11, File 11-11, 'Employment, Women and Negroes, UAW Regions 4-9A, April 1943.
49 ALUA, UAW War Policy Division, Victor Reuther Collection, Box 27, File
'War Policy, Women's Bureau, November 1944 – January 1945,' R.J. Thomas to All Local Union Presidents, 31 October 1944.
50 Ibid., File 'War Policy Women's Bureau, October 1942 – October 1944,'
Women's Bureau Report, 1 May 1944.
51 Ibid., File 'War Policy, Women's Bureau, November 1944 – January 1944,'
'Report of R.J. Thomas.'
52 ALUA, UAW War Policy Division – Women's Bureau Collection, Box 5,
File 5-13, 'Women's Conference – National Committee,' Mildred Jeffrey to
Phoebe Blair, 6 November 1944.
53 ALUA, UAW Region 7 Toronto Sub-Regional Office Collection, Box 11, File
'Meeting, February 1944, Minutes.'
54 ALUA, George Burt Collection, Box 1, File 1-1, 'District Council 26;
Minutes; Burt's Reports and Related Materials; May 1940–41.'
55 ALUA, UAW War Policy Division – Women's Bureau Collection, Box 5,
File 5-12.
56 ALUA, UAW Region 7 Toronto Sub-Regional Office Collection, Box 11, File

'Meeting, June 1942, Minutes and Report,' Minutes, District Council 26
Meeting, 27–8 June 1942; ibid., File 'Meeting, August 1943, Minutes and
Report.'

57 Ibid.
58 Ibid. File 'Meeting, August 1942, Minutes and Reports,' Minutes, District
Council 26 Meeting, 29–30 August 1942; ibid., File 'Meeting, August 1943,
Minutes and Report.' Some locals were highly successful in their implementation efforts. For example, Local 195 in Windsor overcame strong employer opposition and applied the equal pay principle in Gar Wood, Kelsey
Wheel, Canadian Bridge, and to a lesser degree in Gotfredson. Indeed Kel-
sey Wheel hired several women after they agreed to equal pay. ALUA,
UAW Region 7 Toronto Sub-Regional Office Collection, Box 14, File 'Miscellaneous Material, 1942'; ibid., Box 11, File 'Meeting, June 1943, Minutes,'
Minutes, District Council Meeting, 5–6 June 1943. In addition, Local 397
negotiated an equal pay for equal work clause in contracts with Canadian
Durex Abrasives, the Brantford Oven and Rack Company, the Brantford
Coach and Body, and Canadian Car and Foundry. Ibid. File 'Meeting, August 1943, Minutes and Report.'
59 Ibid., File 'Meeting, January 1943, Minutes and Report,' Minutes, District
Council 26, 16–17 January 1943.
60 ALUA, UAW Research Department Acc. No. 350, Box 11, File 11-11, 'Employment, Women and Negroes, UAW Regions 4-9A,' April 1943, 'Questionnaire on Employment in UAW-CIO Plants.'
61 ALUA, UAW Region 7 Toronto Sub-Regional Office, Box 14, File 'Miscellaneous Material, 1942.'
62 Ibid.
63 Ibid., File 'Meeting, November 1942, Minutes and Report'; ibid., Box 11,
File 'Miscellaneous Material, 1942,' Minutes, District Council 26, 7–8 November 1942.
64 Ibid.
65 Ibid.
66 Ibid.
67 Ibid.
68 ALUA, UAW Canadian Region – Companies Collection, Box 136, File 2,
'Ford Motor Company of Canada, Limited, Windsor, 1943,' W.H. Clark to
Regional War Labour Board, 3 June 1943.
69 ALUA, UAW Region 7 Toronto Sub-Regional Office Collection, Box 11, File
'Meeting, June 1943, Minutes.'
70 Ibid., File 'Meeting, August 1943, Minutes and Report.'
71 Gloria Montero, 'George Burt: The UAW and the Ford Windsor Strike 1945'

in *We Stood Together*, ed. Gloria Montero (Toronto: James Lorimer 1979, pp. 91–111); ALUA, UAW Region 7 Toronto Sub-Regional Office, Box 11, File 'Meeting, August 1943, Minutes and Report,' George Burt's Report to the District Council 26 Meeting, 7–8 August 1943.

72 ALUA, UAW Canadian Region – Companies Collection, Box 136, File 'Ford Motor Company of Canada, Windsor, 1945,' Chronological History of Conciliation in Industrial Relations Between the Ford Motor Company of Canada and UAW Local 200.

73 ALUA, UAW Region 7 Toronto Sub-Regional Office, Box 11, File 'Meeting, January 1943, Minutes and Report,' Minutes, District Council 26 Meeting, 16–17 January 1943.

74 ALUA, George Burt Collection, Box 1, File 1-7, 'District Council 26, Brief Submitted to the National War Labour Board c. 1943–44.'

75 Ibid.

76 ALUA, UAW Canadian Region – Companies Collection, Box 136, File 11, 'Ford, Windsor, 1946, Agreements, Negotiations, Awards,' Memorandum of Agreement, Ford Motor Company and UAW-CIO, March 1945.

77 *Oshaworker*, Vol. 3, No. 20, 7 November 1945, p. 1.

78 ALUA, UAW Region 7 Toronto Sub-Regional Office, Box 11, File 'Meeting, June 1943, Minutes,' Minutes, District Council 26, 5–6 June 1943.

79 Ibid. File 'Meeting, August 1943, Minutes and Report.'

80 Union leaders seldom advocated equal pay for work of equal value – a strategy that would have benefited far more women. In a rare instance, in 1943 UAW International representative John Eldon argued for this principle as it was established in the GM Agreement across the border. According to the American settlement, explained Eldon, women do not have to perform exactly the same kind of work as men because the principle was based on labour costs. The Regional War Labour Board verbally agreed with Eldon, but this interpretation was not widely upheld in Canada, and it was seldom used.

81 During the war, the War Labour Board had to approve all wage adjustments. Order in Council P.C. 9384, Section 14, Clause C, provided machinery to rectify 'any gross inequalities and injustices' in established wage rates. ALUA, UAW Toronto Sub-Regional Office Collection, Box 80, File 'National War Labour Board, 1943–44.'

82 ALUA, UAW Canadian Region – Companies Collection, Box 145, File 'GM of Canada, Limited, Oshawa, 1944.'

83 The equation of a sanding machine to an electric floor polisher exemplifies what Milkman (1987) terms the 'idiom of sex-typing.' Milkman states that while sex segregation itself has been a constant feature of industries over time, the specific content of occupational sex-labelling has varied.

84 The National War Labour Board upheld the original decision of the Regional Board, noting that the decision was based on an investigation of the work. Although the women's job was made less arduous since July 1944, they dismissed GM's appeal. The board, however, added that 'the new rate is not to be set up as a reason for increasing any other female rate in the plant.' *Oshaworker*, Vol. 2, No. 23, 6 December 1944, p. 1; ALUA, UAW Toronto Sub-Regional Office Collection, National War Labour Board Decisions, Dominion Labour Service, Book 3, Box 68, National War Labour Board Decision 38-1152, 1 January 1945.

85 ALUA, UAW Canadian Region – Locals Collection, Box 89, File 14, 'Local 222 Oshawa, 1944–46.'

86 ALUA, UAW Canadian Region – Companies Collection, Box 145, File 6, 'GM of Canada Limited, Oshawa, 1945.'

87 ALUA, UAW Canadian Region – Companies Collection, Box 144, File 2, 'GM of Canada Limited, Correspondence, 1943–46.' However, Burt supported the UAW Bargaining Committees's proposal to eliminate the junior or boys' classifications in the plant. When GM turned down this request, Burt wrote, 'Personally, I believe this whole condition should be eliminated.' The boys' classification was unique only to GM, as neither Ford nor Chrysler had instituted such barriers on the basis of age. In both plants the hiring rate on similar operations to those in which boys work in GM was the same as for adult workers. The only difference in Ford and Chrysler between their ordinary rates and those paid to juniors was the apprenticeship for skilled tradesmen. The Bargaining Committee insisted on negotiating a reduction of the age. Burt further stated, 'Our main argument being that eighteen-year-olds are doing a man's job overseas.' The union feared that the existing clause may affect a returning veteran who performed a man's job and received a corresponding man's pay in the army, but would be forced to accept a boys' rate under this clause upon his return to the plant. ALUA, UAW Canadian Region – Companies Collection, Box 144, File 2, 'GM of Canada Limited, Correspondence, 1943–46.'

88 CAW, George Burt Private Papers, Brief Submitted to the National War Labour Board by District Council 26, United Automobile, Aircraft, Agricultural Implement Workers of America Affiliated to the Canadian Congress of Labour, pp. 16–17.

89 Similar dilemmas around the seniority issue arose for unionists in industries such as steel and electrical. In 1945 Local 1005 of the United Steel Workers of America made a bargaining proposal for equal seniority rights of male and female workers. However, this proposal was ultimately dropped, and there was no mention of it in subsequent years. See Robert Storey, 'Workers, Unions, and Steel: The Shaping of the Hamilton Working

Class, 1935–1948' (unpublished Ph.D. Dissertation, University of Toronto 1981). For a detailed discussion of the union's position on seniority and women workers during the Second World War in the United States, see Ronald W. Schatz, *The Electrical Workers* (Urbana: University of Illinois Press 1983, chapter 5).

90 'Reportage of Oshawa Strike, 1937, Vol. 1,' *St Catharines Standard*, 23 April 1937, p. 1.

91 ALUA. Emil Mazey Collection, Box 13, File 13-5, 'Women's Division, 1941–47 – 1,' R.J. Thomas to all UAW-CIO Officers and Regional Directors, 13 November 1944.

92 Ibid.

93 ALUA, UAW Region 7 Toronto Sub-Regional Office, Box 9, File 'Staff Meetings, January–February, 1944, Minutes,' Minutes, Region 7 Staff Meeting, 22–3 January 1944.

94 Ibid.

95 Ibid.

96 *Oshaworker*, Vol. 3, No. 5, 7 March 1945, p. 1.

97 *Oshaworker*, Vol. 3, No. 6, 21 March 1945, p. 3.

98 ALUA, George Burt Collection, Box 2, File 2-2, 'District Council 26, Minutes, Burt's Reports and Related Material, June-October 1945,' George Burt Report to District Council 26 Meeting, 8–9 September 1945.

99 ALUA, UAW Canadian Region – Locals Collection, Box 89, File 14, 'Local 222, Oshawa, 1944–46,' Malcolm Smith to George Burt, 27 August 1945.

100 *Oshaworker*, Vol. 3, No. 16, 5 September 1945, pp. 1–2.

101 *Oshaworker*, Vol. 3, No. 19, 17 October 1945, p. 2.

102 ALUA, UAW Region 7 Toronto Sub-Regional Office Collection, Box 11, File 'Meeting, January 1946, Minutes,' Minutes, District Council 26 Meeting, 19–20 January 1946.

103 'Contract Cancellations,' *McKinnon Doings*, Vol. 8, No. 12, May 1945, p. 3.

104 ALUA, UAW Region 7 Toronto Sub-Regional Office, Box 9, File 'Staff Meetings, January–February, 1944, Minutes,' Minutes, District Council 26 Meeting, 22–3 January 1944; ibid., George Burt Collection, Box 1, File 1-8, 'District Council 26; Minutes, Burt's Reports and Related Materials; ibid., February–April, 1944,' George Burt's Report to District Council 26 Meeting, 19–20 February 1944; ibid., File 1-8, 'District Council 26; Minutes, Burt's Reports and Related Materials, February–April, 1944,' George Burt's Report to District Council 26 Meeting, 19–20 February 1944.

105 ALUA, UAW Region 7 Toronto Sub-Regional Office, Box 9, File 'Staff Meetings, January–February, 1944, Minutes,' Minutes, District Council 26 Meeting, 22–3 January 1944.

106 ALUA, Emil Mazey Collection, Box 13, File 13-5, 'Women's Division, 1941–47 – 1,' R.J. Thomas to all UAW Local Presidents, Regional Directors, and International Representatives, 26 September 1945.

107 *Oshaworker*, Vol 2, No. 10, May 31, 1944, p. 2. This theme also emerged in a dispute at the Hayes Steel plant in Merritton, Ontario, in the following year. In 1945 some Local 676 officials claimed that they were reluctant to oppose the company's plans to replace women with men because it would mean promoting the layoff of low seniority, highly paid workers, and the retention of higher seniority, but lower paid labour. ALUA, UAW Region 7 Toronto Sub-Regional Office Collection, Box 11, File 'Meeting, June 1945 – Minutes,' Minutes, District Council 26 Meeting, 23–4 June 1945. At the District Council meeting in September 1945, Ruth Thompson, Alternate Delegate representing Local 676, elaborated on this. 'The difference in male and female wage rates,' she said, 'makes the female worker a definite threat to the male worker and so, while according to our agreement, women enjoy the same seniority rights as men, we have the majority of male employees opposed to the continued hiring of female help.' ALUA, UAW Region 7 Toronto Sub-Regional Office Collection, Box 11, File 'Meeting, September 1945 – Minutes,' Minutes, District Council 26 Meeting, 8–9 September 1945.

108 ALUA, UAW Region 7 Toronto Sub-Regional Office Collection, Box 11, File 'Meeting, September 1945 – Minutes,' Minutes, District Council 26 Meeting, 8–9 September 1945.

109 Ibid., Box 9, File 'Staff Meetings, January–February, 1944, Minutes,' Minutes, Region 7 Staff Meeting, 21 February 1944.

110 Ibid., Box 11, File 'Staff Meetings, September 1945 – Minutes,' Minutes, District Council 26 Meeting, 8–9 September 1945,' Minutes, Staff Meeting, 22–3 January 1944.

111 ALUA, George Burt Collection, Box 1, File 1-8, 'District Council 26; Minutes, Burt's Reports and Related Materials, February–April, 1944,' George Burt's Report to District Council 26 Meeting, 19–20 February 1944.

112 ALUA, UAW Region 7 Toronto Sub-Regional Office Collection, Box 9, File 'Staff Meetings, January–February, 1944, Minutes,' Minutes, Region 7 Staff Meeting, 21 February 1944.

113 ALUA, Emil Mazey Collection, Box 13, File 13-5, 'Women's Division, 1941–47 '– 1,' R.J. Thomas to all UAW Local Presidents, Regional Directors, and International Representatives, 26 September, 1945.

114 ALUA, George Burt Collection, Box 1, File 1-8, 'District Council 26; Minutes, Burt's Reports and Related Materials, February–April, 1944,' George Burt's Report to the District Council 26 Meeting, 19–20 February 1944; ALUA, UAW Region 7 Toronto Sub-Regional Office Collection, Box

11, File 'February 1944; Minutes,' Minutes, District Council 26 Meeting, 19–20 February 1944.

115 UAW sisters in the United States were more vocal about their seniority rights. Concerned about a general disinterest on the part of government, the public, and even some unionists in ensuring women's equal job opportunities during reconversion, Mildred Jeffrey, Director of the UAW Women's Bureau, declared on behalf of her sisters in the International, 'We feel very strongly that women are going to have to fight and fight hard to get their fair and equal seniority protection both in the layoff period and certainly when it comes to rehiring. Unless women demonstrate now that they are not going to take discrimination lying down, we are going to be in a much weaker position to combat it later on.' ALUA, UAW War Policy Division – Women's Bureau Collection, Box 1, File 1-1, 'Absenteeism and Turnover,' Mildred Jeffrey to Ruth Adlard, 5 July 1945.

In November 1944 a committee of ten UAW women announced that they would try to protect millions of female war workers from being treated as ' "expendable home front soldiers" ' when companies return to domestic production. ALUA, UAW Research Department Collection, Box 32, File: 'Women and the Labor Movement, 1943–44,' 'UAW Moves to Assure Women of Postwar Jobs,' *Detroit News*, 19 November 1944. Thus the theme of the UAW-CIO Women's Conference in Detroit was full employment and women's special interest in achieving the union's goal of 60,000,000 jobs and a decent standard of living in the post-war period. Conference delegates forcefully urged the International Executive Board to assure women of their full and fair seniority rights through the elimination of discriminatory contract clauses, separate seniority lists, sex-based job classifications and wage rates, and laxness on the part of union committeemen, stewards, and negotiating committees in enforcing good seniority contract provisions. ALUA, UAW War Policy Division Victor Reuther Collection, Box 27, File 'War Policy Women's Bureau, November 1944 – January 1944.'

116 ALUA, UAW Region 7 Toronto Sub-Regional Office Collection, Box 9, File 'Staff Meetings, January–February, 1944, Minutes,' Minutes, Region 7 Staff Meeting, 21 February 1944. The Canadian Director reminded members that the UAW International Executive Board had a policy of strict seniority. At the UAW International Convention in Grand Rapids, Michigan, delegates resolved that 'women workers must receive fair and just treatment in seniority rights.' They further stated that the incoming UAW IEB would review all UAW-CIO contracts in order to assist local unions to eliminate sexually discriminatory clauses and add clauses to protect female workers.

The UAW Research Department had reviewed all contracts on file with respect to this resolution. It distributed, as an example, discriminatory contract clauses pertaining to women, and a list of contracts which contain discriminatory, separate sex-based seniority clauses. ALUA, Emil Mazey Collection, Box 13, File 13-5, 'Women's Division, 1941–47 – 1,' R.J. Thomas to UAW Officers and Regional Directors, 13 November 1944.

117 ALUA, George Addes Secretary Treasurer Collection, Box 80, Plant Survey Cards.

118 UAW women in the United States, however, demanded the elimination of separate seniority lists as well as sex-based job classifications. ALUA, UAW War Policy Division – Victor Reuther Collection, Box 27, File 'War Policy, Women's Bureau, November 1944 – January 1944.' In 1946 delegates to the UAW-CIO International Convention presented a resolution for the International to work towards the elimination of separate seniority lists for women. ALUA, UAW Women's Department, Lillian Hatcher Collection, Box 20, Resolution 38, UAW-CIO Tenth Annual Convention, File 20–2 'Conventions and Resolutions, 1955–67.'

119 At the first International UAW Women's Conference in Detroit in December 1944, delegates implied that women workers were expected to perform sexual favours. Women in the southern Ontario auto plants claimed that this was not a pervasive problem after unionization, but they were resigned to the occasional instances.

120 In October 1943 the UAW International Convention issued mandates on maternity provisions for female workers. But generally this was not a significant topic of debate in Canada.

121 Conde and Beveridge Interviews: Olive Farnell/Doug Clark, 20/8/82, UAW 222/15, pp. 3–4.

122 Ibid.: Mary Turner, 2/3/83, UAW 222/29, p. 3.

123 By October 1943 the UAW International boasted 200,000 women among its total of approximately 1,000,000 members. 'Equal Rights Worry UAW,' *Detroit News*, 25 October 1943. By the following month of the same year this figure had risen to approximately 250,000. And one-third of this 250,000 were mothers of children aged under 16 years. ALUA, UAW Toronto Sub-Regional Office Collection, Box 5, File 'Eldon, John, Correspondence, November–December, 1943,' John Eldon to Walter Reuther, 1 November 1943. Most of these women, however, were employed in Detroit and other Michigan war plants.

124 ALUA, Emil Mazey Collection, Box 13, File 13–5, 'Women's Division, 1941–47, – 1.

125 *Oshaworker*, Vol. 2, No. 14, 2 August 1944, p. 2.
126 'Canada Organizes Her Resources for the War,' *McKinnon People*, undated wartime issue, p. 57.
127 Conde and Beveridge Interviews: Elsie Karn, 27/9/82, UAW 222/21, pp. 10–11.
128 Ibid.: Ivy Imerson and Bill Imerson, UAW 222/16, pp. 1–2.
129 Recently, though, there have been some more nuanced accounts of these nineteenth century struggles. For example, in her study of the regulation of women's work in British cotton mills from 1820 to 1850, M. Valverde (1988) shows that the 'public' that became concerned about female labour was not a homogeneous mass. Rather, it was composed of 'groups in conflict.' These groups included legislators and philanthropists, mill owners, factory inspectors, and working-class organizations that were divided by gender and occupational status. In addition, workers themselves were divided by age, occupation, and gender.
130 In her study of the sexual division of labour in the United States auto and electrical industries, Ruth Milkman (1987) demonstrates that the structure of jobs sometimes causes working men's gender interests and class interests to come into conflict, just as men's 'class interests' will, at times, coincide with women's 'gender interests.' In her view the interests of male workers can be against or in support of women depending on the features of the industrial setting. Similarly, in Canada working men sometimes upheld the equal pay principle because it strengthened male unionists' own economic position in the labour market. However, this was also a strategy that benefited women.

CHAPTER 3

1 Workers who were employed by General Motors in the 1930s and 1940s, typically refer to the company as 'The Motors.'
2 Wilson; Manning; Heritz; Anderson; Beaugrand; Wigg; Larkin; Baldwin interviews.
3 This is consistent with general findings on the motives of women workers during the Second World War in Canada. For example, according to a 1943 survey of married women over the age of thirty-five who were seeking employment, over one-half of the respondents reported that they wanted to supplement the family income, while one in ten cited patriotism, and the remainder claimed they were seeking paid work for 'personal needs' (Pierson, 1986: 47).

4 For further discussion of the use of feminine culture and the influence of
   gendered learning and patriarchal constraints on women's coping and resistance strategies, see for example, Hossfeld (1990), McRobbie (1978), Rosen (1987), Westwood (1985), Gregg (1993), Hsiung (1991). Angela Mc-
   Robbie (1978: 108) argues that the culture of adolescent working class girls
   is a response to the material constraints that result from their class position.
   However, she notes that it is also an 'index of, and response to their sexual
   oppression as women.' In her view, these girls are both 'saved by and
   locked within' the culture of femininity.
       In her study of women factory workers in New England, Ellen Israel Ro-
   sen (1987: 68) states that women do not express 'class consciousness and
   resistance to the exploitive nature of the work process' on a daily basis 'in
   militant efforts to challenge or undermine the piece-rate system. Instead,
   women have learned to live with the piece-rate.' For example, they form
   positive relationships with supervisors and friendship with workmates.
   This keeps the shopfloor from 'becoming an armed camp.' 'Most of these
   blue-collar women feel they have been able to carve out a sphere of autonomy and a network of interpersonal communications which make the
   workplace liveable.' This enables them to return to the factory day after
   day and simultaneously retain their dignity. Rosen describes women's resistance as a form of 'self-protection.'
       Karen Hossfeld (1990) also explores this theme in an account of the rela-
   tionship between 'Third World immigrant women production workers'
   and their predominantly white male managers in high-tech manufacturing
   in Silicon Valley, California. Hossfeld argues that in workplaces that are
   divided by sex and race, class struggle takes gender- and race-specific
   forms. Managers encourage women immigrant workers to identify with
   their gender, racial, and national identities in an effort to 'distract' the
   workers from 'class' concerns. In turn, women themselves, turn to conventional gender ideologies and forms of work culture that reaffirm traditional
   conceptions of femininity. According to Hossfeld, this happens because
   women are engaged in roles that are traditionally defined as non-feminine.
   She notes that while 'factory work and wage earning are indeed traditions
   long held by working-class women, the dominant ideology that such tasks
   are "unfeminine" is equally traditional.' Prescriptions about proper identity and behaviour for women have various dimensions. One, the 'definition of "feminine" derives from an upper-class reality in which women
   traditionally did not need ... to earn incomes.' Two, many wage-earning
   women feel ' "unwomanly" ' at work because they are away from home

and family. And three, wage earning is regarded by some men and women as ' "unwifely" ' because it strips men of their identity as ' "breadwinner" ' (Hossfeld, 1990: 158–9).

5 'To the Ladies,' *McKinnon Doings*, Vol. 8, No. 9, January 1945, p. 11.
6 'To Keep Your Hands White,' *McKinnon Doings*, Vol. 6, No. 12, March 1943, p. 9.
7 'The Fair Sex,' *McKinnon Doings*, Vol. 6, No. 1, 24 April 1942, p. 10.
8 *McKinnon Doings*, Vol. 8, No. 4, July 1944, p. 7.
9 'New Safety Regulations Demand Bandanas,' *McKinnon Doings*, Vol. 8, No. 11, March 1945, p. 12.
10 Ibid.
11 'Crown and Glory,' *McKinnon Doings*, Vol. 9, No. 2, 1945, p. 7.
12 There is little evidence that employers attempted to resolve these tensions by either seeking suggestions about preferred headgear from the women themselves or by making the machinery safer and thereby lessening the need for such provisions.
13 'New Zoot,' *McKinnon Doings*, Vol. 6, No. 7, 19 October 1942, p. 8.
14 *McKinnon Doings*, Vol. 5, No. 12, 20 March 1942, p. 5; 'Girls Safety Shoes, Dresses and Coveralls,' *McKinnon Doings*, Vol. 6, No. 1, 24 April 1942, p. 5.
15 'To the Ladies,' *McKinnon Doings*, Vol. 6, No. 7, 19 October 1942, p. 7.
16 Sallie Westwood (1985) and Lois Scharf (1980), for example, also document the importance of marriage rituals in women workers' shop-floor culture.
17 *Oshaworker*, Vol. 5, No. 5, 5 March 1947, p. 4.
18 'To the Ladies,' *McKinnon Doings*, Vol. 6, No. 12, March 1943; ibid. Vol. 7, No. 4, July 1943, p. 7.
19 Though married women whose husbands were serving overseas received a married allowance during the war, it was insufficient to cover the subsistence needs of many people. The Labour Department and NSS officials recognized that most of the married women with children who sought factory work did so out of economic necessity. See Ruth Roach Pierson, *'They're Still Women Afterall': The Second World War and Canadian Womanhood* (Toronto: McCelland and Stewart 1986: 47–8).
20 Violet Towne, 'To the Ladies,' *McKinnon Doings*, August 1945, p. 11.
21 'To the Ladies,' *McKinnon Doings*, Vol. 7, No. 3, June 1943, pp. 9–10; ibid. Vol. 7, No. 4, July 1943, p. 7; ibid. Vol. 7, No. 9, Christmas 1943, p. 11.
22 'The Fair Sex,' *McKinnon Doings*, Vol. 6, No. 3, 25 June 1942, p. 6.
23 In addition, some women *perceived* their socializing as an expression of defiance, whether or not supervision was even aware of these acts. For example, they took delight in reporting that they had 'gotten away with' inces-

sant talking and they had secret codes to inform one another when the supervisor was approaching. Some women described this behaviour with a sense of mischievousness.

24 Many women, for example, noted that although there was also a definite camaraderie in GM's wire and harness department, there was not an equally strong sense of family. 'Everyone in the sewing room seemed to be close knit where I think there were more cliques over in the wiring harness,' reported one woman.

25 Some social historians have suggested that the concentration of women in workplaces and in the Armed Forces during the Second World War provided some women with the opportunity to discover their desire for intimate same-sex relationships. See, for example, Berube (1990). Some of the women I interviewed never married, lived with another woman, and spoke of her with compassion. However, because I did not consider this possibility at the outset of my research, I had assured the women that I would not inquire about such highly intimate matters. I therefore did not pursue this theme, and no one volunteered information on this topic.

26 This theme is explored in a number of recent writings on organizations. See, for example, Hearn and Parkin (1987); Hearn, Sheppard, Tancred-Sheriff, and Burrell (1989).

27 See discussion in Hearn and Parkin (1987: 83).

28 Women's perceptions of what behaviours constitute 'sexual harassment' have probably varied over time. It is likely that during the 1940s, women workers experienced treatment that we would currently regard as 'harassment,' but without the language, resources, and political understanding that we use in discussing the issue today, they may not have perceived, and defined it as such.

29 There were some female supervisors in the women's departments, but for some (unclear) reason these women were eventually demoted to the position of group leader. By far, the majority of supervisors were men.

CHAPTER 4

1 ALUA, George Addes, Secretary-Treasurer Collection, Box 80, Plant Survey Cards.

2 ALUA, UAW Canadian Region, Series V Collection, File 7, GM of Canada Limited, Oshawa, 1955, Box 146, Classification Lists, 1955.

3 'Behind The Sewing Machines of GM's Upholstery Tailors,' *GM Topics*, Vol. 12, No. 1, January 1961; 'Miles of Wire in GM's Wiring Department,' *GM Topics*, Vol. 12, No. 6, June 1961, pp. 6–7.

4 ALUA, George Addes, Secretary-Treasurer Collection, Boxes 80–1, Plant
   Survey Cards, Research and Engineering Department, UAW-CIO.
5 *McKinnon People*, Vol. 13, No. 3, May–June 1950, p. 4. GM (Oshawa) and
   McKinnon Industries were still among the largest employers of women of
   the southern Ontario auto manufacturers. Companies that supplied parts to
   the Big Three auto firms employed women. However, female representation in these companies was limited. For instance, in 1948 UAW Local 252
   reported that Wilkening Manufacturing in Toronto, whose total production
   went to GM, employed 15 (white) women out of a total of 44 workers.
   Wilson Motor Bodies Limited in Long Branch, Ontario, had not hired any
   women, and Westeel in Toronto, a manufacturer of truck bodies, employed
   only two (white) women out of a total workforce of 350. UAW Local 222
   reported that the Skinner Company in Oshawa, a division of the Houdaille-
   Hershey Corporation, employed (white) men exclusively in the production
   of bumpers and buffer plates for GM and Chrysler. Ontario Steel Products,
   whose total production went to GM, Ford, Chrysler, White Truck, Reo, and
   Freuhauf, also employed (white) men only.
      At the end of the Second World War the Ford Motor Company of Can-
   ada had still not hired any women in production jobs. In 1948 there were
   350 (black) men and 9,820 (white) men out of a total bargaining unit of
   10,170 in Ford's Windsor plant. Ford's stockroom in Toronto, employed 260
   (white) men. Similarly, by 1960 there were still no women in the American
   Motors plant, Smith Brothers Motor Bodies, or GM's Frigidaire Products in
   Toronto. In Rootes Motors women worked only in the Parts Department as
   'office girls.' In Somerville Limited 12 women assembled automotive, radio,
   and television panels. Approximately 12 women were employed packaging
   small parts in the Chrysler Parts Depot in Chatham, Ontario.
6 Baldwin interview.
7 ALUA, UAW Canadian Region, General Files Collection, Box 25, File 11,
   'International UAW Women's Department and Canadian Region Women's
   Department, 1960–64, 'Caroline Davis to George Burt, 1 March 1961.
8 *Oshaworker*, Vol. 12, No. 12, 17 June 1954, p. 2.
9 'Sewing Room Department 32,' *Oshaworker*, Vol. 5, No. 10, 6 June 1957, p. 2.
10 Conde and Beveridge Interviews: Maurie Shorten, UAW 222/23, p. 7.
11 For example, an article in a 1955 issue of the *Oshaworker* read, 'Nobody
   wants women to stop being feminine – not that there's any danger of that.
   But they're in a really difficult position when they move into the industrial
   business world, because they have centuries of training behind them –
   training that handicaps them.'
      The author stated that girls are not taught the folklore about men. Rather,

it's 'something they breathe in through the skin.' Men are supposed to in-
stinctively know about such things as money, machinery, politics, and the
like, and women credit them with this knowledge ...' Every man is entitled
to be a hero in his own home, as long as he'll make room for a heroine, too,'
the article read. 'It's when the Little Woman gets out on the job that all this
background training trips her up. And if she isn't married, if she's a girl
going straight from school to work, it's just as bad. She's likely to have the
feeling (a) that she probably isn't as good a worker as the man next to her,
(b) that there are a lot of things that's best to leave to Men, and (c) that her
pay and working conditions don't matter too much because maybe she'll
get married pretty soon and get out of the whole thing. So she leaves thing
[sic] like pressing for equal wages and going to union meetings, to the men
and to few tiresome females who keep pestering her. She has more exciting
things to do with her leisure.' Oshaworker, Vol. 13, No. 1, 6 January 1955,
p. 3.
12 Women were often featured in advertisements for the union. One caption
read, 'Let's take an active part in our union! Attend your union meetings
sign up those non-members.' UAW Local 199 News and Views, Vol. 3, No. 1,
January 1958, p. 10.
13 Oshaworker, Vol. 13, No. 1, 6 January 1955, p. 3.
14 This discussion is based on a systematic review of all grievances and arbitration decisions in the archival collections and private papers for the period of study. Until the 1970s grievances filed by women were easy to isolate because of the given name of the grievant, and because reports often
identified the grievant's sex, if the employee was female.
15 The UAW grievance procedure stated that

An employee having a grievance or one designated member of a group
having a grievance should first take the grievance up with his foreman who
will attempt to adjust it. Any employee may request his foreman to call his
Zone Committeeman without due delay and without further discussion of
the grievance. If the grievance is not adjusted by the foreman it shall be
reduced to writing on an Employee Grievance form provided by the Company and signed by the employee involved and a copy shall be given to the
foreman. The foreman shall give his reply in writing on the Employee
Grievance Form to the Zone Committeeman not later than two working
days following the receipt by foreman of the written grievance.

Stage Two
If the grievance is not adjusted by the foreman an appeal may be lodged by

the Zone Committeeman within two working days thereafter to the Superintendent of the aggrieved employee's department.

The Zone Committeeman will be given an opportunity to discuss the grievance with the Superintendent with or without the employees concerned being present. The Superintendent shall give his decision in writing on the Employee Grievance form to the employee, or to such Zone Committeeman not later than two working days following the presentation to him of the written grievance.

Stage Three
If the written decision of the Superintendent is not satisfactory to the employee, the Grievance Committee may, within five working days thereafter appeal in writing to the Industrial Relations Manager. The Industrial Relations Manager or his designated representative shall consider the written grievance at a meeting with the Grievance Committee. The decision of the Industrial Relations Manager or his designated representative shall be given in writing to the Grievance Committee not later than three working days after the holding of such meeting. An agenda of the written grievances to be considered at any such meeting shall be submitted to the Industrial Relations Manager by a Grievance Committee not later than three working days prior to such meeting ... I would advise the members if this procedure is not adhered to by the foreman, the members that signs [*sic*] the grievance form should refuse to discuss the grievance further in the General Foreman's Office. *Oshaworker*, Vol. 10, No. 2, 23 January 1952, p. 3.

16 *Oshaworker*, Vol. 9, No.18, 5 December 1951, p. 2.
17 See, for example, Richard Herding, *Job Control and Union Structure* (Rotterdam: Rotterdam University Press 1972).
18 ALUA, UAW Local 199 Collection, Box 20, File 'Bargaining, 1950,' Bargaining Committee Meeting, 27 October 1950.
19 Bender interview.
20 Beverly C. Gibson, 'Department 32,' *Oshaworker*, Vol. 21, No. 8, 9 May 1963, p. 4.
21 For example, ALUA, UAW Local 199 Collection, Box 6, File 'Grievances, Step 1 & 2, 1957,' Employee Grievance No. 1087; ibid., Employee Grievance No. 1080; ibid., Box 7, File 'Grievances, Step 1 & 2, 1959–60,' Employee Grievance 1776; ibid., File 'Step 3, January–August, 1958,' H.W. McArthur to James Connell, 18 February 1958; ibid., Employee Grievance No. 2312; ibid., Box 8, File 'Grievances, Step 1 & 2, 1963,' Employee Grievance No. 3103, 18 December 1963; ibid., Employee Grievance No. 1718; ibid., File

'Grievances, Step 3, January–June, 1962,' H.W. McArthur to Gordon Lambert, 1 February 1962; ibid., File 'Grievances, Step 1 & 2, 1963,' Employee Grievance No. 3117; ibid., Box 11, File 'Meetings with Management, July–December 1962,' Employee Grievance 2444; ibid., File 'Meetings with Management, 1958,' Minutes of Meeting with Shop Committee, 13 February 1958.

22 For example, ALUA, UAW Local 199 Collection, Box 8, File 'Grievances, 1962, Step 1 & 2' (second file), Employee Grievance No. 1718; ibid., Employee Grievance No. 1717; ibid., Employee Grievance 2592; ibid., File 'Grievances, Step 1 & 2, 1963,' Employee Grievance No. 2932; ibid., Box 11, File 'Meetings with Management, January–May, 1963,' Employee Grievance 2608.

23 ALUA, UAW Local 199 Collection, Box 6, File 'Grievances Step 1 & 2,' 1957, Employee Grievance No. 10832.

24 Ibid., Box 5, File 'Miscellaneous, 1951,' Employee Grievance No. 2610.

25 ALUA, UAW Local 199 Collection, Box 6, File 'Grievances, Step 1 & 2,' 1957, Employee Grievance No. 107799.

26 ALUA, UAW Local 199 Collection, Box 11, File 'Grievances, Step 3, 1959–60'; ibid., Box 7, File 'Meetings with Management, January–June, 1959,' Employee Grievance No. 1777.

27 Ibid., Box 28, File 'McKinnon Unit Minutes, 1951–64,' 'Delco Workers Study on Bug and Insect Life.'

28 ALUA, UAW Toronto Sub-Regional Office Collection, Box 44, File 'GM of Canada Limited, 1954–57,' Arbitration Case No. CH 18.

29 *Oshaworker*, Vol. 9, No. 5, 7 March 1951, p. 4.

30 Similarly, in her study of immigrant women workers in Silicon Valley, Karen Hossfeld (1990: 171–2) argues that the workers' acts of resistance against management and work arrangements often played on the white male managers' consciousness (both false and real) about gender and ethnic culture. Hossfeld describes this as an instance of turning management's own ideologies 'against them by exploiting their male supervisors' misconceptions about "female problems." ' Insofar as the women themselves adopted these ideas, I do not claim that female auto workers consciously manipulated prevailing gender ideologies. However, the women did draw on these widely held beliefs (as a cultural resource) in their efforts to better working conditions.

31 ALUA, UAW Local 199 Collection, Box 7, File 'Grievances, Step 1 & 2, 1961,' Employee Grievance, No. 2067; ibid., Box 8, File 'Grievances, Step 1 & 2, 1963,' Employee Grievance No. 2620; ibid., Box 8, File 'Grievances, Step 3, May–December 1963,' H.W. McArthur to Gordon Lambert, 12 July

1963; ibid., Box 11, File 'Meetings with Management, July–December 1962,' Employee Grievance No. 669.

32　Ibid., Box 7, File 'Grievances, 1961, Step 1 & 2,' Employee Grievance No. 2064.

33　Ibid., Box 8, File 'Grievances, Step 3, July–December 1962,' H.W. McArthur to Gordon Lambert, 29 November 1962.

34　For example, ALUA, UAW Local 199 Collection, Box 8, File 'Grievances, Step 3, January–March 1963,' H.W. McArthur to Gordon Lambert, 21 February 1963; ibid., Box 11, File 'Meetings with Management – January–May 1963,' Employee Grievance 2614. At times, working men lodged similar complaints, but the tone of their grievances was different. Unlike the women's complaints, they expressed an indignation that supervisors yell or swear at them, but they did not entail a notion of female sensitivity.

35　ALUA, UAW Local 199 Collection, Box 10, File 'Meeting with Management, March–May 1952.'

36　Pat Meagher. 'Cutting and Sewing News Roundup,' *Oshaworker*, Vol. 11, No. 2, 22 January 1953, p. 2.

37　ALUA, UAW Local 199 Collection, Box 11, File 'Meetings with Management, January–May, 1961,' Minutes of Meeting with Shop Committee, 22 December 1960.

38　Ibid., Box 21, Binder 'Bargaining, 1956–62,' Minutes of Meeting of the Radio Department, 6 November 1962.

39　They did not, however, support 'protective' legislation that, for example, would restrict the hours of women's employment. Many women regarded this law to be discriminatory.

40　See, for example, Milkman (1986), Razack (1991), and Scott (1988) for a discussion of the logic of demanding a recognition of 'difference' in a context of inequality, in order to achieve equality of outcome.

41　ALUA, UAW Local 199 Collection, Box 6, File 'Working Conditions, 1952,' H.W. McArthur to John Kramer, 4 December 1952; ibid., Box 10, File 'Meetings with Management, September–December 1952,' Minutes of Meeting with Plant Negotiating Committee, 27 November 1952; ibid., Box 12, File 'Replies from Management, 1956,' H.W. McArthur to Gordon Lambert, 29 May 1956.

42　Ibid., Box 10, File 'Meetings with Management, 1956,' Minutes of Meeting with Shop Committee, 24 May 1956.

43　Ibid., Box 11, File 'Meetings with Management, 1957,' Minutes of Meeting with Shop Committee, 28 March 1957.

44　Ibid., Box 11, File 'Meetings with Management, May–December 1961,' H.W. McArthur to Gordon Lambert, 30 August 1961.

45 Ibid., Box 12, File 'Replies to Items Discussed, 1962,' J.H. Morrow to unidentified UAW representative, 6 July 1962.
46 Ibid., Box 11, File 'Meetings with Management, January–June 1959.'
47 Goddard and Jackson interview; ALUA, UAW Local 199 Collection, Box 11, File 'Meetings with Management, January–June 1959.'
48 Smith, Malcolm, 'President's Column,' *Oshaworker*, Vol. 18, No. 7, 7 April 1960, p. 1.
49 Conde and Beveridge Interviews: Bev McCloskey/Bill Harding, 14/6/82, UAW 222/3, p. 24.
50 ALUA, UAW Local 199 Collection, Box 10, File 'Meetings with Management, April–August, 1951,' 'Conditions in Department 63.'
51 For example, ibid., Box 7, File 'Grievances, Step 1 & 2, 1959–60,' Employee Grievance No. 1157; ibid., Box 8, File 'Grievances, Step 1 & 2, 1963,' Employee Grievance No. 2631.
52 Ibid., Box 6, File 'Grievances, Step 1 & 2, 1957,' Employee Grievance No. 585.
53 Ibid., Box 8, File 'Grievances, Step 3, May–December 1963.'
54 Ibid., Box 8, File 'Grievances, Step 1 & 2, 1963,' Employee Grievance No. 3116.
55 *Oshaworker*, Vol. 6, No. 5, 6 March 1958, p. 2.
56 Wilson, Nels, 'Tidbits from the North Plant,' *Oshaworker*, Vol. 10, No. 17, 1 November 1962, p. 5.
57 ALUA, UAW Local 199 Collection, Box 11, File 'Meetings with Management, January–June 1959,' Minutes of Meeting with Shop Committee, 15 January 1959.
58 Ibid.
59 Ibid., Box 10, File 'Meeting with Management, April–August, 1951,' Minutes of Meeting, 2 May 1951.
60 Conde and Beveridge Interviews: Bev McCloskey/Bill Harding, 14/6/82, UAW 222/3, p. 24.
61 This issue, however, was more complicated than others insofar as it seemed to counterpose workers' health and safety to their personal freedoms. In reviewing much discussion of this matter, however, I have not found any evidence that women themselves were consulted by either their union representatives or employers about an appropriate type of head gear. The women did not have a mechanism for discussion of this issue, and they resented this.
62 ALUA, UAW Local 199 Collection, Box 10, File 'Meetings with Management, April–August, 1951,' Minutes of Meeting, 17 April 1951.
63 Ibid., Box 8, Minutes of Meeting with Shop Committee, 8 November 1962;

ibid., File: 'Grievances, Step 3, July–December, 1962,' H.W. McArthur to Gordon Lambert, 15 November 1962; ibid., Box 11, File 'Meetings with Management, July–December, 1962.'

64 For example, the following year, supervision also reprimanded Jessie Donaldson and Marion Lemsay in McKinnon's A.C. Division regarding the use of bandanas. Ibid., Box 8, File 'Grievances, Step 1 & 2, 1963,' Employee Grievance No. 1805.

65 Ibid., Box 21, Binder 'Bargaining 1956–62,' leaflet, 6 November 1962.

66 Ibid., Box 10, File 'Meetings with Management, 1956,' Minutes of Meeting with Shop Committee, 5 July 1956.

67 Ibid., Box 21, Binder no. 2, 'Bargaining, 1956–62,' Minutes of Meeting with Bargaining Committee, 28 January 1957.

68 Ibid., Box 8, File 'Grievances, Step 1 & 2, 1963,' Employee Grievance No. 2843.

69 For example, ibid., File 'Grievances, Step 3, July–December, 1962,' J.H. Morrow to Gordon Lambert, 6 July 1962.

70 For example, ibid., Box 10, File 'Meetings with Management, September–December, 1952,' Minutes of Meeting with Plant Negotiating Committee, 17 October 1952.

71 For example, ibid., File 'Meetings with Management, January–February, 1952,' Minutes of Meeting with Plant Negotiating Committee, 27 December 1951; ibid., File 'Meeting with Management, September–December, 1951,' Minutes of Meeting with Plant Negotiating Committee, 18 September 1951.

72 For example, ibid., Box 8, File 'Grievances, Step 3, May–December, 1963,' Employee Grievance No. 674; ibid., Box 11, File 'Meetings with Management, July–December, 1962,' Minutes of Meeting with Shop committee, 8 November 1963; ibid., File 'Meetings with Management, August–December, 1960,' Minutes of Meeting with Shop Committee, 24 November 1960; ibid., File 'Meetings with Management, January–June, 1959,' Minutes of Meeting with Shop Committee, 23 April 1959; ibid., File 'Meeting with Management, 1958,' Minutes of Meeting with Shop Committee, 4 July 1958; ibid., File 'Meetings with Management, July–December, 1962,' Minutes of Meeting with Shop Committee, 22 November 1962; ibid., File 'Meeting with Management, January–June, 1959,' Minutes of Meeting with Shop Committee, 23 April 1959; ibid., Box 12, File 'Replies from Management, 1953'; ibid., File 'Replies from Management,' H.W. McArthur to John Kramer, 20 November 1952; ibid., File 'Replies from Management, 1953,' H.W. McArthur to John Kramer, 26 March 1953.

73 For example, Ibid., Box 10, File 'Meetings with Management, September–December, 1951,' Minutes of Meeting with Plant Negotiating Committee,

27 November 1951, p. 9; ibid., Box 12, File 'Replies from Management,' 1952, H.W. McArthur to John Kramer, 5 December 1952.

74 Ibid., Box 11, File 'Meeting with Managements – January–June, 1959,' Minutes of Meeting with Shop Committee, 12 March 1959, p. 3; ibid., Box 1, File 'Appeal Cases, 1959–60, C.I. 1–17, Record of Case C.I. 5 – Grievance 1158.

75 Ibid., Box 7, File: 'Grievances, Step 1 & 2, 1961,' Employee Grievance No. 2067; ibid., Box 8, File 'Grievances, Step 1 & 2, 1963,' Employee Grievance No. 1998.

76 Many employers also expected some groups of working men to display deference, compliance, and a childlike obedience. These expectations were not exclusive to women. Yet, in an effort to secure this compliance among the female workforce, supervision drew on conceptions of proper womanly or ladylike behaviour (which rested on qualities such as politeness, submissiveness, and harmoniousness).

77 Pat McCloskey, 'Zone 31 Sewing Room,' *Oshaworker*, Vol. 4, No. 5, 17 May 1956, p. 4.

78 In comparison, boys (under the age of 18) were employed in the Radiator Room, Rods and Tubing, Sheet Metal Stamping, Truck Body and Hardware, Window Regulator Assembly and Packard Cable, Inspection, Material Handling, Heavy Reject, Final Finish, Passenger Primary Hardware, and Final Body Fit-Up departments. Pat McCloskey, 'Zone 31 Sewing Room,' *Oshaworker*, Vol. 4, No. 5, 17 May 1956, p. 4.

79 PAC, MG 28, I 119, Acc. 83/215, Box 8, File 'General Motors Negotiations, 1955,' Proposed Occupational Classifications, 25 June 1955. Women's jobs included sewing machine operator, door and arm rest trim assembler, bench hand, clicker machine operator, headlining piler and marker, tag writer, vertical and horizontal taping machine operator, wiring harness utility operator, service wiring operator, wiring harness repair operator, Fisher body wiring harness, miscellaneous press operator, solder dipper, rest room supervisor, and matron.

80 In 1951 there were 13 female classifications out of a total of 268 job classifications. In the Foundry, women worked as core makers, inspectors, core cleaners, and core assemblers. In the Fuel Pump, female classifications included special miscellaneous machining, insulator assembly, centre wire welder, key packer, and inspector. In the Bearing, women worked on press and assembly on ballbearing operations, rematching bearing races, and inspection. In the Axle Division, women assembled wheel and master cylinders. In the Commercial Motors, they were employed as slot insulators, main and phase inserters, welder connectors, tapers, shaded pole inserters,

and coil winders. And women were winders, point setters, solderers, arma-
ture assemblers, coil tapers, and special punch press operators in the Delco
Division. ALUA, UAW Local 199 Collection, Box 12, File 'Replies from
Management, 1952,' Job Classification By Divisions – Female Employees.
By 1958, roughly 80 women worked in the Foundry, out of a total of 135.
ALUA, UAW Local 199 Collection, Box 20, File 'Bargaining 1955–1961,'
Special Bargaining Committee Meeting, 6 January 1958.

81 Ibid., Box 1, File 'Agreements, 1953,' McKinnon Industries Supplement No.
7 to the Local Wages Agreement, 6 July 1953.

82 PAC, MG 28, I 119, Acc. 83/215, Box 8, File 'GM – Local 222 Supplement to
Agreement 1963,' Letter – SUB 1956, Appendix 'A' to the local Wage
Agreement, 15 March 1957.

83 ALUA, UAW Local 199 Collection, Box 12, File 'Wage Classifications and
rates, 1951–56,' Unskilled Classifications, 1956.

84 For example, ibid., Box 1, File 'Appeal Cases 1960, CI 29–30, Record of Case
CI-30; ibid., Box 2, File 'Appeal Cases CJ 54–66,' Record of Case CJ–56;
ibid., Series I, Acc. No. 297, Box 6, File 'Working Conditions, 1952,' Em-
ployee Grievance No. 1318; ibid., File 'Wage Classification Rates, 1952–53,'
H.W. McArthur to John Kramer, 8 May 1952; ibid., Box 7, File 'Grievances,
Step 3, 1960,' H.W. McArthur to Gordon Lambert, 6 October 1960; ibid.,
File 'Step 3, January–August, 1958,' Employee Grievance No. 2312; ibid.,
'Grievances, Step 1 & 2, 1959–60,' Employee Grievance No. 1781; ibid., Box
8, File 'Grievances, Step 3, January–March 1963,' Employee Grievance No.
3119; ibid., J.H. Morrow to Gordon Lambert, 7 March 1963; ibid., Employee
Grievance No. 3083; ibid., Box 11, File 'Meetings with Management, January–May 1963,' Minutes of Meeting with Shop Committee, 9 May 1963;
ibid., File 'Meetings with Management, August–December 1960,' Minutes
of Meetings with Shop Committee, 14 October 1960; ibid., File 'Meetings
with Management, 1958,' Minutes of Meeting with Shop Committee, 13
February 1958; ibid., File 'Meetings with Management, August–December,
1960,' Minutes of Meetings with Shop Committee, 14 October 1960.

85 Ibid., Box 4, File 'Wage Classification and Rates, 1949–51,' K.J. Barbeau to
Gordon Lambert, 31 January 1951; ibid., Box 4, File 'Wage Classification
and Rates, 1949–51,' Employee Grievance No. 3079, 30 January 1951.

86 Doug Sutton, 'GM Shop Committee Report,' *Oshaworker*, Vol. 5, No. 9, 16
May 1957, pp. 4–5; ALUA, UAW Local 199 Collection, Box 10, File 'Meet-
ings with Management, March–May, 1952,' Minutes of Meeting with Plant
Negotiating Committee, 1 May 1952.

87 For example, ALUA, UAW Local 199 Collection, Box 7, File 'Grievances,
Step 3, January–June, 1961'; ibid., Box 11, File 'Meetings with Management,
1957,' Minutes of Meeting with Shop Committee, 11 April 1957.

88 'GM Shop Committee Report,' *Oshaworker*, Vol. 4, No. 13, 4 October 1956, p. 6.
89 For example, ALUA, UAW Local 199 Collection, Box 1, File 'Appeal Cases, 1960,' C.I. 29–31, Record of Case CI-37; ibid., Box 2, File 'Appeal Cases, 1961,' C.I. 52–60, Record of Case CI-54; ibid., Box 5, File 'Miscellaneous, 1951,' H.W. McArthur to John Kramer, 5 November 1951; ibid., Box 6, File 'Grievances, Step 3, March–May, 1956,' Employee Grievance No. 387; ibid., File 'Grievances, Step 1 & 2, 1956,' Employee Grievance No. 1485; ibid., File 'Seniority Grievances, 1952–53,' Employee Grievance No. 933; ibid., File 'Grievances, Step 1 & 2, 1956,' Employee Grievance No. 1326; ibid., File 'Seniority Grievances, 1952–53,' H.W. McArthur to John Kramer, March 12, 1952; ibid., File 'Seniority Grievances, 1952–53,' Employee Grievance No. 1029; ibid., Box 7, File 'Grievances, Step 1 & 2, 1961,' Employee Grievance No. 1167; ibid., File 'Grievances, Step 3, 1960,' H.W. McArthur to Gordon Lambert, 20 October 1960; ibid., File 'Grievances, Step 1 & 2, 1958,' Employee Grievance No. 1154; ibid., File 'Grievances, Step 1 & 2, 1958,' Employee Grievance No. 659; ibid., File 'Grievances, Step 1 & 2, 1959–60,' Employee Grievance No. 1162; ibid., Box 8, File 'Grievances, Step 1 & 2, 1963,' Employee Grievance No. 2962; ibid., File 'Grievances, Step 3, May–December, 1963,' J.H. Morrow to Gordon Lambert, 13 June 1963; ibid., File 'Grievances, Step 3, January–March, 1963,' H.W. McArthur to Gordon Lambert, 21 February 1963; ibid., File 'Grievances, Step 1 & 2, 1962' (second file), Employee Grievance No. 2069; ibid., Box 10, File 'Meetings with Management, 1956,' Minutes of Meeting with Shop Committee, 12 April 1956; ibid., File 'Meetings with Management, September–December, 1951,' Minutes of Meeting with Plant Negotiating Committee, 1 November 1951; ibid., Box 11, File 'Meetings with Management, January–May, 1963,' Minutes of Meeting with Shop Committee, 25 April 1963; ibid., File 'Meeting with Management, January–May, 1961,' Minutes of Meeting with Shop Committee, 3 March 1961; ibid., File 'Meetings with Management, January–May, 1961,' Minutes of Meeting with Shop Committee, 16 February 1961; ibid., File 'Meetings with Management, August–December, 1960,' Minutes of Meeting with Shop Committee, 14 September 1960; ibid., Box 20, File 'Bargaining, 1953,' Minutes of McKinnon Bargaining Committee Meeting, 26 October 1953; ibid., Box 146, File 16, 'General Motors of Canada Limited, Oshawa, 1961,' Arbitration Case CI-48, 27 June 1961; CAW, Arbitration Case CI-30, 7 September 1960.
90 *Oshaworker*, Vol. 8, No. 5, 1 March 1950, p. 1.
91 For example, ALUA, UAW Local 199 Collection, Box 7, File 'Grievances, Step 1 & 2, 1958,' Employee Grievance No. 660, No. 621; ibid., File 'Grievances, Step 1 & 2, 1959–60,' Employee Grievance No. 2434. Employers

rarely reclassified work. Most of these grievances were in protest of men temporarily performing a woman's job. The auto manufacturers typically claimed that it was necessary to place men on a woman's job because legislation restricted women from working certain hours, key operations were too heavy for women, females were unavailable in an emergency situation, male employees alone possessed certain skills, or because of past practice. Ibid., Box 6, File 'Grievances, Step 1 & 2, 1957,' Employee Grievance No. 1327; ibid., Box 7, File 'Grievances, Step 3, January–June, 1961,' H.W. McArthur to Gordon Lambert, 22 February 1961; ibid., File 'Grievances, Step 1 & 2, 1959–60,' Employee Grievance No. 1518; ibid., File 'Grievances, 1961, Step 1 & 2,' Employee Grievance No. 1168; Ibid., File 'Grievances, Step 1 & 2, 1958,' Employee Grievance No. 660.

92 Ibid., Box 6, File 'Grievances, Step 1 & 2, 1957,' Employee Grievance No. 1327.

93 Ibid., Box 7, File 'Grievances, 1961, Step 1 & 2,' Employee Grievance No. 1168, No. 2066.

94 Ibid., File 'Grievances, Step 1 & 2, 1959–60,' Employee Grievance No. 1518.

95 Ibid., File 'Grievances, Step 3, January–June, 1961,' H.W. McArthur to Gordon Lambert, 10 March 1961.

96 Shorten interview.

97 PAC, MG 28, I 119, Acc. 88/324, Box 87, 'General Motors Arbitrations,' Arbitration Case 23-54, 18 November 1954; Shorten interview.

98 Shorten interview.

99 CAW, Arbitration Case 29–53, 17 October 1953.

100 Insofar as women did not work past midnight, the company was not in violation of the provincial hours regulations for female employees.

101 ALUA, UAW Canadian Region – Companies Collection, Box 155, File 6, 'McKinnon Industries, Arbitrations, 1950, 1952–54,' Umpire Award – grievance A-17, 11 June 1954; ALUA, UAW Local 199 Collection, Box 20, File 'Bargaining, 1950,' Meeting with Management, 13 October 1950; ibid., Box 1, File 'Agreement, 1950,' Memorandum of Agreement between UAW Local 199 and McKinnon Industries, 15 November 1950.

102 Saxby interview.

103 For example, in December 1951, Canadian UAW member, Zita Bowers, reported that at a recent meeting of the UAW Women's Advisory Council both Canadian and American women discussed, at length, how employers force women to quit working when they marry. They also noted that in some cases, married women would continue to work, without seniority rights. ALUA, UAW Canadian Region – Locals Collection, Box 85, File 12, 'Local 195, Windsor, 1950–51,' Zita Bowers to George Burt, 4 December

1951; Saxby interview; PAC, MG 28, I 119, Acc. 88/324, Box 87, Binder 'General Motors' Arbitrations,' Arbitration Case 22–54, Case No. GMO-23, 30 December 1954.

104 PAC, MG 28, I 119, Acc. 88/324, Box 87, Binder 'General Motors' Arbitrations,' Arbitration Case 22–54, Case No. GMO-23, 30 December 1954.
105 Saxby interview.
106 Ibid.
107 'GM Shop Report,' *Oshaworker*, Vol 12, No. 3, 4 February 1954, p. 2.
108 CAW, *UAW Administrative Letters*, Vol. 1, 1948 – Vol. 10A, 1958, Book 1, UAW-CIO Administrative Letter, 16 June 1954.
109 ALUA, UAW Canadian Region – Series V Collection, Box 146, File 'GM of Canada Limited, Oshawa, 1953–54,' Caroline Davis to Douglas Sutton, 11 February 1954.
110 'GM Shop Report,' *Oshaworker*, Vol 12, No. 3, 4 February 1954, p. 2.
111 ALUA, UAW Canadian Region – Locals Collection, Box 90, File 4, 'Local 222, 1954,' Rosina Saxby to Walter Reuther, 26 January 1954.
112 Ibid., Douglas Fraser to Rosina Saxby, 29 January 1954.
113 Ibid., George Burt to Rosina Saxby, 5 February 1954.
114 ALUA, UAW Canadian Region – Series V Collection, Box 146, File 3, 'General Motors of Canada Limited, Oshawa, 1953–54,' George Burt to Douglas Sutton, 5 February 1954.
115 Ibid.
116 Ibid., Box 146, File 'GM of Canada Limited, Oshawa, 1953–54,' Rosina Saxby to George Burt, 22 June 1954.
117 Ibid., George Burt to Douglas Sutton, 30 June 1954.
118 PAC, MG 28, I 119, Acc. 88/324, Box 87, Binder 'General Motors' Arbitration,' Arbitration Case 22–54, Case No. GMO-23, 30 December 1954.
119 Ibid.; Saxby interview.
120 CAW, Arbitration Case 40–54, 13 January 1955.
121 ALUA, UAW Local 199 Collection, Box 2, File 'Appeal Cases, 1962,' C.J. 29–34, 37–42, Employee Grievance No. 2216.
122 In December 1954 McKinnon Industries management decided to move married women to a new eight-hour, permanent shift, from 3:00 to 11:00 p.m. Eventually, these women were transferred to a day shift, and the company eliminated the temporary employee status. ALUA, UAW Local 199 Collection, Box 20, File 'Bargaining 1954,' Meeting with Shop Committee – McKinnon, 1 December 1954. In July 1956 they discontinued the victory shift. Ibid., Box 10, File 'Meetings with Management, 1956,' Minutes of Meeting with Shop committee, 19 July 1956. Yet after they made this move, McKinnon reinstated its hiring restrictions against married women.

123 Ibid., Box 2, File 'Appeal Cases,' 1962, C.J. 29–34, 37–42, Record of Case CJ-31.
124 Ibid.
125 The UAW had made a few attempts to negotiate a general no-discrimination clause. For example, in 1955, the UAW demanded that General Motors of Canada incorporate the UAW International Non-Discrimination clause regarding race, creed, colour, national origin, political affiliation, sex, or marital status, in the upcoming contract. The company, however, rejected this demand. PAC, MG 28, I 119, Acc. 83/215, Box 3, File '1955 Negotiations,' 'Company reply to union demand on section 4, paragraph 5, of the Agreement,' 9 June 1955. GM spokespersons stated that their position in regard to new employees is none of the union's business. The union subsequently dropped the reference to 'hiring.' The following month, the union made a similar demand. This time, the company claimed that the clause was redundant. In their view, it was unnecessary because workers were protected by the grievance procedure. GM declared that the clause made false implications of company favoritism. The union again withdrew the demand. Ibid., Box 3, File '1955, Negotiations,' Minutes of Meeting with Management, Oshawa, 12 July 1955; ALUA, UAW Canadian Region Collection, Box 148, File 4, 'General Motors of Canada, Limited, 1955,' Company statement to conciliation board, July–August, 1955.
126 CAW, *Proceedings of the Fifteenth UAW-CIO Constitutional Convention,* 27 March to 1 April 1955; ALUA, UAW Women's Department, Lillian Hatcher Collection, Box 20, File 20–2, 'Conventions and Resolutions, 1955–67,' Convention resolutions relative to women workers' rights, 1955.

CHAPTER 5

1 PAC, MG 28, I 119, Acc. 83/215, Vol. 12, Box 12, File 'Memorandum of Understanding McKinnon Industries, St Catharines'; ALUA, UAW Canadian Region Collection, Box 69, File 2, 'Reports of Regional Director, 1963'; 'McKinnon People Visit Windsor Canada's First Automatic Transmission Plant,' *The McKinnon People,* Vol. 26, No. 4, November 1963, pp. 6–7.
2 PAC, MG 28, I 119, Acc. 83/215, Vol. 16, File 'General Motors – Windsor.'
3 McCloskey interview; Shorten interview.
4 May Partridge, 'The End of Old "32",' *Oshaworker,* Vol. 25, No. 19, 2 November 1967, p. 2.
5 ALUA, UAW Canadian Region Collection, Box 61, File 'Courtney, Richard, 1965,' George Burt to R. Hagerman, 13 October 1965.
6 ALUA, UAW Canadian Region, General Files Collection, Box 25, File 4,

'International Union's Research Department and the Canadian Region's Research Department, 1963–67.'

7 ALUA, UAW Canadian Region Collection, Box 61, File 'Courtney, Richard, 1965,' Richard Courtney to George Burt, 27 September 1965.

8 May Partridge Personal Papers, 'A Letter to Mr Walker.'

9 ALUA, UAW Canadian Region Collection, Box 61, File 'Courtney, Richard, 1965,' Petition.

10 Ibid.

11 Ibid., File 'Courtney, Richard, 1965,' George Burt to R. Hagerman, 13 October 1965.

12 Abe Taylor, 'President's Column,' *Oshaworker*, Vol. 25, No. 11, 15 June 1967, p. 1.

13 Steve Nimigon, 'GM Shop Committee Report,' *Oshaworker*, Vol. 25, No. 12, 6 July 1967, p. 2.

14 ALUA, UAW Toronto Sub-Regional Office Collection, Box 80, File 'Miscellaneous Material,' Minutes, Canadian GM Council, 10–11 September 1965, p. 3; Koch interview; Cox interview.

15 ALUA, UAW Canadian Region Collection, Box 61, File 'Courtney, Richard, 1965,' George Burt to R. Hagerman, 13 October 1965.

16 PAC, MG 28, I 119, Acc. 83/324, Vol. 1, File 'GM Windsor Trim Re: Miscellaneous,' Supplement to Memorandum of Understanding, June 1967.

17 Cox interview; Yurkowski interview.

18 As of September 1965 the UAW reported only one instance of dislocation. A few months after the agreement was signed, Ford laid off close to 1,500 workers. However, in Chrysler's Windsor plant the workforce doubled between May and June. In June 1965 there were 7,997 dues-paying members in Local 199 compared with 6,300 the previous year. In Local 222 in Oshawa, membership rose from 15,100 to 17,300 in the one-year period. Furthermore, in May 1965 37,800 individuals were employed in the motor vehicle industry and 26,000 were in the motor vehicle parts industry in Canada, marking the highest level of employment for production workers in the post-war era. Auto workers were also putting in heavy overtime. Production workers in the industry worked an average of 44.5 hours per week in May 1965, 46.2 hours in April, and 47.1 hours in March. ALUA, UAW Canadian Region 7 Collection, Box 52, File 'George Burt, Regional Director, 1965.'

19 CAW, George Burt Papers, James Connell, and Gordon Lambert to James McNulty, 25 April 1966.

20 Ibid.

21 ALUA, UAW Canadian Region – Series III Collection, File 5, 'National Ca-

nadian GM Intra-Corporation Council, 1966,' Minutes, GM Council Meeting, 3–5 June 1966.
22 CAW, George Burt Papers, George Burt to Paul Martin, 24 August 1966.
23 ALUA, UAW Canadian Region – Series III Collection, Box 76, File 5, 'National Canadian GM Intra-Corporation Council, 1966,' Minutes, GM Council Meeting, 18–19 November 1966.
24 'Female Workers on Way out, Architects of Own Predicament?' *St Catharines Standard*, 14 December 1966.
25 Editorial, 'UAW Leaders Meet Government,' *UAW Local 199 News and Views*, Vol. 3, No. 3, March 1967, p. 2.
26 CAW, George Burt Papers, telegram, George Burt to Jean Marchand, C.M. Drury, and John. R. Nicholson, 30 September 1966.
27 'President's Column,' *UAW Local 199 News and Views*, Vol. 3, No. 3, March 1967, p. 1.
28 Abe Taylor, 'President's Column,' *Oshaworker*, Vol. 25, No. 14, 7 September 1967, p. 1.
29 ALUA, UAW Canadian Region Collection, Box 6, File 8, 'Automotive – General, 1967–69,' 'Brief on the Canadian United States Automotive Products Agreement,' 20 February 1969.
30 Ibid., Box 52, File 'George Burt, 1967, Miscellaneous,' Jean Marchand to George Burt, 20 March 1967.
31 ALUA, UAW Canadian Region – Companies Collection, Box 155, File 5, 'McKinnon Industries Limited, St Catharines, 1959–67.'
32 PAC, MG 28, I 119, Acc. 83/215, Vol. 12, File 'Memorandum of Understanding McKinnon Industries, St Catharines,' Memorandum of Understanding, 10 July 1963.
33 *GM Topics*, Vol 16, No. 3, March 1965, pp. 6–7.
34 Ibid.
35 PAC, MG 28, I 119, Acc. 83/215, File 'General Motors Trim – 1967 Negotiations,' Memorandum of Local Seniority Agreement, 27 March 1968.
36 Ibid.
37 'Female Workers on Way out, Architects of Own Predicament?' *St Catharines Standard*, 14 December 1966.
38 'Women Working for Luxuries Put Needy Widows out of Job,' *St Catharines Standard*, 14 December 1966.
39 ALUA, UAW Canadian Region – Companies Collection, Box 155, File 5, 'McKinnon Industries Limited, St Catharines, 1959–67,' Anne Thomson et al. to Lester B. Pearson, 18 November 1966.
40 Ibid.
41 'Job Means Test Impractical, Union Says,' *St Catharines Standard*, 14 December 1966.

42 'Female Workers on Way out, Architects of Own Predicament?' *St Catharines Standard*, 14 December 1966.

43 'Women Working for Luxuries Put Needy Widows out of Job,' *St Catharines Standard*, 14 December 1966.

44 ALUA, UAW Canadian Region – Locals Collections, Box 88, File 4, 'Local 199, 1967,' telegram, Ann Thompson [*sic*] to Walter Reuther, 6 December 1967.

45 'Women Working for Luxuries Put Needy Widows out of Job,' *St Catharines Standard*, 14 December 1966.

46 For a discussion of gender and conceptions of skill, see Jane Gaskell, 'What Counts as skill? Reflections on Pay Equity' in *Just Wages: A Feminist Assessment of Pay Equity*, Judy Fudge and Patricia McDermott, eds. (Toronto: University of Toronto Press, 1991, pp. 141–59); Jane Jenson, 'The Talents of Women, the Skills of Men: Flexible Specialization and Women,' in *The Transformation of Work: Skill, Flexibility, and the Labour Process*, Stephen Wood, ed. (London: Unwin Hyman 1989).

47 *Oshaworker*, Vol. 21, No. 8, 9 May 1963, p. 6; McCloskey interview.

48 Maurie Shorten, 'The Recollections of a Blue Collar Worker,' mimeo. Oshawa, 1983, pp. 3–4.

49 *Oshaworker*, Vol. 25, No. 14, 7 November 1968, p. 3.

50 Ibid., Vol. 28, No. 3, 19 February 1970, p. 4.

51 Ibid., Vol. 26, No. 4, 20 February 1969, p. 7.

52 PAC, MG 28, I 119, Acc. 81/081, Box 52, File '222 Local Correspondence,' Beverly McCloskey to Caroline Davis, 25 October 1968.

53 Ibid.

54 ALUA, UAW Canadian Region – Series III Collection, Box 76, File 4, 'National Canadian GM Intra-Corporation Council, 1964,' Minutes, Special Meeting, Canadian GM Intra-Corporation Council, 21 October 1965.

55 Shorten interview.

56 *Oshaworker*, Vol. 28, No. 4, 5 March 1970, p. 9.

57 I wish to thank Meg Luxton for bringing this point to my attention.

58 The Voice of Women was an organization founded in July 1960 in an effort to 'unite women in concern for the future of the world' and 'to provide a means for women to exercise responsibility for the family of humankind.' By the fall of 1961 it had a membership of 5,000 and a newsletter with a circulation of over 10,000. Although the Voice of Women was primarily a peace organization, it addressed a number of issues, such as biculturalism, women's health and safety, and the legalization of the distribution of birth control information (Adamson, Briskin, and McPhail, 1988: 39).

59 ALUA, UAW Region 7 Toronto Sub-Regional Office Collection, Box 7, File 'Maclean, Thomas, 1960,' George Burt to all UAW International Represen-

tatives, 1 April 1960; ibid., UAW Canadian Region: General Files Collection, Box 25, File 12, 'International UAW Women's Department and Canadian Region Women's Department, 1965–67,' Caroline Davis to George Burt, 15 January 1965; ibid., UAW Women's Department: Lillian Hatcher Collection, Box 20, File 20–3, 'Conventions and resolutions, 1968–73,' 'UAW Policy Established by Convention Resolutions Relative to Women Workers' Rights,' 4–10 May 1968.

60 For example, ALUA, UAW Women's Department, Lillian Hatcher Collection, Box 10, File 10-9, 'Women's Committees; Discussion and Programme Materials, n.d.' workshop materials.

61 *Oshaworker*, Vol. 25, No. 13, 17 October 1968, p. 5. In March 1963, delegates at the UAW Constitutional Convention made local women's committees mandatory in all locals with female members. Article 43, Constitution of the International Union, UAW.

62 *Oshaworker*, Vol. 25, No. 12, 3 October 1968, p. 1.

63 PAC, MG 28, I 119, Acc. 81/081, Vol. 52, File '222 Local Correspondence,' Beverly C. McCloskey to Caroline Davis, 25 October 1968.

64 ALUA, UAW Women's Department, Lillian Hatcher Collection, Box 10, File 10-9, 'Women's Committees; Discussion and Programme Materials,' 'Have you just been elected?,' n.d.

65 May Partridge Personal Papers, 'Guilty???'

66 *Oshaworker*, Vol. 23, No. 8, 15 April 1965, p. 3.

67 Ibid., Vol. 28, No. 10, 21 May 1970, p. 7.

68 Ibid.

69 Ibid., Vol. 28, No. 15, 17 September 1970, p. 6.

70 Ibid., Vol. 25, No. 13, 17 October 1968, p. 5.

71 Ibid., Vol. 25, No. 14, 7 November 1968, p. 3.

72 See Norwood (1990) for a description of the importance of woman-centred techniques in the mobilization and radicalization of women telephone operators in the late 1800s and early 1900s.

73 *Oshaworker*, Vol. 25, No. 14, 7 November 1968, p. 3.

74 May Partridge, 'Women's Committee Forwards Suggestion to Queen's Park,' *Oshaworker*, Vol. 27, No. 18, 6 November 1969, p. 3.

75 *Oshaworker*, Vol. 28, No. 3, 19 February 1970, p. 4.

76 Shorten interview.

77 *Oshaworker*, Vol. 28, No. 3, 19 February 1970, p. 4; ibid., Vol. 28, No. 6, 19 March 1970, p. 6.

78 Ibid., Vol. 28, No. 15, 17 September 1970, p. 6.

79 PAC, MG 28, I 119, Acc. 83/214, Box 48, File 'General Motors of Canada, Oshawa CL 350-374,' 'Notice of Appeal.'

80 Ibid., File 'General Motors of Canada, Oshawa, CL 450-474,' Notice of Appeal, 12 March 1969.
81 PAC, MG 28, I 119, Acc. 83/215, Box 3, File 'Minutes – Appeal Case Meetings, General Motors, Oshawa, 1968,' Minutes of Appeal Meetings.
82 PAC, MG 28, I 119, Acc. 81/081, File 'Local 222 Correspondence' (second file), Richard Courtney to Dennis McDermott, 28 April 1969.
83 PAC, MG 29, I 119, Acc. 83/214, Box 48, File 'General Motors of Canada, Oshawa, CL 375-399,' Notice of Appeal; ibid., Acc. 81/081, File 'Local 222 Correspondence' (second file), Richard Courtney to Dennis McDermott, 28 April 1969.
84 PAC, MG 28, I 119, Acc. 81/081, Box 52, File 'Local 222 Correspondence' (second file), Dorothy Meehan to Dennis McDermott, 6 February 1969.
85 PAC, MG 28, I 119, Acc. 83/215, Box 11, File 'Local 222 Correspondence, Oshawa,' Beverly McCloskey to Dennis McDermott, 26 March 1969.
86 *Oshaworker*, Vol. 28, No. 10, 21 May 1970, p. 7.
87 *Oshaworker*, Vol. 28, No. 10, 21 May 1970, p. 7; May Partridge, 'Women's Committee Report,' *Oshaworker*, Vol. 28, No. 12, 18 June 1970, p. 7.
88 Creighton interview.
89 On 14 May 1970, Minister of Labour, Dalton Bales, presented to the legislature, an Act to amend the Ontario Human Rights Code. This move surprised even members of the legislature. Bales appointed Dr Lita Betcherman to head the board to deal with complaints. Betcherman was head of the Women's Department of the Human Rights Commission since its inception. The act stated that 'no person shall maintain separate seniority lists, etc., refuse to train, promote, or transfer, pregnancy, grant a leave of absence six weeks prior, shall not permit her to work six weeks after, with no loss of opportunity or benefits twelve weeks, every person guilty of an offence and on conviction if a corporation or a trade union, is liable to a fine of $3,000.' 'Women's Committee Report,' *Oshaworker*, Vol. 28, No. 11, 4 June 1970, p. 5.
90 Parts and service was a 'men's department' in which there were no production standards, workers were not tied to a line, and pay was higher than in the 'women's department.'
91 McCloskey interview.
92 'General Motor's Assembly Lines Boast Unique New Models for 1971,' *Oshawa Times*, 14 January 1971; Al Dick, 'Wire and Harness A Job Well Done,' *Oshaworker*, Vol. 29, No. 3, 4 February 1971, p. 3.
93 Tommy Thompson, 'First Vice-President's Report,' *Oshaworker*, Vol. 29, No. 4, 18 February 1971, p. 7.

94 May Partridge, 'Women's Committee Report,' *Oshaworker*, Vol. 29, No. 2, 21 January 1971, p. 8.
95 McCloskey interview.
96 Linda Sutton, 'Wilda Campbell Works Right along with the Men on Line,' *This Week*, 23 June 1971, p. 5.
97 McCloskey interview.

CHAPTER 6

1 For a discussion of the dichotomization of equality and sexual difference, see Joan Scott, 1988, 'Deconstructing Equality-Versus-Difference: Or, the Uses of Poststructuralist Theory for Feminism,' *Feminist Studies* (14) 33–50; Carol Lee Bacchi (1990); Gisela Bock and Susan James (1992).
2 Murphy interview.
3 In March 1973, a UAW committeeman in GM's Oshawa plant wrote, 'I know that the word female has been deleted since our last contract and it has been proven that our females can if given the opportunity do any job in our plant which was traditionally male and now I think it is time that supervision gave our male employees the same opportunity. I can think of two areas where there are no male employees. One is the utility relief classification and I would also like to see our senior male or female employees doing the work that is being done in the methods lab on steady days.' Al Dick, 'Wire and Harness Zone 25 Night Shift in Wire and Harness,' *Oshaworker*, Vol. 31, No. 5, 15 March 1973.
4 PAC, MG 28, I 119, Acc. 86/472, Box 4, File 'UAW Women's Department,' Summary of the Tenth Annual Canadian Women Workers' Conference, 14–16 September 1973.
5 May Partridge, 'Women's Committee Report,' *Oshaworker*, Vol. 29, No. 15, 2 September 1971, p. 6.
6 Ibid., Vol. 29, No. 3, 4 February 1971, p. 4.
7 Ibid., Vol. 29, No. 6, 18 March 1971, p. 2.
8 For example, PAC, MG 28, I 119, Acc. 83/214, Box 50, File 'CL 825–CL 849,' Notice of Appeal, 12 September 1969; ibid., Box 52, File 'GM Trim Windsor CL 50–74,' Management's Statement of Unadjusted Grievance; ibid., File 'GM Trim Windsor CL 75–99,' Statement of Unadjusted Grievance; ibid., Box 55, File 'Oshawa CM 450–CM 474,' Management's Statement of Unadjusted Grievance; ibid., Box 58, File: 'Local 222 – CM 1400–1424,' Union's Statement of Unadjusted Grievance, Appeal Case CM-1404; ibid., Box 71, File 'Local 199 St Catharines Re: Resolved Cases CN 550 – CN 574,' Statement of Unadjusted Grievances, Case CN 561; ibid., Box 72, File 'Windsor

Trim – Resolved Cases CO 25 – CO 40,' Grievance A47717, 9 May 1978; ibid., File 'Windsor Trim – Resolved Cases CO 25 – CO 45,' Grievance 47777.

9 For example, in the wire and harness department, a supervisor told a group of women that GM expected each worker to produce 34 harnesses a day, and that failure to meet this estimate would result in suspension. Allegedly, he harassed and threatened one worker two times in one day. This tactic frightened several 'girls' who were near the bottom of the seniority list and had only recently been recalled. Fearful, the women increased their output from 29 to 30. The supervisor then suspended the other woman for one day. This resulted in a further production increase by two employees to 32 a day and two employees to 34 a day. 'The women are scared,' reported Shorten, and they need their jobs. 'They are doing it in fear of losing their jobs.' According to Shorten, some supervisors had 'become obsessed' with this estimate on Chevelle harnesses. *Oshaworker*, Vol. 26, No. 4, 20 February 1969, p. 7. Shorten declared that harsh production standards and supervision's heavy-handed tactics 'should not have to be tolerated in a society that is increasing productivity by automation and improved methods.' *Oshaworker*, Vol. 26, No. 4, 20 February 1969, p. 7.

See also, PAC, MG 28, I 119, Acc. 83/214, File 'GM Trim – Windsor CL 50–74,' J.D. McKellar to J.J. Morand, 9 September 1968; ibid., Statement of Unadjusted Grievance, Grievance No. 2741, 24 October 1968; ibid., Box 49, File 'General Motors of Canada, Oshawa CL 550–574,' Union's Statement of Unadjusted Grievance, Appeal Case CL-566; ibid., Union's Statement of Unadjusted Grievance, Appeal Case CL-567; ibid., File 'General Motors of Canada, Oshawa CL 700–724,' Union's Statement of Unadjusted Grievance, Appeal Case CL-725; ibid., Box 52, File 'GM Trim – Windsor, CL 150 – CL 174,' Statement of Unadjusted Grievance CL-167; ibid., File 'GM Trim Windsor CL 200 – CL 228,' Statement of Unadjusted Grievance, Grievance 3991; ibid., Box 71, File 'GM St Catharines, Miscellaneous Cases,' Statement of Unadjusted Grievance, Case CN 537.

10 For example, CAW, Arbitration Cases CK–8 and CK–9, Report of the Arbitrator, 2 April 1966; PAC, MG 28, I 119, Acc. 83/214, Box 12, File 'Local 222 – General Motors, Oshawa, January 1971 – December 1973,' Dennis Tyce to Pat Kress, 10 May 1971; ibid., Box 23, File 'GM Windsor Trim, Resolved Cases Re: CO 50 – CO 74,' Grievance A52936; ibid., Box 50, File 'CL 974–999,' Notice of Appeal, Case No. CL 999; Box 52, File 'GM Trim Windsor CL 1–24,' Management's Statement of Unadjusted Grievance; ibid., Notice of Appeal, Case Cl-22; ibid., File 'GM Trim Windsor, CL50-74,' Union's Statement of Unadjusted Grievance, CL 51; ibid., File 'GM Trim Windsor

CL 200 – CL 228,' Management's Statement of Unadjusted Grievance; ibid., Box 54, File 'Oshawa CM 25 – CM 49 closed,' Management's Statement of Unadjusted Grievance, Case No. CM 31; ibid., File 'CM 75 – CM 99 – Resolved, Oshawa,' Management's Statement of Unadjusted Grievance, Appeal Case No. CM 84; ibid., File 'Oshawa CM 25 – CM 49 closed,' Management's Statement of Unadjusted Grievance, Case No. CM 32; ibid., Box 55, File 'Oshawa – CM 300–324,' Union's Statement of Unadjusted Grievance, Appeal Case No. CM 307; ibid., Box 72, File 'Local 1973, Resolved Cases, CO 1 – CO 24,' D.W. Blimke to J.J. Morand, n.d.; ibid., File 'Local 303, CO 75 – CO 99,' Step Three Answer, 7 October 1977; ibid., File 'Local 303, CO 100 – CO 124,' Employee Grievance, 24 November 1977.

11 For example, PAC, MG 28, I 119, Acc. 83/214, Box 55, File 'Oshawa CM 450 – CM 474,' Management's Statement of Unadjusted Grievance, Case No. CM 458; ibid., Union's Statement of Unadjusted Grievance, Appeal Case CM 458; ibid., Box 72, File 'Local 303, CO 75 – CO 99,' Employee Grievance, 26 September 1977; PAC, MG 28 I 119, Acc. 83/215, Box 23, File 'Windsor Trim, Resolved Cases Re: CO 50 – CO 74,' Grievance A52935; PAC, MG 28 I 119, Acc. 83/214, Box 55, File 'Oshawa CM 475–CM 499,' Management's Statement of Unadjusted Grievance, Case No. CM 490; ibid., Exhibit B, CM 490; ibid., Exhibit B CM 491; ibid., Management's Statement of Unadjusted Grievance, Case No. CM 491; ibid., Exhibit B, CM 496.

12 For example, PAC, MG 28, I 119, Acc. 83/215, Box 23, File 'Windsor Trim, Resolved Cases, CO 75 – CO 99,' Grievances A43230 and A43227.

13 For example, PAC, MG 28, I 119, Acc. 83/214, Box 47, File 'General Motors of Canada, Oshawa, CL 100 – 124,' Union's Statement of Unadjusted Grievance, Appeal Case CL 118; ibid., Box 50, File 'CL 925–CL 949,' Notice of Appeal, CL 928; ibid., Box 71, File 'Local 199, St Catharines, Resolved Cases, CN 700 – CN 724,' Statement of Unadjusted Grievance, Appeal Case CN 716; PAC, MG 28 I 119, Acc. 83/215, Box 23, File 'Windsor Trim, Resolved Cases, Re: CO 50 – CO 74,' Management Statement of Unadjusted Grievance, Appeal No. CO 64; ibid., Appeal No CO 74; ibid., File 'Windsor Trim Resolved Cases, Re: CO 75 – CO 99,' Grievance A47852.

14 For example, PAC, MG 28, I 119, Acc. 83/214, Box 52, File 'GM Trim, Windsor, CL 50–74,' Statement of Unadjusted Grievance, CL 74; ibid., CL 72.

15 For example, ibid., Box 50, File 'General Motors, Oshawa, CL 1150 – CL 1174,' Notice of Appeal, Case No. CL 1167; Box 51, File 'General Motors, Oshawa, CL 1175–CL 1199,' Union's Statement of Unadjusted Grievance, Appeal Case CL 1175; ibid., Appeal Case CL 1176; ibid., Appeal Case CL 1179; ibid., File 'General Motors, Oshawa, CL 1300–CL 1324,' Manage-

ment's Statement of Unadjusted Grievance, Appeal Case No. CL 1301; ibid., Box 54, File 'Appeal Cases, 150–174, Oshawa, Resolved,' Management's Statement of Unadjusted Grievance, Case No. CM 164; ibid., File 'Appeals, Resolved, CM 125–149, Oshawa,' Management's Statement of Unadjusted Grievance, Case No. CM 144; ibid., Box 55, File 'CM 325–CM 349, Oshawa,' Union's Statement of Unadjusted Grievance, Appeal Case CM 337; ibid., Appeal Case CM 336; ibid., Box 56, File 'Oshawa, CM 625–649,' Exhibit B, CM 634; ibid., Acc. 83/215, Box 23, File 'Windsor Trim, Resolved Cases, Re: CO 50 – CO 74,' Management's Statement of Unadjusted Grievance, Appeal No. CO 69; ibid., Appeal No. CO 70; ibid., Appeal No. CO 72; ibid., Appeal No. CO 71.

16 For example, ibid., Acc. 83/214, Box 52, File 'GM Trim, Windsor, CL1–CL24,' Management's Statement of Unadjusted Grievance; ibid., J.D. McKellar to J.J. Morand, 8 May 1968; ibid., Acc. 83/215, Box 23, File 'Windsor Trim, Resolved Cases, Re: CO 75–CO 99,' Grievance A53083.

17 For example, ibid., Acc. 83/214, Box 52, File 'GM Trim Windsor, CL 50–74,' Management's Statement of Unadjusted Grievance; ibid., File 'GM Trim, Windsor, CL 175–CL 199,' Management's Statement of Unadjusted Grievance; ibid., File 'GM Trim, Windsor, CL 200–CL 228,' Statement of Unadjusted Grievance, CL 211; ibid., Management's Statement of Unadjusted Grievance; ibid., Statement of Unadjusted Grievance, CL 228.

18 For example, ibid., Box 52, File 'GM Trim, Windsor, CL 75–49,' Statement of Unadjusted Grievance, CL 88.

19 For example, ibid., Box 49, File 'General Motors of Canada, Oshawa, CL 750–774,' Union's Statement of Unadjusted Grievance, Appeal Case CL 754; ibid., Appeal Case CL 760; ibid., Box 50, File 'CL 1050–CL 1074,' Union's Statement of Unadjusted Grievance, Appeal Case CL 1052; ibid., Box 52, File 'GM Trim, Windsor, CL 125–149,' Statement of Unadjusted Grievance, CL 137; ibid., File 'GM Trim, Windsor, CL 175–CL199,' Statement of Unadjusted Grievance, CL 178; ibid., File 'GM Trim, Windsor, CL 25–49,' Employee Grievance No. 2329; ibid., File 'GM Trim, Windsor, CL 75–99,' Statement of Unadjusted Grievance, CL 98; Box 52, File 'GM Trim, Windsor, CL 1–24,' Appeal CL 17; ibid., Management's Statement of Unadjusted Grievance; ibid., Box 55, File 'Oshawa, CM 375–CM399,' Management's Statement of Unadjusted Grievance, Case No. CM 394; ibid., Union's Statement of Unadjusted Grievance, Appeal Case CM 395; ibid., Exhibit B, CM 394; ibid., Box 58, File 'Local 222, CM 1475–CM 1499,' Exhibit B, CM1483; ibid., File 'Local 222, CM 1625–1649,' Exhibit B, CM 1643; ibid., Exhibit B, CM 1644; ibid., Box 71, File 'Local 303, Resolved Cases, CO 26 – CO 51,' Statement of Unadjusted Grievance, Case No. 31; ibid., Box 72, File 'Arbitration

Awards, General Motors of Canada, CL 1–CL 18,' Arbitration Case No. CL 4, Report of the Arbitrator, 6 November 1968; ibid., File 'Resolved Cases, Scarborough, Re: CO 250–CO 274,' CO 264.

20 For example, ibid., Acc. 83/214, Box 52, File 'GM Trim, Windsor, CL 1–24,' Grievance No. 2063; ibid., Management's Statement of Unadjusted Grievance; ibid., File 'GM Trim, Windsor, CL 125–149,' Management's Statement of Unadjusted Grievance; ibid., Box 57, File 'Oshawa, CM 1175–1199,' Union's Statement of Unadjusted Grievance, Appeal Case CM 1175; ibid., Box 71, File 'Local 303, Resolved Cases, Re: 25–49,' Statement of Unadjusted Grievance, Case No. CN 26; ibid., Acc. 83/215, Box 23, File 'Windsor Trim, Resolved Cases, Re: CO 75–CO 99,' Employee Grievance A51103.

21 For example, ibid., Acc. 83/214, Box 52, File 'GM Trim, Windsor, CL 175–CL 199,' Statement of Unadjusted Grievance, CL 190; ibid., Box 56, File 'Oshawa, CM 675–699,' Exhibit B, CM 676.

22 For example, ibid., Acc. 83/215, Box 23, File '303, Scarborough Van Plant, Re: Resolved Cases, CO 375–CO 399,' Statement of Unadjusted Grievance, Case No. CO 382.

23 Personal communication, Pat Clancy, CAW National Representative.

24 PAC, MG 28, I 119, Acc. 83/214, Box 55, File 'Oshawa CM 375–CM 399,' Appeal Case CM–395; ibid., Exhibit 'B.'

25 Ibid., File 'Oshawa CM 300–324,' Appeal Case CM–306.

26 Murphy interview.

27 This would not be a contract provision, however, it would be company policy.

28 *Oshaworker*, Vol 30, No 4, 2 March 1972, p. 5. Also, most of these jobs operated on a shift basis, which meant that high seniority men would be placed on a job that operated on a six-week, two-week-night basis. Many men also resented the company's decision for this reason.

29 'Lead Oxide Readings inside Found Too High,' *Oshawa Times*, 18 November 1975; 'Battery Plant Starts Again,' *Oshawa Times*, 24 November 1975; Bender interview.

30 'Employees Transferred without Pay Reductions,' *Oshawa Times*, 17 December 1975.

31 PAC, MG 28, I 119, Acc. 81/081, Box 46, File 'International Reps, 1970,' Proposed UAW Occupational Health Lead-Acid Battery Manufacturing Survey and Study United States and Canada.

32 'Discrimination Allegation Denied by GM Spokesman,' *Oshawa Times*, 3 December 1975.

33 'Fertile Women Out: GM,' *Oshawa Times*, 2 December 1975.

34 'Employees Transferred without Pay Reductions,' *Oshawa Times*, 17 December 1975; Bender interview; Partridge interview.

35 Bender interview; Partridge interview.
36 Bender interview.
37 By December 1975, the company was testing all battery plant employees, including office workers, catering service, and production workers for lead-oxide levels on a monthly basis. If their urine sample levels were high, the employees would undergo a blood test. GM also planned to replace the (female) nurse in the plant with a male. They monitored female cafeteria workers and office workers, but said their exposure was minimal. 'Monthly Testing of All Employees,' *Oshawa Times*, 19 December 1975.
38 Bender interview.
39 Ibid.
40 PAC, MG 28, I 119, Acc. 88/324, Box 26, File 'Local 222, 1976–79,' May Partridge to Irving Bluestone, 1 February 1978; 'Discrimination Allegation Denied by GM Spokesman,' *Oshawa Times*, 3 December 1975.
41 'Discrimination Allegation Denied by GM Spokesman,' *Oshawa Times*, 3 December 1975.
42 'Sterilization of GM Worker Not Ordered,' *Toronto Star*, 2 February 1976.
43 'HRC Still Investigating Alleged Discrimination,' *Oshawa Times*, 15 April 1976.
44 'But Lead Is Hazardous to Male Workers as Well,' *Union Woman*, Vol. 2, No. 2, November 1978.
45 'Cabinet Ministers Defend GM Move to Protect Women,' *Oshawa Times*, 3 December 1975.
46 'Sterilization of GM Worker Not Ordered,' *Toronto Star*, 2 February 1976.
47 'Cabinet Ministers Defend GM Move to Protect Women,' *Oshawa Times*, 3 December 1975.
48 The union itself was divided on this issue. The UAW International in the United States disagreed with the local's decision to support their women members. American leaders supported the company position that women should be moved out of these areas. Tommy Thompson, a UAW committeeman, claimed that it was only in the heat of this controversy that the UAW-CIO adopted this policy. In Bender's view UAW representatives in Canada only supported the women because they went public with their case. She explained, 'one night I was sitting here watching the news and we came on t.v. with this issue ... I got a call from my sister-in-law in B.C. She had just seen me on t.v. The next evening I got a phone call from a friend of mine on Cape Breton Island. They had seen us on t.v.' The media heard about the incident and called Bender for information. They also requested that she bring any further comments to them. After this, the union representatives told the women that they would check out the case. Bender interview.

49 In addition, a woman in GM's parts department complained to the Ontario Human Rights Commission that her application for a transfer to the battery plant was denied unless she could prove her inability to conceive a child. 'UAW Continues Grievance until GM Proves Harm,' *Oshawa Times*, 17 December 1975.

50 'UAW Continues Grievance until GM Proves Harm,' *Oshawa Times*, 17 December 1975; 'Rights Commission Probes Discrimination Charge at GM Plant,' *Oshawa Times*, 26 November 1975; 'Rights Commission Studies GM Workers' Transfer,' *Oshawa Times*, 3 December 1975. Official complaints with the Human Rights commission were less frequent insofar as women's threat to go to the commission often prompted the company to try to resolve the women's grievances. One worker explained that the women would simply tell their situation to an officer who would 'come down and straighten them [the company] out.' She said, 'We were up at the Human Rights more than we were at work ... we went up and reported them and what they were doing and gradually they've become used to us.' Partridge interview.

51 PAC, MG 28, I 119, Acc. 88/324, Box 23, File 'Local 222, 1976–79,' Ontario Human Rights Commission ruling.

52 CAW, Arbitration Case CO-6.

53 Bender interview.

54 Without documentary evidence from General Motors, one can only speculate about the company's motives in this case. Research on similar cases, however, suggests that employers feared the possibility of legal risks from injury to a fetus. See, for example, the case of atomic energy workers discussed in Women's Bureau, Labour Canada, n.d. *The Selective Protection of Canadian Working Women* (Ottawa: Labour Canada, p. 20).

55 There were isolated cases in which working men also used an equal rights ideology to improve their shop-floor experiences. Ever since women worked in GM, they quit work and punched their time cards five minutes before the men. After women won equal seniority rights, this privilege was the only remaining (contractual) difference between the sexes. However, working men soon claimed that they too should receive an extra five minutes. Orville Faught, a district committeeman in GM, claimed that he would file 1,400 grievances on behalf of male employees protesting the company's discrimination against them. He also planned to lodge a complaint with the Ontario Human Rights Commission. ' "I am not suggesting that the five minutes be taken away from the females,' said Faught. 'I am suggesting though that the male employees be given the right to punch out, with pay, during their wash-up period, the same as the women," he

added.' Ted Murphy Personal Papers, newspaper clipping, source unknown, n.d. This issue was raised through the dispute of a Ted Marshall (Reference number E-5928A). Over 10,000 male employees supported the union's position on the matter. PAC, MG 28 I 119, Acc. 83/215, Box 28, File 'D. Tyce, 1 January – 30 June 1979,' unsigned letter to R.M. Palacio, n.d. GM subsequently reviewed its policies and attempted to eliminate the women's benefit.

56 Conde and Beveridge Interviews: Maurie Shorten, UAW 222/23, pp. 10–11.
57 Murphy interview.
58 Conde and Beveridge Interviews: Maurie Shorten, UAW 222/23, pp. 10–11.
59 May Partridge, 'Women's Committee Report,' *Oshaworker*, Vol. 29, No. 3, 4 February 1971, p. 4.
60 ALUA, UAW Canadian Region – Series III, Box 76, File 'GM Sub-Council, 1961–62,' Proposed Amendments by Council re: GM Master Agreement, 23–24 June 1961; ALUA, UAW Women's Department: Lillian Hatcher Collection, Box 20, File 20–3, 'Conventions and Resolutions, 1968–73,' Resolution re: Working Women, 20–27 March 1964; ALUA, UAW Canadian Region – General Files Collection, Box 48, File 8, 'Canadian UAW Women's Auxiliaries, 1964–67,' Summary, UAW Canadian Women's Department Conference, 11–12 September 1965; ibid., 'Women, 1969–70,' Summary, UAW Canadian Women's Department Conference, 20–21 September 1969; PAC, MG 28, I 119, Acc. 88/324, Box 65, File 'E. Johnston,' Frances I. Nokes to Wendy Cuthbertson, 28 November 1979, Edith Johnston to Bob White, 12 December 1979.
61 For example, ALUA, UAW Women's Department, Lillian Hatcher Collection, Box 20, File 20–30, 'Conventions and Resolutions, 1968–73,' 'UAW Policy Established by Convention Resolutions Relative to Women Workers' Rights,' 4–10 May 1968; ALUA, UAW Canadian Region: Officers' Files Collection, Box 56, File 5, 'Allen Schroeder, Education Director, 1968,' Summary, UAW Canadian Women's Department Conference, 9–10 September 1967; PAC, MG 28, I 119, Acc. 86/472, Box 4, File 'UAW Women's Department,' Summary of the Tenth Annual Canadian Women Workers' Conference, 14–15 September 1973; PAC, MG 28, I 119, Acc. 88/324, Box 67, File 'Women's Advisory Council, 1970–82,' Summary, 15th Annual UAW Canadian Women's Conference, 8–10 September 1978; CAW, *Proceedings, Twenty-Second UAW Constitutional Convention,* 20–24 April 1970.
62 For example, PAC, MG 28, I 119, Acc. 86/472, Box 4, File 'UAW Women's Department, Summary of the Tenth Annual Canadian Women Workers' Conference,' 14–16 September 1973.
63 For example, ALUA, UAW Canadian Region: Officers' Files Collection, Box

56, File 5, 'Allen Schroeder, Education Director, 1968,' Summary, UAW Canadian Women's Department Conference, 9–10 September 1967; PAC, MG 28, I 119, Acc. 81/081, Box 51, File 'Local 27 Correspondence,' Resolution, 'Women in the Canadian Region'; CAW, 'Resolutions,' *Proceedings, Twenty-third UAW Constitutional Convention*, 23–28 April 1972.

64 By the 1970s unionists discussed sexual harassment openly as a shop-floor problem that both labour and management must address. In addition, workers adopted a wider definition of harassment than in the past. For instance, an article in *UAW Local 199 News* defined sexual harassment as

Sexual relations, sexual contact, or the threat of, or coercion for the purpose of sexual relations or sexual contact, which is not freely and mutually agreeable to both parties, including continual or repeated verbal abuse of a sexual nature, graphic commentaries on the victim's body, sexually suggestive objects or pictures in the workplace, sexually degrading language, or propositions of sexual nature, threat or insinuation that lack of sexual submission will adversely affect the victim's employment status, Pornographic pictures get pasted on machines, lunch areas, tool boxes, etc. and obscene notes and literature get attached to her workbench. When she complains her supervisor says, 'If you can't take a bit of fun, you should get out.'

The author furthermore advised female employees on the procedures to follow in contesting such treatment. 'Sexual Harassment on the Job,' *UAW Local 199 News*, Vol. 14, No. 9, 1979, p. 13.

Similarly, Laura Saunders, a longstanding GM employee explained that 'they didn't talk about it then like they will now ... Now of course, there's different rules, laws, regulations ... that you don't have to take this kind of abuse and sexual remarks being said to you by bosses and by supervisors and by men in general on the floor ... You can stand up and you have a little bit to fight with. But back then, we did it on our own.'

Some women even filed individual grievances on sexual harassment. For instance, in May 1979, a sewing machine operator in GM's Windsor Trim plant formally complained that she was sexually harassed by supervision and protested her foreman's use of profane language. PAC, MG 28, I 119, Acc. 83/215, Box 23, File 'Windsor Trim – Resolved Cases Re: CO75 to CO99,' Employee Grievance A43206; ibid., File 'Windsor Trim – Resolved Cases Re: CO-75 to CO-99,' Appeal Case CO-88; ibid., File 'Windsor Trim – Resolved Cases Re: CO-75 to CO-99,' Notice of Intention to Appeal.

65 For instance, a Canadian delegate to the Fifth UAW-CIO Women's Confer-

ence in 1978 wrote in the Local 199 newspaper, 'A fact remains, women outlive men. Are we able to receive the same insurance benefits as men? How about pensions?' 'Women Conference – Black Lake,' *UAW Local 199 News*, p. 9. Local union newspapers furthermore featured articles on women and pensions, and the current legislation. Julia Majka, 'Women and Pensions,' *UAW Local 199 News*, Vol. 14, No. 7, June 1979, p. 3; *Oshaworker*, Vol. 36, No. 13, 7 September 1978.

66 The UAW had made some settlement gains on maternity leave during the early-to-mid 1960s, such as the elimination of a waiting period for Sickness and Accident Benefits for female employees for disability due to pregnancy in 1964. PAC, MG 28, I 119, Acc. 83/215, Box 8, File 'General Motors Negotiations, 1964,' GM Settlement Gains, Insurance and Health Care Improvements, 1964. In subsequent years, women in union locals frequently discussed the status of pregnant workers and tried to improve on these gains. ALUA, UAW Canadian Region – Series IV Collection, Box 81, File 2, 'Correspondence, All Locals, 1966,' Summary, UAW Canadian Women's Conference, 10–11 September 1966; PAC, MG 28, I 119, Acc. 86/472, Box 4, File 'UAW Women's Department,' Summary, Tenth Annual UAW Women's Conference, 14–16 September 1973; ibid., UAW Canadian Region – Series III Collection, Box 76, File 4, 'National Canadian GM Intra-corporation Council, 1964,' Minutes, GM Canadian Intra-corporation Council, 26–27 February 1965. In March 1970, the Local 222 membership meeting endorsed resolutions on Sickness and Accident benefits for pregnancy. PAC, MG 18, I 119, Acc. 81/081, Box 29, File 'Collective Bargaining, 1969–70,' Beverly C. McCloskey to Dennis McDermott, 1 April 1970. And at the September 1970 Canadian Region Women Workers' Conference, women sought to extend the six-week maternity leave in their contract with GM. PAC, MG 28, I 119, Acc. 81/081, Box 46, File 'Allen Schroeder,' Summary, Seventh Annual UAW Canadian Women Workers' Conference, 26–27 September 1970. Also in September 1971, women in the GM plant could receive pregnancy benefits for up to fifteen weeks, which would be paid for nine weeks prior to confinement and for the week of confinement, and would continue for five weeks after the week of confinement. The benefit paid would be the same as your regular benefit from unemployment insurance. 'District #9 Report,' *Oshaworker*, Vol. 29, No. 16, 16 September 1971, p. 8. In 1974, Local 195 adopted a resolution on maternity leave stating that a twelve-week leave is inadequate. PAC, MG 28, I 119, Acc. 81/081, Box 50, no file, Canadian UAW Council, Windsor, 26–27 January 1974. By the 1979 Canadian Women's Conference, delegates discussed extended maternity and paternity

leave. PAC, MG 28, I 119, Acc. 83/215, Box 12, File 'Toronto Office – Education Department, January 1971 – December 1973,' Summary of the Ninth Annual Canadian Women Workers' Conference, 22–24 September 1972.

67 CAW, *Proceedings*, Twenty-Second UAW Constitutional Convention, 20–24 April 1970.

68 PAC, MG 28, I 119, Acc. 83/215, Box 12, File 'Toronto Office, Education Department, January 1971 – December 1973,' Allen Schroeder to Delegates to the UAW Women's Conference, Recording Secretaries, Chairmen, Women's Committees, UAW Canadian Region, 11 February 1972; ibid., 'Summary, Ninth Annual UAW Canadian Women Workers' Conference, 22–24 September 1972; PAC, MG 28, I 119, Acc. 88/324, Box 67, File 'Canadian UAW Council Women's Committee,' Minutes, UAW Canadian Women's Conference, 28 April 1973; ibid., File 'Women's Advisory Council, 1970–82,' Summary of the Fifteenth Canadian UAW Women's Conference, 8–10 September 1978; PAC, MG 28 I 119, Acc. 86/472, Box 4, File 'UAW Women's Department,' Summary, Twelfth Annual UAW Canadian Women's Conference, 19–21 September 1975.

69 PAC, MG 28, I 119, Acc. 88/324, Box 67, File 'Canadian UAW Council Women's Committee, 1972–81,' Proceedings of the Eighth Annual Canadian Women's Conference, 16–17 October 1971.

70 For example, PAC, MG 28, I 119, Acc. 83/215, Box 12, File 'Toronto Office – Education Department, January 1971 – December 1973,' Summary of the Ninth Annual Canadian Women Workers' Conference, 22–24 September 1972; PAC, MG 28 I 119, Acc. 81/081, Box 50, File 'April 20–21, 1974,' Resolution re: Child Care Centres; ibid., Box 56, File 'Canadian UAW Council, 1970,' Resolution 3, re: child care; PAC MG 28 I 119, Acc. 86/472, Box 4, File: 'UAW Women's Department,' Summary of the Tenth UAW Canadian Women's Conference, 14–16 September 1973. CAW, *Proposed Resolutions to the Twenty-Fourth Constitutional Convention of the UAW*, 2–7 June 1974; ALUA, UAW Canadian Region – Series IV Collection, Box 81, File 2, 'Correspondence, All Locals, 1966,' Summary of the UAW Canadian Women's Conference, 10–11 September 1966; ibid., UAW Canadian Region – Officers' Files Collection, Box 56, File 6, 'Allen Schroeder, Education Director, 1969,' Summary of the UAW Canadian Women's Conference, 7–8 September 1968.

71 For example, PAC, MG 28, I 119, Acc. 86/472, Box 4, File 'UAW Women's Department, Summary of the Tenth Annual Canadian Women Workers' Conference, 14–16 September 1973.'

72 ALUA, UAW Women's Auxiliaries – Series III Collection, Box 10, File 10–11, 'Canadian Region, 1955–76,' Agenda, UAW Canadian Women's

Conference, 9–10 September 1967; ibid., UAW Canadian Region: General Files Collection, Box 25, File 12, 'International UAW Women's Department and Canadian Region Women's Department, 1965–67,' Agenda, UAW Canadian Women's Conference, 9–10 September 1967; ALUA, UAW Canadian Region – Officers' Files Collection, Box 56, File 5, 'Allen Schroeder, Education Director, 1968,' Summary of the UAW Canadian Women's Conference, 9–10 September 1967.

73 May Partridge, 'Women's Committee Report,' *Oshaworker*, Vol. 28, No. 9, 7 May 1970, p. 8.

74 PAC, MG 28, I 119, Acc. 88/324, Box 67, File 'Canadian UAW Council Women's Committee, 1972–81,' Proceedings of the Eighth Annual Canadian Women's Conference, 16–17 October 1971.

75 For example, delegates to the 1970 Canadian UAW Women's Conference discussed Bill 83 with a spokesperson from the Ontario Women's Bureau, Department of Labour. They also reviewed current provincial legislation, in particular, laws regarding separate wage scales and job classifications. In addition, they argued that protective legislation conflicts with equal opportunity. PAC, MG 28, I 119, Acc. 81/081, Box 46, File 'Allen Schroeder,' Summary of the Seventh UAW Canadian Women's Conference, 26–27 September 1970; ibid., Acc. 83/215, Box 12, File 'Toronto Office – Education Department, January 1971 – December 1973,' Summary of the Ninth Annual UAW Women's Conference, 22–24 September 1972. Over time, they continued to address these issues. For example, the program of the Canadian UAW Women's Conference in September 1977 dealt exclusively with three pieces of legislation: health and safety, the Employment Standards Act, and Human Rights legislation. Ibid., Acc. 81/081, Box 51, File 'Fourteenth Annual Canadian Region UAW Women's Conference,' Summary of the Fourteenth Canadian UAW Women's Conference, 16–18 September 1977; ibid., Acc. 88/324, Box 67, File 'Canadian UAW Council Women's Committee, 1972–81,' Minutes of UAW Canadian Women's Conference, 28 April 1973.

76 For example, ALUA, UAW Women's Auxiliaries – Series III Collection, Box 10, File 10–11, 'Canadian Region, 1955–76,' Agenda, UAW Canadian Women's Conference, 9–10 September 1967; ibid., UAW Canadian Region: General Files Collection, Box 25, File 12, 'International UAW Women's Department and Canadian Region Women's Department, 1965–67,' Agenda, UAW Canadian Women's Conference, 9–10 September 1967; ibid., UAW Canadian Region – Officers' Files Collection, Box 56, File 5, 'Allen Schroeder, Education Director, 1968,' Summary of the UAW Canadian Women's Conference, 9–10 September 1967.

77 'How Can We Help You?,' *UAW Local 199 News*, October–November 1979, Vol. 14, No. 8, p. 10.
78 McCloskey interview.
79 PAC, MG 28, I 119, Acc. 88/324, Box 67, File 'Canadian UAW Council Women's Committee, 1972–81,' Proceedings of the Eighth Annual Canadian Women's Conference, 16–17 October 1971.
80 Ibid.
81 'General Motor's Assembly Lines Boast Unique New Models for 1971,' *Oshawa Times*, 14 January 1971.
82 Partridge interview.
83 PAC, MG 28, I 119, Acc. 88/324, Box 67, File 'Canadian UAW Council Women's Committee, 1972–81,' Cele Carrigan to conference delegates, Proceedings of the Eighth Annual Canadian Women's Conference, 16–17 October 1971.
84 Yurkowski interview.
85 *UAW Local 199 News*, Vol. 8, No. 3, April 1972, p. 4.
86 Linda Sutton, 'Wilda Campbell Works Right Along with the Men on Line,' *This Week*, 23 June 1971, p. 5.
87 'GM's "Undercover" Pin-Ups,' *GM Topics*, Vol. 12, No. 3, March 1961, p. 11.
88 Lepitsky interview.
89 Cox interview.
90 Conde and Beveridge Interviews: Maurie Shorten, UAW 222/23, pp. 5–6.
91 Ibid.
92 Partridge interview.
93 For example, PAC, MG 28, I 119, Acc. 83/214, Box 46, File 'International Correspondence, Detroit,' UAW Proclamation on International Women's Year; ALUA, UAW Canadian Region – Officers' Files Collection, Box 56, File 6, 'Allen Schroeder, Education Director, 1969,' Summary of the UAW Women's Conference, 7–8 September 1968; ibid., UAW Women's Department, Lillian Hatcher Collection, Box 2, File 2–8, 'Correspondence and Materials, August–December 1967,' 'Why Women Love the UAW.'
94 CAW, 'Women's Department Report,' *Report of Walter P. Reuther Part III*. 19th UAW Constitutional Convention, 20–27 March 1964.
95 For instance, in April 1970, Pat Kress (Creighton), secretary of the Local 222 Women's Committee, wrote to Dennis McDermott requesting the names of UAW locals in both the United States and Canada which still practice sexual discrimination. McDermott curtly replied that sexual discrimination exists in Kress's Local [222] itself. PAC, MG 28, I 119, Acc. 81/081, Box 52, File 'Local 222 Correspondence, second file,' Pat Kress to Dennis McDermott, 15 April 1970; Dennis McDermott to Pat Kress, 4 May 1970; ALUA, UAW

Women's Department, Lillian Hatcher Collection, Box 2, File 2–8, 'Correspondence and Materials, August–December 1967,' 'Introduction by President Walter P. Reuther.'

96 ALUA, UAW Canadian Region – General Files Collection, Box 25, File '3, International Union, Research Department, 1968,' George Burt to Carrol Coburn, 13 February 1968.

97 ALUA, UAW Canadian Region – Officers' Files Collection, Box 54, File 6, 'Dennis McDermott, Regional Director, October 1968,' Dennis McDermott to Lee Chiodo, 4 October 1968; ibid., UAW Canadian Region – Series III Collection, Box 73, File 7, 'Canadian UAW Council, 1968,' Minutes of the UAW Canadian Council, 14–15 September 1968.

98 ALUA, UAW Canadian Region – Locals Collection, Box 91, File 1, 'Local 222, Oshawa, 1966,' Abe Taylor to Olga Madar, 28 September 1966; ibid., Olga Madar to Abe Taylor, 5 October 1966; PAC, MG 28, I 119, Acc. 86/472, Box 4, File 'UAW Women's Department, Proceedings of the Thirteenth Annual Canadian Women's Conference, 17–19 September 1976; ibid., Summary of the Eleventh Annual Canadian UAW Women Workers' Conference, 13–15 September 1974; ibid., Acc. 81/081, Box 47, File 'Olga Madar,' Olga Madar to 'Chalesta and Dick,' 17 May 1972; CAW, *Proposed Resolutions to the 24th Constitutional Convention of the UAW*, 2–7 June 1974, pp. 270–5.

99 PAC, MG 28, I 119, Acc. 86/472, Box 4, File 'UAW Women's Department,' Summary of the Tenth Annual Canadian Women Workers' Conference, 14–16 September 1973.

100 Ibid., Acc. 81/081, Box 46, File 'Allen Schroeder,' Allen Schroeder to Delegates to the UAW Women's Conference, 3 November 1970.

101 Ibid., Acc. 88/324, Box 67, File 'Women's Advisory Council, 1970–82,' Edith Welch to Leonard Woodcock, 8 July 1970; CAW, Resolutions, *Proceedings*, 22nd UAW Constitutional Convention, 20–25 April 1970; ibid., Box 65, File 'E. Johnston,' inter-office communication re: 'Women Membership in UAW,' May 11, 1977'; ibid., *Proceedings*, 22nd UAW Constitutional Convention, 20–25 April 1970.

102 Shorten interview.

103 PAC, MG 28, I 119, Acc. 81/081, Box 51, File 'Fourteenth Annual UAW Canadian Region Women's Conference,' Summary of the Fourteenth Annual Canadian Women Workers' Conference, 16–18 September 1977.

104 Ibid., Acc. 88/324, Box 67, File 'Canadian UAW Council Women's Committee, 1972–81,' Summary of the Eighth Annual Canadian Women's Conference, 16–17 October 1971; ibid., Acc. 83/215, Box 12, File 'Toronto Office, Education Department, January 1971 – December 1973,' Allen Schroeder to

Delegates to the UAW Women's Conference, Recording Secretaries, Chairmen, Women's Committees, 11 February 1972.

105 Ibid., Acc. 86/472, Box 4, File 'UAW Women's Department,' Proceedings of the Tenth Annual Canadian Women Workers' Conference, 14–16 September 1973.

106 PAC, MG 28, I 119, Acc. 81/081, Box 51, File 'Fourteenth Annual Canadian Region UAW Women's Conference,' Summary of the Fourteenth Annual Canadian Women's Conference, 16–18 September 1977.

107 Ibid.

108 Ibid., Acc. 88/324, Box 67, File 'Canadian UAW Council Women's Committee, 1972–81,' Proceedings of the Eighth Annual Canadian Women's Conference, 16–17 October 1971.

109 Ibid., Acc. 86/472, Box 4, File 'UAW Women's Department,' Summary of the Tenth Annual Canadian Women Workers' Conference, 14–16 September 1973.

110 Ibid., Acc. 81/081, Box 51, File 'Fourteenth Annual Canadian Region UAW Women's Conference,' Summary of the Fourteenth Annual Canadian Women Workers' Conference, 16–18 September 1977.

111 Ibid.

112 May Partridge, 'Women's Committee Report,' *Oshaworker*, Vol. 29, No. 8, 15 April 1971, p. 8.

113 PAC, MG 28, I 119, Acc. 86/472, Box 4, File 'UAW Women's Department,' Summary of the Tenth Annual Canadian Women Workers' Conference, 14–16 September 1973.

114 Ibid., Acc. 83/215, Box 12, File: 'Toronto Office – Education Department, January 1971 – December 1973,' Summary of the Ninth Annual Canadian Women Workers' Conference, 22–24 September 1972.

115 May Partridge, 'Women's Committee Report,' *Oshaworker*, Vol. 29, No. 5, 4 March 1971, pp. 3, 5.

116 CAW, *Proceedings*, Twentieth UAW Constitutional Convention, 16–21 May 1966.

117 PAC, MG 28, I 119, Acc. 86/472, Box 4, File 'UAW Women's Department,' Summary of the Eleventh Annual Canadian UAW Women Workers' Conference, 13–15 September 1974.

118 May Partridge, 'Liberation – No ... Equality – Yes,' *Oshaworker*, Vol. 29, No. 4, 18 February 1971, p. 2.

119 For a discussion of working-class feminism, see Heather Jon Maroney, 1986, 'Feminism at Work,' *What Is Feminism?*, in Juliet Mitchell and Ann Oakley, eds. (New York: Pantheon Books, pp. 101–26).

120 See Linda Briskin, 'Union Women and Separate Organizing' in *Women*

Challenging Unions, Linda Briskin and Pat McDermott, eds. (Toronto: University of Toronto Press, 1993).

121 ALUA, UAW Canadian Region – Officers' Files Collection, Box 56, File 1, 'Allen Schroeder, Education Director, 1964,' Summary of the UAW Canadian Women's Conference, 12–13 September 1964; Doc 594 – ibid., UAW Canadian Region – General Files Collection, Box 48, File 8, 'Canadian UAW Women's Auxiliaries, 1964–67,' Summary of the UAW Canadian Women's Conference, 11–12 September 1965, p. 5; Doc 639B – ibid., UAW Women's Department: Lillian Hatcher Collection, Box 20, File 20–3, 'Conventions and Resolutions, 1968–73,' 'UAW Policy Established by Convention Resolutions Relative to Women Workers' Rights,' 4–10 May 1968.

122 PAC, MG 28, I 119, Acc. 86/472, Box 4, File 'UAW Women's Department,' Proceedings of the Thirteenth Annual Women's Conference, 17–19 September 1976.

123 Ibid., Acc. 81/081, Box 51, File 'Fourteenth Annual Canadian Region UAW Women's Conference,' Summary of the Fourteenth Annual Canadian UAW Women Workers' Conference, 16–18 September 1977.

124 Ann Bailey, 'Women's Committee,' mimeo, n.d.

125 May Partridge, 'Women's Committee Report,' *Oshaworker,* Vol. 30, No. 5, 6 April 1972, p. 7.

126 In March 1971 GM's London diesel plant employed only 15 women out of a total workforce of 778. There was not one female employee out of a total workforce of 2,800 at GM's Ste Therese plant in Quebec; 150 women were working in GM's Scarborough van plant (Delco) in Toronto, out of a total workforce of 875. At GM's Trim plant in Windsor, there were 896 females out of a total plant workforce of 1,379. GM's Transmission plant in Windsor did not employ one woman out of a total plant workforce of 846. And at GM's St Catharines plant, there were a mere 255 women workers left out of a total plant workforce of 6,435. PAC, MG 28, I 119, Acc. 83/215, Box 12, File 'Toronto Office – Education Department, January 1971 – December 1973,' Dennis Tyce to Allen Schroeder, 18 March 1971.

127 *Oshaworker,* Vol. 29, No. 6, 18 March 1971, p. 2.

128 *Windsor-Essex Manufacturers' Directory* (Greater Windsor Industrial Commission. Windsor: 1976, 1979).

129 Murray interview.

CHAPTER 7

1 This theme touches on current debates about rights, equality, and difference in the United States and Canada. In the United States, the equality-

difference debate has revolved around the sex discrimination case brought before the Equal Employment Opportunity Commission against Sears, Roebuck and Company. The case was tried in 1984 and 1985, and in 1986 Judge John A. Nordberg ruled in favour of Sears, Roebuck (see Milkman, 1986; Scott, 1988). In Canada, the Women's Legal Education and Action Fund (LEAF) set an important precedent in 'Law Society of British Columbia v. Andrews et al.' Andrews, a British lawyer, argued that the B.C. rule restricting the practice of law to Canadian citizens violated his equality rights under the Canadian Charter of Rights, on the basis of citizenship. Acting on Andrews' behalf, LEAF urged the Court to reject the 'similarly situated test,' arguing that the test 'presumes that all persons are similarly situated in most respects.' They noted that the erroneousness of this assumption is evident in cases of sex equality. Insofar as their reproductive capacities set men and women apart, the rule is said to permit different treatment where there is a biological difference. In February 1989, the Court accepted the concept that section 15 was designed to protect groups who suffer social, political, and legal disadvantage and it rejected the 'similarly situated test' as 'seriously deficient.' Justice McIntyre recognized that 'identical treatment may frequently reproduce serious inequality' ('Andrews Case,' *Leaf Lines* (3) 1989: 7).

2 I wish to thank Carl Cuneo for bringing this point to my attention, especially in reference to women's failure to challenge the seniority principle itself.

3 For example, activist Bev McCloskey continued to protest masculine dominance on the shopfloor at GM. In 1983, McCloskey wrote Donald E. Hackworth, then president and general manager of GM of Canada, complaining about the pin-ups and other 'sexist culture' in the plants. Acting on her complaints, in 1984 CAW National Representative Pat Clancy negotiated an affirmative action clause with General Motors of Canada. The focus of this clause, however, stressed education. The company refused to bargain hiring 'quotas' or numerical 'targets.' In the same year, the union negotiated similar clauses in contracts with Ford and Chrysler. However, these firms did not implement the clause for several years. Ontario Women's Directorate and the Canadian Auto Workers, *Affirmative Action at Work: The Case of the Canadian Auto Workers and General Motors of Canada*. (Toronto: Ontario Women's Directorate 1987).

4 I thank Graham Knight for bringing this point to my attention.

Bibliography

PRIMARY SOURCES

Manuscript Collections

Archives of Labor and Urban Affairs (ALUA), Wayne State University, Detroit, Michigan

UAW Canadian Region – Series III Collection
UAW Canadian Region – Companies Collection
UAW Canadian Region – General Files Collection
UAW Canadian Region – Series V Collection
UAW Canadian Region – Officers' Files Collection
UAW Canadian Region – Locals Collection
UAW Canadian Region 7 Collection
UAW Local 199 Collection
UAW Region 7 Toronto Sub-Regional Office Collection
George Burt Collection
UAW Research Department Collection
UAW War Policy Division – Women's Bureau Collection
UAW War Policy Division, Victor Reuther Collection
UAW Women's Department: Lillian Hatcher Collection
Emil Mazey Collection
George Addes – UAW Secretary-Treasurer Collection

Public Archives of Canada (PAC), Ottawa, Ontario

Accession 81/081
Accession 83/314

Accession 83/215
Accession 86/472
Accession 88/324

Windsor Public Library, Windsor, Ontario Local History Collection

Private Papers

Isabel Baird Papers, Oshawa, Ontario
Canadian Auto Workers Union (CAW) National Office, North York, Ontario
CAW Legal Office, Toronto, Ontario
CAW Local 222, Oshawa, Ontario
CAW Local 199, St Catharines, Ontario
Pat Clancy Papers, North York, Ontario
Ted Murphy Papers, North York, Ontario
May Partridge Papers, Oshawa, Ontario

Interviews

Interviews conducted by author; in possession of author (The asterisk indicates a pseudonym.)

Effie Baldwin, 9 July 1990, Oshawa (McLaughlin – GM)
Helen Beaugrand (Forestall), 18 February 1991, Whitby, Ontario (GM, Chrysler)
Fay Bender, 22 October 1990, Oshawa (GM)
Jean Cormier, 4 February 1991, St Catharines (McKinnon – GM)
Martha Cox (Campbell), 2 August 1990, Oshawa (GM)
Pat Creighton (Kress), 27 June 1990, Oshawa (GM)
Ann Brisbois, 8 August 1990, Oshawa (GM)*
Elsa Goddard (Cardinal), 18 July 1990, Oshawa (GM)
Helen Graham (Lott), 20 July 1990, Lindsay, Ontario (GM)
Margaret Heritz, 30 October 1990, St Catharines (McKinnon – GM)
Joan Jackson, 18 July 1990, Oshawa (GM)
Janet Kent, 29 August 1990, Oshawa (McLaughlin – GM)*
John 'Jack' King, 29 August 1990, Oshawa (McLaughlin – GM)
Dorothea ('Doe') Koch, 26 July 1990, Port Perry, Ontario (GM)
Mabel Larkin, 28 January 1991, St Catharines (McKinnon)*
Doris Lepitsky, 11 March 1991, St Catharines (McKinnon – GM)

Marion Manning (with Bud Manning), 11 July 1990, Oshawa (GM)
Beverly McCloskey (Gibson), 4 October 1990; 10 October 1990, Oshawa (GM)
Marguerite McGrath, 27 August 1990, Oshawa (GM)
Ted Murphy, 6 February 1991, North York, Ontario (GM – Local 222 – CAW
    National Office)
Betty Murray, 1 August 1990, Belleville, Ontario (GM)
Richard Nicholson, 18 October 1990, St Catharines (McKinnon – GM)
Bea Parkin (Taillon), 25 July 1990, Oshawa (GM)
May Partridge, 18 June 1990, Oshawa (GM)
Nora Paterson, 25 June 1990, Oshawa (GM)
Pat Roy, 24 October 1990, Oshawa (Chrysler)
Mary Salter, 30 July 1990, Oshawa (GM)
Laura Saunders, 24 September 1990, Oshawa (GM)*
Rosina Saxby (with Bill Saxby), 9 August 1990, Port Hope, Ontario (GM)
Maurie Shorten, 24 June 1990, Oshawa (GM)
Marie Smith (Taillon), 25 July 1990, Oshawa (GM)
Kay Suddard, 24 October 1990, Oshawa (Chrysler)
Amy Swanson, 17 December 1990, St Catharines (McKinnon – GM)
Alice Torosian, 11 February 1991, St Catharines (McKinnon)
Hygus Torosian, 11 February 1991, St Catharines (McKinnon)
Ann Whyte (Taillon), 25 July 1990, Oshawa (GM)
Celia ('Sibby') Wigg, 3 July 1990, Oshawa (McLaughlin – GM)
Marie Willson, 17 July 1990, Oshawa (GM)
Phyllis Yurkowski (Holman) (with Walter Yurkowski), 5 July 1990, Oshawa
    (GM)

Interviews conducted by Carol Conde and Karl Beveridge, Toronto, Ontario
(also on deposit in the Public Archives of Canada)

Harry Benson/W. Grant/Ted Nichols/Jack Johnson/Doug Clark/Nip
    Tucker
George Burt
Olive Farnell/Doug Clark
Ivy Imerson (Bartlett) and Bill Imerson
Elsie Karn
Bev McCloskey/Bill Harding
Maurie Shorten
Ethel Thomson
Mary Turner

Personal Communication

Leroy Bell, St Catharines, Ontario
Pat Clancy, North York, Ontario
Cliff Pilkey, Toronto, Ontario

Periodicals and Newspapers

Canadian Fiction Magazine
Canadian Geographic Journal
The Detroit News
Detroit Times
Ford Times
GM Topics
The Guardian
Leaf Lines
McKinnon Doings
McKinnon People
Oshawa Times
Oshaworker
Progress
St Catharines Standard
This Week
Toronto Daily Star
UAW Local 199 News
UAW Local 199 News and Views
Union Woman
Windsor Daily Star
Windsor–Essex Manufacturers' Directory

SECONDARY SOURCES

Books

Adamson, Nancy, Linda Briskin, and Margaret McPhail. 1988. *Feminist Organizing for Change: The Contemporary Women's Movement in Canada.* Toronto: Oxford University Press.

Anderson, Karen. 1981. *Wartime Women: Sex Roles, Family Relations, and the Status of Women During World War II*. Westport, Connecticut: Greenwood Press.

Bacchi, Carol Lee, 1990. *Same Difference: Feminism and Sexual Difference*. Sydney, Australia: Allen and Unwin.

Balser, Diane. 1987. *Sisterhood and Solidarity: Feminism and Labor in Modern Times*. Boston: South End Press.

Baron, Ava, ed. 1991. *Work Engendered: Toward a New History of American Labor*. Ithaca: Cornell University Press.

Berube, Allan. 1990. *Coming Out Under Fire: The History of Gay Men and Women in World War Two*. New York: Free Press.

Beynon, Huw. 1973. *Working for Ford*. Harmondsworth: Penguin.

Blewett, Mary H. 1988. *Men, Women, and Work: Class, Gender, and Protest in the New England Shoe Industry, 1780–1910*. Urbana: University of Illinois Press.

Bock, Gisela, and Susan James, eds. 1992. *Beyond Equality and Difference: Citizenship, Feminist Politics and Female Subjectivity*. London: Routledge.

Briskin, Linda, and Patricia McDermott, eds. 1993. *Women Challenging Unions: Feminism, Democracy, and Militancy*. Toronto: University of Toronto Press.

Chinoy, Eli. 1955. *Automobile Workers and the American Dream*. New York: Doubleday.

Chodorow, Nancy. 1978. *The Reproduction of Mothering*. Berkeley: University of California Press.

Cobble, Dorothy Sue, ed. 1993. *Women and Unions: Forging a Partnership*. Ithaca: ILR Press.

Cockburn, Cynthia. 1986. *Machinery of Dominance: Women, Men, and Technical Know-How*. London: Pluto Press.

– 1983. *Brothers: Male Dominance and Technological Change*. London: Pluto Press.

Cook, Alice H., Val R. Lorwin, and Arlene Kaplan Daniels. 1992. *The Most Difficult Revolution: Women and Trade Unions*. Ithaca: Cornell University Press.

Drake, Barbara. 1984. *Women in Trade Unions*. London: Virago Press.

Dunk, Thomas W. 1991. *It's a Working Man's Town: Male Working-Class Culture in Northwestern Ontario*. Montreal: McGill-Queen's University Press.

Eisenstein, Sarah. 1983. *Give Us Bread But Give Us Roses: Working Women's Consciousness in the United States, 1890 to the First World War*. London: Routledge and Kegan Paul.

Fantasia, Rick. 1988. *Cultures of Solidarity: Consciousness, Action, and Contemporary American Workers*. Berkeley: University of California Press.

Frager, Ruth. 1992. *Sweatshop Strife*. Toronto: University of Toronto Press.

Gabin, Nancy. 1990. *Feminism in the Labor Movement: Women and the United Auto Workers, 1935–1975*. Cornell University Press.

Game, Ann, and Rosemary Pringle. 1983. *Gender at Work*. Sydney: George Allen and Unwin.

Gannage, Charlene. 1986. *Double Day, Double Bind: Women Garment Workers*. Toronto: Women's Press.

Hearn, Jeff, and Wendy Parkin. 1987. *'Sex' at 'Work': The Power and Paradox of Organisation Sexuality*. Sussex: Wheatsheaf Books.

Hearn, Jeff, Deborah L. Sheppard, Peta Tancred-Sheriff, and Gibson Burrell. 1989. *The Sexuality of Organization*. London: Sage.

Herding, Richard. 1972. *Job Control and Union Structure*. Rotterdam: Rotterdam University Press.

Hochschild, Arlie. 1989. *The Second Shift: Working Parents and the Revolution at Home*. New York: Viking Penguin.

Honey, Maureen. 1984. *Creating Rosie the Riveter: Class, Gender, and Propaganda during World War II*. Amherst: University of Massachusetts Press.

Hunt, Pauline. 1980. *Gender and Class Consciousness*. London: Macmillan Press.

Hutchins, B.L., and A. Harrison. 1903. *A History of Factory Legislation*. London: P.S. King and Son.

Jeffreys, Steven. 1986. *Management and Managed: Fifty Years of Crisis at Chrysler*. Cambridge: Cambridge University Press.

Kesselman, Amy. 1990. *Fleeting Opportunities: Women Shipyard Workers in Portland and Vancouver during World War II and Reconversion*. Albany: State University of New York Press.

Kingsolver, Barbara. 1989. *Holding the Line: Women in the Great Arizona Mine Strike of 1983*. Ithaca: ILR Press.

Laxer, Robert. 1976. *Canada's Unions*. Toronto: James Lorimer.

Lichtenstein, Nelson. 1989. *On the Line: Essays in the History of Auto Work*. Urbana: University of Illinois Press.

Light, Beth, and Ruth Roach Pierson. 1990. *No Easy Road: Women in Canada, 1920s to 1960s*. Toronto: New Hogtown Press.

Mackie, Marlene. 1991. *Gender Relations in Canada: Further Explorations*. Toronto: Butterworths.

Meier, August, and Elliott Rudwick. 1979. *Black Detroit and the Rise of the UAW*. New York: Oxford University Press.

Milkman, Ruth. 1987. *Gender at Work: The Dynamics of Job Segregation by Sex during World War II*. Urbana: University of Illinois Press.

– 1985. *Women, Work, and Protest: A Century of Women's Labour History*. London and New York.

Norwood, Stephen. 1990. *Labor's Flaming Youth: Telephone Operators and Worker Militancy, 1878–1923*. Urbana: University of Illinois Press.

Ontario Women's Directorate and the Canadian Auto Workers. 1987. *Affirmative*

Action at Work: The Case of the Canadian Auto Workers and General Motors of Canada. Toronto: Ontario Women's Directorate.

Parr, Joy. 1990. *The Gender of Breadwinners: Women, Men, and Change in Two Industrial Towns, 1880–1950.* Toronto: University of Toronto Press.

Pierson, Ruth Roach. 1986 *'They're Still Women After All': The Second World War and Canadian Womanhood.* Toronto: McClelland and Stewart.

– 1983. *Canadian Women and the Second World War.* Ottawa: Canadian Historical Association.

Pollert, Anna. 1981. *Girls, Wives, Factory Lives.* London: Macmillan Press.

Pringle, Rosemary. 1988 *Secretaries Talk: Sexuality, Power, and Work.* London: Verso.

Razack, Sherene. 1991. *Canadian Feminism and the Law: The Women's Legal Education and Action Fund and the Pursuit of Equality.* Toronto: Second Story Press.

Rinehart, Sue Tolleson. 1992. *Gender Consciousness and Politics.* New York: Routledge, Chapman, and Hall.

Rosen, Ellen Israel. 1987. *Bitter Choices: Blue-Collar Women in and out of Work.* Chicago: University of Chicago Press.

Rubin, Lillian. 1983. *Intimate Strangers.* New York: Harper and Row.

Sargent, Lydia, ed. 1981. *Women and Revolution.* Montreal: Black Rose Books.

Scharf, Lois. 1980. *To Work and Wed: Female Employment, Feminism, and the Great Depression.* Westport, Connecticut: Greenwood Press.

Schatz, Ronald W. 1983. *The Electrical Workers: A History of Labor at General Electric and Westinghouse 1923–60.* Urbana: University of Illinois Press.

Serrin, William. 1973. *The Company and the Union.* New York: Knopf.

Steibner, Jack. 1962. *Governing the UAW.* New York: Wiley.

Tentler, Leslie Woodcock. 1979. *Wage-Earning Women: Industrial Work and Family Life in the United States, 1900–1930.* New York: Oxford University Press.

Westwood, Sallie. 1985. *All Day, Every Day: Factory and Family in the Making of Women's Lives.* Urbana: University of Chicago Press.

White, Julie. 1993. *Sisters and Solidarity: Women and Unions in Canada.* Toronto: Thompson Educational Publishing.

– 1990. *Mail and Female: Women and the Canadian Union of Postal Workers.* Toronto: Thompson Educational Publishing.

Widick, B.J. ed. 1976. *Auto Work and Its Discontents.* Baltimore: Johns Hopkins University Press.

Women's Bureau, Labour Canada. n.d. *The Selective Protection of Canadian Working Women.* Ottawa: Labour Canada.

Yates, Charlotte. 1993. *From Plant to Politics.* Philadelphia: Temple University Press.

Articles

Abella, Irving M. 1974. 'Oshawa 1937,' p. 93–128 in *On Strike: Six Key Labour Struggles in Canada, 1919–1949*, Irving M. Abella, ed. Toronto: James Lorimer.

Baron, Ava. 1991. 'An "Other" Side of Gender Antagonism at Work: Men, Boys, and the Remasculinization of Printers' Work, 1830–1920,' p. 47–69 in *Work Engendered: Toward a New History of American Labor*, Ava Baron, ed. Ithaca: Cornell University Press.

Benenson, Harold. 1984. 'Victorian Sexual Ideology and Marx's Theory of the Working Class,' *International Labor and Working Class History* (25) 1–23.

Blewett, Mary H. 1991. 'Manhood and the Market: The Politics of Gender and Class among the Textile Workes of Fall River, Massachusetts, 1870–1880,' p. 92–113 in *Work Engendered: Toward a New History of American Labor*, Ava Baron, ed. Ithaca: Cornell University Press.

Bordo, Susan. 1992. 'Anorexia Nervosa: Psychopathology as the Crystallization of Culture,' p. 90–109 in *Knowing Women: Feminism and Knowledge,*. Helen Crowley and Susan Himmelweit, eds. Cambridge: Open University Press.

Brenner, Johanna, and Maria Ramas. 1984. 'Rethinking Women's Oppression,' *New Left Review* (144) 33–71.

Briskin, Linda. 1993. 'Union Women and Separate Organizing,' p. 89–108 in *Women Challenging Unions*, Linda Briskin and Pat McDermott, eds. Toronto: University of Toronto Press.

Collinson, David, and David Knights. 1986. ' "Men Only": Theories and Practices of Job Segregation in Insurance,' p. 140–78 in *Gender and the Labour Process*, David Knights and Hugh Willmott, eds. Hampshire, England: Gower Publishing.

Creese, Gillian. 1988. 'The Politics of Dependence: Women, Work, and Unemployment in the Vancouver Labour Movement before World War II.' p. 121–42 in *Class, Gender, and Region: Essays in Canadian Historical Sociology*, Gregory S. Kealey, ed. St John's Newfoundland: Committee on Canadian Labour History.

Fox, Bonnie. 1990. 'Selling the Mechanized Household: 70 Years of Ads in Ladies Home Journal,' *Gender and Society* (4) 25–40.

– 1987 'Conceptualizing "Patriarchy," ' *Canadian Review of Sociology and Anthropology* (25) 163–83.

Frager, Ruth. 1989. 'Class and Ethnic Barriers to Feminist Perspectives in Toronto's Jewish Labour Movement, 1919–1939,' *Studies in Political Economy* (30) 143–65.

Gaskell, Jane. 1991. 'What Counts as Skill? Reflections on Pay Equity.' p. 141–59 in *Just Wages: A Feminist Assessment of Pay Equity.* Judy Fudge and Patricia McDermott, eds. Toronto: University of Toronto Press.

Gersuny, Carl, and Gladys Kaufman. 1985. 'Seniority and the Moral Economy of U.S. Automobile Workers, 1934–46,' *Journal of Social History* (18) 463–73.

Gregg, Nina. 1993. 'Trying to Put First Things First: Negotiating Subjectivities in a Workplace Organizing Campaign,' pp. 172–204 in *Negotiating at the Margins: The Gendered Discourses of Power and Resistance,* Sue Fisher and Kathy Davis, eds. New Brunswick, New Jersey: Rutgers University Press.

Hartmann, Heidi. 1979. 'The Unhappy Marriage of Marxism and Feminism: Towards a More Progressive Union,' p. 1–43 in *Women and Revolution,* Lydia Sargent, ed. Boston: South End Press.

– 1976. 'Capitalism, Patriarchy, and Job Segregation by Sex.' p. 206–48 in *Capitalist Patriarchy and the Case for Socialist Feminism,* Zillah Eisenstein, ed. New York: Monthly Review Press.

Hossfeld, Karen J. 1990. "Their Logic Against Them": Contradictions in Sex, Race, and Class in Silicon Valley.' p. 149–78 in *Women Workers and Global Restructuring,* Kathryn Ward, ed. Ithaca: New York: ILR Press.

Humphries, Jane. 1977. 'The Working Class Family, Women's Liberation, and Class Struggle: The Case of Nineteenth Century British History,' *The Review of Radical Political Economics* (9) 23–41.

Jenson, Jane. 1989. 'The Talents of Women, the Skills of Men: Flexible Specialization and Women.' in *The Transformation of Work: Skill, Flexibility, and the Labour Process,* ed. Stephen Wood. London: Unwin Hyman.

Lewchuk, Wayne. 1993. 'Men and Monotony: Fraternalism at the Ford Motor Company,' *Journal of Economic History* (53) 1–30.

Livingstone, David, and Meg Luxton. 1989. 'Gender Consciousness at Work: Modification of the Male Breadwinner Norm among Steelworkers and Their Spouses,' *Canadian Review of Sociology and Anthropology* (26) 240–75.

Maroney, Heather Jon. 1986. 'Feminism At Work,' p. 101–126 in *What Is Feminism,* Juliet Mitchell and Ann Oakley, eds. New York: Pantheon Books.

May, Martha. 1985. 'Bread before Roses: American Workingmen, Labor Unions, and the Family Wage.' p. 1–21 in *Women, Work, and Protest: A Century of U.S. Women's Labor History,* Ruth Milkman, ed. Boston: Routledge and Kegan Paul.

McRobbie, Angela. 1978. 'Working-Class Girls and the Culture of Femininity,' p. 96–108 in *Women Take Issue: Aspects of Women's Subordination,* Centre for Contemporary Cultural Studies, ed. London: Hutchinson.

Milkman, Ruth. 1986. 'Women's History and the Sears Case,' *Feminist Studies* (12) 394–5.

Montero, Gloria. 1979. 'George Burt: The UAW and the Ford Windsor Strike

1945,' p. 91–111 in *We Stood Together*, Gloria Montero, ed. Toronto: James Lorimer.

Phelps, Edwin S. 1972. 'The Statistical Theory of Racism and Sexism,' *American Economic Review* (62) 659–661.

Pierson, Ruth Roach. 1990. 'Gender and the Unemployment Insurance Debates in Canada, 1934–1940,' *Labour/Le Travail* (25) 77–103.

Piore, Michael J. 1972. 'The Dual Labor Market: Theory and Implications,' p. 90–4 in *Problems in Political Economy: An Urban Perspective*, David Gordon, ed. Lexington, Massachusetts: D.C. Heath.

Pollert, Anna. 1983. 'Women, Gender Relations, and Wage Labour,' in *Gender, Class, and Work*, E. Garmarnikow et al., eds. London.

Rose, Sonya O. 1986. ' "Gender at Work": Sex, Class, and Industrial Capitalism.' *History Workshop Journal* (21) 113–31.

Rubery, Jill. 1980. 'Structured Labour Markets, Worker Organization, and Low Pay,' p. 242–70 in *The Economics of Women and Work*, Alice H. Amsden, ed. Harmondsworth: Penguin.

Scott, Joan W. 1988. 'Deconstructing Equality-Versus-Difference: Or, the Uses of Poststructuralist Theory for Feminism.' *Feminist Studies* (14) 33–50.

Sen, Gita. 1980. 'The Sexual Division of Labor and the Working-Class Family: Towards a Conceptual Synthesis of Class Relations and the Subordination of Women,' *Review of Radical Political Economics* (12) 76–86.

Storey, Robert. 1994. 'The Struggle Over Job Ownership in the Canadian Steel Industry: An Historical Analysis,' *Labour/Le Travail* (in press).

Swidler, Ann. 1986. 'Culture in Action: Symbols and Strategies,' *American Sociological Review* (51) 273–86.

Valverde, M. 1988. ' "Giving the Female a Domestic Turn": The Social, Legal, and Moral Regulation of Women's Work in British Cotton Mills, 1820–1850,' *Journal of Social History* (21) 619–34.

Wells, Don. 1986. 'Autoworkers on the Firing Line,' p. 327–32 in *On the Job*, Craig Heron and Robert Storey, eds. Kingston: McGill-Queen's University Press.

Willis, Paul. 1979. 'Shop Floor Culture, Masculinity, and the Wage Form,' p. 185–98 in *Working-Class Culture: Studies in History and Theory*, J. Clarke, C. Critcher, and R. Johnson, eds. New York: St Martin's Press.

Unpublished Works

Gabin, Nancy Felice. 1984. 'Women Auto Workers and the United Automobile Workers' Union (UAW-CIO), 1935–1955.' Unpublished PhD Dissertation, University of Michigan.

Hsiung, Ping-Chun. 1991. 'Class, Gender, and the Satellite Factory system in Taiwan.' Unpublished PhD Dissertation, University of California, Los Angeles.

Meyerowitz, Ruth. 1984. 'Organizing and Building the UAW: Women at the Ternstedt General Motors Part Plant, 1936–1950.' Unpublished PhD Dissertation, Columbia University.

Sugiman, Pamela H. 1992. 'Labour's Dilemma: The Meaning and Politics of Worker Resistance in a Gendered Setting.' Unpublished PhD Dissertation, University of Toronto.

Shorten, Maurie. 1983. 'The Recollections of a Blue Collar Worker.' Mimeo. Oshawa.

Storey, Robert. 1981. 'Workers, Unions, and Steel: The Shaping of the Hamilton Working Class, 1935–1948.' Unpublished PhD Dissertation, University of Toronto.

Yates, Charlotte Alyce Bronwen. 1988. 'From Plant to Politics: The Canadian UAW 1936–1984.' Unpublished PhD Dissertation, Carleton University.

Index

Picture Credits

CAW National Office Private Collection: woman war worker; women doing each other's hair; drawing women into union activity, photograph by Don Sinclair, *St Catharines Standard*; a lone woman delegate; District Council Meeting; women auto workers

CAW Local 222 Private Collection: women playing cards

City of Toronto Archives: Labour Day parade 92274-S; UAW men fighting for a family wage SC 266-100057

City of Toronto Archives, *Globe and Mail* Collection: marching women auto workers 44073; victory dance 44279

Marie Smith, Marie Smith Private Papers: group portrait